.C8
E895
2013
v. 3

EVANGELICAL CHRISTIANS AND POPULAR CULTURE

Pop Goes the Gospel

VOLUME 3:
PUBLIC FIGURES, POPULAR PRESS, PLACES, AND EVENTS

Robert H. Woods Jr., Editor

Foreword by Mark A. Noll

Colo. Christian Univ. Library
8787 W. Alameda Ave.
Lakewood, CO 80226

PRAEGER

AN IMPRINT OF ABC-CLIO, LLC
Santa Barbara, California • Denver, Colorado • Oxford, England

Copyright 2013 by ABC-CLIO, LLC

All rights reserved. No part of this publication may be reproduced, stored in a retrieval system, or transmitted, in any form or by any means, electronic, mechanical, photocopying, recording, or otherwise, except for the inclusion of brief quotations in a review, without prior permission in writing from the publisher.

Library of Congress Cataloging-in-Publication Data

Evangelical Christians and popular culture : pop goes the gospel / Robert H. Woods Jr., editor ; foreword by Mark A. Noll.
   p. cm.
   Includes bibliographical references and index.
   ISBN 978–0–313–38654–1 (hardback) — ISBN 978–0–313–38655–8 (ebook) 1. Popular culture—Religious aspects—Christianity. 2. Evangelicalism. I. Woods, Robert, 1970–
BR115.C8E895   2013
261.0973—dc23   2012014133

ISBN: 978–0–313–38654–1
EISBN: 978–0–313–38655–8

17 16 15 14 13   1 2 3 4 5

This book is also available on the World Wide Web as an eBook.
Visit www.abc-clio.com for details.

Praeger
An Imprint of ABC-CLIO, LLC

ABC-CLIO, LLC
130 Cremona Drive, P.O. Box 1911
Santa Barbara, California 93116-1911

This book is printed on acid-free paper ∞

Manufactured in the United States of America

Contents

Foreword by Mark A. Noll	vii
Acknowledgments	ix
Introduction by Robert H. Woods Jr.	xiii
Chapter Summaries for Volume 3	xxix
1. Rick Warren: Evangelical Media and Ministry *Michael A. Longinow*	1
2. Evangelical Political Engagement *Denise P. Ferguson*	16
3. Evangelicals, Politics, and the 2008 Presidential Campaign *Martin J. Medhurst*	33
4. Constructions of Evangelicalism in Media Coverage of Sarah Palin *Kevin Healey*	62
5. Johnny Cash, Evangelicals, and Popular Culture *Stephen J. Nichols*	79
6. Navigating the Treacherous Waters of Celebrity Culture: A New Challenge for Evangelicals *Benson P. Fraser and William J. Brown*	94
7. Scandalous Evangelicals: Sex, Greed, Politics, and the Arts *Judith M. Buddenbaum*	110
8. Evangelical Media Cults *Quentin J. Schultze*	128

9. How Evangelicals Are Covered in the News: From Curiosity through Obscurity to the Mainstream — 149
   Judith M. Buddenbaum

10. Daring to Believe: Evangelical News and Journalism — 169
    Michael A. Longinow

11. Charles M. Sheldon's Jesus Newspaper and the Reformist Impulse in Evangelical Publications — 182
    Michael Ray Smith

12. Evangelical Magazines — 195
    Kenneth E. Waters

13. *Christianity Today*: Uniting Evangelicals, Changing the Culture — 212
    Phyllis E. Alsdurf

14. Evangelical Film Festivals — 229
    Terrence R. Wandtke

15. Themed Destinations, Museums, and Evangelicals — 244
    Annalee R. Ward

16. Evangelical Theater in a New Century: Redefining the Redemptive Theatrical Event — 261
    Paul D. Patton

17. Jesus People: The Forgotten Evangelical Offspring of the Counterculture — 278
    Larry Eskridge

18. Evangelical Women's Movements and Leaders — 296
    Kathleen Osbeck Sindorf

About the Contributors to Volume 3 — 315

Index — 325

Foreword

Mark A. Noll

The editor has assembled a superb crew of expert authorities in preparing this work on *Evangelical Christians and Popular Culture*. In recent years, popular media have occasionally paid some attention to the phenomena treated in these volumes. They have noticed the occasional best-selling CD or DVD by a contemporary Christian musician, they might be aware of the record sales wracked up by the *Left Behind* series of end-times thrillers, they know that public figures like Sarah Palin have roots in evangelical or Pentecostal or fundamentalist churches, and they could tell that the United States's conservative Protestants accounted for much of the surprising success of Mel Gibson's *The Passion of the Christ*. But these references are usually ad hoc. They almost never provide responsible historical background, and they do not indicate the scope or depth of evangelical investment in radio, television, popular merchandise, novels, music festivals, video games, and more. The well-researched chapters that make up this work are different. They proceed from a careful definition of the meaning of *evangelical*; they trace some of the background, going back centuries, that lies behind contemporary expressions of evangelical popular culture; several of them spotlight the crucial role of the 1960s "Jesus People" in bringing popular music and communication into conservative Protestant churches; and they provide a well-grounded sense of how deep and wide the streams of popular culture run in the contemporary evangelical world. In addition, the specific attention given to topics such as singers like Johnny Cash and groups like U2, evangelical magazines like *Christianity Today*, important innovators like C. S. Lewis in *The Screwtape Letters*, popular painters like Thomas Kinkade, and usually neglected forms like evangelical tattoos and evangelical candy ensure that these volumes are as lively and interesting as they are instructive.

The evangelical engagement with popular modes of communication goes back at least three centuries. German pietists, who wrote hymns designed to be sung by laypeople, were pioneers. The young British evangelist George Whitefield, who electrified crowds in the mid-eighteenth century with his dramatic gospel message, solidified the link between evangelicalism and the populace. Since then, evangelicals' attitudes have gone through cycles. In earlier periods, the reading of novels was sometimes considered a dangerous waste of time, and music with a syncopated beat was thought to be satanic. But also from earlier periods came the effective writing campaigns of Hannah More, a British evangelical who in the early nineteenth century published a great number of edifying stories aimed deliberately at the working classes, and the sprightly music of Ira Sankey written to captivate mass audiences for D. L. Moody's urban preaching campaigns. The whys and wherefores of such shifting attitudes provide the backdrop for many of the chapters found here.

Evangelicals have always moved toward the populist side of the Christian churches. They pioneered theologies of personal conversion, encouraged lay appropriation of scripture, favored democratic means of church organization, recruited ordinary men and women for missionary service, and often looked suspiciously at the markers of elite society. Negative effects of these tendencies have included a propensity toward anti-intellectualism and a susceptibility to irresponsible demagogues. Positive results have included great success in mobilizing large numbers of middle-class believers for active Christian service and unusual creativity in fashioning innovative modes of organization and communication. Both the negative and positive aspects of the democratic populism that has always been so prominent in evangelical circles are fully on display in the chapters that follow.

Even before the path-breaking labors of Marshall McLuhan, who underscored how much insight could be gleaned from careful study of popular culture, it had become commonplace for scholars to expect rich rewards from studying the artifacts of popular culture. For evangelical Christians, whose history has been fully engaged with an immense range of popular cultural forces, the rewards are particularly great. Even casual readers of these volumes will understand why. Those who attend to their pages carefully will reap an especially rich harvest of understanding and insight.

Acknowledgments

A project like this has 1,000 details and requires many selfless hands working in concert over an extended period of time. I owe a deep debt of gratitude to several individuals and groups of people who have labored tirelessly during the past three years to bring this project to publication.

Quentin J. Schultze, of Calvin College, recommended me for this project, and his wise council early on allowed me—among many other things—to collect an outstanding group of scholars who were committed to the task. As with other projects I've worked on, this one would not have happened without him. A better academic mentor and role model than Quentin would be difficult to find.

Mark A. Noll took time out of his busy schedule to write the foreword to this collection. Mark's scholarship over the past three decades has provided a strong foundation for the study of American evangelicalism. His leadership and influence in the field are visible throughout this collection, and his foreword wonderfully foreshadows the depth and breadth of scholarship represented herein.

Additionally, a collection such as this is not possible without a top-flight group of experts who can speak with authority on the subject matter. Special thanks are due, both individually and collectively, to the fifty-seven authors whose work spans fifty-four chapters across the three volumes. Their patience and persistence throughout the process were impressive. I especially appreciated their willingness to revise—and to keep revising—so their work would serve the needs of the target audience. I asked a lot from them during the past three years, and they delivered each time with a smile.

Several of the authors provided additional assistance throughout the project, including but not limited to supplying photographs and images for their own and in some cases others' chapters. Additional thanks to Phyllis E. Alsdurf, Diane M. Badzinski, William J. Brown, Judith M. Buddenbaum, Thomas J. Carmody, Paul A. Creasman, Terri Lynn Cornwell,

Samuel E. Ebersole, Larry Eskridge, Denise P. Ferguson, John P. Ferré, Michael V. Firmin, Benson P. Fraser, Janie Harden Fritz, Roddy Knowles IV, Michael A. Longinow, Gerald D. Mast, Lynn S. Neal, Paul D. Patton, Kevin P. Schut, Kathleen Osbeck Sindorf, Michael Ray Smith, Luke M. Tse, Terrence R. Wandtke, Annalee R. Ward, Mark Ward Sr., and Kenneth E. Waters.

Marsha Daigle-Williamson served as copyeditor on this project and provided additional content review. Marsha was an English professor for nearly twenty-five years who earned "teacher of the year" honors five times during her tenure. She is a master of languages: she speaks French and Italian and has some knowledge of German, Latin, and Greek, which come in handy, she explains, in doing translations and checking English speakers' use of those languages. Marsha makes what is "good" somehow "great" and what is "great" truly "awesome." Without her, this project and others I have worked on would not have been completed on time or with such high quality. A debt from me that can never be repaid is due her. Everyone needs a "Marsha."

Spring Arbor University's (SAU) library staff (Robbie Bolton, Roy Meador, Kami Moyer, Karen Parsons, and Susan Panak), and Dave Burns, formerly of SAU, provided ongoing and timely research support that allowed me to stay on schedule. Other SAU staff, colleagues, students, and friends provided much-needed support of varying kinds: Dave Buchanan, Rachel Buchanan, Jay Cordova, Darcy Drake, Nate Evans, David Goodrich, Benjamin Rupp, Shawn Rutan, and Jason Thiede. The consistent and reliable support of SAU master's of communication graduate assistants Alyse Lehrke and Annette Ford freed me up to spend extra time working on the project. My non-SAU colleague Naaman Wood provided support as well.

During the first several months of this project's formation, Kim Chimenti, formerly of the Gainey Institute for Faith and Communication at Calvin College, provided important administrative and organizational support. She created spreadsheets, managed author contracts, and helped me to stay two steps ahead of where I needed to be at all times.

SAU graciously granted me a reduction in teaching load during the early stages of the project. Paul D. Patton, chair of SAU's Department of Communication and Media, and Wally Metts, master's of communication program director, offered words of encouragement and other tangible support for my work on this project.

Praeger and ABC-CLIO deserves appreciation for recognizing the importance and timeliness of such a project. Thanks to Praeger editor Jane

Messah-Ericksen and former Praeger editor Dan Harmon for their patience throughout the project. Jane took over for Dan as editor about two months before final submission and handled the transition with professionalism and grace. Thanks to Erin Ryan, preproduction and media editor for ABC-CLIO, who patiently guided me through the photo selection process and who helped secure several images that were difficult to find. Thanks also to Nicole Azze, ABC-CLIO production coordinator, and N. Magendra Varman, senior project manager for PreMediaGlobal. Magendra managed the day-to-day production of the three volumes, providing excellent oversight of the copyediting, typesetting, proofreading, and indexing for all three volumes.

Finally, I'm extremely grateful for my wife, partner, and friend, Rebekah Starr Woods, who gives me time and space to work on such projects. She is a constant source of joy.

I absolve all my friends and colleagues of any responsibility for the weaknesses that remain.

Introduction

Robert H. Woods Jr.

Over the past two decades, the study of media and religion has changed significantly. Researchers were initially concerned about the effect of televangelists and other institutional religious media on society, but in the early 1990s, a major shift in the sociology of religion appeared as researchers began to document new religious cultures.[1] The focus on televangelism and institutional religion failed to notice that while institutional religion was declining, religion as cultural practice was growing in importance. The lines between the sacred and secular were blurring. Media and popular culture were increasingly becoming popular sites and sources for constructing and expressing religious identities for individuals and religious groups of all kinds—from monks to Mormons, Buddhists to Muslims, and, of course, Christians.

Evangelicals and Popular Culture

Popular culture, explains Andrew Greeley, is the "locus theologicus" of our age;[2] that is, pop culture is the place where we live, where we "do" theology, and where we encounter God. And, in this respect, American evangelicals (a sub-group within Christianity) are well suited to the task. In an effort to fulfill the biblical command to "make disciples of all nations" (Matt. 28:19), evangelicals have been some of the earliest pioneers in new media, persistently packaging biblical truths in popular culture formats. Evangelicals also tend to get some of their theology from popular culture. They learn about the end-times from the *Left Behind* book series, the creation story from the Creation Museum in Kentucky, and the gruesome details of Christ's crucifixion from *The Passion of the Christ* and the Holy Land Experience theme park in Orlando, Florida. Christian television, despite several high-profile scandals, continues to draw millions of faithful viewers each day, and the Contemporary Christian Music (CCM) radio format continues to be one of the most popular formats in the country.

Evangelical insiders in the academy have long been interested in the various cultural forces shaping American evangelicalism and how evangelicalism has shaped mainstream culture. For more than two decades, the evangelical exemplar has been historian of religion Mark A. Noll, who has successfully explored the development and dimensions of this sub-culture of American Christianity.[3] Religious historians like Randall Balmer and Joel A. Carpenter, to name a few, drew our attention to evangelicalism's adoption of new media, from film to radio and television, and its imitation of popular trends in the mainstream entertainment industry.[4] Scholars of religion and media such as Quentin J. Schultze showed the history of Christianity and mass media in the United States to be one of democratic accommodation, demonstrating how religion and the media in the United States have borrowed each other's rhetoric.[5] From social-scientific perspectives, others demonstrated how formal and informal evangelical groups provide spaces for expression of personal and communal faith.[6] Still others showed how evangelical leaders and churches are engaged in a highly competitive market for religious consumers and how certain well-known celebrity evangelical innovators market themselves in ways that challenge religious experience.[7]

Despite the short list of outstanding and multi-layered work listed above, the study of American evangelicalism and related movements in the academy is relatively scant compared with those of other religious subjects and movements. Recently, within the last decade or two, there has been a growing interest—what some insiders would call *renewed* interest—in the subject among non-evangelical readers inside and outside the academy. This growing interest has resulted in a publication boom led by several mainstream publishers. Several outstanding works from scholars of media and religion, religion and popular culture, sociology of religion, and religious history illuminate the landscape, and some of their research and insights are included in these three volumes.

There are several factors contributing to the growing interest in American evangelicalism in the last decade. To begin, the explosion in Christian-themed product sales, blogs, cyberchurches, and literature in the early 2000s may be attributed, in part, to a spiritual revival led by evangelicals in response to the 9/11 terrorist attacks and the war in Iraq. Additionally, the role evangelicals played in the presidential elections of 2000 and 2004 garnered significant attention from individuals on the left and right. The role of the evangelical vote in the elections of presidents Jimmy Carter and Ronald Reagan are well documented, but George W. Bush's back-to-back victories in 2000 and 2004 prompted renewed interest in evangelicals' relationship with the public sphere. On the heels of the 2004 election was the record-breaking success of Mel Gibson's *The Passion of the Christ*, which became one of the top ten highest grossing films of all time. *The Passion*'s success led to several popular films and television shows with Christ-centered themes produced by evangelicals for mainstream audiences. The way in which evangelicals were assuming the role of Hollywood insiders drew mainstream attention. And the continued mainstream cross-over success of popular evangelical musicians (Amy Grant, Switchfoot, Relient K, and Lifehouse), painters (Thomas Kinkade), and best-selling authors (Rick Warren, Joel Osteen, and T. D. Jakes) meant that such merchandise—once only available at Christian bookstores—was readily accessible at mainstream retailers (like Wal-Mart and Target).

Moreover, several popular trade books about evangelical popular culture have been written by non-evangelicals who provide first-person accounts of their immersion in particular evangelical communities.[8] To these outsiders, evangelical popular culture seems like a "parallel universe,"[9] often mocked for its insularity, triteness, poor production quality, manipulative practices, and tendency to mimic mainstream trends for spiritual ends. To be fair, many of these criticisms are ones that evangelicals themselves level against evangelical popular culture these days.

Yet while such work by non-evangelicals provides harsh critique, it also positively demonstrates how many evangelical Christians are engaged in complex dialogue with popular culture rather than simply rejecting it. Furthermore, such works draw attention to a new generation of evangelicals raised on the Internet, social media, and downloadable music who struggle with making clear dividing lines between the sacred and the secular. These evangelicals watch Steven Colbert and Jon Stewart for their news and are as likely to find something "redemptive" in a Stephen King novel as in a Sunday morning sermon. Their performances and publications are changing the way non-evangelicals perceive Christian cultural engagement and, in many ways, how evangelical churches do ministry. The work of these evangelicals has led even the harshest non-evangelical critics to recognize the potentially transformative effect that evangelical popular culture might have on mainstream culture.

The three volumes presented here may be viewed as additional support for the ways American evangelicalism in general, and evangelicals and popular culture in particular, are becoming subjects of serious academic study inside and outside the academy and beyond only those who identify with it as insiders. The fifty-seven authors across three volumes and fifty-four chapters represent nearly fifty institutions of higher learning, both public and private. The authors teach and write in the areas of history, English, theology, music, psychology, sociology, new media, journalism, communication and media studies, rhetoric and cultural studies, film and television studies, advertising, and public relations. Individually and collectively, they have been called upon to explore the following intersections between evangelicals and popular culture:

- how evangelicals produce traditional and non-traditional forms of popular culture;
- how evangelicals are portrayed in popular culture created by non-evangelicals;
- how evangelicals are viewed by the wider public and the mainstream media;
- how evangelicals and their faith have shaped and been shaped by popular culture;
- how evangelical critiques can be brought to bear on popular culture; and
- how evangelicals use, or make use of, popular culture for spiritual or religious purposes.

Key Definitions

At the outset, defining *evangelicalism* for a project such as this has its difficulties. *Evangelical* has become so vague that even the world's most famous evangelical, Billy Graham, had difficulty defining the term at one time.[10] Some evangelicals call the Irish rock band U2 evangelical, while other evangelicals think their music comes from the devil. Outsiders also find difficulty in defining the word. To journalists, *evangelical* is political, while to many non-evangelicals it is synonymous with "Christian" or "fundamentalist" or the most extreme fringes of conservative Christian theology. But the term actually represents a broad range of different Christian theologies, practices, and movements.

For the purposes of the current project, evangelicals are defined as individuals who believe in Jesus Christ alone for personal salvation, view the Bible as the word of God, and seek to share their faith with others. *Christians* is a term that describes everyone who follows Jesus Christ; Christians are "Christ-followers." As such, evangelicals are a subgroup of Christians who reside within many denominations: there are evangelical Presbyterians,

Methodists, Baptists, and even Roman Catholics. Some entire denominations define themselves as evangelical (the Evangelical Free Church, for example), although this is the exception. Many independent Protestant congregations consider themselves evangelical; the phrase *Bible Church* is a give-away.

In addition, the term *Christian media* is used throughout these volumes to refer to the larger grouping of all media claimed to be Christian by one or another Christian group—including Roman Catholic and mainline Protestant media ("mainline" Protestants being those who would not describe themselves as evangelicals). The term *evangelical media* refers to media that evangelicals consider their own media. Along the way, authors refer to "non-Christian" media as "mainstream media" rather than "secular media" to avoid making knee-jerk or superficial judgments about media that do not seem to be very religious, at least on the surface. The idea that particular media are "Christian" and others are merely "secular" does not work very well for understanding the real world. It simplistically suggests that "Christian" media are entirely godly while "secular" media are entirely godless. Using *mainstream* opens up rather than closes off a discussion about how evangelicals are using popular culture and media for spiritual purposes.

Organization of the Three Volumes

In Volume 1, authors focus on evangelicals' use of electronic media in the twentieth and twenty-first centuries, specifically, film, radio and television, and the Internet. Because evangelicals emphasize *evangelization*, they have been among the world's earliest and most innovative users of media, from the printing press to the personal computer and just about everything in-between. Films about Jesus are among the most significant means through which mainstream culture has formed impressions of Jesus Christ and learned about the gospel story. Evangelical interest in film has spurred the development of the academic study of theology and film, birthed several institutes and programs at universities devoted to the subject matter, hatched dozens of popular books for popular consumption, and, in the process, further promoted the role of the "evangelical" critic in American society. Several chapters in Volume 1 describe the history and development of evangelicals in the North American film history and illustrate several models and approaches evangelicals use to critique and interpret film.

Other chapters in Volume 1 describe how evangelicals were some of the earliest radio and television broadcast pioneers in the United States. In the

1950s, television allowed Graham to "preach to more people in one night on TV than perhaps [the Apostle] Paul did in his whole lifetime."[11] In the 1970s and 1980s, evangelicals were among the first to push forward with satellite technology. Today, evangelicals are among the first to use the Internet to form cyberchurches, build online gaming communities, and experiment with the use of social media.

In short, few media bear witness to the evangelical impulse to spread the gospel to all nations as clearly as electronic media. More important perhaps, in the popular mind evangelicals and electronic media are inextricably linked. As the chapters in Volume 1 demonstrate, this linkage comes with its own unique set of benefits and burdens for evangelicals.

In Volume 2, authors address the areas of literature, popular art, music, and merchandise. Evangelicals are known for being people of the "Book"—the Bible—so their love for literature should come as little surprise. Since World War II, religious book sales have increased dramatically, with the 1970s producing religious blockbusters such as *The Late Great Planet Earth* that helped promote evangelicalism for a time. Today, best-selling evangelical cross-over titles such as *The Purpose-Driven Life*, *The Shack*, and the *Left Behind* Series, to name a few, demonstrate the ongoing significance of this medium for evangelical cultural engagement.

Volume 2 further demonstrates how the explosion of popular art and music among evangelicals owes much to the Jesus Movement of the late 1960s and 1970s, which helped to create the Contemporary Christian Music (CCM) industry and simultaneously provide new inroads for evangelicals into mainstream popular culture. Today, CCM is a thriving industry, and its music appeals to evangelicals and non-evangelicals alike. Significant growth within the Christian music industry over the past three decades has helped to promote an evangelical popular culture based on commercialism that in some cases elevates consumer tastes above good theology. The growth of Christian music and merchandise of all kinds further demonstrates the role of evangelical consumption communities in the production of popular culture. Although consumption communities can help strengthen individuals' faith, they also run the risk of commercial exploitation of spiritual desires. Chapters at the end of Volume 2, devoted to the Jesus merchandise phenomenon, Christian candy, and advertising, highlight evangelicals' consumeristic impulse in the name of evangelism, edification, and entertainment.

Finally, in Volume 3, authors explore public figures, popular press, places, and events that demonstrate the ways evangelicals create, consume, and critique popular culture. As the opening chapters in Volume 3 demonstrate, evangelicals remain one of the most powerful political blocs in the nation and continue to influence elections at the local, state, and national levels. Evangelicals who run for office or serve as public figures tend to draw significant press coverage that regularly highlights mainstream press bias against evangelicals and existing religious tensions among Americans. Evangelicals, fed up with mainstream coverage, often turn to their own brand of journalism that provides cultural commentary from biblical perspectives. Chapters on Charles M. Sheldon's Jesus newspaper and evangelical magazines highlight the prominent role that the evangelical press has played in upholding evangelicalism and transforming mainstream culture. Furthermore, several chapters in Volume 3 illustrate that many leading evangelical figures are evangelical celebrities known for their megachurches or broadcast ministries, music careers, or politics. Although these public figures promote the causes of evangelicalism and provide support and encouragement to the faithful, they sometimes become embroiled in scandals that expose the dark side of the intersection between religion and popular culture.

Chapters toward the end of Volume 3 highlight several key evangelical movements and events that are less publicized but nonetheless significant in terms of showcasing evangelical influence in mainstream culture. Although the Jesus Movement is referenced throughout Volume 2, an entire chapter is devoted to it in Volume 3. Leading evangelical women and their national movements are also highlighted, along with lesser-known evangelical film festivals, theme parks, and theatrical events. By the late mid-1980s, evangelical festivals, tourist sites, and theaters were regular destinations in the Midwest and on both coasts. The Jesus Movement had clearly succeeded in promoting a growing comfort among evangelicals with such "worldly" amusements and entertainments.

Key Themes of Popular Culture Engagement among Evangelicals

To help the reader navigate the diverse topics and conclusions spread across the fifty-four chapters that comprise these three volumes, I present several key themes that emerge regardless of the medium, genre, style, or group being discussed. The following themes are by no means intended to be exhaustive or represent every nuance in evangelical popular culture expression in the United States; rather, they are intended to provide a backdrop for the more in-depth analysis of the artifacts, phenomena, and events that appear in the individual chapters.

Contemporary Evangelical Popular Culture Is Grounded in Historical Precedent

The relationship between evangelicals and the broader society is often called the "Christ and Culture" paradox.[12] How should followers of Jesus Christ relate to the world around them and even to their own churches and local communities? Put another way, how should Christians live *in* the world without becoming fully *of* the world (see John 17:14–16)?

These contemporary "Christ and Culture" questions have ancient roots that many evangelicals draw upon in their conversations about popular culture. The main issue for the early Christian Church was how to relate Jesus's teachings to mainstream Roman and tribal Jewish culture. Early Christians discussed whether they should go to Roman games and theater, dance at "non-Christian" festivals, or read Aristotle's "pagan" philosophy. The Apostle Paul, writing letters to early churches endorsing Christian "freedom" against excessive legalism, also cautioned that even though most cultural "things" were permissible, not all of them were "beneficial" for community (1 Cor. 10:23).

The dilemma today includes not just how to engage "secular" theater and books but also how to engage new media such as social networking websites, podcasting, and high-tech worship. Evangelicals face a dizzying array of media and popular culture, from high-tech Bible theme parks to fantasy computer games to intense public relations campaigns for political candidates and megachurch celebrities. Because many of the same arguments used in the early Church are still used today to support or condemn certain forms of evangelical cultural engagement, authors in these volumes were asked to situate their contemporary cases in historical contexts. This allows readers not only to make important connections deep within evangelicals' past but also to predict future modes of engagement.

Evangelical Criticism of Popular Culture Tends to Be Moralistic or Analytical

Broadly speaking, apart from evangelical groups that outrightly reject popular culture and those that accept it with few limitations, regardless of the media or popular culture, most North American evangelicals demonstrate two types of criticism: *moralistic* and *analytical*. The work of both types is illustrated and critiqued across the three volumes.

For some evangelicals, criticism of popular culture tends to be *moralistic*.[13] Such criticism is usually not grounded in a full review of the particular event or pop culture artifact, its context, or its apparent meaning for a given audience. This criticism appears rules based at times (e.g., all R-rated movies, even *The Passion of the Christ*, should be avoided) and often says more about the critic's personal biases or his or her denomination's fears than about the Christian metanarrative. To avoid the negative influences of an ungodly media environment, many evangelicals simply recommend avoiding morally questionable content (mainly sex, violence, and profanity); boycotting media with the most offensive content; and choosing family-friendly programming. Not surprisingly, evangelicals who support moralistic criticism tend to promote or create Christian versions for nearly every form of popular media as a way to teach, encourage, and strengthen faith among believers.

For other evangelicals, criticism of popular culture tends to be *analytical*, that is, exegetical or hermeneutical.[14] This criticism includes close readings of popular myths found in popular media. Analytical critics first define the event or media content, then explain its context, and then identify a dominant reading or interpretation. Finally, they look for "points of tension, synergy, allegory, and irony between the TV series' [or other stories'] meaning and Christian faith." This cultural critique is "lower criticism with a higher purpose, or using a religious metanarrative to exegete the patterns and meaning of mass media's mythological formulas."[15] Rather than placing the Church in opposition to society as moralistic critics tend to do, critics operating within this mode tend to see the Church in dialogue with the world. Put another way, God not only gave Christians the Great Commission (Matt. 28:18–20) but also a mandate to form and inform culture, which calls them to redeem not just individuals but cultural institutions, including the media. Since "all truth is God's truth"—as the popular Christian saying goes—evangelicals should search for faith-affirming interpretations among all types of popular media content. Analytic critics are the first to write books that teach Christians how to "find God" or "look for God" in popular culture of all kinds—from *LOST* to *Harry Potter*, *The Simpsons*, or *The Sopranos*.[16] Such criticism has helped to elevate the role of the evangelical critic among evangelicals and mainstream communities.

Both types of evangelical critics do criticism with one foot in mainstream popular culture and the other firmly grounded in their basic Christian beliefs. Whether dealing with comic books, video games, music, or film, both types try to challenge popular notions of truth embedded in popular culture while asserting their own biblical notions of truth. And both support critical functions of Christian communication and the Church in the world, including evangelism, teaching, and cultural critique.

Yet in assuming that most mainstream popular culture is evil at worst, and unedifying at best, moralistic critics tend to be insensitive to the ways individuals can receive valuable religious truths. They also tend to voice somewhat narrow concerns about media content while ignoring media's promotion of racial and gender stereotypes and consumerism, for instance. Analytical critics, on the other hand, address broader concerns about media content and social institutions yet struggle with walking a fine line between understanding the world and sacrificing good theology. On the plus side, analytical critics are significantly more likely than moralistic critics to consider how technologies are value-laden human constructions that shape the messages they send as well as the people who use them.Several chapters in Volume 1, in particular, address various approaches evangelicals have toward technology and the consequences for evangelical criticism of adopting a particular view of technology.

Evangelical Media "Preaches to the Choir"

Despite their good intentions to reach non-evangelicals, evangelical popular culture is consumed mainly by individuals from the in-group. With notable exceptions, evangelicals often create their own gospel ghettos. Christian books are consumed mainly by those who are "born again," and Christian television attracts overwhelmingly older, already committed evangelicals. Nearly all evangelical magazines and newspapers speak to specific audiences intensely interested in their content. In fact, most evangelical media stay afloat from the support they get from evangelicals audiences, not advertisers. Granted, such media often provide important instruction and cultural critique not found in mainstream media, but it is mainly for Christians.

The downside to all of this, of course, is that in an effort to maintain audiences, evangelical media often self-propagandize, telling already-loyal viewers what they want to hear. Like mainstream media, evangelical media must transform their brands into "destinations," serving their targeted audience "better and in more ways than anyone else."[17] But in preaching to the choir, Christian media tend to promote ideological divisions already present among Christians. In the final analysis, perhaps the most significant impact of evangelical media has been to make various evangelical groups and denominations more cohesive, with shared identities and common understandings of who they are and how they should relate to mainstream culture.

There are exceptions, of course: evangelical painters (Thomas Kinkade), musicians (U2, Brandi, Johnny Cash), actors (Patricia Heaton, Zachary Levi, Tony Hale), and public figures and politicians (Jimmy Carter, George W. Bush, Sarah Palin) who reach beyond the in-group with great success. Some evangelical literature has reached well beyond the in-group, finding a place on best-selling mainstream book lists across the country. The history of evangelicalism in the United States is filled with such examples of evangelicals with "mass" appeal. Although most evangelicals who reach outside the in-group tend to avoid the label "evangelical" because of its negative political connotations, they remain committed to their faith. Such outliers seem to be on the rise among younger evangelicals today (just as they were among the younger evangelicals of the Jesus Movement), and they make for interesting case studies in several chapters across the three volumes.

Evangelicals Avoid Self-Criticism about Their Media

Evangelicals are quick to criticize mainstream media but not always their own media. As explained in Volume 3, the biggest evangelical scandals of the 1980s and 1990s were first reported by mainstream journalists, even though the evangelical press knew about them much earlier. Evangelicals also tend to avoid self-criticism while hurling insults at non-conformists even within their own ranks. Magazines on the evangelical right accuse magazines on the evangelical left of being overly concerned about social justice to the exclusion of other important social issues such as abortion, while evangelical magazines on the left accuse those on the right of imposing their views on every else.

And it seems that many innovative evangelical media artists receive more criticism from insiders than from mainstream audiences. In the process, they get marginalized, pushed underground, or accused of "selling out" or "watering down" their message to appeal to wider audiences. Evangelicals who question the efforts of a popular media "ministry" themselves can become the victims of harsh and often unfair condemnation. As a result, it is difficult to find sustained evangelical community discourse about media and popular culture.

Evangelical Popular Culture Lacks Originality and Artistic Quality

Although evangelicals historically were among the most creative artists, writers, dramatists, and so forth, few of today's North American evangelicals set the trend in mainstream culture. Instead, most tend to follow or mimic mainstream culture and offer a Christian version of just about everything mainstream—does GodTube sound familiar? As one evangelical writer observed, "If imitation is the highest form of flattery, then Christians have become pop culture's most devoted admirers."[18]

Creative or *cutting-edge* would not be words used to describe many evangelical productions. Serious evangelical films are sometimes a joke (although not to most evangelicals). Many evangelical websites are amateurish, with poor grammar and bad graphics. What about the sets used on some evangelical television programs? It is probably fair to say that evangelical productions not only suffer from a lack of originality but also from a lack of artistic quality.

What explains this lack of originality and artistic quality? It could be argued that evangelicals' overemphasis on evangelization as the main goal of all media use has contributed to confusion about the purpose of art and entertainment in human life. For some evangelicals, the only real justification for popular art, including television and film, is evangelism. There is little room for the idea that art might be prophetic, that is, art that is devoted to social justice in that it willingly battles untruths and "lies of corrupt regimes."[19] The measuring stick for good art among evangelicals often becomes how well the particular work sets forth the plan of salvation or points to Christ as "the answer" to any number of (usually individual) problems.

Despite such low marks in the areas of originality and quality, several evangelical stand-outs have risen, and continue to rise, above the norm. *VeggieTales*, for instance, discussed in Volume 1, set new standards for children's animation and enjoyed several years as a top-rated NBC children's show. *Touched by an Angel*, also discussed in Volume 1, was a top-rated show on CBS for many years, led by evangelical writer/producer Martha Williamson, and opened the door for other faith-based programming. Contemporary Christian Music, the topic of several chapters in Volume 2, once criticized for low production quality, has now reached the same production quality as most mainstream music. Other evangelical stand-outs are represented in these volumes in the areas of film, literature, journalism, and popular art.

Evangelical Media Lack Ethnic Diversity

A significant percentage of evangelical popular culture is a Caucasian affair. That is not to say evangelicals are not African American or they do not create, critique, or consume what others would consider evangelical popular culture. African Americans such as T. D. Jakes, for instance, rank at the top of many lists of evangelical leaders and authors. Since the twentieth century, black evangelists have been on the cutting edge of using media in ministry. But for the most part, African Americans are underrepresented in evangelical popular culture outside of two key areas: Contemporary Christian Music and Black Gospel music.[20]

Although North American evangelicals include many ethnic groups and races, audiences would hardly know it. Even more than their mainstream counterparts, evangelical media are owned and operated primarily by Caucasians. These three volumes correspondingly say very little about African American, Hispanic, and Asian media. Is it perhaps because many African Americans, Hispanics, and Asians do not use *evangelical* to identify themselves or their "Christian" media? Whatever the cause, it will not likely last. A large part of the growth of evangelicalism in North America is especially among Hispanic and Asian populations. It is expected that evangelical entrepreneurs within these groups will increasingly launch media, as is already happening among Hispanics in some major cities.

In closing, to trace the history of American evangelicalism through the twentieth and twenty-first centuries is to observe the radio, television, literature, and political involvement of evangelicals. How evangelicals negotiated the "Christ and Culture" paradox in early theater, film, radio, television, music, and popular art offers special insight into the depth and breadth of evangelical modes of cultural engagement and expression. The contents of these volumes demonstrate how evangelicals' personal and communal identities are closely tied to the media they use, the media celebrities they admire, and the artists they appreciate. These volumes further demonstrate that American evangelicals take seriously their challenge to be in the world but not of it, to form and transform culture for the Kingdom of God. As religion and popular culture continue to converge, and as popular culture increasingly becomes a place where the spiritual and transcendent meaningfully work, evangelicals appear uniquely positioned to play a leading role.

Notes

1. For example, see Robert N. Bellah et al., *Habits of the Heart: Individualism and Commitment in American Life* (Berkeley: University of California Press, 1985); Wade Clark Roof, *A Generation of Seekers: The Spiritual Journeys of the Baby Boom Generation* (San Francisco: Harper, 1993); and Wade Clark Roof, *Spiritual Marketplace: Baby Boomers and the Remaking of American Religion*

(Princeton, NJ: Princeton University Press, 2001). Later works in this same vein of scholarship include Stewart M. Hoover and Lynn Schofield Clark, eds., *Practicing Religion in the Age of the Media: Explorations in Media, Religion, and Culture* (New York: Columbia University Press, 2002); and Peter Horsfield, Mary Hess, and Adán M. Medrano, eds., *Belief in Media: Cultural Perspectives on Media and Christianity* (Burlington, VT: Ashgate, 2004), to name only a few.

2. Andrew M. Greeley, *God in Popular Culture* (Chicago: Thomas More, 1988), 9.

3. Some of Noll's significant work includes *A History of Christianity in the United States and Canada* (Grand Rapids, MI: Eerdmans, 1992); *The Scandal of the Evangelical Mind* (Grand Rapids, MI: Eerdmans, 1995); *Turning Points: Decisive Moments in the History of Christianity* (Grand Rapids, MI: Baker Academic, 1997); *American Evangelical Christianity: An Introduction* (Malden, MA: Blackwell, 2000); and *The Rise of Evangelicalism: The Age of Edwards, Whitefield, and the Wesleys* (Downers Grove, IL: InterVarsity, 2004).

4. Randall Balmer, *Mine Eyes Have Seen the Glory: A Journey into the Evangelical Subculture in America* (New York: Oxford University Press, 1989); and Joel A. Carpenter, *Revive Us Again: The Reawakening of American Fundamentalism* (New York: Oxford University Press, 1997).

5. Quentin J. Schultze, *Christianity and the Mass Media in America: Toward a Democratic Accommodation* (East Lansing: Michigan State University Press, 2003).

6. For example, see Nancy T. Ammerman, *Bible Believers: Fundamentalists in the Modern World* (New Brunswick, NJ: Rutgers University Press, 1987) and *Congregation and Community* (New Brunswick, NJ: Rutgers University Press, 1997); Robert Wuthnow, *Sharing the Journey: Support Groups and America's New Quest for Community* (New York: Free Press, 1994) and *Sharing the Journey: Support Groups and the Quest for a New Community* (New York: The Free Press, 1996).

7. See, for example, Roof, *Spiritual Marketplace*, and Shane Lee and Phillip L. Sinitiere, *Holy Mavericks: Evangelical Innovators and the Spiritual Marketplace* (New York: New York University Press, 2009).

8. Jeff Sharlet, *The Family: The Secret Fundamentalism at the Heart of American Power* (New York: Harper Perennial, 2008); and Kevin Roose, *The Unlikely Disciple: A Sinner's Semester at America's Holiest University* (New York: Grand Central, 2009).

9. Daniel Radosh, *Rapture Ready!: Adventures in the Parallel Universe of Christian Pop Culture* (New York: Scribner, 2008), 19.

10. Billy Graham, quoted in Terry Mattingly, "Who or What Is an Evangelical Christian," in *Understanding Evangelical Media: The Changing Face of Christian Communication*, eds. Quentin J. Schultze and Robert H. Woods Jr. (Downers Grove, IL: InterVarsity, 2008), 21.

11. Billy Graham, "The Future of TV Evangelism," *TV Guide* 31, no. 10 (1983): 8.

12. See H. Richard Niebuhr, *Christ and Culture* (New York: Harper and Row, 1951). For a critical update on the *"Christ and Culture"* perspective, see Craig A. Carter, *Rethinking Christ and Culture: A Post-Christendom Perspective* (Grand Rapids, MI: Brazos, 2007).

13. See Schultze, *Christianity and the Mass Media in America*, 201, for a discussion or moralistic criticism.

14. Ibid., 199 for an explanation of analytical criticism.

15. Ibid., 200–201.

16. For example, see John Ankerberg and Dillon Burroughs, *What Can Be Found in LOST: Insights on God and the Meaning of Life* (Eugene, OR: Harvest House, 2008); Connie Neal, *The Gospel According to Harry Potter* (Louisville, KY: Westminster/John Knox, 2002); David Dark, *Everyday Apocalypse: The Sacred Revealed in Radiohead, The Simpsons, and Other Pop Culture Icons* (Grand Rapids, MI: Brazos, 2002); Chris Seay, *The Gospel According to Tony Soprano: An Unauthorized Look into the Soul of TV's Top Mob Boss and His Family* (Lake Mary, FL: Relevant, 2002). More generally, see John Wiley Nelson, *Your God Is Alive and Well and Appearing in Popular Culture* (Philadelphia: Westminster, 1976); Kenneth A. Myers, *All God's Children and Blue Suede Shoes: Christians and Popular Culture* (Westchester, IL: Crossway, 1989); Richard J. Mouw, *Consulting the Faithful: What Christian Intellectuals Can Learn from Popular Religion* (Grand Rapids, MI: Eerdmans, 1994); Rodney Clapp, *Border Crossings: Christian Trespasses on Popular Culture and Public Affairs* (Grand Rapids, MI: Brazos, 2000); Craig N. Detweiler and Barry Taylor, *A Matrix of Meanings: Finding God in Pop Culture* (Grand Rapids, MI: Baker Academic, 2003); and William D. Romanowski, *Eyes Wide Open: Looking for God in Popular Culture*, rev. ed. (Grand Rapids, MI: Brazos, 2007).

17. Ray Richmond, "Thinking outside the Box," *Hollywood Reporter*, October 12, 2006, S-1.

18. Skye Jethani, *The Divine Commodity: Discovering a Faith Beyond Consumer Christianity* (Grand Rapids, MI: Zondervan, 2009), 19.

19. Grace Emmerson, ed., *Prophets and Poets: A Companion to the Prophetic Books of the Old Testament* (Nashville, TN: Abingdon, 1997), 16.

20. See Jonathan L. Walton, *Watch This! The Ethics and Aesthetics of Black Televangelism* (New York: New York University Press, 2009). Walton explains that even African American media theorists and religious historians, in general, have ignored African American broadcasters in their scholarship.

Chapter Summaries for Volume 3

Chapter 1: "Rick Warren: Evangelical Media and Ministry," by Michael A. Longinow. Nationally known evangelical pastor and best-selling author Warren knows people, his Bible, and the ways of American popular culture. That is demonstrated in the massive sales of his book *The Purpose Driven Life*, but it can also be seen in the national and international reach of his ministries through Saddleback Church in California. This chapter analyzes the somewhat controversial work of Warren as twenty-first-century heir to the ministry legacy of another Southern Baptist preacher, Billy Graham, noting the deft, seamless ways Warren navigates questions—from secular news media as well as from Christians around him—about the work he believes God has given him to do in a generation that has become increasingly disenchanted with organized religion.

Chapter 2: "Evangelical Political Engagement," by Denise P. Ferguson. This historical chapter focuses on the involvement of influential evangelical groups in national political elections and public policy from 1980 to 2010. Sections address influential evangelical groups (the Moral Majority, Christian Coalition, and Sojourners); their rhetoric, communication and media strategies, mobilization efforts, and lobbying in advocating for and against public policy and presidential candidates; and their attempts to influence presidents. The chapter also addresses the rhetoric of group leaders and how such groups have shaped, and been shaped by, popular culture.

Chapter 3: "Evangelicals, Politics, and the 2008 Presidential Campaign," by Martin J. Medhurst. This chapter examines the changing nature of evangelical politics by analyzing how three types of evangelicals—progressives, centrists, and conservatives—participated in the 2008 presidential election. Three campaign issues of particular concern to evangelicals (abortion, poverty, and war) are used to illustrate the differences between and among evangelical political voices. These diverse voices are treated as signs of an evolving political consciousness among evangelicals and as possible indicators that the evangelical vote may be far more fluid—and unpredictable—in the future than it has been in the past thirty years.

Chapter 4: "Constructions of Evangelicalism in Media Coverage of Sarah Palin," by Kevin Healey. Palin's religious background has generated intense public debate. Supporters portray her as a mainstream evangelical with benign political beliefs. Detractors claim that she downplays her Pentecostal roots and her ties to controversial religious networks. This chapter argues that, in favoring the former narrative, media coverage of Palin has overlooked important ideological tensions within contemporary evangelicalism. In short, the story of Palin demonstrates how media coverage can influence evangelicals' self-perception as well as the perception of evangelicals by the public at large.

Chapter 5: "Johnny Cash, Evangelicals, and Popular Culture," by Stephen J. Nichols. Following (one of) his conversion(s), Cash, along with his wife June, trekked off to Jerusalem to make the film *The Gospel Road*. In the 1970s, he made frequent appearances alongside Billy Graham. And, when he met up with Rick Rubin, the partnership first produced *My Mother's Hymnbook*. Cash certainly has his evangelical credentials in order. As he has embraced evangelicalism, with his distinctive Southern accent, evangelicals have also embraced him. This chapter explores that relationship.

Chapter 6: "Navigating the Treacherous Waters of Celebrity Culture: A New Challenge for Evangelicals," by Benson P. Fraser and William J. Brown. This chapter focuses on how religious media consumers become involved with religious leaders through parasocial interaction, identification, and celebrity worship. It discusses the influence of celebrity culture on the evangelical leaders and the Church. Numerous religious and spiritual leaders have gained national prominence in recent years, yet how these leaders develop and maintain their followers (audience) is often more the product of a consumer society than it is a serious spiritual endeavor. The chapter discusses the ways in which many of these religious celebrities present the face of evangelical Christianity to mainstream culture and the implications for the Church.

Chapter 7: "Scandalous Evangelicals: Sex, Greed, Politics, and the Arts," by Judith M. Buddenbaum. This chapter examines conventional scandals created by evangelical religious leaders who killed, lied, cheated, and committed adultery in spite of their faith. While the media framed most of those scandals as individual instances of sin and hypocrisy, over time even those scandals took on political overtones as evangelicals became increasingly prominent in the public arena. Therefore, this chapter also examines evangelical political scandals that, through media framing, have tended to tarnish the image of the many through the actions of a few.

Chapter 8: "Evangelical Media Cults," by Quentin J. Schultze. As a form of popular religion, American evangelicalism is organized partly around well-known media personas that function somewhat like the emperors in ancient Roman imperial cults. From their rise during the Protestant Reformation, evangelical-styled Christian media figures have used mass media to create influential religious movements. Contemporary evangelical leaders rely upon print, broadcast, and increasingly online media to establish a particular evangelical movement's public identity and to coalesce supporters around key issues and common interests. The result is influential, symbolic, charismatic evangelical personas that represent evangelicalism to evangelicals and to non-evangelicals.

Chapter 9: "How Evangelicals Are Covered in the News: From Curiosity through Obscurity to the Mainstream," by Judith M. Buddenbaum. This chapter traces mainstream news media coverage of evangelicals from their first appearance on the American religious scene during the First Great Awakening to the present time with emphasis on the period since the mid-1970s when the media discovered evangelicalism through the rise of the electronic church and the political candidacy and subsequent election of Jimmy Carter as president. Although coverage during the past thirty years has focused on politics, and much of that coverage has been negative, attention to evangelicals has also tended to make them the de facto face of American Christianity.

Chapter 10: "Daring to Believe: Evangelical News and Journalism," by Michael A. Longinow. Evangelicals have been involved in news—good and bad—since before the ratification of what we now know as the First Amendment to the U.S. Constitution with its protections for a free press. The saddlebags of circuit-riding preachers plodding through Western territories carried Bibles as well as news from the ports and major cities of the East. Technology through the generations has only sharpened the grip of evangelicals on news that has been crucial to their survival as a people of faith. This chapter brings a critical historical analysis to the news interest and news-gathering of evangelicals over time, noting the connection between the latest technological trends and patterns established over the centuries.

Chapter 11: "Charles M. Sheldon's Jesus Newspaper and the Reformist Impulse in Evangelical Publications," by Michael Ray Smith. Evangelical Christians want to transform the culture, but that impulse appears counter to the conventions used by mainstream newspapers. Among the richest examples of an editor using his faith to reform the mainstream press is that of the Reverend Dr. Charles M. Sheldon. From March 13 to 17, 1900, Sheldon edited the *Topeka Daily Capital* in an experiment to produce a daily newspaper according to explicitly Christian principles. Sheldon had, in fact, proposed just such a newspaper in his 1897 novel, *In His Steps.* While Sheldon did not succeed in his quest to remake mainstream journalism in the image of something sacred as well as newsy, his efforts demonstrate how evangelicals make use of mainstream culture for religious purposes and how an evangelical critique can be brought to bear on popular culture.

Chapter 12: "Evangelical Magazines," by Kenneth E. Waters. In their relationship with mainstream culture, evangelicals are just as diverse and sometimes as contentious as they are when discussing their patterns of worship, church organization, and doctrines. Amid this babble of voices vying for influence stands the myriad of publications created by evangelicals to help them create, maintain, repair, and transform their identity as a co-culture. This chapter explores the history of evangelical publications and shows the important role they still play in influencing both evangelical and mainstream culture and politics. Several examples drawn from independent evangelical magazines such as *Christianity Today*, *Sojourners*, and *WORLD* illustrate this critical role.

Chapter 13: "*Christianity Today:* Uniting Evangelicals, Changing the Culture," by Phyllis E. Alsdurf. The founding of *Christianity Today* magazine in 1956 was the fulfillment of a dream by the Reverend Billy Graham to create a rallying point for evangelicals and encourage their engagement with the culture. As this chapter demonstrates, *Christianity Today* soon became the voice of a marginalized group of evangelicals and helped them coalesce into a more unified social movement. Under the leadership of capable editors, past and present, the magazine has articulated an evangelical response to the culture and provided coverage of a growing and diverse community of evangelicals for more than fifty years. Today *Christianity Today* is a well-established media system with several publications and media services designed to serve more as a gathering place for evangelical opinion shapers than as a means of redeeming the culture.

Chapter 14: "Evangelical Film Festivals," by Terrence R. Wandtke. The essay traces the development of the Christian film festival from its formal inception in the 1990s through the last two decades. By placing this development within the related contexts of U.S. evangelical and film festival histories, this essay argues that certain ideological forces fundamentally shape the culture of the Christian film festival. In particular, as prominent Christian film festivals are profiled, the chapter demonstrates how the festivals belong to categories that emphasize different aspects of mainline evangelicalism: personal conversion and sharing the gospel on one hand and well-founded interpretation and the centrality of Jesus on the other.

Chapter 15: "Themed Destinations, Museums, and Evangelicals," by Annalee R. Ward. Evangelical tourist destinations may vary in purpose, means, and messages, but all demonstrate a mindset of entertainment. How do they express their faith? Why are they drawing attention, and are they viable tourist destinations? To answer these questions, the author set out to visit sites from Florida to Arkansas, Missouri to Ohio, observing and interviewing managers, employees, and visitors at various Christian tourist destinations in the United States. From themed destinations reflecting historical precedence to museums, these evangelical attractions entertain and inspire, but they also raise issues of how evangelicals faithfully engage popular culture.

Chapter 16: "Evangelical Theater in a New Century: Redefining the Redemptive Theatrical Event," by Paul D. Patton. This chapter provides an overview sketch of evangelical engagement in the theater arts, from the many centuries of the church's antagonism to the Roman arenas of entertainment to late-Victorian restrictions on Christian propriety. It demonstrates how the explosion of interest and involvement in theater is also characterized by a unique tension between a concern for Christian witness and a perceived competing loyalty to artistic excellence. The chapter suggests that the key to understanding the strengths and limitations of evangelical engagement in the theater arts is traced to competing aesthetic visions—one "rhetorical" and the other "poetic."

Chapter 17: "Jesus People: The Forgotten Evangelical Offspring of the Counterculture," by Larry Eskridge. The Jesus People movement arose in the late 1960s. This unique combination of the counterculture and evangelical Christianity spread from California to many parts of the United States during the 1970s, briefly attracting much media and academic attention. While the movement faded, as demonstrated throughout this chapter, its effect upon the evangelical subculture was significant both as the source of burgeoning groups like Calvary Chapel and the Vineyard and for its lasting impact upon evangelicals' relationship to youth and popular culture.

Chapter 18: "Evangelical Women's Movements and Leaders," by Kathleen Osbeck Sindorf. Throughout biblical history, women have had important roles, but as Christianity became more organized, women were usually relegated to supporting roles. Only a few extraordinary women gained prominence in the early days of evangelicalism (i.e., Aimee Simple McPherson, Kathryn Kuhlman, and Henrietta Mears), but in the last few decades, especially through the electronic media, more evangelical women leaders have emerged. Women such as Beth Moore, Joyce Meyer, and Kay Arthur are respected as authors, broadcasters, and Bible teachers. Victoria Osteen is now copastor of the largest congregation in the United States. Gatherings like Women of Faith draw thousands of grassroot evangelical women who are poised to be activists for significant issues. While evangelicals still debate the issue of women as elders or deacons, women are exploring new spiritual roles inside and outside the church.

Chapter 1

Rick Warren: Evangelical Media and Ministry

Michael A. Longinow

Rick Warren was on the front page again, but this time it was different. He was looking like a televangelist—the crazy kind. A color picture in the *New York Daily News* on New Year's Eve in 2009 showed him in a sharp-looking navy-blue suit, with cufflinks and a kerchief in the breast pocket, arms upstretched, mouth open. And he was asking for money.[1]

For years, Warren had avoided the look of what were typically "turn-offs" to hip churchgoers in Southern California. Pastors who ask for money are not "cool." Now here he was, shortly after Christmas on the down-slope of one of the nation's worst recessions since the 1930s, telling his church that because typical Christmas-time donations were down, Saddleback Church, in Lake Forest, California, needed $900,000.

For most churches in the United States, such a deficit would be catastrophic. But this church, with an average weekly attendance of more than 20,000, is one of the largest and most influential in the United States. It has a $20 million youth ministry facility and runs four satellite campuses. Its pastoral teaching programs, built on elements of *The Purpose Driven Life* (Pastor Warren's best-selling book), have national impact on how ministers across American evangelicalism approach their pulpits and their church leadership. Clergy in other parts of the world, including developing regions of Africa, use Purpose-Driven church materials.[2]

The New York news media got the photo but failed to "get the picture." This was less an emergency than a family discussion in a really big church family. The news tip had been a note from Warren on the church's website, opening with "THIS IS AN URGENT LETTER." Within a week, the *Los Angeles Times* was reporting that Saddleback had received an estimated $2.4 million more than had been in hand when Warren's appeal letter hit the Web. Warren had pulled out of what the news media had misdiagnosed as a crisis and had done it with grace—again.³

Such is the news equilibrium of perhaps the most media-connected Southern Baptist preacher since Billy Graham.⁴ In fact, there are tangible connections between Graham and Warren. The Saddleback pastor, it was famously reported, wore a winter cap given to him by Graham at Barack Obama's inauguration, a hat Graham had worn at a presidential inauguration years earlier. The Religion Newswriters Association, at the end of 2009, voted Warren the "Religion Newsmaker of the Year."⁵

Rick Warren, pastor of Saddleback Church, Lake Forest, California, shown here (center) while mentoring others. (Courtesy of gregschneider.com.)

Evangelical pastors who use media in their ministries are becoming increasingly common. Those with the media smarts of Warren are not. This chapter looks at Warren as a target for media attention and as a media message shaper. He and a growing number of megachurch pastors have media connections that have historic roots but are a work in progress—a work that has ramifications for media and ministry in this country and around the world for decades to come. This chapter suggests that Warren is atypical of the majority of evangelical clergy in that he understands the ways of news media and can navigate their questions in ways that not only satisfy journalists but pre-empt some of their inquiry. His approach stands in sharp contrast to the ranting of clergy on cable news stations about the politics of abortion, school prayer, or wars in the Middle East. He is not the next Billy Graham. He is not necessarily a prototype for what megachurch evangelical pastors should be in the twenty-first century. But Warren is part of an emerging movement of church and ministry leaders who are figuring out how the Christian mandate of making "disciples of all nations" (Matt. 28:19) relates to public policy trends, global compassion, and the media that interweave them. It is an approach that will be expected, as the twenty-first century unfolds, from an increasingly skeptical American public inside and outside the church.

Warren's Knack for Gaining Media Credibility

What is it about this minister that sets his relationship with media apart from clergy across the nation? Privilege? Specialized training? Political aspiration? It is nothing that sophisticated—except when the sophistication shines through.

Like Protestant clergy tracing back to John Wesley (and even to Martin Luther), Warren is a news commentator (in some ways, a kind of news outlet) that some will heed when they have canceled their newspaper subscription and stopped watching or listening to broadcast news. Warren is among the best at this approach in that he knows his Bible as well as he knows his newspaper and the popular culture that drives his listeners. Others like him in this exclusive group include John Piper, a Minnesota pastor whose writing and speaking have national connections; Bill Hybels, of the widely influential Willow Creek Community Church in the Chicago suburbs; T. D. Jakes, who leads the Potter's House, a media-intensive church in Dallas, Texas; Max Lucado, popular author and teaching pastor of Oak Hills Church in San Antonio, Texas; Charles Stanley, pastor and radio/television ministry host at First Baptist Church of Atlanta; Chuck Smith of Calvary Chapel in Costa

Mesa, California; pastor and church planter Wayne Cordeiro of New Hope Church in Honolulu; and Joel Osteen, a pastor and author with a widely popular television ministry whose church attendees pack the former Houston Rockets stadium in numbers the NBA franchise could rarely muster.[6]

In election years, a mixture of biblical perspective and public affairs and pop culture insight matter more than ever. During the 2008 presidential campaign—a first of its kind in the United States because an African American had won the Democratic party's nomination—Warren was talking about political news.

He wanted his church to care about it. In the early going, he persuaded Hillary Clinton and Barack Obama—not figures beloved by some evangelicals—to speak at Saddleback. Later, he organized an event he called a Civil Forum, for which he brought presidential candidates Obama and John McCain onto the stage at Saddleback for what became an internationally televised moment of political dialogue. Warren came away much talked about but essentially unscathed. "One thing I wanted to do in this forum is say: The church is at the table, the church is intelligent, and the church believes in the common good, not just the Good News," Warren told *Christianity Today* shortly before the presidential election.[7]

Warren was able to succeed with this political event largely because he kept his promise to make the event civil rather than a verbal sparring match between political debaters. Even his critics looked at it as a useful, if comparatively non-combative, moment in the history of the campaign.[8]

A key element of Warren's media credibility is his timing. Whenever possible, he is pre-emptive. Rather than wait for news media to come to him, to his ministry, or to his causes, Warren goes to them. The tendency for many churches in their approach to media is to wait too long to respond to media inquiry. Some fail to reply altogether.[9] At a Pew Forum conference in 2005, Warren told a small group of journalists he had accepted their invitation to speak to them "because I only speak to influencers. . . . I read your stuff all the time."[10]

And he does. It helps him learn what to say and how to say it when news journalists ask tough questions—like whether public speaking is hard for him. Turns out it is. He had to tame a stuttering problem that he still has not completely overcome.[11] And he will talk about it, along with other foibles, to reporters. Such self-deprecation by high-profile clergy goes a long way with journalists who too often have to deal with ego-inflated celebrity interviewees, whether clergy or not.[12]

When Obama chose Warren to give the invocation during an inauguration that was historic in many ways, Warren accepted without hesitation. Like Graham before him, Warren's decision to give that invocation, to step into the political limelight, was not a calculated partisan move. He went there as a minister, with ministry uppermost in his intentions and in the outcome of his words. Washington invocations, which tend to be more than prayer, are scrutinized by news media, pundits, and scholars as statements of political and social significance.

The reactions to his invitation were varied. Episcopal bishop Eugene Robinson, a national spokesman for gays in the clergy, decried Warren's selection as a "slap in the face" to the homosexual community. Conservative evangelicals accused Warren of selling out in a way that could hurt their credibility in the public sphere. In a media world where appearance can be larger than reality, Warren's decision to stand on the platform with those whose rhetoric had fueled decades-long culture wars was, for some, cause for offense even before he opened his mouth.

Some mainstream media in the United States and around the world looked at Warren in this invocation moment as an audacious agitator. Talk radio buzzed about Warren's use of Jesus's name—along with references to Christ that made his deity clear—in the prayer. For some it was too much; for others, not enough.[13]

Yet despite the flurry of criticism, there was at the same time a civility to the onslaught. "He walks the walk," said *Washington Post* columnist Sally Quinn about Warren in a piece prior to his inaugural prayer that defused uninformed criticism of the pastor as a hate-monger.[14] One *Newsweek* writer said, "Many on the cultural left worry that [in his selection to pray at the inauguration] . . . Warren has gained new stature as counselor to presidents. They worry, in other words, that Obama has made Warren the twenty-first century's Graham. They can rest easy. Warren is not Graham. First, the two men see their callings differently; and second, they came to fame in very different eras."[15] Warren does not do stadium evangelism, and he is not a product of the post–World War II evangelical push to counteract the evils of popular culture embodied in entertainment media—such as the swiveling hips of Elvis Presley. Warren is a Southern Baptist pastor doing ministry in the shadow of Hollywood and Disneyland, overseeing a church that has dared to bridge the twentieth and twenty-first centuries armed with an approach to the gospel message that approaches public policy issues through media in cutting-edge ways.

Let it never be said that Warren looks with favor on all news media that show up at his door. Like many evangelical clergy, he views some journalists, whether they are Christian or mainstream, as a kind of necessary evil—particularly those looking for a hype angle rather than trying to really understand what he is trying to say or do. "Why don't you wear Hawaiian shirts any more?" asked *Christianity Today* managing editor Tim Morgan in an interview in 2008. "I threw them all away," Warren said. "It started becoming shtick. Every time I'd read a newspaper (it would) say: 'Rick Warren, the Hawaiian-shirted preacher.' " In reference to news journalists, he added, "Most media have only two stories: build you up or tear you down."[16]

Part of what makes Warren so effective in media appearances is his ability to think on his feet. He can turn a phrase, on cue, on camera, at precisely the right moment. Yet despite all the deftness of Warren's media decisions, there is a careful calculation underlying them. Warren chooses his media moments as carefully as his media advisers. A. Larry Ross, a Texas-based public relations strategist, is one who has helped Warren navigate national talk shows, prayer breakfasts, and international summits. Some of Ross's clients have been Mel Gibson (of Icon Productions), Dreamworks, and the Discovery Channel.[17]

Ross and a team of media strategists help Warren filter out the good from the best invitations in his extensive speaking tours. Warren's time is too precious, and the planet too wide, to accept every request, so they choose opportunities bringing the highest return on his time investment. Warren's chief of staff, David Chrzan, says the big question in deciding Warren's media exposure is whether that medium or that speaking moment will "influence a culture."[18] This is another distinction of Warren's media approach. Whether through aides' help or on his own, he not only grasps the power of media exposure, he senses which of it will target the right audiences at the right time.

When Hurricane Katrina hit the Gulf Coast, he was soon in a skybox beside Oprah Winfrey. He sat across the studio desk of CNN's former talk-show host Larry King explaining why and how megachurches do relief work; he shared the platform in speaking events about social reform with Microsoft founder Bill Gates; he talked through the connections of music and disaster relief with U2's Bono.[19] What is his secret? When Warren shows up for a media moment, he is smooth and affable. People trust him, and he is as comfortable in front of news cameras as he is in front of his sanctuary cameras.

One Sunday, he took to the church stage with a gauze swab and wiped it inside his mouth, holding it up for all to see. Had a preacher ever self-administered an HIV test in church? Perhaps, but never with the media buzz of Warren. "The AIDS test was his idea," Ross told the *Orange County Register*. It was a move that had about it all the insight into audience and media that Ross would have suggested if Warren had asked.[20]

Warren's Media Messages: Connecting at a Life Level

Warren's unique touch as a pastor in a media-saturated culture comes through in his grasp of how his congregation views friendship, power, wealth, the poor, the diseased, and the disenfranchised. Like many churches its size, Saddleback is a media hub. It uses video, audio, print media, podcasting, and the Internet to communicate with those who attend the church.

Saddleback Church's website, shortly before Christmas in 2010, featured a video clip of a woman diagnosed with HIV. Viewers had to click a button over her face to start the clip. In that heart-gripping video, she said she connected with Saddleback because it was a place where nobody asked how she got her infection. They just helped her. Warren spoke briefly in the clip, as did the originator of Saddleback's HIV/AIDS initiative, his wife Kay. More gripping were images of children and entire families walking up to displays that explained what the disease is and what Jesus would say about it today.[21]

Saddleback's Internet media and use of video and audio files is part of a national trend among the largest evangelical church ministries. Research in 2005 showed that 83 percent of churches with 2,000 or more weekly attendees made video files available on a download service such as iTunes. About 30 percent offered video in real time to Web audiences.[22] Saddleback's media approach is not unique in its ability stay on point. But what Saddleback's media tries to do is avoid making its media all about Warren. The point is for those who attend to get increasingly more involved and to pursue a purpose-driven life—one that serves Jesus Christ actively through practical help to the poor, the marginalized, and those in pain in Southern California and in other countries.

A small percentage of pastors in the largest evangelical churches blog regularly on the church website. But a key to the effectiveness of blogs that people know and follow is their ability to break into people's routines with the wonder of the unique. On December 3, 2010, Warren was waiting for a flight in an airport in Dallas typing up a blog post about church leadership. He had just finished a sentence referring to our trust in God for finances: "You don't get scared, you get excited, after you've seen God miraculously provide time and again." Then he broke in with a new segment that began, "You Won't Believe What Just Happened!" On the plane he had just deboarded, a couple had been sitting behind him and told him that though they live in Texas, they believed in the vision of Saddleback Church—and handed Warren a check for $10,000. "How random is that!" Warren wove that anecdote into the blog he was finishing, noting that if total strangers were stepping up in support, maybe Saddleback members ought to as well.[23]

The Saddleback website serves as a hub for Twitter feeds, Facebook activity, and a host of Web pages, video clips, and slideshows. Jay Kranda, part of Saddleback's social media team, says the church has not had an easy road taking Saddleback into the era of instant response on Web-driven devices like smartphones and similar emerging devices. A significant majority of the estimated 22,000 weekend attendees are "boomers" (born in the late 1950s or early 1960s) and are hesitant to go entirely to the Web for their media about Saddleback or to hear from Warren. Saddleback was among the first of the nation's larger churches to move significant parts of its ministry to the Web, but the church still uses paper bulletins on Sunday. Kranda believes that within the next decade the church will be moving closer to a paperless media approach to reaching those who attend Saddleback and those around the world who want to keep up with Warren's teaching. Kranda said the church's media team tracks how many "hits" the church's Web media receive (tens of thousands each week), and they have found the audience for Saddleback's Web media is mostly women, predominantly English speakers, who are between the ages of 35 and 54. Devotees of Warren's online writing are also mostly women, more than 60 percent of them.[24]

Warren's pop culture connection through media harkens back to techniques of nineteenth-century preachers who used what was then cutting-edge media technology—the steam-driven rotary press—to crank out leaflets, tracts, pamphlets, magazines, and newspapers that told stories of real people and their pursuit of faith in Christ. When they could, they tied soul-stirring music to the message. The idea was a precursor to today's convergent media: if one sent people out of a service in the 1880s with an unforgettable phrase ringing in their ears, something in their hands to read later, and a tune on their lips, they would be back, maybe bringing others.[25]

In the late 1800s, the power of Christianity was exploding across the American frontier through "the transforming power of the word, spoken, written and sung," observes religious historian Nathan O. Hatch. Those who showed the greatest mastery of spiritually hungry audiences—people like John and Charles Wesley, Charles Finney, and later Dwight L. Moody and Billy Sunday—were communicators who were "supremely confident that the vernacular and the colloquial were the most fitting channels for religious expression."[26]

Warren's time-tested but media-adapted approach to evangelicals is part of a movement in megachurches that Peter Drucker, a mentor of Warren's with a national following in business leadership, says is as significant as the growth of corporations in the early twentieth century.[27] Warren's management style focuses on new ideas with a flexibility to their development.[28] Media innovation, after all, is a process requiring enormous patience.

Warren was editor-in-chief of *Purpose Driven Connection*, a magazine published in 2009 through Home Service Publications, a subsidiary of Reader's Digest Association.[29] The name of the magazine evoked Warren's best-selling book, *The Purpose Driven Life*. The 144-page slick-cover magazine lasted only four editions before being discontinued.[30] Why so short a run? The reasons are as complicated as the tremors shaking the country's larger media landscape. Americans do not read as they used to. They also increasingly do not want to pay for what they read.[31] But Warren's magazine fizzle should not be considered a failure. It led to more exploration in media that connect people to people in communities to which he is building bridges.

Like media at other megachurches, one strength of Saddleback's media approach is that it is less about media than it is about people. If Saddleback's media can connect the church with the women, the men, the teens, the senior adults—and they find ways of measuring whether they are making such connections—the response is even more powerful in scope than the media that is aimed at reaching them. But it has to be personal, connected with someone like Warren (or those in the leadership team he has assembled) who evokes an "I'm there with you" feel. People touched by this kind of media message will stick around and do things, lots of things, some of them potentially global in scope. It is this connectedness that brings newcomers to Saddleback Church, and it draws mainstream media attention to the church as well.

For Warren, that mainstream media has given him opportunity to craft unique approaches to pastoral advice, some of them in the context of public policy trends. At the level even the most uninitiated can grasp, what has helped Warren draw the distinction as compared with clergy at other megachurches is his knack for pivotal sound bites—short, clipped responses to interview questions that are easily aired or inserted into featured narrative. Warren's way of communicating works in church as well as it does on a news set.

Warren's Purpose Driven Pen: Plain-Spoken Power in Hardback

By Warren's own account, his book *The Purpose Driven Life* was a surprise hit. In 2004, *Publishers Weekly* called the first two years of the book's sales statistics "nothing less than amazing." By then it was pushing 20 million in unit sales with another million sold in a Spanish-language version. It had been translated into fifty-eight languages. Saddleback had sold 4 million "ancillary products" ranging from Purpose Driven journals to Purpose Driven calendars to camouflage editions of the book for military chaplains. (More than 50,000 copies have been sent to U.S. forces in Iraq, 25,000 to the military in South Korea, and 40,000 to the Pentagon.)[32] The book has spawned Purpose Driven study programs that have become part of the ministries of an estimated 10 percent of U.S. evangelical churches; the programs have also been used at Ford, Wal-Mart, Coca-Cola, and the U.S. Air Force. With 30 million copies sold, the book is far and away the best-selling non-fiction work in the recorded history of U.S. publishing.[33]

The Purpose Driven Life has about it an inescapable quality that disarms readers from the opening sentence: "It's not about you," Warren writes. But of course he is wrong, or teasing. It is about the reader. That is why Warren took up the book in the first place. But what the reader does with life's decisions is what the book is getting at. Media scholar Stewart M. Hoover has argued that what audiences look for in the post–September 11, 2001, era is a kind of schizophrenic pursuit of the self while seeking escape from self. Warren's message of Christ—evident in *The Purpose Driven Life* and in much of Warren's media approaches—fits squarely into this seemingly impossible continuum.[34]

Not all evangelicals agree with Warren's approach to readers in the book. Noted evangelical pastor John McArthur has publicly criticized *The Purpose Driven Life* as a dangerous watering down of the message of Christ—one that neglects any reference to repentance from sin and, because it lacks a thorough exegesis of the Bible, can contribute to dangerous misunderstanding of what the Bible means. McArthur, whose church is also in Southern California, has a media presence of his own, hosting a nationwide radio and television ministry. McArthur, who is also president of a Christian college north of Los Angeles, has appeared on King's interview show opposite such notable ideological opponents as former San Francisco mayor Gavin Newsom.[35]

It is Warren's in-your-face approach in the book that grabs readers and will not let them go—even if they disagree with where he is going. A writer for the Roman Catholic publication *Commonweal*, in reviewing Warren's book, recoiled at his notion of purpose-driven pursuit of knowing God. To him, such a pursuit was more intangible than knowable. However, Warren had persuaded him to keep up the pursuit, for "a God this mysterious is clearly more fascinating than the alternative."[36]

Warren and the Media Skill of Avoiding Politics

It could be said that what separates Warren from other prominent evangelicals of the last forty years is his skillful approach to political causes. He has had his moments of political confusion, but Warren is no Jerry Falwell; he will never be mistaken for Pat Robertson. He refuses to be caught up in the momentary—or long-term—battles of culture war. But the battles explode around him constantly.

In this avoidance, Warren does somewhat resemble Graham, who through his career met with presidents ranging from John F. Kennedy to Obama. Graham was more a chaplain than a political ally; he never overtly endorsed any political party and dealt with presidents as people, not political icons.[37] Warren has adopted this pattern. "I'm always asked, 'Are you left wing or are you right wing?' and I say, 'Well, I'm for the whole bird,'" says Warren—a canned quote he brings to press conferences, interviews, and a website called Big Think.[38]

Perhaps the most controversial issue facing evangelical Christians in the late twentieth century has been the homosexual lifestyle and the AIDS epidemic. An estimated 14,000 are infected with HIV each day, a phenomenon that has rocked the U.S. entertainment industries as well as nations on the African continent.[39]

When Warren made AIDS and HIV infection key elements of his ministry outreach, he aligned himself, by default, with gay activists in California and around the nation. That made for tricky media explanations. He put it this way to *USA Today* in 2008: "All of a sudden I started having people of goodwill who were not Christian or not church members saying, 'We'd like to do that. We'd like to partner with you on helping the poor. We'd like to help end AIDS. We'd like to help end corruption and injustice.'"[40]

It makes for a great quote, but in practice, such alliances can make for prickly ongoing policy, especially when it involves leaders of other nations who make decisions with disturbing political implications. In late 2009, Warren made a public statement condemning a law in Uganda that would have made homosexual activity criminal. One *Newsweek* columnist called it a reversal for Warren, who earlier had said, "It is not my personal calling as a pastor in America to comment or interfere in the political process of other nations."[41] Nevertheless, however unwittingly, Warren had interfered, joining himself to a growing movement of evangelical churches in Uganda that critics said had ties to corrupt governmental activity that was abusive of those unwilling to affiliate with evangelical doctrines.

Conclusion

Warren, in the early twenty-first century, stands as a leader among evangelical clergy at the nation's largest churches. He has navigated media inquiry without bringing to the encounters the mistrust and suspicion of journalists so common from church leaders under the news-camera glare. He is a pastor who has refused to allow his people to neglect what he believes is Christ's mandate to take the gospel into all the world (Matt. 28:18–20)—including the sphere of public policy discussion. Yet he has done so without staining himself, at least in any devastating way, in the marketplace of ideas. News media see this and appear, for the most part, to respect it. Warren's global vision is one that has a media-driven focus tying aid for the poor and marginalized to the message of Christ. Other megachurches have international ministries, as do Christian non-profits such as the Salvation Army. Many large churches have a strong media presence, some of them being accepted by local or even national mainstream media; some have preceded Warren by decades with ministry outreach to places like AIDS-ravished central Africa. The difference, though, is that they are not "purpose driven." Warren's is a media voice that connects his message of purpose-driven Christianity with audiences in unique ways by means of his internationally acclaimed book and its parallel study materials. His influence is palpable in the pulpits of evangelical churches both tiny and enormous, in the book aisles of Wal-Marts, in the Pentagon, on upper floors of major U.S. business complexes, and through the scrolling pages of Amazon.com. Yes, Osteen's church is bigger than Saddleback. Hybels was on a first-name basis with Bill Clinton when he was in the White House. Jakes has better appeal to ethnic-minority evangelicals and has appeared in a feature film. But what sets Warren apart is the uncanny shrewdness of his relationship to news media that come calling. He also stands apart from other evangelical Christian leaders in the ways he engages the world of ideas and public policy initiatives with biblical insight woven into simple, straightforward media language—words as well as photos, video, events, and combinations of them all. Not all agree with what Warren has done as an evangelical pastor and media spokesperson to speak on behalf of and to exemplify a simple faith in Christ tied into profound compassion. But they cannot escape the influence of his ministry in a world increasingly skeptical of evangelicals, their churches, and the ways they tell the story of life-transforming power in Christ in the midst of a world of despair.

Notes

1. Catey Hill, "Saddleback Church Pastor, *The Purpose-Driven Life*, Author Rick Warren, Begs Parishioners for $900K," *New York Daily News*, December 31, 2009. http://www.nydailynews.com/news/money/saddleback-church-pastor-purpose-driven-life-author-rick-warren-begs-parishioners-900k-article-1.434038 (accessed June 21, 2012).

2. "Saddleback Church: One Family, Many Locations," http://www.saddleback.com/.

3. Howard Blume, "O. C. Pastor Asks for $900,000, Receives $2.4 million," *L.A. NOW—Southern California, This Just In*, January 2, 2010, http://latimesblogs.latimes.com/lanow/2010/01/pastor-rick-warren-asks-for-900000-gets-24-million-for-saddleback-church.html (accessed February 14, 2010).

4. David Van Biema and Alex Perry, "The Global Ambition of Rick Warren," *Time*, August 18, 2008, http://www.time.com/time/magazine/article/0,9171,1830390,00.html (accessed March 11, 2011).

5. Tim Townsend, "Obama's Cairo Speech Voted Top Religion Story, California Megachurch Pastor Rick Warren Is Named 2009 Newsmaker of the Year," *St. Louis Post Dispatch*, January 2, 2010, A9.

6. Nathan O. Hatch, *The Democratization of American Christianity* (New Haven, CT: Yale University Press, 1989), 24–26.

7. Quoted in Timothy C. Morgan, "After the Aloha Shirts: Retooling Saddleback's International Work and Hosting a Presidential Forum Serve a Common Purpose, Says Rick Warren," *Christianity Today*, October 2008, 42–45.

8. Lynn Neary, "After Saddleback Forum, Some Questions Still Unanswered," *Tell Me More*, National Public Radio, August 22, 2008, http://www.npr.org/templates/story/story.php?storyId=93869924 (accessed December 14, 2010).

9. Eileen Wirth, "The Church and the Media," *America*, August 26, 2002, 22–23.

10. Quoted in Event Transcript, "Myths of the Modern MegaChurch," *Pew Forum on Religion & Public Life*, May 23, 2005, http://pewforum.org/Christian/Evangelical-Protestant-Churches/Myths-of-the-Modern-Megachurch.aspx (accessed December 12, 2010).

11. Tim Stafford, "A Regular Purpose-Driven Guy," *Christianity Today*, November 18, 2002, 42.

12. Biema and Perry, "The Global Ambition of Rick Warren," 36.

13. Stephanie Gaskell, "Warren Foes Say Time to Move On," *New York Daily News*, January 21, 2009, A26; Colbert I. King, "It's Prayer, Not Policy," *Washington Post*, December 20, 2008, A17.

14. Sally Quinn, "On Faith: Pastor Rick's Evolution," *Washington Post*, January 20, 2009, A25.

15. Jonathan Darman, "An Inexact Analogy: The Left Can Breathe Easy, Rick Warren Is Not Obama's Billy Graham," *Newsweek*, January 12, 2009, 47.

16. Quoted in Morgan, "After the Aloha Shirts," 43.

17. http://www.alarryross.com/clients.html (accessed December 14, 2010).

18. Gwendolyn Driscoll, "Rick Warren's Spiritual Spin Doctor," *Orange County Register*, November 7, 2006, 1.

19. Marc Gunther and Christopher Tkaczyk, "Will Success Spoil Rick Warren?" *Fortune*, October 31, 2005, 108–120.

20. Driscoll, "Rick Warren's Spiritual Spin Doctor."

21. "Saddleback Observes World AIDS Day," http://www.saddleback.com/mediacenter/home/Default.aspx (accessed December 16, 2010).

22. Scott Thuma and Dave Travis, *Beyond Megachurch Myths: What We Can Learn from America's Largest Churches* (New York: John Wiley and Sons, 2007), 163–164.

23. Rick Warren, "News & Views," December 3, 2010, http://saddleback.com/blogs/newsandviews/news—views-12310/.

24. Jay Kranda, interview by author, December 17, 2010.

25. George M. Thomas, *Revivalism an Cultural Change: Christianity, Nation-Building and the Market in the Nineteenth Century United States* (Chicago: University of Chicago Press, 1989), 1–2.

26. Hatch, *The Democratization of American Christianity*, 127.

27. See Gunther and Tkaczyk, "Will Success Spoil Rick Warren?" 108–120.

28. Ibid.

29. Marissa Miley, "Reader's Digest Communes with Rick Warren," *Advertising Age* 80, no. 3 (January 26, 2009): 33–35.

30. *Purpose Driven Connection*, Premier Issue, 2009.

31. "Highlights from the Magazine Reader Experience Study Toolkit," Media Management Center of Northwestern University, 2003, http://www.mediamanagementcenter.org/research/magazinetoolkit.asp (accessed December 18, 2010).

32. Daisy Maryles, "Statistics on *Purpose*," *Publishers Weekly*, September 27, 2004, 20.

33. Wendy Kaminer, "Rick Warren, 'America's Pastor,'" *Nation*, September 12, 2005, 28–30. See also Michele Vu, "Christian Books Still Dominate Best-Seller Lists," *Christian Post*, July 4, 2007, http://www.christianpost.com/news/christian-books-still-dominate-all-time-best-sellers-lists-28293/ (accessed March 11, 2011).

34. Stewart M. Hoover, *Religion in the Media Age* (London: Routledge, 2006), 86–87.

35. "John MacArthur on the *Purpose Driven Life*," Bororean.blogspot.com, taken from McArthur sermon, "Apostates Be Warned, part 2," http://www.gty.org, http://www.youtube.com/watch?v=nI9EzMWZoag (accessed March 13, 2011).

36. Thomas Baker, "Purpose-Driven Spirituality: How Deep Does Warren Go?" *Commonweal*, February 24, 2006, 22–23.

37. David Frost, *Billy Graham: Personal Thoughts of a Public Man, 30 Years of Conversations* (Colorado Springs, CO: Chariot Victor, 1977), 97–107.

38. Quoted in http://bigthink.com/ideas/3005 (accessed December 14, 2005).

39. "Where We Stand: Close Encounters with HIV," *Christianity Today*, February 2006, 30–31.

40. Quoted in Cathy Lynn Grossman, "Warren Driven to Expand His Reach," *USA Today*, December 11, 2008, D9.

41. Quoted in Lisa Miller and Katie Paul, "What Took You So Long? Rick Warren Does the Right Thing," *Newsweek*, December 21, 2009, 31.

Chapter 2

Evangelical Political Engagement

Denise P. Ferguson

Flanked by Speaker of the House Newt Gingrich, Senate Minority Whip Trent Lott, Senator Phil Gramm of Texas, and other leading House conservatives, Christian Coalition executive director Ralph Reed Jr. unveiled the Coalition's *Contract with the American Family* at a Capitol Hill press conference just six months after the historic 1994 Republican takeover of both houses of Congress and two-thirds of the nation's governorships.[1] The "contract" was built on a "Survey of American Values," which found that churchgoing Americans were concerned not only about "hot-button" issues such as abortion and homosexuality but also about education and the economy. With its broadened agenda supported by more than 60 percent of Americans, the contract was the opportunity for the Christian Coalition and religious conservatives to make their mark on the new congressional term and U.S. culture.

This chapter focuses on the involvement of influential evangelical groups such as the Christian Coalition in national political elections and public policy from 1980 to 2010. I first review some of the approaches to the intersection of evangelical faith and politics. Second, I discuss the emergence of modern evangelicals' political engagement with the election of "born-again" president Jimmy Carter and exemplified by the conservative Moral Majority and progressive Sojourners. Third, I explain how evangelicals' political involvement gained momentum in the 1980s and 1990s through the combined efforts of the powerful Christian Coalition and other evangelical faith-based organizations. Fourth, I explore how the power of the evangelical vote affected the election of born-again president George W. Bush. Finally, I conclude by exploring evangelical mobilization and voting in the 2008 presidential and 2010 midterm congressional elections and other indications that point to a shift in issues emphasis and political involvement of the next generation of evangelicals.

Influential Philosophies of Evangelical Political Engagement

The role of evangelical Christianity in the public arena is a contentious and hotly debated topic, with a range of political theologies and perspectives on the nature of the interaction between Christian persons, congregations, and government.[2] During the twentieth century, evangelicals experimented with three approaches to public engagement: "*movement politics* (challenges to political institutions), *quiescent politics* (detachment from political institutions), and *regularized politics* (adaptation to political institutions)."[3] Between 1920 and 1940, movement politics and quiescent politics were predominant. After 1940, the founding of the National Association of Evangelicals introduced regularized politics. Since 1970, movement politics (e.g., the Christian Right) and regularized politics have been predominant.

Evangelicals' distance from or involvement in U.S. politics reflects the thinking of a number of influential twentieth-century theologians and philosophers. H. Reinhold Niebuhr, the United States' leading Protestant theologian in the mid-1900s, argued that the United States must exercise global responsibility and maturity as the post–World War II leader.[4] Niebuhr developed an enduring taxonomy or framework explaining several ways Christians may respond to their culture.[5] Three types are particularly relevant to Christians' engagement in the political sphere. The "Christ against Culture" view finds expression in faith traditions such as Anabaptists and Mennonites who distance themselves from culture and avoid political engagement.[6] The "Christ and Culture Paradox" view emphasizes the ongoing conflict between Christ and human culture; these faith traditions encourage believers to participate in government to promote cultural regeneration and prevent degeneration.

Another of Niebuhr's views, "Christ Transforming Culture," recognizes the corruption of culture but is hopeful about the possibility of cultural renewal. Taking this approach, many contemporary evangelicals have participated in the public sphere with the goal of transforming U.S. politics and culture. Christians, as individuals or as churches, can and should participate in government, as in all spheres of life, advocating public policy and organizing political action.

Carl F. H. Henry was a leading voice in urging the evangelical world to regain its social and political voice. Considered by some as the father of the modern evangelical movement,[7] Henry was a leader in the founding of Fuller Theological Seminary, the National Association of Evangelicals, and *Christianity Today*. Henry called evangelicals to translate the gospel to the "political, economic, sociological, and educational realms, local and international," and to "endeavor to provide the leadership, basic principles, and moral energy for movements of justified reform."[8] Likewise, theologian Francis Schaeffer offered a wide-ranging analysis of corrupt modern American culture and, as historian and author Patrick Allitt explains, "urged evangelicals to concentrate on rescuing their world from moral decay."[9] Schaeffer urged fellow evangelicals to get involved in the crucial issues of the day, such as abortion.[10] Schaeffer is credited with first making evangelicals aware in the 1970s of the "culture war" and, more than any other writer, of activating and politicizing evangelicals.

Emergence of Modern Evangelicals' Political Engagement (1970s)

Many evangelicals were uncomfortable with the results of the 1960s, which was the catalyst for Christians to put the concepts of evangelical theologians and philosophers into action in the public sphere. This voice found expression in a variety of new faith-based organizations that reflected the diversity of evangelical attitudes toward political engagement.

The U.S. Supreme Court decision in *Roe v. Wade*, which legalized abortion in 1973, and the Equal Rights Amendment (ERA) to the Constitution, proposed in 1972, were particularly important in shaping conservative evangelical opposition. These issues launched a neo-evangelical movement, commonly known as the Christian Right, that was dedicated to restoring "traditional values" to public policy."[11] This movement was made up of "born-again, evangelical Christians who take seriously Christ's charge to spread the gospel to the entire world."[12] The driving factors behind the rise of this movement were changes in American culture that evangelicals saw as threats to the traditional nuclear family and Judeo-Christian values, including legalized abortion, no-fault divorce, pornography, and homosexuality. Related threats to the family included trends in public education, limitations on the public expression of religion, the state of popular culture (especially television), and the changing role of women. Conservative religious women led the opposition to the ERA's ratification in 1972. Phyllis Schlafly started StopERA in 1972 (renamed Eagle Forum in 1975) to fight states' ratification of ERA. Thousands of evangelical women, including Concerned Women of America founder Beverly LaHaye, joined Schlafly's effective coalition of grassroots activists, who demonstrated outside state assembly buildings when ratification came up for a vote.[13] As the 1970s progressed and the combined efforts of evangelicals gained momentum, legislators and states pulled their support from the amendment.

The civil rights, women's, environmental, and anti-war movements contributed to the appearance of liberal voices as well in the evangelical community. Arising largely from colleges and seminaries, a new group of progressive evangelicals supported an expansion of the public engagement advocated by the neo-evangelicals.[14] The important Chicago Declaration, published in 1973, connected traditional evangelical beliefs to a social justice agenda.[15] The oldest and perhaps best-known of these progressive groups is Evangelicals for Social Action (ESA). Founded in 1973 by the signers of the Chicago Declaration, ESA is committed to social justice, holding liberal views on poverty, foreign policy, and the environment, as well as being prolife and pro-family.[16] Another progressive evangelical organization, Sojourners, founded by Rev. Jim Wallis, began in Washington, D.C., in 1975.[17]

American evangelicals turned out in record numbers for the 1976 presidential election, supporting Georgia governor Jimmy Carter. Comprising nearly a quarter of the entire population, born-again Christians showed they were, "latently, a political force of the first magnitude."[18] Carter promised a foreign policy grounded in the Micah 6:8 principles of Christian decency and respect for human life; he was heavily influenced by Niebuhr's writings about the connection between Christ's teachings and practical politics as a way to alleviate human suffering and align with God's will.[19] Carter's approach was to work toward creating an ethical and just society rather than to right a list of "society's moral wrongs."

Carter was more openly and actively evangelical than any other president of the twentieth century. His election brought the prospect of uniting the evangelical community and "pointed to the ascendancy of Evangelicals into the centers of power."[20] Evangelicals, misreading Carter's brand of evangelism, anticipated a "sweeping spiritual change" in the nation that did not occur.[21] Soon Carter disappointed evangelicals by supporting the ERA, failing to act to stop federally funded abortions, and advocating homosexual rights. Believing the evangelical president had not done enough to support other conservative public policy positions, the Christian Right re-energized itself.

By the end of Carter's presidency in 1980, the New Christian Right arose as a loose coalition of evangelical ministers and lobbyists united by a concern for an increasingly immoral American culture. Its three most prominent organizations were Christian Voice (launched in 1979 and dependent on television evangelists like Pat Robertson, founder of the Christian Broadcasting

Network); the Moral Majority (established in 1979 by televangelist Dr. Jerry Falwell and Paul Weyrich, founder of the Free Congress Foundation); and Religious Roundtable (created in 1980 for conservative ministers uncomfortable with Christian Voice or the Moral Majority).[22]

Falwell had an inclusive vision, believing that a majority of Americans from many religious backgrounds shared a common morality that was under assault in modern society. The Moral Majority's success in mobilizing evangelicals has been credited to substantial financial resources, an extensive communications network between the organization and its constituents that focused on grassroots activism, and organizational expertise and leadership that took advantage of evangelicals' growing dissatisfaction with American popular culture.[23]

The Moral Majority campaigned vigorously against Carter in his reelection bid, and, instead, the New Christian Right supported California governor Ronald Reagan, who held conservative positions on profamily issues of concern to evangelicals. Christian Voice, the Moral Majority, and Religious Roundtable worked within both major political parties, having their greatest success with Republicans, and evangelicals were a much-noticed presence at the 1980 Republican Convention.[24] After poll data indicated that only 55 percent of all evangelicals were registered to vote, the alliance of organizations urged ministers to get their congregants enrolled, resulting in an estimated 2 million new registered evangelical voters.[25] Falwell and other New Christian Right leaders claimed some credit for Reagan's victory, and even pollster Louis Harris's results showed that evangelical turnout for Reagan put him in the White House.[26] Schlafly proclaimed that Reagan won the nomination and election because he "rode the rising tides of the pro-family movement," and although the economy was the main issue, the social issues were "motivating" ones.[27] Thus, after Reagan's inauguration, evangelicals insisted that the president and new Congress act quickly on social issues.

Evangelicals Gain Momentum (1980s)

Reagan's election, aided by the votes of born-again white Protestants, raised expectations for action on a variety of social issues that were not fulfilled. The Reagan administration directed its attention to the most urgent issues and policy agenda—the economy, defense, and federalism, respectively—despite Reagan's campaign promises to quickly move on social issues.[28] During this period, Reagan's challenge was to rally the country behind his economic program while reassuring evangelicals that he had not modified or abandoned their goals. In the spring of 1982, amid criticisms from social conservatives about unfulfilled campaign pledges, the new administration proposed a School Prayer Amendment to the Constitution to overturn the 1962 and 1963 Supreme Court decisions outlawing Bible reading and state-sponsored prayer. Although controversial and opposed by some within Christian circles, "it was a historic change on school prayer and the role of government."[29]

Despite the energized re-entry of evangelicals into public life, evangelicals achieved few legislative successes by the end of Reagan's second term. Few evangelicals were named to federal posts, and there was no significant change in widespread abortion, tuition tax credit, gay rights, and school prayer policy. The lack of success on those fronts only increased the determination of evangelicals to advance their agenda, and in 1988 they began looking for a new champion.[30]

Evangelicals' continuing influence was evident in the presidential election of 1988 when Pat Robertson ran for the Republican nomination, showing strongly in the Iowa caucuses and six state primaries. Robertson had "made history by applying the tools and skills of modern television evangelism to presidential politics."[31] Two days before the Iowa precinct caucuses, it was clear that a real fight had developed for the evangelical vote. The two Republican candidates who claimed the most support were Jack Kemp, a Republican congressman from upstate New York, and Robertson. Robertson was said to have the superior organization and promised to surprise the pundits with his showing, claiming that he would "bring in thousands of conservative evangelicals, many of whom had never participated in caucuses before."[32] When the straw poll was tallied, Robertson received thirty-eight votes, nearly 50 percent of the Republicans present, with Bob Dole second.

Meanwhile, Vice President George H. W. Bush was being instructed on how to communicate appropriately with evangelicals and their leaders; one advisor recommended he read C. S. Lewis and Francis Schaeffer.[33] The vice president was cautioned to make sure "that his own early encounters with leaders of the Evangelical Movement do not reveal a lack of understanding of the values,"[34] and was coached on what to say to evangelicals—proof of their voting bloc power. Ultimately, reservations about Robertson's religious beliefs and occasional outlandish statements, the inexperience of his political machine, and scandals involving other prominent televangelists proved barriers to a successful nomination bid. In the end, Christians shifted their Reagan loyalty to George H. W. Bush, giving him an astounding 81 percent of the evangelical vote—higher than the 75 percent for Reagan in 1984.

In brief, the 1980s were spectacular for American evangelicals and witnessed their powerful reentry into political life. However, evangelicals' success in achieving the attention of political leaders and the media failed to translate into significant public policy change. One sign of the evangelicals' disappointment as the decade ended was Falwell's decision to disband the Moral Majority, although he claimed that the goal of solidifying the Religious Right had been achieved.[35] Evangelicals would continue to influence U.S. politics and culture, and the rise of another organization to take the Moral Majority's place—the Christian Coalition—demonstrated conservative evangelicals' belief that outside pressure on politicians would be as necessary in the 1990s as it had been in the 1980s.

Change in Power (1990s)

After the Moral Majority disbanded, other Christian Right groups came to prominence in the late 1980s and early 1990s. One important cluster of groups grew out of Focus on the Family, founded in 1977 by Dr. James Dobson as a para-church organization devoted to family life and traditional values. Most of Focus's efforts were nonpolitical, but it did support three avenues for evangelical political engagement.[36] First, it encouraged the formation of "community impact committees" in local churches, thus creating a grassroots structure for activism in local school and government bodies. Second, Focus merged with Family Research Council in Washington, D.C., in 1988 and formed organizations in many state capitals. Third, Dobson and other movement leaders founded the Alliance Defense Fund (1993) to carry out litigation, as well as Focus on the Family Action (2004) to engage in nonpartisan electoral work. Other important groups continuing into the 1990s included Concerned Women for America (1979), the Traditional Values Coalition (1983),[37] and the American Family Association (1977).[38]

The most influential evangelical political organization through most of the 1990s, however, was the Christian Coalition, with the motto "Giving Christians a Voice in Their Government." Building on his 1988 campaign, Robertson founded that grassroots organization in 1989 and hired Reed, a former national director of the College Republicans with a recent doctorate in history, to start the Christian Coalition, leading it as executive director for almost a decade. The Coalition poured its resources into grassroots training workshops, voter guides, and phone banks, "transforming evangelicals into precinct workers and party leaders, and training them to run for office themselves."[39] Whereas Falwell and Robertson had previously focused on the national political scene, Reed focused on local politics. He organized politically conservative Christians to win elections to local school boards and to run for county and township offices.

Just as opposition to President Carter had motivated the Christian Right movement, dislike of President Bill Clinton's policies, which were contrary to most of the conservative evangelicals' values, provided a strong impetus for the second phase of evangelical action in the 1990s. Clinton's "peripheral attachment to the evangelical community (having been raised among Baptists in the South) and his extensive use of evangelical language (his platform in 1992 was called 'the new covenant') appear to have intensified the hostility among Christian Rightists."[40]

The Christian Coalition was energized after its successful 1992 voter turnout. Exit polls showed that 24 percent of all voters were self-identified evangelicals.[41] The organization also began implementing its plan to broaden its issues base to encompass economic issues, although moral issues, focusing on abortion and homosexuality, continued to receive high priority.

The Coalition's staff and membership was composed of people of faith across a variety of Christian traditions, including Baptists, Presbyterians, Methodists, Pentecostals, and Catholics. The organization "was not established to further a particular sectarian dogma but rather to see religious conservatives elected to office, and to encourage governments to pass legislation that strengthens families and protects religious freedom."[42] In 1994, founder Robertson joined Chuck Colson and other well-known Protestants in signing "Evangelicals and Catholics Together," a document that encouraged cooperation between the two largest Christian groups.

The Coalition's ultimate focus for 1994 was the midterm congressional elections. The $25 million-a-year operation produced and distributed 60 million pieces of literature for that election, including 33 million voting guides.[43] Post-election surveys showed an increase in religious conservative voters from 24 percent in 1992 to 33 percent in 1994; nearly half of religious conservatives who had voted for winning candidates had seen a Christian Coalition voter guide.[44] Evangelicals and pro-family Catholics comprised 40 percent of all Republican votes. For the first time in forty years, the Republicans had gained control of Congress, and evangelicals had played a central part in those victories and in Republican wins in two-thirds of state governorships.

During the mid-1990s, however, the Christian Coalition's fortunes changed. One of the most influential factors in the Coalition's declining influence was the resignation of Executive Director Reed in 1997. Due to

24 Evangelical Christians and Popular Culture

Ralph Reed Jr., executive director of the Christian Coalition, gestures while appearing on NBC's *Meet the Press* in this May 21, 1995 photo. (AP Photo/Joe Marquette.)

leadership changes, financial difficulties, and staff departures, the late 1990s saw a steep decline in the group's political power.

The Christian Coalition was a powerful force in evangelicals achieving influence on a national conservative political agenda—by some considered to be "the most successful social conservative organization in this country."[45] Its focus on mobilizing evangelicals to gain office in local, state, and national elections; to pass family-friendly laws at all levels of government; and to exercise their citizenship as never before is still being felt in the twenty-first century.

Evangelicals and the Born-again Presidency of George W. Bush (2000–2008)

The crowded field for the Republican nomination for president in 2000 included the second evangelical candidate, former Family Research

Council head Gary Bauer, and U.S. senator John McCain. Attacks McCain made on conservative evangelical leaders Robertson and Falwell energized faith-based conservatives and resulted in the disintegration of his campaign for the Republican nomination, becoming "the turning point in the entire Republican presidential nomination."[46] Exit polls showed that an estimated 68 percent of evangelicals voted for George W. Bush in 2000,[47] and the percentage of evangelical voters mobilized by faith-based groups declined in 2000.[48] Nonetheless, the united voice of the Christian Right was crucial to Bush's win.

In Bush, evangelicals "found a born-again Christian who, unlike Jimmy Carter, spoke their language and subscribed to their views."[49] To the presidential debate question, "Which philosopher has made the greatest impact in your life?" Bush responded, without hesitating, "Christ. Because He changed my heart." His response was predicted to be "the most memorable sound bite of the early season.... [It] was an extraordinary moment where secular politics and religious faith intersected."[50] Had it not been for evangelicals' prominence in public life during the previous decade, "Bush's answer to the question would not have been a major story for days to come."[51] According to a former Christian Coalition leader, far more than Reagan or George H. W. Bush, President George W. Bush believed that "religious groups should participate actively in public life and should receive their fair share of public funds."[52] However, his first term showed a mixed record on social issues dear to evangelicals. His most significant effort to integrate faith into public policy was creating the Office of Faith-Based Initiatives, yet the program was criticized by prominent Christian leaders.[53] Evangelicals were dismayed at some of Bush's federal appointments and nuanced position on the controversial stem cell issue but pleased with his signing the ban on late-term abortions, the executive order banning federal funding for international agencies that provide abortions, and support for education vouchers.[54]

Past efforts to mobilize evangelicals had been dominated by groups such as the Moral Majority and the Christian Coalition, but in 2004 the largest organizations were Focus on the Family and the Family Research Council. There were also many smaller groups and individual pastors involved in get-out-the-vote efforts. In early October, Focus on the Family released a "must-read election message," signed by Dobson and more than eighty prominent evangelical Protestants, stating that the Bible teaches lessons about proper government, including not only opposition to abortion and same-sex marriage but also support for the war in Iraq. Focus on the Family radio and online broadcasts were part of a vigorous campaign to galvanize the 25 million Christians they estimated did not vote in the 2000 election.[55] By October 30, the organization had mailed more than 1 million voter registration kits modeled after a similar initiative by the Southern Baptist Convention (SBC).[56] The 16.3 million-member SBC, never before actively involved in a national voter registration drive, also worked to mobilize Christian voters. The SBC outfitted an eighteen-wheel tractor-trailer as a mobile registration center, set up a website—iVoteValues.com—and helped Focus on the Family create a similar website, iVoteValues.org.[57] Both were Internet-based versions of the older voter guides earlier distributed by the Christian Coalition.

Reed, heading the Bush-Cheney campaign's Southeast efforts after leaving the Christian Coalition, said that "what's most different about 2004 is that for the first time, the effort to get out the socially conservative faith community has been fully integrated into the presidential campaign."[58] All along, Bush's chief campaign strategist Karl Rove had argued that if Bush could turn out millions of conservatives and evangelical Christians who stayed home in 2000, he could win.[59] What was important, said Reed, was that "there has been an evolution of the conservative faith vote from a marginal position to a mainstream position within the Republican Party."[60]

Many political and media experts claim the "values vote" was the deciding factor in the 2004 national elections, and evangelicals (especially those who attended church more than once a week) were influential in Republican wins.[61] Contrary to media predictions that "it's the economy, stupid," exit polls of voters nationwide showed 22 percent citing "moral values" as their top issue.[62] Of voters who cared most about moral values, 80 percent voted for Bush. In a year of increased turnout across many demographic characteristics, conservative Christians appeared to have increased more than the national average. Whereas the percentage of the electorate identified as "religious right" had declined from 17 percent in 1996 to 14 percent in 2000, in 2004 they made up 23 percent of the electorate, with 78 percent voting for Bush-Cheney.[63]

Bush's re-election stimulated the evangelical left to offer an alternative moral vision and agenda to that of the Religious Right. While many conservatives applauded Falwell's call to "take back the culture," other evangelicals contested it as a distortion of true evangelicalism. Sojourners leader Wallis urged believers to "take back the faith" that had been "co-opted by the Right."[64] Wallis charged the Religious Right with getting the "public meaning of religion mostly wrong—preferring to focus only on sexual and cultural issues while ignoring the weightier matters of justice."[65] Through the presidential election of 2004, the Religious Right had been able to point to more influence in the political arena. Falwell and others mobilized their conservative base and kept it united to a far greater extent than those sympathetic to Wallis's views.

While the continuing trend of Christian voters was apparent in the 2008 elections and benefited Republican McCain, the percentage was weaker than in 2004. President-elect Barack Obama made modest gains among evangelicals and mainline Protestants, and especially strong gains among minority Christians.[66] A sharp shift to economic issues may have been largely responsible for the vote softening; election results offered "a counterpoint to the 2000 and 2004 results, revealing the traditionalist alliance's strengths and weaknesses under sharply different political circumstances."[67] Another explanation is that, after 2004, Democrats tried to close the "God gap" between churchgoing voters and less religious Americans.[68] Wallis was invited by Democratic hopefuls Hillary Clinton, Obama, and John Edwards to discuss religion, values, and liberal social policy. In 2008, candidates for the Democratic nomination courted the evangelical vote. Clinton talked about her prayer life and Obama talked about his faith during a candidate forum at Rick Warren's Saddleback Church. After "clinching the nomination, Obama announced his intention to expand the role of churches in social spending."[69] In his campaign, Obama worked hard on an outreach to moderate evangelicals and was successful in some states, especially among young voters. The Pew Center on Religion and Public Life found that 30 percent of under-thirty white evangelicals voted for Obama, compared to the 22 percent who voted for McCain. An even more dramatic result was that young evangelicals gave Bush and the Republican Party negative ratings.[70]

The question is whether the Democratic Party will take advantage of this negative Republican brand and make greater inroads with young evangelicals, or whether the Republican Party will rehabilitate its image to attract these young voters. Centrist evangelicals are strongly against abortion, gay marriage, and euthanasia, but they also see room in a broad, holistic agenda for human rights for the plight of the poor and peacemaking.[71] Sixty percent of evangelicals identified themselves as interested in "protecting the environment, tackling HIV/AIDS, alleviating poverty, and promoting human rights,"[72] according to a July 2008 online BeliefNet poll (with a younger sample). Among the issues most concerning them were reducing poverty, improving health care and education, and stopping torture. Seventy percent still said that ending abortion was important or very important; almost 50 percent opposed same-sex marriage. Another 2008 preelection poll, by

Relevant, a magazine targeting evangelicals under twenty-five, asked respondents who they believed "Jesus would vote for," and a plurality said Obama.[73] These results indicate that young evangelicals lack a connection to the traditional Religious Right, differ strongly on domestic policy issues related to poverty, and are dissatisfied with the United States' foreign policy and the war.

Conclusion

As the 2010 mid-term elections approached, there was little coordinated political activity on the part of evangelical groups; however, a political movement of loosely affiliated local and national protests was growing. The Tea Party movement, made up of Americans self-described as conservative and libertarian, is unlike the evangelical movements of the 1980s and 1990s that were energized primarily by narrowly defined moral issues. The Tea Party movement is primarily a reaction to policies proposed and implemented since January 2009. Tea Partiers' concerns center on the federal deficit and taxes, a federal government that has too much control over individual liberty, and Washington officials who do not listen to them.[74] While the mainstream media and some politicians claim Tea Partiers are another brand of the Religious Right, that may not be a valid generalization. Although 44 percent say they are Christian fundamentalists, Tea Party supporters are more likely to be older, white, and male, according to a Bloomberg national poll.[75] Another poll, by the Public Religion Research Institute, indicates that nearly half (47 percent) of Americans who identify with the Tea Party consider themselves part of the Christian conservative movement and that the movement makes up 11 percent of the adult population, which is half the size of the conservative Christian movement.[76] In addition, more than three-quarters prefer the Republican Party, and 63 percent say abortion should be illegal in most or all cases.

These demographics show significant overlap, yet there is a lesser percentage of young evangelicals who are active in the Tea Party movement. There are moderate and progressive evangelical voices that caution evangelicals against aligning themselves too closely to the Tea Party's libertarian positions. They argue that because Christians are called to care for the poor and underprivileged, Christians "belong outside the tea party."[77]

Evangelicals may be at a crossroads in their thinking and propensity to engage in political and social life. Many conservative evangelical organizations that mobilize the grassroots to gain local and national pressure to produce change in elections and public policy have lost strength, and their repeated attempts to transform culture through legislating morality have been limited. A new generation of evangelicals is rising with a broader scope of moral concern for social justice and demanding authenticity and unity between thought, or belief, and action.[78]

Notes

1. Joel Vaughn, *The Rise and Fall of the Christian Coalition* (Eugene, OR: Wipf and Stock, 2009).

2. Jay Budziszewski, *Evangelicals in the Public Square* (Grand Rapids, MI: Baker Academic, 2006); H. Reinhold Niebuhr, *Christ and Culture* (New York: Harper and Row, 1951); and Francis Schaeffer, *How Should We Then Live?* (Wheaton, IL: Crossway, 1976).

3. J. C. Green, "Seeking a Place," in *Toward an Evangelical Public Policy*, eds. Ronald J. Sider and Diane Knippers (Grand Rapids, MI: Baker, 2005), 15.

4. See Patrick Allitt, *Religion in America since 1945: A History* (New York: Columbia University Press, 2003).

5. Niebuhr, *Christ and Culture*. See also George Marsden, "Christianity and Cultures: Transforming Niebuhr's Categories," *Insights: The Faculty Journal of Austin Seminary* 115, no. 1 (Fall 1999), http://religion-online.org (accessed January 5, 2011).

6. Amy E. Black, *Beyond Left and Right* (Grand Rapids, MI: Baker, 2008).

7. Budziszewski, *Evangelicals in the Public Square*, i.

8. Quoted in ibid., 6.

9. Allitt, *Religion in America*, 156.

10. Schaeffer, *How Should We Then Live?* 254–265.

11. Green, "Seeking a Place," 26.

12. Frank Lambert, *Religion in American Politics* (Princeton, NJ: Princeton University Press, 2008), 184.

13. Allitt, *Religion in America*, 165.

14. Jorstad Erling, *Evangelicals in the White House: The Cultural Maturation of Born-again Christianity, 1960–1981* (New York: Edwin Mellen, 1981), 153.

15. Green, "Seeking a Place," 25.

16. Ibid., 30.

17. Sojourners, http://www.sojo.net/index.cfm?action=about_us.mission (accessed December 15, 2010).

18. Allitt, *Religion in America*, 154.

19. Ibid., 150.

20. Paul Toews, book review, *Direction*, 12, no. 4 (April 1983), http://www.directionjournal.org/article/?472, para. 1 (accessed December 15, 2010).

21. Janis Johnson, "A Born-again Style at the White House," *Washington Post*, January 21, 1977, A18.

22. See Robert C. Liebman and Robert Wuthnow, *The New Christian Right* (New York: Aldine, 1983).

23. Robert Booth Fowler, *A New Engagement: Evangelical Political Thought, 1966–1976* (Grand Rapids, MI: Eerdmans, 1982), 55–57.

24. Ibid.

25. Ibid., 37.

26. Louis Harris, "Pollster Gives Conservative Groups Credit for Reagan Win," *Greenville News* (Greenville, SC), November 15, 1980, 3A.

27. Quoted in "The Conservative Pro-family Movement Nominated, Elected Ronald Reagan," *Conservative Digest*, January 1981, 21.

28. Martin J. Medhurst, "Postponing the Social Agenda: Reagan's Strategy and Tactics," *Western Journal of Speech Communication* 48 (1984): 262–276.

29. Richard Cizik, "A History of the Public Policy Resolutions of the National Association of Evangelicals," in *Toward an Evangelical Public Policy*, eds. Ronald J. Sider and Diane Knippers (Grand Rapids, MI: Baker, 2005), 51.

30. Randall Balmer, *Mine Eyes Have Seen the Glory* (New York: Oxford University Press, 1993), 173.

31. Dudley Clendinen, "Robertson Sets Condition for Making a Run in 1988," *New York Times*, September 18, 1986.

32. Quoted in William Martin, *With God on Our Side* (New York: Broadway, 1997), 148.

33. Ibid., 262.

34. Ibid., 263.

35. Allitt, *Religion in America*, 198.

36. Green, "Seeking a Place." See also John C. Green et al., *The Values Campaign?: The Christian Right and the 2004 Elections* (Washington, DC: Georgetown University Press, 2006).

37. Traditional Values Coalition, http://www.traditionalvalues.org/ (accessed January 4, 2011).

38. "Our Mission," American Family Association, http://www.afa.net/Detail.aspx?id=31 (accessed January 4, 2011).

39. Vaughn, *The Rise and Fall of the Christian Coalition*, 3.

40. Green, "Seeking a Place," 27.

41. Ralph Reed Jr., "Casting a Wider Net," *Policy Review*, July–August 1993, 31–35.

42. Ibid., 55.

43. Denise P. Ferguson, "Rhetorical Public Relations and Issues Management Strategies of Social Movement Organizations: The Communication of Values and Policy Preferences," PhD diss., Purdue University, 1999, 54.

44. Vaughn, *The Rise and Fall of the Christian Coalition*, 74.

45. Mark Rozell, quoted in Vaughn, *The Rise and Fall of the Christian Coalition*, 200.

46. Jeff Greenfield, "CNN Super Tuesday Wrap-up," CNN, March 7, 2000.

47. "Religion and the Presidential Vote," Pew Research Center for the People and the Press, December 6, 2004, http://people-press.org/commentary/?analysisid=103.

48. Mark J. Rozell, "Bush and the Christian Right," in *Religion and the Bush Presidency*, eds. Mark J. Rozell and Gleaves Whitney (New York: Palgrave/Macmillan, 2007), 25.

49. Lambert, *Religion in American Politics*, 205.

50. Vaughn, *The Rise and Fall of the Christian Coalition*, 200.

51. Ibid.

52. Ibid., 205.

53. Rozell, "Bush and the Christian Right," 20; and Lambert, *Religion in American Politics*, 206.

54. Ibid., 20.

55. Denise P. Ferguson, "Evangelical Fervor: Energizing Conservatives to Go to the Polls in 2004," Religious Communication Association Pre-Conference, Chicago, IL, November 2004.

56. Judith Kohler, "GOP Looks to Solid Backing from Conservative Christian Groups," Associated Press State & Local Wire, October 30, 2004.

57. Alan Cooperman, "Evangelical Leaders Appeal to Followers to Go to Polls; Efforts Are Planned to Amplify Religious Conservatives' Voice," *Washington Post*, October 15, 2004, A06.

58. Quoted in ibid.

59. Todd Purdum, "President Found Believers in Nation's Center," *New York Times*, November 4, 2004, http://www.nytimes.com.

60. Quoted in Cooperman, "Evangelical Leaders Appeal," A06.

61. Rozell, "Bush and the Christian Right," 22.

62. Tina Susman, "Polls Show Faith, Morality Issues Drew Voters to Bush," November 4, 2004, http://www.newsday.com.

63. "Religion and the Presidential Vote," Pew Research Center for the People and the Press, December 6, 2004, http://people-press.org/commentary/?analysisid=103.

64. Jim Wallis, *God's Politics: A New Vision for Faith and Politics in America* (New York: HarperSanFrancisco, 2005), 3–4.

65. Ibid., 4.

66. "How the Faithful Voted," Pew Forum on Religion and Public Life, http://pewforum.org/Politics-and-Elections/How-the-Faithful-Voted.aspx (accessed December 29, 2010).

67. John C. Green, "Exploring the Traditionalist Alliance: Evangelicals, Protestants, Religious Voters, and the Republican Presidential Vote," in *Evangelicals and Democracy in America*, vol. 1, eds. Steven Brint and Jean Reith Schroedeel (New York: Russell Sage Foundation, 2009), 150.

68. David Paul Kuhn, "The Gospel According to Jim Wallis: For Democrats to Win Back the White House, They May Well Have to Rely on the Power of the Almighty. And It's Not Bill Clinton," *Washington Post*, November 26, 2006.

69. Steven Brint and Jean Reith Schroedel, *Evangelicals and Democracy in America. Vol. 2: Religion and Politics* (New York: Russell Sage Foundation, 2009), 78.

70. Michael Cromartie, "A Post-Election Look at Religious Voters in the 2008 Election," Pew Forum on Religion and Public Life, Faith Angle Conference, Key West, FL, December 8, 2008.

71. Daniel Burke, "A Crash Course in God and Politics: Books on Faith and Public Life Proliferate as Election Near," *Washington Post*, February 9, 2008, B09.

72. David Kuo, "It's Not Your Father's Religious Right," *Washington Post*, February 24, 2008, B01.

73. Quoted in Nicholas Kristof, "Who Is More Electable?" *New York Times*, February 7, 2008.

74. Dan Well, "Rasmussen: Tea Party Shows Weakness of GOP Establishment," Newsmax.com, September 18, 2010, http://www.newsmax.com/InsideCover/ScottRasmussenReportspollster/2010/09/18/id/370770.

75. Heidi Przybla, "Tea Party Advocates Who Scorn Socialism Want a Government Job," Bloomberg, March 25, 2010, http://www.bloomberg.com/apps/news?pid=newsarchive&sid=aLBZwxqgYgwI&pos=8 (accessed January 5, 2011).

76. Robert P. Jones and Daniel Cox, "Religion and the Tea Party in the 2010 Election: An Analysis of the Third Biennial American Values Survey," Public Religion Research Institute, October 2010.

77. David P. Gushee, "Christians Belong outside the Tea Party," *Christianity Today*, October 27, 2010, http://www.christianitytoday.com/ct/2010/october/32.55.html (accessed December 15, 2010).

78. Robert E. Webber, "The Younger Evangelicals: Facing the Challenges of the New World," http://www.facingthechallenge.org/webber.php (accessed June 21, 2012).

Chapter 3

Evangelicals, Politics, and the 2008 Presidential Campaign

Martin J. Medhurst

The 2008 presidential campaign provides a compelling backdrop for the examination of evangelical politics in the United States. From the reemergence of evangelicals into national politics in the 1976 presidential campaign to the overwhelming mandate that white evangelicals delivered to George W. Bush in the 2004 presidential election, evangelical Christians have been one of the most important electoral demographics, comprising between 25 and 33 percent of the electorate.[1] Evangelicals are distinguished from other types of Christians by their theological beliefs, chief among them the necessity for a new birth in Christ Jesus (often referred to as being "born again"), reliance upon the Bible as the written and authoritative word of God, a calling to share the "good news" of the gospel with other people, and a general belief that all of life—including politics and government—is under God's control and subject to his will and direction.

Having won the popular vote yet lost the presidency by the narrowest of margins in 2000, the Democratic Party was expecting a victory in 2004. Yet Bush pulled out a narrow Electoral College win over John Kerry, propelled in large measure by a larger-than-expected turnout among white evangelical Christians, whose votes increased by more than 3 million over those cast in the 2000 presidential election.[2] In the crucial state of Ohio—the state that gave the 2004 victory to Bush—a combination of white and black evangelical votes provided the margin of victory.[3] In the immediate aftermath of this unexpected loss, the national Democratic Party made the strategic decision to compete for what some referred to as the "God vote." Part of this new strategic approach would involve the active courting of certain segments of the evangelical electorate, particularly young evangelicals (ages 18 to 29), minority evangelicals, and progressive and centrist evangelicals. At no time did the Democrats target conservative evangelicals, although the Barack Obama campaign did make contact with a handful of evangelical conservatives in the hope of taking the edge off of what was expected to be their bitter opposition to his candidacy.[4]

At the same moment that the Democratic Party was deciding to compete for the evangelical vote, evangelicals themselves were beginning to back away from what many considered a "too close" relationship with the Republican Party. This realization, which had been building for some years, came to a climax in 2004 because of three converging issues: (1) increasing dismay over the Bush administration's decision to launch a pre-emptive war in Iraq; (2) the failure of the Religious Right, led by conservative evangelicals, to rally behind a successor to Bush; and (3) the emergence of a new evangelical center, led by the National Association of Evangelicals (NAE) and codified in their 2004 statement "For the Health of the Nation: An Evangelical Call to Civic Responsibility." Each of these three issues had profound implications for how evangelicals would respond to the appeals of Obama and John McCain in the 2008 presidential election. Three years later, in 2007, a fourth issue—the congressional debate over comprehensive immigration reform—would lead directly to the disaffection of Hispanic evangelicals, a group that had supported Bush in the 2004 presidential election.[5]

I have written elsewhere about the efforts of the Obama campaign to court evangelical voters.[6] Therefore, in this chapter I want to focus on the response of evangelicals to that courting effort as well as their responses to one another, as some evangelicals supported Obama and others supported McCain. First, I will set the background to the campaign. Second, I will describe three ways in which to think of evangelicals as a political demographic—as progressives, centrists, and conservatives. Third, I will examine how evangelicals responded to three specific issues—abortion, war, and poverty—that all three factions consider to be important areas of concern. In this examination, I am less concerned with the horse-race aspect of the campaign—a campaign in which McCain ended up winning 74 percent of the white evangelical vote[7]—and more interested in what the rhetoric of political evangelicals says about the nature of evangelicalism, the tensions inherent within the evangelical movement, and the lessons that can be learned from the 2008 campaign—for evangelicals, for Democrats, and for Republicans. Specifically, I will argue that evangelicals as a political demographic are in the process of change—not rapid or radical change, but a slow movement away from political conservatism to a more moderate, centrist stance. Moreover, I will argue that as this movement continues and deepens, it will eventually confront one of the central tensions of Bible-based politics—how to square unbridled capitalism with the biblical call to do justice. And finally, I contend that once this tension comes into clearer focus, evangelicals will become much more of a swing vote than they are today.

Background to the Campaign

Nothing clarifies thought like losing a close election. In the aftermath of their ticket's loss in the 2004 presidential campaign, the Democratic Party read the exit polls and quickly realized that among their biggest losses were people who attended church regularly. In fact, the more regular a person's church attendance was, the greater the likelihood they had voted for the Republican ticket.[8] This came to be called the "God gap," and the Democrats, belatedly to be sure, decided to do something about it. In early 2005, House Minority Leader Nancy Pelosi established a Faith Working Group. That same year, Democratic National Committee (DNC) chairman Howard Dean established an arm of the DNC called Faith in Action and put Leah Daughtry, a Pentecostal minister, in charge of it. Obama, who had anticipated the importance of the religious vote long before his other colleagues by proclaiming in his DNC keynote address that "We serve an awesome God in the blue states,"[9] became the first presumptive candidate to hire a religious affairs coordinator and placed Joshua DuBois, also a Pentecostal minister, on his payroll. Both the party as a whole, and Obama in particular, were determined not to cede the religious vote in the next election.

Three events in 2006 helped to shape the electoral landscape leading into the 2008 campaign season. First, Obama reached out to progressive evangelicals in a speech to Call to Renewal, an anti-poverty organization founded by Jim Wallis, on June 28, 2006. This speech, which would be Obama's most comprehensive statement on his religious views as well as the basis for his chapter on faith in his best-selling book *The Audacity of Hope*, set forth a defining proposition: "I think we make a mistake when we fail to acknowledge the power of faith in people's lives—in the lives of the American people—and I think it's time that we join a serious debate about how to reconcile faith with our modern, pluralistic democracy."[10] The specifics of the speech would later become subject to controversy during the 2008 campaign, but the important point in 2006 was that Obama had signaled his willingness to engage religious voters, and he had done so in front of an explicitly evangelical audience composed primarily of people associated with the Sojourners ministry of progressive evangelical and social activist Wallis.

On December 1, 2006, Obama would make an appearance on World AIDS Day at Saddleback Church in Orange County, California, where he made a brief speech and clasped hands with church pastor and best-selling author Rick Warren, who described Obama as one of his "friends."[11] Unlike Wallis, who had long been associated with liberal causes, Warren was known as a theological conservative whose positions against abortion and gay marriage were well known.[12] But Warren had also become committed to the fight against AIDS, especially on the African continent. On this subject, he and Obama were in full agreement. Although Warren had also invited Republican senator Sam Brownback to the AIDS conference, it was his embrace of Obama that received note in the evangelical world. As one writer observed in *Christianity Today*, "Senator Obama's political team, or whoever's making the decision, was smart to associate him with Warren. It suggests that there are evangelical moderates that they can work with, or reach, or maybe even attract their vote."[13] Warren was just one of several evangelical leaders who had begun to embrace a larger social agenda. In their 2004 document "For the Health of the Nation," the NAE had explicitly noted,

> The Bible makes it clear that God cares a great deal about the well-being of marriage, the family, the sanctity of human life, justice for the poor, care for creation, peace, freedom, and racial justice. While individual persons and organizations are at times called by God to concentrate on one or two issues, faithful evangelical civic engagement must champion a biblically balanced agenda.[14]

Warren was committed to adding AIDS activism to that agenda.

Other evangelicals, especially those from the Hispanic community, were committed to adding comprehensive immigration reform to the social agenda. Evangelical Hispanics had supported Bush in 2004 precisely because they thought that Bush, as a fellow believer, would support their cause. Bush did indeed support their cause by supporting the immigration reform bill introduced in the U.S. Senate in May 2007, but he could not convince most of his Republican colleagues in the Senate to support his proposed reforms. During the debates on immigration reform, some of the Republican members made comments that were deeply offensive to all Hispanics, including Hispanic evangelicals. As Luis Cortes, president of Esperanza USA, a network of 10,000 evangelical churches, put it, "All of a sudden we're a security problem? We're the drug dealers who are destroying the nation? If the Republicans choose a candidate who takes a negative stance on immigration, then I believe you will see a large defection."[15] The vitriolic nature of the immigration reform debate made Hispanic evangelicals an available audience to the Democratic Party, even though the Republicans eventually nominated the pro-immigration reform candidate, McCain.

By the time the various candidates announced their intentions to run for the presidency of the United States in early 2007, the political situation looked very bad for the Republicans. They had an unpopular president waging an unpopular war, as well as a group of potential presidential nominees, led by Rudy Guiliani, Mitt Romney, Fred Thompson, and McCain, who collectively failed to excite the base of the party or to gather much support from evangelicals. Even the Religious Right was divided, with Pat Robertson supporting Guiliani, Paul Weyrich and Bob Jones III supporting Romney, the National Right to Life Committee and Gary Bauer supporting Thompson, and virtually no major figure on the Religious Right coming out in support of McCain. McCain would later gain the endorsements of pastors John Hagee and Rod Parsley, only to have to repudiate those endorsements. Perhaps the most important leader of the evangelical right, James Dobson, found some fault with all of the leading Republican candidates, specifically going out of his way to say that he could never vote for McCain.[16] While conservative evangelicals were searching for a perfect candidate, younger evangelicals, turned off by the war in Iraq and the tone of some of the debates over same-sex marriage during the 2004 campaign, were abandoning the Republican Party in droves. Having supported Bush's re-election with 84 percent of their votes in 2004, support for Republicans from evangelicals ages 18 to 29 had fallen to just 45 percent by August 2007.[17] This was the situation for evangelical voters as the presidential campaign began in earnest.

The Political Demographics of Evangelicalism

When Obama chose the Call to Renewal conference as the venue in which to make his major speech about religion and politics, he was playing to one of his natural bases—progressive evangelicals. Since the late 1960s and early 1970s, progressive evangelicals have been a small but dedicated force both within the evangelical movement and within the larger world of social activism. To properly understand progressive evangelicalism, it is important to begin at the beginning, and for our purposes the beginning was the late 1960s at Trinity Evangelical Divinity School in Deerfield, Illinois, where a young seminarian, Jim Wallis, and a handful of his fellow students became convinced that the Vietnam War was immoral, both in its rationale and its execution, and that commitment to the war effort was diverting the attention of Christians away from the real biblical issues of poverty and social justice. Though they did not come out of the civil rights movement or the black church, the critique made by Wallis and his associates was very close to that offered by Dr. Martin Luther King Jr. in his famous speech at Riverside Church on April 4, 1967. In that speech, King had not only called for an end to the Vietnam War but went on to call for a "true revolution of values," which "will soon cause us to question the fairness and justice of many of our past and present policies."[18] That is precisely what Wallis did.

As Wallis recounted in his 2005 best-seller, *God's Politics: Why the Right Gets It Wrong and the Left Doesn't Get It*, true Christianity calls for a transvaluation (or revaluation) of values. Commenting on Matthew 25:40, where Jesus says "whatever you did for one of the least of these brothers and sisters of mine, you did for me," Wallis writes,

> What's always been striking to me is that the people gathered in front of the throne of Christ in this story all really believe that they are among his followers. And they must be completely stunned to learn that they will be separated and judged by how they have treated the poor—the poor! This judgment is not about right doctrine or good theology, not about personal piety or sexual ethics, not about church leadership or about success in ministry. It's about how we treated the most vulnerable people in our society, whom Jesus calls "the least of these." Jesus is, in effect, saying, I'll know how much you love me by how you treat them. Whatever you do for them, it's like you've done it for me. And, conversely, ignoring them is like ignoring me. Jesus is casting his lot with the poor, almost taking up residence among them. Mother Teresa once said about this Scripture that Jesus appears in "the distressing disguise of the poor." As a young student and activist, I had never encountered anything like this passage before and had never heard about it in the church. None of the radical writers that I was reading in the late 1960s were as radical as this. It was enough to make me sign up and decide to try to be a follower of this radical Jesus.[19]

And a radical follower of Jesus Wallis has been ever since. For Wallis and other progressive evangelicals such as Brian McLaren and Tony Campolo, policies that promote peace and justice are always to be preferred. As McLaren said in September 2006, "When we present Jesus as a pro-war, anti-poor, anti-homosexual, anti-environment, pro-nuclear weapons authority figure draped in an American flag, I think we are making a travesty of the portrait of Jesus we find in the gospels."[20] Likewise, Campolo, who founded

Red-Letter Christians (RLC) in September 2006 as a way to distinguish progressive evangelicalism from that of the Religious Right, claimed that the RLC would "struggle to convince our fellow believers to think, act, give, and vote according to the teachings of Jesus."[21]

Progressive evangelicals, generally speaking, hold to progressive policy positions but do so from explicitly biblical warrants. Some, but not all, are pacifists. Others are advocates of what ethicist David Gushee calls "strict just-war theory," an approach he describes as

> characterized by a strongly articulated horror of war, a strong presumption for peace and against violence and war; a tendency to be skeptical of government claims about the need for military buildups and military action; an inclination to use just-war theory as a tool for citizen discernment and prophetic critique; a pattern of trusting the efficacy of international treaties and multilateral approaches (over against U.S. unilateralism) and the information and perspective offered by global peace and human rights groups and the international press (over against those offered by the U.S. government and American media outlets).[22]

The decision to go to war in Iraq was a key moment in the political decision making of many progressive evangelicals. Although it is doubtful that Bush had many supporters among progressive evangelicals at any point, those he might have had were clearly disturbed not only by the turn to war in Iraq but also by the virtual abandonment of the compassionate conservative agenda, the politicization of the Office of Faith-Based and Community Initiatives—which originally had promised massive aid to the poor—and other Bush-era policies that were perceived to be anti-environmental or unnecessarily hurtful toward homosexuals. The one Bush policy that progressive evangelicals could and did applaud was his African AIDS initiative and his pledge of $15 billion through the Millennium Challenge Account.

Progressive evangelicals were an obvious target of opportunity for the Democratic Party and one that both Obama and Hillary Clinton tried to exploit. The fact that Wallis had known Obama since 1997 and had been talking with him for almost a decade about the need for a coalition of religious and secular progressives gave the Illinois senator a leg up on capturing this part of the evangelical electorate.[23] Obama's 2006 speech to Call to Renewal further solidified his hold on this group. In truth, there was not much persuasion needed to convince progressive evangelicals that they should be in Obama's camp. That was not the case, however, with centrist evangelicals.

There is no doubt that evangelical centrists were a target of Obama's presidential campaign. Presumably they were a target of McCain's campaign as well, although the evidence for that proposition is not nearly as strong. A more accurate statement would be that McCain's campaign seemed to presume that mainstream evangelicals would be with him, with little or no need to appeal to them.[24] Evangelicals, after all, are one of the main bases of the modern Republican Party, and one normally assumes that the base will be with the party's nominee. In 2008, however, that proved to be a dangerous presumption. Part of the reason was a change in the self-identity of mainstream evangelicals between 2004 and 2008. Many factors entered into this change of identity, but among them were (1) the widespread perception that evangelicalism had become, in the words of one scholar, "the Republican Party at prayer";[25] (2) the resulting danger that was perceived to follow from allowing the gospel to become captive to any single political orientation or philosophy; (3) a widespread perception that evangelicals had been "used" during the 2004 Bush re-election campaign, particularly with regard to the many state-level ballot propositions concerning same-sex marriage that just happened to appear during a presidential election; (4) widespread evangelical angst about the Iraq War; (5) deep disappointment about the way compassionate conservatism had disappeared from the political radar of the Bush administration; (6) a rising evangelical consciousness with respect to issues of creation care (or stewardship of the environment), poverty, and religious freedom around the world; and (7) a clearer sense that it was both inaccurate and unwise to allow the media to continue to equate evangelicalism with the Religious Right, even though many members of the Religious Right were, in fact, evangelicals.

Other issues were also at play, but it is important to remember that even before the 2004 presidential election, the NAE had released "For the Health of the Nation," a report that held, among other things, that

> God identifies with the poor (Ps. 146:5–9).... God measures societies by how they treat the people at the bottom.
>
> God's prophets call his people to create just and righteous societies (Isa. 10:1–4, 58:3–12, Jer. 5:26–29, 22:13–19, Amos 2:6–7, 4:1–3, 5:10–15). The prophetic teaching insists on both a fair legal system (which does not favor either the rich or the poor) and a fair economic system (which does not tolerate perpetual poverty)....
>
> Economic justice includes both the mitigation of suffering and also the restoration of wholeness.... Health care, nutrition and education are

important ingredients in helping people transcend the stigma and agony of poverty and reenter community....

We further believe that care for the vulnerable should extend beyond our national borders. American foreign policy and trade policies often have an impact on the poor. We should try to persuade our leaders to change patterns of trade that harm the poor and to make the reduction of global poverty a central concern of American foreign policy.[26]

Nothing quite like this document had ever been issued by a group representing upwards of 30 million evangelicals. It would be easy to presume that this document represents a take-over of the NAE by the evangelical left, but that would be a mistaken judgment. The document represents a wide swath of evangelical opinion, extending from the progressive left to the center-right. Drafted primarily by David Neff, long-time editor of the evangelical monthly *Christianity Today*, "For the Health of the Nation" represented a consensus document that included all but the right and far-right of the evangelical community. And it was but one source of this new evangelical centrism.

According to Gushee, this new

center has emerged organically from within core institutions in U.S. evangelicalism, including the churches (especially certain key mega-churches), the Christian college networks, important evangelical publishers, the massive evangelical relief and development community, key umbrella bodies such as the National Association of Evangelicals, key evangelical leaders in the black and Hispanic communities, and younger evangelicals.[27]

In short, there are multiple sources and inspirations for this new political centrism. However, one of the common outcomes is an expanded sense of what counts as an issue of concern to evangelicals. It was, in fact, precisely a revolt against this agenda expansion that separated the evangelical right from some within the evangelical center.

Perhaps no group of Christians has attracted more media attention than the members of the Religious Right. Starting with the formation of the Moral Majority by Jerry Falwell in 1979, the Religious Right has been a major force in U.S. politics. The story of how fundamentalists and conservative evangelicals came to be aligned with the Republican Party is too complex to recount here, but several recent works explain this somewhat paradoxical pairing very well.[28] Suffice it to say that Falwell (Moral Majority), Robertson (Christian Coalition), Dobson (Focus on the Family), Donald Wildmon (American Family Association), Lou Sheldon (Traditional Values Coalition), Tony

Perkins (Family Research Council), Beverly LaHaye (Concerned Women for America), Richard Land (Ethics and Religious Liberty Commission of the Southern Baptist Convention) and other lesser-known leaders within the world of political religion have largely set the agenda for evangelical political involvement for most of the last thirty-five years.

The chief instrument for forging the alignment of theologically conservative Protestants with key elements of the Republican Party was the *Roe v. Wade* decision of 1973 that legalized abortion in the United States by wiping out the various state-level restrictions on the practice. Though coming late to a full realization of what that decision meant, conservative evangelicals soon joined Roman Catholics as the staunchest foes of abortion on demand. Abortion, along with issues such as school prayer, school-based health clinics, government regulation of private Christian schools, infanticide, the changing nature of American households, and other "family" issues drove the formation of the Religious Right in the late 1970s and early 1980s. Later, other issues such as gay rights, public display of the Ten Commandments, nativity scenes on public property, defending the phrase "under God" in the pledge of allegiance, and fighting against same-sex marriage became important parts of the Christian Right agenda.

It is not true, as many of their critics allege, that conservative evangelicals have been concerned only with "one or two issues."[29] It is true that only a handful of issues has received the lion's share of the media attention directed to the Christian Right, and that this narrow focus has been intentionally maintained for primarily strategic political reasons. And it is both the narrowness of the focus and the strategic political reasoning behind that focus that has led to a recent fracturing of the Christian Right. Conservative evangelical leaders maintain—correctly—that from a political point of view their influence in U.S. politics is proportionately greater if they are viewed as speaking on behalf of all of evangelicalism, which is variously estimated at between 30 and 40 million voters. The way to make sure that they speak for all evangelicals, the conservatives have reasoned, is to emphasize only those issues on which the vast majority of evangelicals agree, namely opposition to abortion on demand, opposition to same-sex marriage, and support for pro-family policies.

It was widespread evangelical opposition to same-sex marriage that brought several million new evangelical voters to the polls in the 2004 presidential election and that may have been the deciding factor in the re-election of Bush. This is precisely the kind of influence that the evangelical right has long sought to wield. But no sooner had that "victory" been achieved than widespread disillusionment with the Bush presidency began to set in. This disillusionment, combined with such new evangelical initiatives as "For the Health of the Nation" (2004), "Climate Change: An Evangelical Call to Action" (2006), and "An Evangelical Declaration against Torture" (2007)[30] resulted in a situation in which millions of evangelical votes that might normally have gone to the Republican nominee—whoever that nominee might be—were now seen as being "in play" for the Democratic Party. This set of situational circumstances combined with two other factors in the 2008 presidential campaign: (1) the Republicans nominated a candidate who was basically tone-deaf to evangelical language and concerns, and (2) the Democrats nominated a candidate who spoke the language of evangelical religion far better than either his Republican opponent or previous Democratic nominees.

Given these divisions, it is not surprising that progressive evangelicals largely supported Obama, conservative evangelicals largely supported

In 2008, then Democratic presidential candidate Sen. Barack Obama (right) and Republican presidential candidate Sen. John McCain (left) court the evangelical vote during a nondebate forum moderated by Pastor Rick Warren (center) at Warren's Saddleback Church in Lake Forest, California. (AP Photo/Richard Vogel, File.)

McCain, and centrist evangelicals found themselves being courted by both sides in an effort to break the decades-long stranglehold of the Republican Party on the evangelical electorate. To compare how these three factions of evangelicalism contended during the 2008 campaign, I will examine how representative spokespersons for each faction addressed three key issues—abortion, poverty, and war.

Abortion

If there is one issue on which the vast majority of evangelicals agree, it is opposition to abortion on demand. As people who believe that God is the creator of life, evangelicals are fierce defenders of the unborn, committed laborers in crisis pregnancy centers, strong advocates of adoption, and generous contributors to social support agencies. Over the last thirty years, the abortion issue has been a clear point of demarcation between the two major parties and their respective presidential candidates. As such, the abortion issue has been the leading edge—some would say wedge—in an effort to separate pro-life people from the Democratic Party and to identify those people with the Republican Party. In large measure, that strategy has worked. Whereas evangelicals divided their votes fairly equally between Gerald Ford (the last pro-choice Republican nominee) and Democrat Jimmy Carter (the personally opposed but pro-choice-anyway Democratic nominee) in the 1976 presidential race, evangelicals have broken for the Republican candidate by large margins in every presidential race since.[31] Abortion is a large part of the reason for that.

On the surface, it would seem that the 2008 presidential election should have been an easy call for all evangelicals inasmuch as the Democratic nominee, Obama, was a long-time supporter of abortion rights and had even gone so far as to vote against the Born Alive Infant Protection Act in the Illinois legislature—at least three times. But because of the expanded agenda being advocated by the evangelical center and the efforts by evangelical progressives to present Obama as a more fully pro-life candidate notwithstanding his views on abortion, the abortion issue did not seem to have the traction it had gained in previous elections. Part of the reason for this failure of the abortion issue to become definitive was Obama's own handling of it. Over the course of the campaign, Obama met with various kinds of evangelical audiences. He explained his thinking on the abortion issue, clearly identified it as in part a moral issue, lamented the number of abortions in the United States, said that he could support limitations on late-term abortions as long as the life of the mother was protected, and pledged to work for policies that would reduce the need for abortions.

In an interview with *Christianity Today* in January 2008, Obama said,

> I don't know anybody who is pro-abortion. I think it's very important to start with that premise. I think people recognize what a wrenching, difficult issue it is. I do think that those who diminish the moral elements of the decision aren't expressing the full reality of it. But what I believe is that women do not make these decisions casually, and that they struggle with it fervently with their pastors, with their spouses, with their doctors.
>
> Our goal should be to make abortion less common, that we should be discouraging unwanted pregnancies, that we should encourage adoption whenever possible. There is a range of ways that we can educate our young people about the sacredness of sex and we should not be promoting the sort of casual activities that end up resulting in so many unwanted pregnancies.
>
> Ultimately, women are in the best position to make a decision at the end of the day about these decisions.[32]

To conservative evangelicals, such reasoning was unpersuasive. Land of the Southern Baptist Convention's Ethics and Religious Liberty Commission charged, "Barack Obama has never met an abortion that he couldn't, at least, live with."[33] Michael Gerson, the evangelical former speechwriter for Bush, noted that "An evangelical vote for Obama requires a large mental adjustment: 'I like his views on poverty or torture or climate change, even though he cannot bring himself to oppose the most brutal form of abortion.'"[34] It was, in fact, Obama's earlier votes as an Illinois state legislator to which many conservative evangelicals pointed when criticizing the Democratic candidate. Janet Folger, the president of Faith2Action, said of Obama, "He's the only Senator in the entire Senate in Illinois who actually stood on the floor and spoke against protecting babies that were completed severed from the mother, that had survived the assault of an abortion."[35] Wendy Wright of Concerned Women for America argued, "When a politician speaks against the Born Alive Infant Protection Act, there seems to be a disconnect between his rhetoric and his record."[36]

The further to the right one went, the more extreme the charges became. The Family Research Council ran a video during the fall campaign ostensibly directed to Obama himself: "Senator Obama, why did you vote against protecting infants that survived late-term-abortions not once, but four times? Even Congress unanimously supported protections identical to those you blocked in Illinois. The Supreme Court upheld the ban on partial-birth abortion, and yet today you keep working to roll back this law. Call Senator Obama. Tell him to stop trying to overturn these basic human rights."[37] Appearing on Sean Hannity's radio program, Dobson of Focus on the Family charged, "[T]he man is dangerous, especially in regard to this issue of morality.... Do you remember the position that he's taken on the Born Alive Protection Act that was passed in Congress in 2002? ... Am I required in a democracy to conform my efforts in the political arena to his bloody notion of what's right in regard to tiny babies?"[38]

While conservative evangelicals railed against Obama's support for current abortion laws, the evangelical center was clearly conflicted. Many of those who liked Obama personally or supported him politically found themselves in a difficult position. When Warren was asked whether he agreed with Obama's answer to the question "at what point does a baby get human rights," to which Obama responded, "answering that question with specificity, you know, is above my pay grade,"[39] Warren confessed,

> I happen to disagree with Barack on that. [T]o me, I would not want to die and get before God one day and go, "Oh, sorry, I didn't take the time to figure out" because if I was wrong, then it had severe implications for my leadership if I had the ability to do something about [it].... But just to say "I don't know" on the most divisive issue in America is not a clear enough answer for me.[40]

Other centrists tried to contextualize Obama's abortion stance within the larger matrix of evangelical concern. Ron Sider of Evangelicals for Social Action, a center-left group, noted, "If we ask what the Bible says God cares about, the implications of our political agenda becomes obvious: We must be pro-life *and* pro-poor, pro-family *and* pro-creation care, pro-racial justice *and* pro-peacemaking."[41] Other centrists acknowledged the contradiction but refused to give the abortion issue the highest place on the evangelical agenda. Wilfredo DeJesus, an evangelical pastor who switched his support from Bush in 2000 and 2004 to Obama in 2008, proclaimed, "I'm still pro-life, I believe in the sanctity of marriage ... but I'm not going to be put in a corner."[42]

It is clear that many of the evangelical centrists, people who almost to a person were pro-life in their own beliefs and convictions, were impressed by Obama the man. DeJesus spoke of learning of Obama's "heartbeat" from a meeting in Brownsville, Texas. Richard Cizik, a long-time NAE official who was one of the forty-three people, most of them evangelicals, who met secretly with Obama at a Chicago law office in June 2008, reported,

"His genuine faith seemed obvious."[43] Steven Strang, the evangelical publisher of *Charisma* magazine, who was also at the Chicago meeting, came away convinced that Obama was personally opposed to abortion even while maintaining his pro-choice position.[44] Some of these centrists, like DeJesus, publicly supported Obama's candidacy. Others, like Strang, let it be known that they were supporting McCain, mostly because of the abortion issue. Even such a staunch conservative as Land realized the appeal of Obama's candidacy when he noted, "But if you take the abortion issue off the table then a lot of these other issues get oxygen they aren't getting now, such as the environment and social justice and racial reconciliation, all of which Evangelicals care about."[45]

It was precisely to give these "other issues" the oxygen they needed to catch fire that evangelical progressives were early converts to Obama's campaign. Many of them signed up immediately following Obama's June 2006 speech to Call to Renewal; some had signed up even before that event. One of Obama's early supporters was McLaren, one of the founders of the Emergent Church movement. As early as April 2005, McLaren was arguing that "there are more moral issues out there than two—abortion and homosexual marriage."[46] On the subject of abortion, McLaren held that "to just say 'okay, let's pass laws about it' seems to me to skip a number of important steps, like honest and open dialogue, persuasion and seeking to remove the conditions that make abortion so prevalent."[47] No progressive evangelical that I could find verbally supported abortion on demand, yet all supported Obama. Like McLaren, they generally expressed that support either by attacking the Republican position as misdirected ("pass laws") or ineffective, and argued that Obama's approach was better because it would reduce the need for abortion and thus result in fewer abortions actually being performed.

Appearing on the *Tavis Smiley Show*, Campolo of RLC claimed, "[W]e are pro-life people, but we are saying it's not enough simply to pass a law. We have to change the economic circumstances that are driving people to abortions, and that's going to be a big issue."[48] McLaren, taking aim at the Republicans, charged, "Again and again over the last 30 years, Republican presidents and other politicians have used the issue of abortion to get elected and raise funds, but then, once in office, they have said little about abortion and done even less."[49] This theme of Republican duplicity runs throughout the rhetoric of progressive evangelicals. Donald Miller, the author of the evangelical best-seller *Blue Like Jazz*, expressed this view, saying, "I really felt like the Republican Party was taking advantage of the evangelical community by throwing us abortion and gay marriage, really not giving the heart of

Christ more thought. I felt like it was the party of the extremely wealthy and they needed this conservative base in order to get a majority and so they pandered to us."[50]

The main argument of progressive evangelicals, however, was a positive one—that Obama's approach would do more to actually reduce the number of abortions. According to McLaren, "if we really care about seeing fewer pregnancies ending in abortion, a greater concern for 'the least of these'—demonstrated through better health care, more vigorous job creation, better education, and other needed initiatives for people in poverty—could bring us greater results than a strategy of criminalization. And Senator Obama is the stronger candidate in these areas."[51] Casting a vote for Obama, McLaren held, was "fully consistent with our desire to celebrate the sacredness of life."[52] The Obama campaign picked up this line of argument when it placed the following language on its *ProLifeProObama.com* website:

> An Obama administration will do more than a McCain administration for the cause of life, by drastically reducing abortions through giving women and families the support and the tools they need to choose life. Barack Obama will strive to promote life with dignity for all from the beginning of life to the end—by making sure health care is affordable, combating poverty, providing good paying jobs, and ensuring security in life's final years.[53]

Poverty

From the perspective of evangelical progressives, the topic of abortion was directly linked to that of poverty. Poverty was seen by the progressives and some of the centrists as the primary causal factor in the demand for access to abortion. A cut in the poverty rate would thus automatically lead to a reduction in the number of abortions. Conservative evangelicals, while often mentioning the poor as an object of Christian concern, virtually never link abortion to poverty. For conservatives, the evangelical agenda is a vertical hierarchy, with abortion clearly at the top. For progressives and centrists, however, the agenda is envisioned as horizontal, with all of the major issues calling for equal concern. Sider captured the centrist position when he wrote, "Mainstream evangelicalism—precisely because it seeks biblical balance—understands that 'moral issues' include not just the sanctity of human life and marriage, but also justice for the poor, human rights, freedom, peacemaking, and care for creation."[54]

Because the Bible so clearly speaks to God's love and concern for the poor, all evangelicals recognize the obligation to provide for "the least of these."

The differences arise when it comes to the question of how to express and embody that concern. Historically, evangelicals have believed that charity and relief organizations were the best pathway toward restoration and renewal. Evangelicals thus founded and sponsored such agencies as the Salvation Army, World Relief, and World Vision. Many individual evangelical churches and entire denominations sponsor food pantries and thrift stores. Even today, it is not unusual to find evangelical church and para-church organizations serving the poor in the urban centers through soup kitchens, men's shelters, and drug or alcohol rehabilitation programs.

But in the early 1970s, this traditional focus on charity and relief organizations was challenged by a small group of progressive evangelicals, led by Wallis, founder of the Sojourners ministry. Not only had Wallis come to believe that poverty was the central concern of biblical social justice, but he also began to identify structural and governmental obstacles that impeded the fight against poverty. As Wallis writes in *God's Politics*,

> [I]t was the powerful who were most often the prophets' target audience; those in charge of things were the ones called to greatest accountability. And whom were the prophets usually speaking for? Most often, the dispossessed, widows and orphans (read: poor single moms), the hungry, the homeless, the helpless, the least, last, and lost. Is God into class warfare? No, God wants the "common good," but speaking for the common good can get one accused of calling for class warfare—usually by the elites who control the public discussion and do not want too much conversation about what God thinks of our political priorities.[55]

Wallis moved the Sojourners ministry to the heart of Washington, D.C., in 1975 to both live among and serve the poor. Since then, he has consistently called for more spending on social welfare programs aimed at reducing the rate of poverty in the United States. During the 2008 campaign, Wallis sounded many of the same themes he had trumpeted for more than thirty years—that "God hates injustice" and that the church should function as "the conscience of the state, holding it accountable."[56]

Because he has a policy of refusing to endorse political candidates, Wallis did not formally endorse Obama during the presidential campaign. Even so, he did advise Obama and may well have been the single most important influence on Obama's stances regarding poverty, including Obama's decision that the revamped the White House Office of Community and Neighborhood Partnerships (formerly called the White House Office of Faith-Based and Community Initiatives under the Bush administration) should henceforth "be targeted specifically at the issue of poverty and how to lift people up."[57] Profiling the evangelical political activists, all of them progressives, who worked for Obama's presidential campaign, *World Magazine* noted, "Their method is to equate federally-funded poverty, health-care, and foreign-aid programs with biblical mandates to help the poor."[58] One of those advisers, Burns Strider, acknowledged that the government budget is "where our priorities and our values are put into action."[59] These evangelical advisors were simply putting into Obama's policy stances the view that Wallis had earlier articulated in a chapter of *God's Politics* titled "Isaiah's Platform: Budgets Are Moral Documents." Progressive evangelicals have little doubt that it is the morally right thing to use tax and fiscal policies to redistribute wealth. Like Wallis, Campolo believes that "Christians should engage in efforts to change the political and economic structures of society."[60] This is the philosophy that separates most progressive evangelicals from some centrists and almost all conservative evangelicals.

Yet even some centrists and conservatives recognize a difference between traditional Republican economic principles and the demands of the gospel. Gerson, a center-right evangelical who has worked for such notable conservatives as Chuck Colson, Senator Dan Coats (R–IN), and Bush, has written,

> This evangelical centrism is not libertarian. It's engaged in a significant conflict on the visions of justice within the Republican Party. A libertarian definition of justice is generally the impartial application of rules—the rule of law, markets, everyone is treated equally. But it's impossible to avoid the fact that the Christian and Jewish definition of justice is quite different. It's measured by the treatment of the poor, the weak, the powerless, the voiceless.[61]

How evangelicals try to reconcile their biblical principles with their policy stances often seems to reflect the structural position they occupy or the position of the groups they represent. Kirbyjon Caldwell, an African American center-left evangelical who had supported Bush in 2000 and 2004, endorsed Obama in 2008. Part of Caldwell's motivation was Obama's stances on the reduction of poverty. As Caldwell noted, "[W]e have approximately one half of all African American children aged six years and younger left at or below poverty.... [S]lightly more than one third of all African Americans families live at or below poverty."[62] Given such statistics, it is small wonder that most of the prominent African American evangelicals, including T. D. Jakes, Eugene Rivers, and Charles Blake, ended up supporting Obama. Colson is doubtless right when he says that "to be an evangelical is to defend life at every stage, help the poor, and strive for justice."[63] However, the ways in which one chooses to do these things vary substantially along the evangelical political spectrum.

War

Evangelicals have long been committed to biblical justice, but on certain subjects discerning what the biblical demands of justice are is difficult. War falls within that domain. Historically, Christians have been divided into two groups—those who oppose all wars as inherently against the teaching of Christ (pacifists) and those who believe that war should only be a last resort once all other reasonable measures have been exhausted (just-war doctrine proponents). Evangelicals are represented in both groups, with evangelical Quakers, Mennonites, and Brethren congregations adopting a pacifist stance, and most other evangelical groups adopting some version of just-war theory. Because the war in Iraq was a major issue during the 2008 campaign—and because evangelicals had been among the strongest supporters of President Bush's pre-emptive strike in Iraq—both parties had reason to compete for the evangelical vote on the issue of war.

One of the chief targets of Obama's political operatives was young evangelicals, ages 18 to 29. Polling data revealed that this demographic had moved from 87 percent for Bush in 2002 to only 45 percent by 2007—a 42-point swing.[64] Data also indicated that this group was opposed to Bush on the Iraq War and was much more tolerant of homosexuality than were their parents' generation. That was the good news for the Democrats. The bad news was that on the subject of abortion, this younger generation was at least as conservative as their parents, if not more so. Even so, the Democrats decided to target younger evangelicals (focusing on the war, poverty, and environmental issues), minority evangelicals (focusing on poverty and immigration issues), and progressive and centrist evangelicals (focusing on the environment, human rights, and poverty issues). Few voices in the mainstream media seemed to realize how important the war in Iraq was to evangelical voters of all stripes, but particularly to younger evangelicals. The cause of this concern is apparent to all evangelicals—the biblical call to be peacemakers. As Wallis put it in *God's Politics*, "Christian peacemaking always calls churches to seek alternatives to war in resolving conflicts. Both the just war and pacifist traditions agree with that."[65]

During the run-up to the Iraq War in late 2002 and early 2003, several major evangelical leaders, organizations, and organs endorsed the Bush Doctrine and gave their blessing to a pre-emptive strike. In an editorial on

September 1, 2002, *Christianity Today* published an editorial in which it concluded, "If all the prudential and practical questioning points to the conclusion that Iraq or its proxies are about to use weapons of mass destruction—and that military action would not create catastrophe and chaos—then we believe, though with heavy hearts, that a pre-emptive strike could be considered just, and perhaps an act of Christian charity and duty."[66] Five prominent evangelicals—Land, Colson, Bill Bright, D. James Kennedy, and Carl D. Herbster—signed an open letter to Bush on October 3, 2002. In that letter, they wrote, "[W]e believe that your stated policies concerning Saddam Hussein and his headlong pursuit and development of biochemical and nuclear weapons of mass destruction are prudent and fall well within the time-honored criteria of just war theory."[67] In that same month, it was reported that "69 percent of conservative Christians favor military action against Baghdad."[68]

While conservative evangelicals were almost uniformly behind the push toward war, many centrist and progressive evangelicals remained unconvinced of the need for war and unsympathetic to the doctrine of pre-emption. By the time the 2008 presidential campaign began in earnest, many centrist evangelicals had already turned against the war effort, thus giving the Democrats a potential opening both for those centrists and for the many conservative evangelicals who sat in the pews. It was not just progressives who questioned the war effort. As megachurch pastor Bill Hybels put it, "the quickness to arms, the quickness to invade, I think that caused a desertion of what has been known as the Christian right."[69] Although evangelicals are among the most patriotic of Americans, they know their Bibles well enough to realize that one should always go the extra mile for peace. Bush did not go the extra mile, and by 2007 evangelicals knew it. The fact that McCain was promoting a redoubled effort in Iraq while Obama was making it clear that he had opposed the war from the outset—and opposed it still—provided an opening that Obama might otherwise not have had. As one source noted, many traced "the current identity crisis of the Christian right to differences over the Iraq war."[70]

Evangelical progressives continued to underscore the differences between Obama and McCain on the war issue. McLaren wrote, "Instead of dividing the world into 'us' and 'them,' Obama's narrative seeks to bring people together in an expanding us. While McCain's narrative only offers enemies surrender and defeat, Obama's offers them the possibility of reconciliation.... I believe a narrative of reconciliation is in harmony with the teachings of Jesus."[71] Progressive evangelicals who were specifically targeting the youth vote played heavily on the anti-war theme. Campolo, who plainly proclaimed that "Jesus is anti-war,"[72] lambasted the results of the Iraq War when he told a reporter that his RLCs

> are really raising some very serious questions as to whether or not democracy has come to play [in Iraq]. The president talks about the war having created democracy. What he means by that is that there was a free election; but a free election does not create a democracy. A democracy is when it is safe to be in the minority, and young people know that Christians in Iraq are being persecuted right now. There was about 1.5 million Christians in Iraq prior to the war, but over a million have fled. . . . [A]bove all, they really raise questions about the morality of the war.[73]

The center-left evangelical author Miller, who was dispatched by the Obama campaign to Christian college campuses during the fall of 2008, focused his arguments on what the war implied about U.S. Christianity: "America represents Christianity to the rest of the world," Miller noted. "What we have is Christianity being represented by what is perceived as arrogance, bullying, an inability to negotiate peace, an inability to listen. People assume that Christianity is that way."[74]

A handful of conservative evangelical and Roman Catholic intellectuals continued to defend the Bush administration and its war policies publicly, among them Jean Bethke Elshtain and George Weigel,[75] but for the most part conservative evangelicals were noticeably quiet on the topic of the Iraq War, preferring to change the topic from whether the United States should have invaded to the more pressing issue of whether it should stay. According to a board member of the NAE, "We should not have gone in. . . . But we are going to need to stay in long enough to prevent chaos and to stabilize the country."[76] Though most conservatives continued to support the president—as late as July 2008, 57 percent of evangelicals still believed that "the U.S. did the right thing in taking military action against Iraq"[77]—they did so through in-house publications and private networks rather than in the mainstream media.

Conclusion

It is difficult to make generalizations about evangelicals and politics because neither evangelicals nor politics are a static entity—both change continuously. It is accurate to say that at the beginning of the twenty-first century the majority of evangelicals tend toward the center-right. The majority at this moment in history have chosen to affiliate with the Republican Party. However, in other historical eras, evangelicals have been associated with the Democratic Party or its predecessors. What makes evangelicals who they are is their commitment to the Bible as the word of God and their determination to live out their understanding of that word in every aspect of their lives, including the political. God demands no less.

This situation raises the intriguing issue of what would happen if evangelical voters should determine that biblical values were better embodied by the Democratic rather than the Republican Party. In the 2008 presidential election, Hispanic evangelicals made exactly that determination, and one-third of evangelicals under the age of 30 made that determination. Will older, white evangelicals eventually follow? The movement of groups such as the NAE and the editorial page of *Christianity Today* suggests that such a movement may already be underway. This will not be a movement from the Religious Right to the progressive left, but it may well be a movement to the center or even center-left. Evangelicals are too stitched into the capitalist fabric of American life to embrace the radical, often anti-capitalist politics of Wallis. However, when confronted with clear biblical mandates that contradict current conservative policies, evangelicals could become an alluring target of opportunity for Democrats or other political parties. They could become the ultimate swing vote in U.S. politics.

Today, there are evangelicals who occupy all parts of the U.S. political spectrum. When the final votes were tallied in the 2008 presidential election, McCain and Sarah Palin had won 74 percent of the overall white evangelical vote. How much of that percentage is attributable to Palin's presence on the ticket is unknown, but her selection was clearly motivated, in large part, by the perceived need to keep the evangelical base of the Republican Party satisfied. It seems unlikely that there will be large migrations of the evangelical faithful to the Democratic Party as long as that party continues to embrace abortion on demand, an issue that most evangelicals will not negotiate or compromise. Even a candidate as articulate as Obama could claim only 26 percentage of the white evangelical vote—seven percentage points less than Bill Clinton won in 1996. Of course, should the Republican Party move away from its pro-life platform or the Democratic Party succeed in its recent attempts to make the party a more welcome home for pro-life Democrats, including most progressive and many centrist evangelicals, current alignments could change. The reason those alignments could change is that there is one proposition on which all evangelicals—left, right, and center—agree: God calls us to study his word and to put into practice the ideas, actions, and values found therein, both in our personal lives and in the life of the nation.

Notes

1. Scott Keeler, "Will White Evangelicals Desert the GOP?" *Pew Research Center Publications*, May 2, 2006, http://pewresearch.org/pubs/22/will-white-evangelicals-desert-the-gop (accessed January 4, 2011), and "American Evangelicalism: New Leaders, New Faces, New Issues," *Pew Research Center Publications*, June 30, 2008, http://pewresearch.org/pubs/883/american-evangelicalism (accessed January 4, 2011).

2. For the role of the evangelical vote in the 2004 presidential election, see Bill Schneider, "Bush's Secret Weapon," *CNN.com*, November 8, 2004, http://www.cnn.com/2004/ALLPOLITICS/11/05/karl.rove/index.html?iref=allsearch; "Religion and the Presidential Vote: Bush's Gains Broad-Based," Pew Research Center, December 6, 2004, http://www.people-press.org/2004/12/06/religion-and-the-presidential-vote/ (accessed May 22, 2012); and "2004 Election Exit Poll Results," *beliefnet.com*, http://beliefnet.com/story/155/story_15546.html (accessed January 4, 2011).

3. Although many sources point to the large increase in the white evangelical voter turnout in the state of Ohio in 2004, far fewer comment on the substantial increase—from 8 percent in 2000 to 16 percent in 2004—in the black evangelical voter turnout for Bush. See David Kuo, *Tempting Faith: An Inside Story of Political Seduction* (New York: Free Press, 2006), 252; and Earl Ofari Hutchinson, "Black Evangelicals: Bush's New Trump Card," *AlterNet.org*, January 27, 2005, http://www.alternet.org/module/printversion/21096 (accessed January 4, 2011).

4. Obama met with several evangelical conservatives, including Franklin Graham and Steve Strang, at the June 10, 2008, meeting in Chicago. For Strang's report on that meeting, see Steve Strang, "Obama's 'Off the Record' Meeting with Christian Leaders," *Strang Report*, June 11, 2008, http://www.strangreport.com/2008/06/obamas-off-record-meeting-with.html (accessed January 4, 2011). Around the same time, Joshua DuBois of the Obama campaign made an overture to executives at Focus on the Family about a possible meeting between Obama and James Dobson, but nothing ever came of the effort. On July 6, 2008, Obama told reporters on board his campaign plane, "if we show up, if we let folks know that we're interested in them and we share a lot of common values, then we're not going to win 100 percent of the evangelical vote. We might not win 50 percent of the evangelical vote. But we will at least take some of the sharp edges off the divide that's existed in our politics. And that hopefully will allow people to listen to each other, and that will help me govern over the long term." Obama, quoted in Jonathan Weisman, "Obama Addresses His Faith; Senator Describes Spiritual Journey," *Washington Post*, July 6, 2008, http://www.washingtonpost.com/wp-dyn/content/article/2008/07/05/AR2008070501854.html (accessed January 4, 2011).

5. Bob Allen, "Poll: Latino Protestants Switching Back to Democrats This Election," Associated Baptist Press, October 21, 2008, http://www.abpnews.com/archives/item/3579-poll-latino-protestants-switching-back-to-democrats-this-election (accessed May 22, 2012); and "Hispanic Protestant: We're Not the Christian Right,"

Christian Post, October 21, 2008, http://www.christianpost.com/article/20081021/hispanic-protestant-we-re-not-the-christian-right (accessed January 4, 2011).

6. See Martin J. Medhurst, "Barack Obama and the Politics of Faith," in The Obama Phenomenon Conference, Texas A & M University, March 4–7, 2010.

7. "Voting Religiously," *Pew Research Center Publications*, November 5, 2008, http://pewresearch.org/pubs/1022/exit-poll-analysis-religion (accessed January 4, 2011).

8. Peter Steinfels, "In Politics, the 'God Gap' Overshadows Other Differences," *New York Times*, December 9, 2006, http://nytimes.com/2006/12/09/us/politics/09beliefs.html (accessed January 4, 2011).

9. Barack Obama, "We Are One People! Keynote Address to the Democratic National Convention," in *Barack Obama Speeches 2002–2006*, eds. Maureen Harrison and Steve Gilbert (Carlsbad, CA: Excellent, 2007), 18.

10. Barack Obama, "Politics and Faith: A Call to Renewal," in *Barack Obama Speeches 2002–2006*, 100.

11. Rick Warren, quoted in Deborah White, "Sen. Barack Obama's Speech on World AIDS Day 2006," December 1, 2006, http://usliberals.about.com/od/barackobama/a/ObamaWarren.htm (accessed January 4, 2011).

12. According to the *New York Times*, "Although he does not speak from the pulpit about politics, [Warren] sent a letter before the 2004 presidential election to pastors in a vast network who draw advice from him, urging them to weigh heavily 'nonnegotiable' issues like abortion, stem cell research and same-sex marriage from a biblical perspective." See Michael Luo and Laurie Goodstein, "Emphasis Shifts for New Breed of Evangelicals," *New York Times*, May 21, 2007, http://nytimes.com/2007/05/21/us/21evangelical.html (accessed January 4, 2011).

13. Collin Hansen, quoted in David Van Biema, "The Real Losers in the Obama–Warren Controversy," *Time*, December 1, 2006, http://www.time.com/time/printout/0,8816,1565076.html (accessed January 4, 2011).

14. National Association of Evangelicals, "For the Health of the Nation: An Evangelical Call to Civic Responsibility," quoted in David P. Gushee, *The Future of Faith in American Politics: The Public Witness of the Evangelical Center* (Waco, TX: Baylor University Press, 2008), 226.

15. Quoted in Eve Conant, "The Miracle Workers: For 25 Years, Evangelicals Have Voted Republican. But the Democrats Are Courting, and Their Efforts May Have a Prayer," *Newsweek*, October 1, 2007, http://www.newsweek.com/id/41735 (accessed January 4, 2011).

16. See Bob Unruh, "Dobson Says 'No Way' to McCain Candidacy," *WorldNetDaily*, January 13, 2007, http://www.wnd.com/?pageId=39667 (accessed January 4, 2011).

17. Dan Cox, "Young White Evangelicals: Less Republican, Still Conservative," *Pew Forum*, September 28, 2007, http://pewforum.org/docs/?DocID=250 (accessed January 4, 2011).

18. Martin Luther King Jr., "Speech at Riverside Church," in *Words of a Century: The Top 100 American Speeches, 1900–1999*, eds. Stephen E. Lucas and Martin J. Medhurst (New York: Oxford University Press, 2009), 461.

19. Jim Wallis, *God's Politics: Why the Right Gets It Wrong and the Left Doesn't Get It* (New York: HarperSanFrancisco, 2005), 218–219.

20. Quoted in Caryle Murphy, "Evangelical Author Puts Progressive Spin on Traditional Faith," *Washington Post*, September 10, 2006, http://www.washingtonpost.com/wp-dyn/content/article/2006/09/09/AR2006090901155.html (accessed January 4, 2011).

21. Tony Campolo, "Stan Guthrie's Red Letter Blues," *Sojourners*, October 9, 2007, http://blog.sojo.net/2007/10/09/stan-guthries-red-letter-blues-by-tony-campolo/ (accessed January 4, 2011).

22. Gushee, *The Future of Faith in American Politics*, 204.

23. On February 29, 2008, Wallis wrote, "I have known Barack Obama for more than 10 years, and we have been talking about his Christian faith for a decade.... We have talked about our faith and its relationship to politics many times since." See Jim Wallis, "Defending the Facts on Obama's Faith," *Huffington Post*, February 29, 2008, http://www.huffingtonpost.com/jim-wallis/defending-the-facts-on-ob_b_89271.html (accessed January 4, 2011).

24. Marlys Popma is identified as McCain's coordinator of evangelical outreach, but precisely who she was coordinating with is unclear. The NAE's Richard Cizik reported in October 2008 that "the NAE has been receiving weekly communication from the Obama camp, but nothing from McCain." It was not until October 27, 2008—one week before the election—that McCain's campaign added an "Americans of Faith" section to the campaign website. There was some effort to reach out to evangelical colleges. See Cizik, quoted in John W. Kennedy, "The Faith Factor," *Christianity Today*, October 2008, 28; Dan Gilgoff, quoted in Kyle, "Better Late Than Never," *Right Wing Watch*, October 27, 2008, http://www.rightwingwatch.org/category/individuals/john-mccain (accessed January 4, 2011); and Catherine Guiles, "Christian Campuses Play More Visible Role in Campaigns," *Medill Reports*, November 3, 2008, http://news.medill.northwestern.edu/chicago/news.aspx?id=103485 (accessed January 4, 2011).

25. Several scholars, including Mark A. Noll, Stephen Mansfield, and Marvin Olasky, made this comparison. See, for example, Noll, quoted in Frances Fitzgerald, "The New Evangelicals; This Election, a Growing Movement Presents a Challenge to the Religious Right," *New Yorker*, June 30, 2008, http://www.newyorker.com/reporting/2008/06/30/080630fa_fact_fitzgerald (accessed January 4, 2011).

26. National Association of Evangelicals, "For the Health of the Nation," in Gushee, *The Future of Faith in American Politics*, 231.

27. See "David Gushee Q & A," *Dallas Morning News*, March 18, 2008, http://web.archive.org/web/20080516222718/http:/www.dallasnews.com/sharedcontent/dws/news/longterm/stories/031808dnedigusheeinterview.2770644.html (accessed January 4, 2011).

28. See, for example, Andrew P. Hogue, *Religion on the Stump: How the 1980 Election Changed American Politics* (Waco, TX: Baylor University Press, forthcoming); D. Michael Lindsay, *Faith in the Halls of Power: How Evangelicals Joined the American Elite* (New York: Oxford University Press, 2008), 1–71; Gary Scott Smith, *Faith and the Presidency* (New York: Oxford University Press, 2006); and William C. Martin, *With God on Our Side: The Rise of the Religious Right in America* (New York: Broadway, 1996).

29. The list of critics who make this charge is long and includes progressive evangelicals Jim Wallis and Brian McLaren. The charge became so prevalent during the 2008 campaign that Charles Colson felt he had to argue that "we have been much more than a one-or-two-issue movement, as the press characterizes us." See Colson with Anne Morse, "No Utter Collapse," *Christianity Today*, February 29, 2008, http://www.christianitytoday.com/ct/article_print.html?id=53912 (accessed January 4, 2011).

30. A description of all these initiatives can be found in Gushee, *The Future of Faith in American Politics*, 223–234, 253–270, 275–281.

31. See David Domke and Kevin Coe, *The God Strategy: How Religion Became a Political Weapon in America* (New York: Oxford University Press, 2008), 22–27.

32. See "Q & A: Barack Obama," *Christianity Today*, January 23, 2008, http://www.christianitytoday.com/ct/2008/januaryweb-only/104-32.0.html (accessed January 4, 2011).

33. "Richard Land: How Evangelicals View Election 2008," National Public Radio, February 28, 2008, http://m.npr.org/news/front/46457288?singlePage=true (accessed January 4, 2011).

34. Michael Gerson, "A Tactical Leap of Faith," *Washington Post*, June 27, 2008, http://www.washingtonpost.com/wp-dyn/content/article/2008/06/26/AR2008062603654.html (accessed January 4, 2011).

35. Quoted in "Rick Warren: Obama's Abortion Answer Not Clear Enough," *Christian Post*, August 19, 2008, http://www.christianpost.com/article/20080819/rick-warren-obama-s-abortion-answer-not-clear-enough (accessed January 4, 2011).

36. Quoted in Kennedy, "The Faith Factor," 29.

37. Family Research Council Video, quoted in Jim Brown, "Abortion Stance Continues to Haunt Obama," *OneNewsNow*, October 10, 2008, http://www.onenewsnow.com/Election2008/Default.aspx?id=280554 (accessed January 4, 2011).

38. Quoted in "James Dobson Terrified by President Obama," *Newsmax*, June 25, 2008, http://newsmax.com/InsideCover/dobson-mike-huckabee/2008/06/25/id/324253 (accessed January 4, 2011).

39. Quoted in "Saddleback Presidential Candidates Forum," CNN, August 16, 2008, http://transcripts.cnn.com/TRANSCRIPTS/0808/17/se.01.html (accessed January 4, 2011).

40. Quoted in "Rick Warren: Obama's Abortion Answer Not Clear Enough."

41. Ron Sider, "McCain or Obama?" *Prism*, September–October 2008, 46.

42. Quoted in Eric Gorski, "Hispanic Protestants Swinging Back to Democrats," *Real Clear Politics*, October 21, 2008, http://realclearpolitics.com/news/ap/politics/2008/Oct/21/hispanic_protestants_swinging_back_to_democrats.html (accessed January 4, 2011).

43. Quoted in Adelle M. Banks and Daniel Burke, "Pastors Focus on Faith, Morals in Private Meeting," *Washington Post*, June 21, 2008.

44. Steve Strang, "We Endorse John McCain," *Strang Report*, September 3, 2008, http://www.strangreport.com/2008/09/we-endorse-john-mccain.html (accessed January 4, 2011).

45. Richard Land, quoted in Nancy Gibbs and Michael Duffy, "How the Democrats Got Religion," *Time*, July 12, 2007, http://www.time.com/time/politics/article/0,8599,1642649,00.html (accessed January 4, 2011).

46. Quoted in Chris Keller, "An Interview with Brian McLaren," *The Other Journal*, April 4, 2005, http://theotherjournal.com/2005/04/04/an-interview-with-brian-mclaren/ (accessed May 22, 2012).

47. Quoted in Murphy, "Evangelical Author Puts Progressive Spin on Traditional Faith."

48. Tony Campolo, interview, *Tavis Smiley Show*, PBS, March 10, 2008, http://www.locatetv.com/tv/tavis-smiley/season-13/4480058 (accessed January 4, 2011).

49. Brian McLaren, "Why I'm Voting for Barack Obama . . . and I Hope You Will Too. Reason 5: The Sacredness of Life," October 27, 2008, http://www.brianmclaren.net/archives/blog/why-im-voting-for-barak-obama-and-i-hope-you-will-too-reason-5.html (accessed January 4, 2011).

50. Donald Miller, quoted in Sarah Pulliam, "Donald Miller to Give DNC Benediction," *Christianity Today*, August 22, 2008, http://blog.christianitytoday.com/ctpolitics/2008/08/donald_miller_t.html (accessed January 4, 2011).

51. McLaren, "Why I'm Voting for Barack Obama . . . Reason 5: The Sacredness of Life."

52. Ibid.

53. Quoted in Drew Zahn, "Christian Campaign Website Endorses Obama as Pro-Life," *World Net Daily*, October 3, 2008, http://www.wnd.com/2008/10/76920/ (accessed June 24, 20121).

54. Ron Sider, "The Religious Right Has Lost the Evangelical Center," *Prism*, July–August 2007, 40.

55. Wallis, *God's Politics*, 32.

56. Quoted in Chris Satullo, "Religious Right Gives Way to a New Prophet: Jim Wallis Writes of Americans Hungry for Justice," *Philadelphia Inquirer*, February 19, 2008, A11, http://www.sojo.net/index.cfm?action=news.display_article &mode=s &NewsID=6542 (accessed January 2011).

57. Barack Obama, quoted in "Democratic Candidates Compassion Forum," CNN, April 13, 2008, http://transcripts.cnn.com/TRANSCRIPTS/0804/13/se.01.html (accessed January 4, 2011).

58. Mark Bergin, "Prodigal Party," *World Magazine*, January 27, 2007, http://www.worldmag.com/articles/12612 (accessed January 4, 2011).

59. Quoted in Bergin, "Prodigal Party." Strider was still working for Hillary Clinton, but after Obama won the nomination, he worked for the Obama campaign.

60. Quoted in Stan Guthrie, "When Red Is Blue: Why I Am Not a Red Letter Christian," *Christianity Today*, October 2007, 100.

61. Quoted in "Religious Voters in the 2008 Election: What It Means for Democrats, Republicans," *Pew Forum*, May 5, 2008, http://pewtrusts.org/news_room_detail.aspx?id=39622 (accessed January 4, 2011).

62. Quoted in "Evangelicals Take a Second Look at Obama," NPR, July 7, 2008, http://www.npr.org/templates/story/story.php?storyId=92280874 (accessed January 4, 2011).

63. Colson with Morse, "No Utter Collapse."

64. Cox, "Young White Evangelicals."

65. Wallis, *God's Politics*, 109.

66. Editorial, "Bully Culprit," *Christianity Today*, September 1, 2002, http://www.christianitytoday.com/ct/article_print.html?id=7103 (accessed January 4, 2011).

67. Richard Land, "The So-Called 'Land Letter,'" Ethics and Religious Liberty Commission, October 3, 2002, http://erlc.com/article/the-so-called-land-letter/ (accessed January 4, 2011).

68. Jim Lobe, "Conservative Christians Biggest Backers of Iraq War," *Common Dreams*, October 10, 2002, http://www.commondreams.org/headlines02/1010-02.htm (accessed January 4, 2011).

69. Quoted in David D. Kirkpatrick, "The Evangelical Crackup," *New York Times*, October 28, 2007, http://nytimes.com/2007/10/28/magazine/28Evangelicals-t.html (accessed January 4, 2011).

70. Peter S. Canellos, "New Concerns Crack Unity of Religious Right: Conservative Campus Shows Divisions on Candidates, Iraq," *Boston Globe*, November 18, 2007, http://www.boston.com/news/nation/articles/2007/11/18/new_concerns_crack_unity_of_religious_right (accessed January 4, 2011).

71. Brian McLaren, "Why I'm Voting for Obama, and Why I Hope You Will Too: Reason #1: Framing Story," September 12, 2008, http://www.brianmclaren.net/archives/blog/why-im-voting-for-obama-and-why.html (accessed January 4, 2011).

72. Campolo, "Stan Guthrie's Red Letter Blues."

73. Tony Campolo, interview, *Tavis Smiley Show*.

74. Quoted in Pulliam, "Donald Miller to Give DNC Benediction."

75. Jean Bethke Elshtain, "Just War Theory: More Relevant Than Ever," *Beliefnet*, March 2003, http://www.beliefnet.com/News/2003/03/Just-War-Theory-More-Relevant-Than-Ever.aspx (accessed January 4, 2011); George Weigel, "Just War and Iraq Wars," *First Things*, April 2007, 14–20; and George

Weigel, "Moral Clarity in a Time of War," *First Things*, January 2003, 20–27. For a critique of these views by more liberal evangelicals and Elshtain's reply to them, see Stanley Hauerwas et al., "War, Peace, and Jean Bethke Elshtain," *First Things*, October 2003, 41–46.

    76. Ethan Cole, "Most US Evangelical Leaders Still Support Iraq War," *Christianity Today*, February 13, 2008, http://www.christiantoday.com/article/most.us.evangelical.leaders.still.support.iraq.war/16812-2.htm (accessed January 4, 2011).

    77. Naomi Schaefer Riley, "Left Behind: Evangelicals Haven't Embraced the Democrats' Agenda," *Wall Street Journal*, July 18, 2008, http://online.wsj.com/article/SB121633761975563839.html (accessed January 4, 2011).

Chapter 4

Constructions of Evangelicalism in Media Coverage of Sarah Palin

Kevin Healey

When John McCain announced his choice of Sarah Palin as vice presidential (VP) candidate on August 29, 2008, scholars and journalists rushed to identify Palin's religious faith. Throughout the campaign, many speculated that McCain would choose a running mate who could appeal to the Republican Party's white evangelical base. The issue was clearly important to evangelicals: the following day, *Christianity Today* ran an article with the headline, "Is Palin an Evangelical?"[1] Religion scholars and mainstream newspapers described Palin as evangelical, but *Christianity Today* questioned their definition of the term. The Southern Baptist Convention, the Christian Coalition, and the Family Research Council voiced support for Palin, but she did not say that she was an evangelical.[2] Much was at stake: for better or worse, a high-profile nominee would serve as the public face of evangelicalism. For many, the question was not "Is Palin an evangelical?" but "What kind of evangelical is she?"

Palin's nomination came at a time of significant tension within American evangelicalism. In recent years, sociologists have observed a struggle for evangelical leadership between "populists" and "cosmopolitans."[3] The former represent the "old" face of the Religious Right[4]—emphasizing issues like abortion and gay marriage—while the latter voice concerns about environmentalism or poverty. Younger evangelicals, in particular, hold positions on social and economic issues that diverge from the traditional emphases of the Religious Right.[5] Moreover, these tensions unfold against a backdrop of increasing ethnic and racial pluralism. Evangelicals' ambivalence toward such pluralism echoes developments at the turn of the twentieth century, when many turned away from their long-standing engagement with social issues

Alaska governor and Republican vice-presidential hopeful Sarah Palin speaks to a crowd estimated at 60,000 during a campaign stop in Florida in 2008. (AP Photo/Phelan M. Ebenhack.)

in what one historian calls the "Great Reversal."[6] With regard to political, sexual, racial, and environmental issues, therefore, American evangelicals stand at a crossroads.

Palin's rise to stardom is a significant development in this juncture. In her policy positions, Palin aligns herself with the old leadership of the Religious Right, leading younger evangelicals to complain that Palin has ignored issues of concern to them.[7] Furthermore, Palin's support for the Tea Party echoes the antipathy toward pluralism and social justice issues exhibited by evangelicals at the turn of the last century.[8] For these reasons, while younger and more moderate evangelicals remain wary of Palin, she has become immensely popular among one group in particular: Palin's favorability rating among white evangelical Republicans reached 85 percent in October 2008 and held steady through the following summer.[9] By fall of 2009, Palin was the most popular and well-known conservative political leader, edging out both Mike Huckabee and McCain.[10]

In contrast to Huckabee especially, Palin's rise to prominence in the Republican Party represents a "revival" of the old-guard Religious Right.[11] Huckabee, who openly expressed his desire to become McCain's running mate, aligned himself more closely with the new evangelical leadership and distinguished himself from prominent figures like Tony Perkins and James Dobson.[12] While the wedge-issue politics of the old-guard Religious Right tend to resonate in commercial media, the moderate and rhetorically nuanced evangelicalism of the new leadership does not.[13] At least in part, Huckabee failed to secure the VP nomination because he was "a reluctant culture warrior."[14] Palin, by contrast, "fit the role perfectly."[15]

In other words, Palin's rise to prominence does not represent the undivided will of evangelicals so much as the peculiar dynamics of the political and media institutions that drive U.S. electoral politics. The ideological tensions within evangelicalism unfold during a critical juncture in which professional journalism—especially the newspaper industry—is in a state of crisis, if not outright decline.[16] As commercial values displace civic ones, mass media increasingly function as an "evangelical-capitalist resonance machine" that strengthens the alliance between old-guard social conservatism and free-market Republicanism.[17] Rather than encouraging a nuanced discussion, media coverage of Palin has favored a narrow definition of "mainstream" evangelicalism that obscures its inner tensions and rich diversity. While Palin does not represent all evangelicals, some politicians, religious leaders, and media pundits may have an interest in having it appear so.

As this chapter shows, the dominant narrative of Palin's background portrays her faith as mainstream, simple, authentic, and non-political. While some print journalists provided a broader context for her beliefs, the flittering rush of the cable news cycle allowed Palin's "pastor problems" to remain largely below the public's radar screen. The relative lack of media attention to Palin's beliefs allowed the Grand Old Party (GOP) to court its white evangelical base while avoiding the controversies plaguing the Obama campaign. The result has normalized views that cause concern among more moderate evangelicals while hindering the latter's efforts to focus on environmentalism, social justice issues, and a more civil political discourse. In these ways, Palin's story shows how media coverage can impact evangelicals' self-perception as well as the perception of evangelicals by the public at large. Considering their influential role in U.S. political history, evangelicals and non-evangelicals alike have an interest in critically examining the quality of such coverage in the months and years to come.

A Testy Start

After McCain's VP announcement, bloggers and journalists rushed to report all available information about Palin, who at that time was largely unknown outside of Alaska. Adding to the intrigue, reports suggested that

McCain's campaign had failed to vet the candidate properly. The *New Yorker* reported that when he made his announcement, McCain had spent less than three hours with her.[18] *Vanity Fair* reported that the campaign sent its own team of lawyers and researchers belatedly, after national reporters had already arrived.[19] The race to define Palin had begun.

Almost immediately, the blogosphere and popular press became mired in conspiracy theories. The most prominent was the erroneous claim that Palin had faked her own pregnancy to cover up her daughter's pregnancy. Emerging initially from readers' posts on the *Daily Kos* website, the rumor spread rapidly in celebrity gossip magazines like *National Enquirer*, *US Weekly*, and *OK!* magazine.[20]

As the pregnancy issue made headlines, questions about Palin's religious background and policy positions fell by the wayside. Palin dominated news coverage, but reports mostly focused on her family and personal life.[21] She and her campaign condemned the media as unfair and elitist. Howard Kurtz described this early coverage as "testy" but defended the efforts of "serious journalists" to "answer fundamental questions about Palin's record"; "That, by the way, is our job," Kurtz added.[22] Despite such protests, initial coverage put journalists on the defensive, making substantive questions about Palin's background more difficult to broach.

Evasiveness from Palin and her campaign made substantive coverage of her faith more difficult. Palin spent most of her life attending Wasilla Assembly of God, a Pentecostal church. When she ran for lieutenant governor in 2002, however, she began attending the non-denominational Wasilla Bible Church.[23] After her VP nomination, reports suggested that the McCain campaign was deliberately downplaying Palin's Pentecostal roots[24] and discouraging her former pastors from talking to the news media.[25] Her campaign insisted that she is "not a Pentecostal," stressing instead her Roman Catholic baptism.[26] Palin denied belonging to any church.[27]

A Task from God?

The *Wall Street Journal* issued the first serious critique of Palin's religious background. Citing statements from Wasilla Assembly of God pastor Ed Kalnins, the *Journal* article highlights themes of divine prophecy and apocalypse. Kalnins appears to believe that "America is locked in a 'holy war' with terrorists," which he calls "a war of gods." When asked about such beliefs, a McCain spokeswoman replied simply, "I am not going to get into that."[28]

But Kalnins's remarks provide important context for Palin's own statements. In June 2008, Palin spoke to a group of young missionaries at

Wasilla Assembly of God. In a video of the event, Palin asks the audience to "Pray for our military men and women . . . that our national leaders are sending them out on a task that is from God."[29] In another video, Palin asks the audience to pray for a proposed natural-gas pipeline, saying, "I think God's will has to be done in unifying people and companies to get the gas line built. So, pray for that."[30] The *Journal* raises concerns about such statements, noting that Christian ethicist David P. Gushee "is troubled that a public official might presume that government action could be God's intent."[31]

Though Wasilla Assembly of God removed the videos from its website, they began to circulate on YouTube, cable news, and blogs. The *Huffington Post* posted the videos with additional quotes from Kalnins, including his suggestion that the war in Iraq is "a manifestation of what's going on in this unseen world called the spirit world."[32] Keith Olbermann ran the "pipeline" video on *Countdown*, and guest Rachel Maddow wondered whether Palin believes that "God is directing troop movements in Fallujah."[33] On *Good Morning America*, Diane Sawyer raised similar concerns about the "task from God" video, citing statements from another of Palin's former pastors.[34] The McCain campaign finally issued a statement defending Palin's prayer as "an incredibly humble statement . . . and a sentiment that any religious American will share."[35]

Taking a cue from Palin's campaign, Fox News framed her prayer as mainstream and non-political. Fox's Dan Springer accused critics of "trying to show that Sarah Palin's beliefs are out of the mainstream," suggesting they were "looking for any 'gotcha' moment that would . . . create a 'Reverend Wright' moment for Sarah Palin."[36] Springer's guest, a *Washington Examiner* columnist, lamented that "far-left blogs" and mainstream journalists "just don't understand [. . .] normal evangelical Christians." Fox's Brit Hume suggested that since leaving her Pentecostal church, she had been attending "a garden variety Bible church."[37] Hume's guest, a *Weekly Standard* columnist, argued that Palin is "an evangelical, pretty much in the mainstream of American Christianity." Another guest argued that while Wright's controversial statements were political, Palin's were not.

While defending Palin's faith, supporters also maligned journalists who raised substantive questions. Fox's Hume and Bill O'Reilly each accused journalists of "attacking"[38] Palin's faith by taking "little snippets" of church videos out of context.[39] At the height of the controversy, ABC's Charles Gibson ran the "task from God" video and asked her bluntly, "Are we fighting a holy war?"[40] Palin argued that she was merely repeating a similar quote from Abraham Lincoln. Critics dismissed her argument as "scripted by political strategists,"[41] suggesting that she may, in fact, see the job of government "as carrying out God's tasks."[42] But defenders insisted that it was journalists, not Palin or her pastors, who deserved scrutiny. O'Reilly portrayed Gibson's interview as an example of how "the secular media generally dismisses any faith-based people."[43] Newt Gingrich called Gibson's interview "a sad commentary on the growing anti-religious hostility of the elite media."[44] Such strategies deflected attention from Palin's background and put journalists on the defensive once again.

Preacher Problem!

A second wave of coverage developed after Olbermann aired a clip from Wasilla Assembly of God in which Palin credits her successful gubernatorial campaign to Thomas Muthee, bishop of the Word of Faith church in Kiambu, Kenya.[45] Muthee had faced scrutiny when the *Christian Science Monitor* reported his involvement in evangelical groups espousing radical interpretations of "spiritual warfare." Interpreting the concept literally, radical groups implement strategies of "spiritual mapping" and "strategic prayer" in order to locate and drive out demons from communities.[46] Muthee had targeted a woman named "Mama Jane," accusing her of practicing witchcraft and allegedly driving her out of Kiambu. Theologians suggest that these aggressive, confrontational techniques flourish in the more literal approach of Pentecostalism but raise concerns among many evangelicals.[47]

Palin's public comments indicate her familiarity with such views. In the video featured by Olbermann, Palin credits Muthee's "bold" prayer for her success: "And he's praying not, Oh, Lord, if it be your will, may she become governor. No, he just prayed for it. He said, Lord make a way and let her do this next step. And that's exactly what happened."[48] Such comments shed doubt on the claim that her "task from God" and "pipeline" prayers had been mischaracterized. Indeed, Palin's references to "prayer warriors"— in an interview with Dobson[49] and in her book[50]—are consistent with the views of evangelical groups that advocate aggressive forms of strategic prayer.[51] Drawing from scriptural passages, these groups' leaders have launched controversial campaigns targeting specific ethnic groups, geographic areas, and "strategic towns."[52] Citing the *Christian Science Monitor*, Olbermann argued that Muthee "makes Jeremiah Wright look like Father Flanagan of Boys Town."[53]

The controversy gathered momentum when the *Daily Kos* website posted a video of Muthee's prayer under the headline "Preacher Problem!"[54] In the clip, Muthee places his hand on Palin and prays, "Make a way for Sarah even in the political arena.... In the name of Jesus ... every form of witchcraft is what we rebuke." This is the prayer for which Palin would thank Muthee after she had been elected governor. That evening, Olbermann suggested that this "witchcraft" video undermined Palin's average "hockey mom" image.[55] Olbermann's guest, a *Chicago Tribune* columnist, briefly joked that Palin "could bring a witch hunter to Washington with her, and maybe chase out some demons from Capitol Hill." But then he turned serious, adding, "I've covered a number of countries in Africa. This kind of thing has a terrible reputation. A lot of innocent women have been killed, mutilated on these witch hunts."

As the Muthee videos circulated among cable news, YouTube, and blogs, more substantive coverage of spiritual mapping networks emerged. The Associated Press (AP) reported that violence against accused witches—including children—is rampant in present-day Africa. "In Congo," the article reports, "children have been thrown out of their homes and in Rwanda alleged witches have been beaten by mobs."[56] Similar coverage, providing sketches of Pentecostalism and Muthee's radical interpretations of spiritual warfare, appeared in sources such as the *Guardian*, the *Los Angeles Times*, and *Newsday*.

Some journalists began to question the McCain campaign's vetting process. Citing the Muthee video, *Time* magazine asked, "Does Sarah Palin Have a Pentecostal Problem?" "Evangelicals' swoon for Palin might fade," the article suggests, "if it turns out that she continues to hold fast to Pentecostal practices and beliefs."[57] The *New York Times* highlighted the belief among Palin's former pastors that Alaska would be "one of the refuge states in the Last Days." The *Times* claims that Palin's ties to radical prayer networks are more than tenuous, adding that "the movement's fixation on demons, its aggressiveness and its leaders' claims to exalted spiritual authority have troubled even some Pentecostal Christians."[58] Contrary to her supporters' claims, the *Times* describes these networks as explicitly political, advocating a seven-point strategy for exerting influence over societies and governments.[59]

Though newspaper coverage provided important context for Palin's views, cable news coverage largely dismissed the political aspects of Muthee's prayer networks. While CNN's Amy Holmes found "a political component" in Wright's sermons, she failed to see the problem with Muthee's videos: "There was rebuking witchcraft. I mean, where's the news in that?"[60] As noted earlier, even Palin's critics treated Muthee's reference to witchcraft jokingly. Regarding Muthee's prayer to protect Palin from "every form of witchcraft,"

Kurtz asked, "Is it potentially offensive to witches?" His guest replied sarcastically, "They'll lose the Wiccan vote."[61]

In contrast to more substantive print coverage, the dismissive tenor of cable news lent credence to Palin's claim that "Not just my faith, faith and God in general has been mocked through this campaign."[62] In fact, research indicates that mainstream media did not "dwell on religion" and exhibited a "relative lack of attention to Palin's religious biography."[63] Coverage of Palin's background paled in comparison to the Wright controversy, which was the single largest press narrative in the presidential campaign.[64] But while racial prejudice and a lack of context turned Wright into a liability for Barack Obama, the same factors allowed Palin's pastor problems to slip off the radar screen.[65] Pundits who accused Obama of dishonesty about his faith portrayed Palin as authentic, down-to-earth, and forthcoming about hers. While claiming to defend Palin's Christian faith, such portrayals only served to hinder an open discussion of race within American evangelicalism.

Hockey Moms and Joe Six-Packs

Indeed, from the campaign's beginning, supporters portrayed Palin as an "authentic" voice of the public. Palin's self-identification as a "hockey mom" was inseparable from the representation of her faith as mainstream and benign. As one religion scholar notes, Palin began to "divide the country into real and unreal America," and "as she presented it, the real America is the America of (among other things) religion."[66] Her supporters continually linked Palin's down-home authenticity to her faith. For example, in an interview on Fox News shortly after the election, Rev. Franklin Graham suggested that "first of all, she's real. What you see is what you get with her. And she is a woman of faith. And she's not afraid to let that come out."[67]

But in the construction of Palin's authenticity, religious faith is inseparable from race. Scholars suggest that through her repeated references to "hockey moms" and "Joe six-packs," Palin has established herself as an icon of "archetypal whiteness."[68] While sounding generic, such expressions appeal specifically to white, working-class men. Indeed, just after Palin's biographer appeared on Fox News to defend Palin's authenticity,[69] pollster Scott Rasmussen told Sean Hannity that Palin "has a cultural appeal to those white working class voters" in the Mid-western states where Obama struggled in the primaries.[70]

Some journalists critique Palin on this point. For example, columnist Mary Mitchell suggested that when Palin claimed "[w]e grow good people

70 Evangelical Christians and Popular Culture

in our small towns with honesty, sincerity, and dignity," she was deliberately invoking racial prejudice.[71] Yet just as the campaign dismissed issues of Palin's religious background, supporters disavowed the importance of race in her populist appeals. O'Reilly dismissed Mitchell's criticism of Palin by suggesting that for her, "everything is racial."[72] Speaking to O'Reilly from Wasilla the following day, Fox News's Greta Van Susteren reinforced Palin's claims of authenticity. "Everyone here calls her Sarah," said Van Susteren, "And everyone seems to know her. It's all on a first-name basis."[73] Speaking to O'Reilly several days later, pollster Frank Luntz agreed that "there's one word that people use to describe her, both positive and negative. Authentic. They believe that they see what she is, and she is what people see."[74]

The repeated claims that Palin is an ordinary American with nothing to hide stand in stark contrast to the narrative that plagued Obama during the Wright controversy—namely that Obama is disingenuous, elitist, and politically radical. Obama's critics waged a highly racialized campaign that portrayed Obama as dishonest about his religious and political background. After Obama had left Trinity United Church and condemned Wright's controversial statements, Palin's supporters continued to link Obama to Wright, whom they portrayed as racist. As Palin invoked race implicitly in her appeals to white voters, supporters again projected racial intolerance onto the Obama campaign. Rush Limbaugh portrayed any discussion of Palin's whiteness as a racist ploy and claimed that the Obama campaign deliberately "incites racism."[75]

Of course, such accusations of anti-white racism prioritize the concerns of white voters, raising fears that whites will face discrimination from an African American president. In portraying Palin as an authentic representative of mainstream religious and political values, supporters frame Palin as an icon of white entitlement. In this way, the narrative of authenticity surrounding Palin serves as a flip side to the Wright controversy. Each narrative appeals to a "four-centuries-old white racial frame"[76]—a set of background assumptions that label blacks as threatening, dangerous, and dishonest while portraying whites as non-threatening, honest, and trustworthy.[77]

Palin's rhetoric of patriotism plays into this white racial frame. "We believe that the best of America is in these small towns that we get to visit," she told one crowd in North Carolina. She described such towns as "the real America," and expressed her delight at visiting the "very patriotic" and "pro-America areas of this great nation."[78] Limbaugh continued this populist narrative, claiming that "the Democrat [sic] Party tried to destroy an average citizen, this Joe the plumber guy"[79]—a reference to Joe Wurzelbacher, a figure whom McCain and Palin invoked in debates and speeches. In response to unflattering information that had been uncovered about Wurzelbacher, Limbaugh suggested that "Governor Palin has a genuine, rich American life that she has lived, and she has hundreds of people to vouch for it. She doesn't have anything in her past that's hidden."[80] In the wake of the racially charged campaign against Obama and Wright, however, figures such as Joe the Plumber invoke the same racial codes as Palin's references to "Joe Six-Pack."[81] Coupled with her defense of racial profiling, Palin's expressed concern for "Americans desiring representation"[82] amounted to a call for the representation of white voters' interests in the face of shifting demographics and the possible election of an African American president. Such rhetoric likely contributed to Palin's steady approval ratings among white evangelical Republicans.[83]

The importance of Palin's whiteness became clearer after the election as she assumed a leadership role in the Tea Party movement. Research indicates that Tea Party activists are not simply concerned about the size of government; they are also motivated by concerns about race. A *New York Times*/CBS News poll found that Tea Party activists "tend to be white, male, and married," are "loyal Republicans," and "are significantly more likely than all adults to say that too much has been made of the problems of black people."[84] These attitudes—along with continued claims that Obama is Muslim, born in Kenya, overly sympathetic to the Third World, and a socialist—contribute to a racialized campaign to define Obama's inherent "otherness." As Palin assumes a leadership role within the Tea Party movement, then, she serves as an icon for white voters harboring "fears of disenfranchisement."[85]

Why Palin Matters

As theologian Richard Mouw explains, the leadership of the Tea Party by Palin and other partisan conservatives echoes the "Great Reversal" of the late nineteenth century, when evangelicals' discomfort with increasing cultural pluralism led many to turn away from their long-standing engagement with social justice issues.[86] Along with the racially charged campaign against Obama, the vilification of out-groups such as immigrants and gays has revived a sense that "they're taking something away from us and we got to get it back."[87] For evangelicals like Mouw, who seek to foster a more civil public discourse, such developments are troubling. As George Shulman explains, while engagement with social justice issues invigorates the democratic process, absolutism and claims of divine prophecy "engender self-righteousness and violence, which close spaces for political contest."[88]

Especially in contrast to media coverage of Obama and Wright, Palin's rise to stardom demonstrates that while advocates of social justice struggle to gain a foothold in the commercial media environment, leaders subscribing to a mixture of religious apocalyptism, U.S. exceptionalism, and free-market ideology can achieve rapid success. For decades, professional journalism has enabled this imbalance by failing to adequately cover the U.S. black Church and by neglecting politically significant developments in global Christianity. Without this broader context, coverage of Wright aggravated racial stereotypes while substantive coverage of Palin's background simply "sounded outlandish."[89] Thus while Wright still appears in political attack ads, Palin's "pastor problems" are far behind her. Since resigning from her governorship, she has launched a lucrative media career, securing six-figure speaking fees and cable television contracts. As one critic notes, Palin has become "a singular national industry."[90]

Palin's success is partly a measure of her personal ambition. In contrast to her campaign's narrative of authenticity, *Vanity Fair* describes a long-standing "counter-narrative" portraying Palin as "a woman who saw her opportunities and coolly seized them."[91] *Slate* suggests that "Palin's only actual message is the importance of loving and understanding Palin," adding that "Palin's political skill lies in selling a persona but not a message."[92] This counter-narrative resonates with recent scholarship indicating that in many cases "authenticity is a hook employed either to sell products and services ... or a hegemonic discourse through which various ideologies are articulated."[93] Indeed, while Palin complained of being mocked either for her religion or for her unwillingness to conform to the values of the Washington elite, much of the satire she faced aimed directly at the fissures in a heavy-handed campaign that transformed Palin's idiosyncratic style into a strategic marketing tool.[94] Thus Palin's down-home "wink" became yet another campaign tactic, lending itself to parody of the type seen on *Saturday Night Live*.

From Billy Graham to David Kuo, the history books are filled with evangelicals who, having flown to close to the flame of political power, turned away for fear of getting burned. Many have expressed concern for the integrity of their faith, noting how difficult it is to speak truth to power when one is too comfortable walking its halls. Time will tell whether Palin will experience a similar revelation. In the meantime, audiences and voters will benefit from a healthy skepticism toward popular definitions of mainstream evangelicalism and those who claim to champion it. Beneath the clamor of voices on cable news and YouTube, each claiming the mantle of authentic, mainstream faith, there is another generation struggling to find its voice. Regardless of how her political career develops, Palin's story highlights an ongoing struggle at the heart of American evangelicalism. It is a struggle as old as the United States itself: over leadership, values, and the role of faith in U.S. public life.

Notes

1. Sarah Bailey, "Is Palin an Evangelical?" *Christianity Today*, August 30, 2008, http://blog.christianitytoday.com/ctpolitics/2008/08/is_palin_an_eva.html (accessed April 6, 2010).

2. Ibid. Also see Sarah Bailey, "McCain Picks Alaska Gov. Sarah Palin for VP," *Christianity Today*, August 29, 2008, http://blog.christianitytoday.com/ctpolitics/2008/08/mccain_picks_al.html (accessed April 6, 2010).

3. William McKenzie, "The Tension Growing in Evangelicalism Is Healthy," *Dallas Morning News*, October 16, 2007, http://www.nacdweb.org/files/Press room/The_tension_growing_in_evangelicalism.pdf (accessed May 20, 2008).

4. Ed Stoddard, "Is Palin New Face of Religious Right, Or Old?" *Reuters.com*, September 16, 2008, http://www.reuters.com/article/idUSN1625146420080916 (accessed April 7, 2010).

5. "A New Generation Expresses Its Skepticism and Frustration with Christianity," Barna Group, September 24, 2007, http://www.barna.org/barna-update/article/16-teensnext-gen/94-a-new-generation-expresses-its-skepticism-and-frustration-with-christianity (accessed May 20, 2008).

6. George M. Marsden, *Fundamentalism and American Culture: The Shaping of Twentieth-Century Evangelicalism 1870–1925* (New York: Oxford University Press, 1980).

7. Lisa Miller, "A Religious-Right Revival," *Newsweek*, September 6, 2008, http://www.newsweek.com/2008/09/05/a-religious-right-revival.html (accessed April 7, 2010).

8. Richard Mouw, speaking to radio host Krista Tippett, "Restoring Political Civility," *Krista Tippett on Being*, American Public Media, October 14, 2010, http://being.publicradio.org/programs/2010/restoring-civility/transcript.shtml (accessed November 5, 2010).

9. "Romney's Image Improves; Palin Well Regarded by Republican Base," Pew Research Center for the People and the Press, June 24, 2009, http://people-press.org/report/524/republican-favorability (accessed December 4, 2010).

10. John C. Green et al., "Faithful, Engaged, and Divergent: A Comparative Portrait of Conservative and Progressive Religious Activists in the 2008 Election and Beyond," Public Religion Research, September 2009, http://publicreligion.org/site/wp-content/uploads/2011/06/Progressive-and-COnservative-REligious-Activists-Report.pdf (accessed May 22, 2012).

11. Miller, "A Religious-Right Revival."

12. Mark Silk, "What Makes Huckabee Run?" *Spiritual Politics*, February 17, 2008, http://www.marksilk.com/2008/02/what_makes_huckabee_run/ (accessed May 22, 2012).

13. Joel C. Hunter, *Right Wing, Wrong Bird: Why the Tactics of the Religious Right Won't Fly with Most Conservative Christians* (Longwood, FL: Distributed Church, 2006).

14. Mark Silk, "That Woman," *Spiritual Politics*, November 25, 2008, http://www.marksilk.com/2008/11/that_woman/ (accessed May 22, 2012).

15. Ibid.

16. Robert W. McChesney and John Nichols, *The Death and Life of American Journalism: The Media Revolution That Will Begin the World Again* (Philadelphia: Nation, 2010).

17. William E. Connolly, "The Evangelical-Capitalist Resonance Machine," *Political Theory* 33, no. 6 (2005): 870.

18. Jane Mayer, "The Insiders: How John McCain Came to Pick Sarah Palin," *New Yorker*, October 27, 2008, http://www.newyorker.com/reporting/2008/10/27/081027fa_fact_mayer (accessed April 12, 2010).

19. Todd Purdum, "It Came from Wasilla," *Vanity Fair*, August, 2009.

20. Howard Kurtz, "Palin & Press: A Testy Start," *Washington Post*, September 8, 2008 (accessed from Lexis-Nexis).

21. "The Palin Phenomenon Drives Campaign Coverage," Pew Research Center's Project for Excellence in Journalism, 2008, http://www.journalism.org/node/12693 (accessed September 22, 2010).

22. Kurtz, "Palin & Press: A Testy Start."

23. Amy Sullivan, "Are Evangelicals Really Sold on Palin?" *Time*, September 6, 2008, http://www.time.com/time/politics/article/0,8599,1839190,00.html (accessed April 6, 2010).

24. "How the Media Have Handled Palin's Faith," Pew Forum on Religion and Public Life, September 22, 2008, http://pewforum.org/Politics-and-Elections/How-the-Media-Have-Handled-Palins-Faith.aspx (accessed December 4, 2010).

25. Laurie Goodstein, "Palin's Faith Is Linked to Form of Pentecostalism Known as Spiritual Warfare," *New York Times*, October 25, 2008 (accessed from Lexis-Nexis).

26. Amy Sullivan, "Does Sarah Palin Have a Pentecostal Problem?" *Time*, October 9, 2008, http://www.time.com/time/politics/article/0,8599,1848420-1,00.html (accessed April 15, 2010).

27. Mark Silk, "Her Personal Faith," *Spiritual Politics*, October 1, 2008, http://www.marksilk.com/2008/10/her_personal_faith/ (accessed May 22, 2012).

28. Quoted in Suzanne Sataline, "Palin's Faith Is Seen in Church Upbringing," *Wall Street Journal*, September 4, 2008, http://online.wsj.com/article/SB122048406528596987.html (accessed December 4, 2010).

29. Ibid.

30. "Palin's Church May Have Shaped Controversial Worldview," *Huffington Post*, September 2, 2008, http://www.huffingtonpost.com/2008/09/02/palins-church-may-have-sh_n_123205.html (accessed September 9, 2008).

31. Sataline, "Palin's Faith Is Seen in Church Upbringing."

32. "Palin's Church May Have Shaped Controversial Worldview," 2008.

33. Keith Olbermann, "Countdown for September 8, 2008," *Countdown*, MSNBC, September 8, 2008 (accessed from Lexis-Nexis).

34. Diane Sawyer, "Sarah Palin Uncensored; Tapes from the Past," *Good Morning America*, ABC News, September 9, 2008 (accessed from Lexis-Nexis).

35. "McCain/Palin Campaign Goes on the Dole," *New York Sun*, September 9, 2008, http://www.nysun.com/national/mccain-palin-campaign-goes-on-the-dole/85431/ (accessed March 6, 2009).

36. Dan Springer, "America's Election Headquarters for September 9, 2008," *America's Election Headquarters*, Fox News Network, September 9, 2008 (accessed from Lexis-Nexis).

37. Brit Hume, "Interview with Bill Sammon," *Fox Special Report with Brit Hume*, Fox News Network, September 9, 2008 (accessed from Lexis-Nexis).

38. Ibid.

39. Bill O'Reilly, "Personal Story," *O'Reilly Factor*, Fox News Network, September 9, 2008 (accessed from Lexis-Nexis).

40. Charles Gibson, "Exclusive: Task from God," *World News with Charles Gibson*, ABC News, September 11, 2008 (accessed from Lexis-Nexis).

41. Sullivan, "Does Sarah Palin Have a Pentecostal Problem?"

42. Mark Silk, "God's Plan," *Spiritual Politics*, September 11, 2008, http://www.marksilk.com/2008/09/gods_plan.html (accessed May 22, 2012).

43. Bill O'Reilly, "Analyzing Palin Interview," *O'Reilly Factor*, Fox News Network, September 12, 2008 (accessed from Lexis-Nexis).

44. Quoted in Howard Kurtz, "Palin Gives Interview to ABC News," *CNN Reliable Sources*, September 14, 2008 (accessed from Lexis-Nexis).

45. "Sarah's Blessed Quest," *Weekend Australian*, September 27, 2008 (accessed from Lexis-Nexis).

46. Jane Lampman, "Targeting Cities with 'Spiritual Mapping' Prayer," *Christian Science Monitor*, September 23, 1999, http://www.csmonitor.com/1999/0923/p15s1.html (accessed April 21, 2010).

47. Ibid.

48. Keith Olbermann, "Countdown for September 19, 2008," *Countdown*, MSNBC, September 19, 2008 (accessed from Lexis-Nexis).

49. Goodstein, "Palin's Faith Is Linked to Form of Pentecostalism Known as Spiritual Warfare."

50. Sarah Palin, *Going Rogue: An American Life* (New York: HarperCollins, 2009), 411.

51. Mark Silk, "Spiritual Warfare," *Spiritual Politics*, October 26, 2008, http://www.marksilk.com/2008/10/spiritual_warfare.html (accessed May 22, 2012).

52. Jane Lampman, "Operation Prayer," *Christian Science Monitor*, September 16, 1999, http://www.csmonitor.com/1999/0916/p11s1.html (accessed April 21, 2010).

53. Olbermann, "Countdown for September 19, 2008."

54. David Waldman, "Preacher Problem!" *Daily Kos*, September 24, 2008, http://www.dailykos.com/storyonly/2008/9/24/171613/532 (accessed September 22, 2010).

55. Keith Olbermann, "Countdown for September 24, 2008," *Countdown*, MSNBC, September 24, 2008 (accessed from Lexis-Nexis).

56. Associated Press, "Video Shows Pastor Protecting Palin from 'Witchcraft,'" *New Zealand Herald*, September 26, 2008 (accessed from Lexis-Nexis).

57. Sullivan, "Does Sarah Palin Have a Pentecostal Problem?"

58. Goodstein, "Palin's Faith Is Linked to Form of Pentecostalism."

59. See, for example, Bruce Wilson, "Spiritual Mapping and Spiritual Warfare: Muthee and the 'Transformations' Franchise," Talk to Action, September 5, 2008, http://www.talk2action.org/pages/docs/Transformation.pdf (accessed May 5, 2009).

60. Howard Kurtz, "Coverage of Presidential Debate Examined," *CNN Reliable Sources*, September 28, 2008 (accessed from Lexis-Nexis).

61. Ibid.

62. David Brody, "Palin: Faith, God in General Has Been Mocked through This Campaign," *Brody File*, CBN News, October 20, 2008, http://blogs.cbn.com/thebrodyfile/archive/2008/10/20/palin-faith-god-in-general-has-been-mocked-through-this.aspx (accessed December 4, 2010).

63. "How the Media Have Handled Palin's Faith," Pew Forum on Religion and Public Life.

64. "How the News Media Covered Religion in the General Election," Pew Forum on Religion and Public Life, November 20, 2008, http://pewforum.org/docs/?DocID=372 (accessed February 17, 2011).

65. Kevin Healey, "For a Culture and Political Economy of the Prophetic: Critical Scholarship and Religious Politics after the 2008 Election," *Cultural Studies Critical Methodologies* 10, no. 2 (2010): 157–170.

66. Mark Silk, "Anti-Palinism," *Spiritual Politics*, November 20, 2008, http://www.marksilk.com/2008/11/anti-palinism.html (accessed May 22, 2012).

67. Greta Van Susteren, "Interview with Rev. Franklin Graham," *On the Record with Greta Van Susteren*, Fox News Network, November 13, 2008 (accessed from Lexis-Nexis).

68. Jessie Daniels, "Sarah Palin: Archetypal Whiteness," *Racism Review*, October 5, 2008, http://www.racismreview.com/blog/2008/10/05/sarah-palin-archetypal-whiteness/ (accessed December 4, 2010).

69. Sean Hannity and Alan Colmes, "Interview with Palin Biographer," *Hannity & Colmes*, Fox News Network, September 8, 2008 (accessed from Lexis-Nexis).

70. Sean Hannity and Alan Colmes, "Interview with Scott Rasmussen," *Hannity & Colmes*, Fox News Network, September 8, 2008 (accessed from Lexis-Nexis).

71. Mary Mitchell, "Is Attack Dog's Bite Even Worse Than Her Bark?" *Chicago Sun Times*, September 5, 2008, http://www.suntimes.com/news/mitchell/1146696, CST-NWS-mitch05.article (accessed December 4, 2010).

72. Bill O'Reilly, "Personal Story: Sarah Palin," *O'Reilly Factor*, Fox News Network, September 8, 2008 (accessed from Lexis-Nexis).

73. Bill O'Reilly, "Personal Story." *O'Reilly Factor*, Fox News Network, September 9, 2008 (accessed from Lexis-Nexis).

74. Bill O'Reilly, "The Palin Factor," *O'Reilly Factor*, Fox News Network, September 19, 2008 (accessed from Lexis-Nexis).

75. Greta Van Susteren, "Rush Limbaugh Says New Obama Ad Incites Racism," *On the Record with Greta Van Susteren*, Fox News Network, September 19, 2008 (accessed from Lexis-Nexis).

76. Adia Harvey Wingfield and Joe Feagin, *Yes We Can? White Racial Framing and the 2008 Presidential Campaign* (New York: Routledge, 2009), 155.

77. Ibid., 15, 106.

78. Quoted in Sam Stein, "Palin Explains What Parts of Country Not 'Pro-America,'" *Huffington Post*, October 17, 2008, http://www.huffingtonpost.com/2008/10/17/palin-clarifies-what-part_n_135641.html (accessed November 29, 2010).

79. Greta Van Susteren, "Radio Talk Show Host Rush Limbaugh Talks Politics," *On the Record with Greta Van Susteren*, Fox News Network, October 27, 2008 (accessed from Lexis-Nexis).

80. Ibid.

81. Daniels, "Sarah Palin: Archetypal Whiteness."

82. Sean Hannity and Alan Colmes, "Interview With Sarah Palin," *Hannity & Colmes*, Fox News Network, October 27, 2008 (accessed from Lexis-Nexis).

83. "Romney's Image Improves; Palin Well Regarded by Republican Base," 2009.

84. "Polling the Tea Party," *New York Times*, April 14, 2010, http://www.nytimes.com/interactive/2010/04/14/us/politics/20100414-tea-party-poll-graphic.html?ref=politics#tab=5 (accessed December 4, 2010).

85. Frank Rich, "The Rage Is Not about Health Care," *New York Times*, March 27, 2010, http://www.nytimes.com/2010/03/28/opinion/28rich.html?hp (accessed April 20, 2010).

86. Marsden, *Fundamentalism and American Culture*.

87. Tippett, "Restoring Political Civility."

88. George Shulman, *American Prophecy: Race and Redemption in American Political Culture* (Minneapolis: University of Minnesota Press, 2008), xii.

89. Bill Berkowitz, "The New Christianity: What the Mainstream Media Has Missed," *Religion Dispatches*, April 2, 2009, http://www.religiondispatches.org/

archive/politics/1275/the_new_christianity%3A_what_the_mainstream_media_has_missed_/ (accessed May 22, 2012).

90. Gabriel Sherman, "The Revolution Will Be Commercialized," *New York Magazine*, April 25, 2010, http://nymag.com/news/politics/65628/ (accessed April 28, 2010).

91. Purdum, "It Came from Wasilla."

92. Dahlia Lithwick, "Lost in Translation: Why Sarah Palin Really Quit Us," *Slate*, July 8, 2009 (accessed from Lexis-Nexis).

93. Phillip Vannini and J. Patrick Williams, "Authenticity in Culture, Self, and Society," in *Authenticity in Culture, Self, and Society*, eds. Phillip Vannini and J. Patrick Williams (Burlington, VT: Ashgate, 2009), 10.

94. Healey, "For a Culture and Political Economy of the Prophetic."

Chapter 5

Johnny Cash, Evangelicals, and Popular Culture

Stephen J. Nichols

They had the routine worked out pretty well. Celebrated evangelist Billy Graham, during any one of his stadium-packed crusades, would tell of a drunken man getting on an airplane and taking a seat in the first-class cabin next to him. The flight crew was unsure how to handle their inebriated, belligerent passenger, but Graham offered calm assurances that the situation would be okay and that he could handle it. By the time wheels touched down, the man, presumably having sobered up, had in fact calmed down, had repented, and had accepted Christ. With tears in his eyes, this once-gruff man apologized for his behavior towards the flight crew and the other passengers. That drunk was a new man, allowing Graham to end the story with a punch: Jesus will, as he did for that drunken man on a plane, "change your life too." Graham's signature stirring testimony never failed to hit its mark.

And then Johnny Cash would be introduced to the great crowd. As Cash would lift the guitar strap over his shoulder, he would step up to the microphone and, with a wink, say, "I don't know why he always tells that story just before *I* come on the stage." And Johnny Cash had the audience. And he still does.

One needs no other evidence for status as an evangelical than association with Graham. Graham defined twentieth-century evangelicalism, with its emphasis on evangelism, inter-denominational cooperation, and being "salt and light" in American culture. Graham gave evangelicalism its rallying cry; his simple message sincerely declared, "You must be born again." U.S. presidents, star athletes, actors, and musicians stood at Graham's side, and Cash stood tall among them.

They were an odd couple. Graham was well-groomed and calm; throughout the 1950s, 1960s, and 1970s, he looked the part of any mother's wish for a son or son-in-law. Then there was Cash—a man with a history, a history etched in the lines of his face, hardened already in the prime of his life. From his early days, Graham knew he wanted to be an evangelist and lived a saintly life accordingly. No hint of scandal ever touched Graham in those decades of fallen heroes and plastic saints. Then there was Cash—dogged by stories of philandering, drug use, and rehab treatment (again). Graham would see a cameraperson and flash a smile and a princely wave. Cash would see a cameraperson, grit his teeth, and make an obscene gesture.

Singer and songwriter Johnny Cash, shown here performing at the Grand Ole Opry in 1974. Cash performed at a number of Billy Graham crusades over a period of more than two decades. (AP Photo/John Duricka.)

At the Graham Museum at Wheaton College and the one in Charlotte, North Carolina, there are letters between Graham and Cash. There are also photographs of Graham and Cash alongside world leaders and presidents. Graham and Cash not only took the platform together at crusades; their families vacationed together and celebrated birthdays together. When June Carter Cash died, Graham was there. When Cash died a few months later, Graham was there again. Graham offered a press release that sums up his estimation of the man:

> Johnny Cash was not only a legend, but was a close personal friend. Johnny was a good man who also struggled with many challenges in his life. Johnny was a deeply religious man. He and June came to a number of our Crusades over a period of many years. Ruth and I took a number of personal vacations with them at their home in Jamaica and in other places. They both were like a brother and sister to Ruth and me. We loved them. We are praying that God will comfort his family and staff at this critical time. I look forward to seeing Johnny and June in heaven one day.[1]

Cash is a legend among evangelicals, his life and his songs providing great fodder for sermons and books and the telling of inspiring tales among evangelicals. However, Cash had far more different kinds of friends than Graham. His role as exemplar in the evangelical community, then, comes with not a little dose of irony. Divorced and drug-addled, Cash knew quite a bit about and sang often of life on the dark side. What serves to knock others off the evangelical platform—drugs and dalliances—somehow served to endear Cash to evangelicals.

Evangelicals like stories of the drunk on the plane *before* conversion. However, Cash was drunk (or high) *after* conversion, and by some reports was often so.[2] Cash is an unlikely hero among evangelicals, singing of cocaine-aided homicide and of wandering eyes and of reckless hearts, but he is a hero nevertheless. Perhaps he is a hero among evangelicals precisely because of the times when his "better angels" lost out. Perhaps evangelicals are drawn to Cash because, like Cash, they too see their "better angels" losing from time to time.

This chapter explores Cash as an evangelical and his influence on evangelicalism. First, Cash's own journey as an evangelical bears scrutiny and offers an intriguing perspective on defining and understanding evangelicalism. Second, the chapter looks at the places Cash shows up in the evangelical landscape. Third, this chapter explores Cash's contribution to evangelicalism. All of this raises the following questions: Why are evangelicals so fond of him?

And for the skeptic, why *should* evangelicals be fond of him? The short answer has to do with Cash's unequaled life, legacy, and music. He forged his own way as a musician, as a poet, and as a prophet. For evangelicals looking for a model for engaging culture they clearly find one in Cash. Cash took his faith into arenas (literally!) where faith seldom gets heard. Cash also never fit the notion of what some have sarcastically referred to as being a "plastic saint." Cash shows all dimensions, both highs and lows, both the noble and the ignoble, of real life. The following pages expand on these themes.

Cash's Evangelical Journey

Cash's journey was not the typical evangelical journey. Cash had a childhood conversion in 1944 at a revival meeting in a Southern Baptist Church, but that did not remove the dark side that was there.

One of those who got close enough to Cash to see the dark side of the performer was bassist and long-time member of the Tennessee Two Marshall Grant. Cash first met Marshall in Memphis, Tennessee. Marshall went with Cash to Sun Studio on Union Avenue, where he, Luther Perkins, and Cash won over Sam Phillips. Phillips, who gave the world Elvis Presley and Roy Orbison—and the list goes on—had a steady stream of would-be stars line up behind his microphones at Sun, many fresh from the cotton fields with wide-eyed dreams of success. Few made it. Cash, Grant, and Perkins did.

Grant went on the road with Cash in those early years, along with the likes of Orbison and a young Presley as the "Louisiana Hayride" crisscrossed the byways of the South. Grant watched as Cash took his first amphetamines just before they opened for Faron Young, and then he watched his friend spiral down into drugs for the first time. That was in the mid-1960s.[3]

By 1967, with June Carter in his life, Cash sobered up and underwent a religious experience. But here the tale is not so clear. Evangelicals, especially those of the 1960s, tended to place a high premium on the moment of decision to follow Christ. This is the conversion experience, the moment when a person, using the famous slogan of Graham, is "born again." Other versions of Christianity, especially those stressing more sacramental approaches such as Roman Catholicism or Anglicanism, follow a different paradigm. However, evangelicals know the when and where and even vivid details of the time of their conversion to Christ, not at all unlike the New Testament account of Paul on the road to Damascus.

The question this raises concerning Cash is, what happened in 1967? Was his experience in 1967 a "rededication"? A rededication is yet another peculiar evangelical practice. It refers to someone who, having experienced conversion, has backslidden and drifted away from commitment to Christ and living as a disciple. Cash, however, saw it as deeper than a rededication and took it as his conversion. This was the event of the "poor sinner coming home," taking a line from a favorite altar-call hymn, "Softly and Tenderly," a hymn Cash himself would sing on one of his American recordings for Rick Rubin.[4]

The question of what happened in November 1967 gets even more complicated when Cash answered yet another altar call on May 9, 1971. Jimmy Snow, son of Hank Snow and pastor at Evangel Temple where Cash walked down the aisle during an altar call, must have had a way with sermons. In that same year, 1971, songwriter, musician, and sometime actor Kris Kristofferson also heard a similar altar call, walked that same aisle that his hero did, knelt at the same altar, and made his own confession.[5]

In the wake of Cash's 1971 experience, Steve Turner points out in his authorized biography that "Cash became noticeably more diligent about his faith."[6] And he applied that diligence to a demanding project. Though Turner calls it diligence, it may be better to call it—despite the fact that Cash was an evangelical *Protestant*—penance. And so he set out to do his penance in the desert. Cash shepherded a studio film and a soundtrack on the life of Jesus, all shot entirely on location in Israel. In 1972, Cash released both the movie and the soundtrack of *The Gospel Road*.

The timing was impeccable, as the very same year witnessed Explo '72, the debut for the Jesus Movement and Christian rock, which would quickly evolve into Contemporary Christian Music (CCM).[7] Cash, of course, was there in Houston. He even managed to talk Kristofferson into appearing.[8] Through most of the 1970s, Cash was a full-throttled evangelical.

Then something happened in 1977. In the authorized biography, Turner notes, "The first signs of a disturbance in Cash's otherwise placid new life came when he stopped attending Evangel Temple in 1977." Turner adds, "The reasons he left are unclear."[9] Cash suggested it had something to do with his celebrity status making it quite a problem for him to attend church. Cash did not feel that fending off autograph seekers and would-be singer-songwriters coalesced well with an attitude of worship.

Grant has a different theory. According to Grant, during a brutal road tour in 1977, Cash relapsed in New Haven, Connecticut, and went back to drugs. Again, Grant was there, and all he could ask of Cash was, "Why? Why?" Cash mustered enough focus to shoot back, "Marshall, have you ever been through the shit of life?"[10] Cash was still haunted by his demons, even after he had made his profession of faith and had answered the altar call three times. The relapse into drugs and the lapse from church would mean that the 1970s would not end for Cash as they had begun.

The "Man in Black" *and* the "Man in White"

At the end of the 1970s, Cash wrote a novel—Christian fiction, actually. After finishing a correspondence course on the Bible, Cash could not shake his fascination with the life of the Apostle Paul. "I lay awake nights back in 1978 and 1979 thinking about Paul," Cash writes in the preface to the *The Man in White*.[11] It was the transformation that intrigued him.

Cash, often referred to as "the Man in Black," liked the outlaw persona, and he nurtured it through his songs. If truth be told, however, his imprisonments totaled nothing more than a few nights. This was not hard time. He was held for attempting to smuggle amphetamines in from Mexico in his guitar case. He also spent a night in the drunk tank at Starkville, Mississippi, for picking flowers from the flower beds of the unsuspecting Copeland family home along Highway 182.

While his outlaw image was more hype than substance, Cash nevertheless knew the dark side of the human heart. However, he also knew of the power of transformation, so he was drawn to Paul. When Paul first appears in the biblical narrative, he is still called Saul, and he is holding the coats of those stoning Stephen to death (Acts 7:58). When he next appears, he is dragging early Christians from their homes to be martyred (Acts 8:1–3). Paul led a reign of terror so intense that the mere mention of his name sent Christians into hiding. By the end of the book of Acts, though, Saul has been converted, his name has been changed to Paul, and he emerges as the leader of Christianity. The thirteen New Testament epistles attributed to him constitute the essential foundation or base of Christian theology and practice. Cash's fascination with Paul's transformation, with Paul's "character and personality," makes perfect sense.[12]

Perhaps what Cash saw first and foremost in the character and personality of Paul was a mirror image of himself. Perhaps Cash liked even more the idea that Paul's dark side was far darker than Cash's own. Could it be that here, in the story of Paul, was an even more despicable person than himself?

The Final Stage of the Journey

The next decade, the 1980s, saw Cash weaving on and off drugs and drifting, musically and spiritually, so the Graham organization dropped Cash from their crusades.[13] Again, though, Cash sobered up.

In the 1990s, Cash embarked on what would come to be, in the eyes of many, the most creative decade of his life. As Cash was poised to turn out some hit records, he was also poised to return to his gospel emphasis. In 1990, he hired Jack Shaw, an evangelist, to enlist his support. Shaw was Cash's mobile pastor and counselor. Cash also made Shaw available to his audiences for spiritual counsel. Shaw would say of this arrangement that Cash "was so glad that he was doing something to affect people's lives with the gospel of Jesus Christ."[14] Cash soon got invited back on to the crusade platform with his old friend Graham. Cash was back, musically and spiritually.

Cash teamed up with Rubin to begin the release of the American Recordings with a variety of songs: some new, some old, some originals, some covers (rerecordings of someone else's songs), some songs of the lost sinner, and some songs of the redeemed saint. (Cash as saint, though, tended towards a bent halo.)

In an interview with Turner, Cash looked back over the 1980s and said, "I never lost my faith during that time, but I lost my contact with God," adding, "I wasted a lot of time and energy. I mean we're not just talking days, but months and years."[15] Cash had a lot of time to make up, and that is what he did from the 1990s right up to the end of his life on September 12, 2003.

Cash's life has all the right ingredients for his place as an evangelical exemplar, starting with a churchgoing and Bible-reading upbringing. Like the rest of the group of Sun artists who gave birth to rock 'n' roll and like the earlier generation of blues singers or of early country music singers, Cash learned to sing in the church at his mother's side. Cash also had the essential ingredient of conversion. In fact, he had three conversions, not to mention as many baptisms—his third baptism in the Jordan River in 1979. He had piety, the heartfelt and life-evidenced warmth, compassion, and zeal of a disciple. He had a love for the Bible.

But he did not have a straight path. Evangelicals typically prefer straighter journeys in their heroes. A person's life prior to conversion is one thing, but after conversion one's life should be a bit cleaner, the path of life straighter and narrower. However, Cash's meandering ways, on and off drugs, in and out of gospel phases, might actually have served to endear him to evangelical audiences.

David Bebbington, in his often-repeated quadrilateral for defining evangelicalism, lists Biblicism, crucicentrism (a stress of Christ's sacrifice on the cross), conversionism, and activism as the tell-tale marks.[16] Cash had all four, but in his own way. His was not the way of Graham. Graham was the image for post–World War II evangelicalism. His clean-cut looks and squeaky-clean image fit well with the *Ozzy and Harriet* and *Leave It to Beaver* American culture of the baby-boom generation.

As American culture veered away from "plastic values" toward a quest for authenticity, evangelicals also began to see the cracks in the "plastic saint" approach. Cash told *Rolling Stone*'s Anthony DeCurtis in 2000, "There is a spiritual side to me that goes real deep, but I confess right up front that I'm the biggest sinner of them all."[17] For an up-and-coming generation looking for authenticity, Cash could not present a better model. If Graham fit the bill as poster-boy for the baby boom generation of evangelicals, Cash fit the bill as poster-boy for post-modern evangelicals. And when those post-modern evangelicals listen to his aging vocals on the American Recordings—sometimes punching along to a hard beat, sometimes gently lifting over the gentle strumming of a lone guitar—they hear in Cash exactly what they need and what they want.

Cash across the Evangelical Spectrum

Cash has appeal in many places along the broad and vast evangelical horizon. His appearance at two opposite two poles shows this to be true. Russell Moore, at Southern Baptist Theological Seminary in Louisville, Kentucky, and Rob Bell, an Emergent Church leader in Michigan, both hold up Cash to their respective constituencies. Moore and Bell agree on very little, representing rather different paradigms within evangelicalism. Nevertheless, both see Cash as a healthy corrective to problematic tendencies among American evangelicals.

While noting that "Cash's Christian testimony is a mixed bag," Moore muses out loud about the good that could potentially come "if Christian churches modeled themselves more after Johnny Cash." To Moore, Cash is the perfect antidote to the "prevailing saccharine mood of pop Evangelicalism."[18]

Bell, of the wildly popular NOOMA videos and founding pastor of Mars Hill Bible Church in Grand Rapids, Michigan, commends the marriage of Johnny and June to his audiences. Bell speaks of admirable marriages as "Johnny and June marriages."[19] Bell appreciates Cash for the same reason as Moore: the gritty reality that Cash's life, music, and faith presents.

That Cash is admired by the polar opposites of the traditionalist Moore and of the Emergent Bell is a commentary on both Cash and evangelicalism. Evangelicalism can be rather elastic. While there are certainly elements that define it, such as those proffered in Bebbington's quadrilateral—biblicism, crucicentrism, conversionism, and activism—there are rather divergent emphases within it. Beyond theological commitments, evangelicals may also be defined by their engagement of culture.

Those who would self-identify as "fundamentalists" tend more towards a "culture-warrior" paradigm, adopting a defensive stance against "worldly" influence. Fundamentalism advocates more of a withdrawal from culture, viewing worldly influence as subtle, numbing, and, ultimately, deadly. This withdrawal from culture may be felt most acutely in the arts, in music, literature, and film. Mainstream works are worldly and to be avoided. That much defines fundamentalism.

Evangelicalism, on the other hand, advocates engaging culture.[20] This is actually what Graham did, by holding crusades in Los Angeles and then New York—the cultural centers of the United States. Graham was walking into the proverbial lion's den. As Graham did that, evangelicalism, in its post–World War II American manifestation, came into being.

Although Graham graced the television sets of American living rooms, evangelical influence in the arts lagged far behind. However, by the 1970s, a distinct evangelical music scene emerged. The boundaries were clearly defined between sacred and secular music. Some artists, like Michael W. Smith and Amy Grant (who both, incidentally, appeared with the Cashes and the Grahams in a 1996 TV Christmas special) attempted to cross over from Christian to mainstream markets and were severely criticized in the process. Music was clearly lagging behind.

But then Cash came along. Cash achieved what many other musicians with similar convictions were unable to do. His recording of Nine Inch Nails's song "Hurt" and the accompanying video produced by Mark Romanek redirected the song for his own purposes. The song, which appears on Cash's *American IV: The Man Comes Around* (2003), is a nihilistic anthem of the grunge set with rather transparent references to drug use and even cutting. However, Cash, in the words of the song's author Trent Reznor, stole it and made the song about Christ.[21] In the song, Christ becomes Cash's "sweetest friend," the one whom Cash hurts and the one who "hurts" profoundly and viscerally for Cash on the cross. The video shows Cash's conversion, as he breaks down in tears before a crucified Christ. Humbled and forgiven, Cash is redeemed. And all of this gets played out not on some Christian radio station but on MTV and VH1—the ultimate worldly bastions of mainstream culture.

In 2003, in the last year of his life, Cash assumed the role of preacher and evangelist to the teens and twenty-somethings locked into the endless cycle of videos on MTV. If evangelicals are looking for a model of how to engage culture, they certainly can find one in Cash. And that is partly why Cash is appreciated by such divergent poles as the Southern Baptist Seminary's Moore and Mars Hill's Bell.

Cash's famed video received no less than six nominations at the MTV awards in 2003, including video of the year. It ended up winning one of the six, the one for cinematography. However, Justin Timberlake, whose own work clinched video of the year for him, felt that the Man in Black had been robbed. In Timberlake's acceptance speech, he reprimanded the judges for choosing him over Cash, a rare occurrence in such a narcissistic event.

In his own inimitable and winsome way, he spoke the gospel to culture, which evangelicals desire to do. Cash long ago shed pretensions of "having it all together." He could never be accused of presenting a saccharine-coated evangelicalism. Cash was truly authentic. Evangelicals see in him how they can in turn engage culture. To put the matter another way, if, at the age of 71, Cash could connect meaningfully with the MTV generation, then evangelicals have hope that they can do so too.

Cash's Contribution to Evangelicalism

Cash is well embraced by evangelicals partly because he is a model of connecting with culture. First and foremost, he contributes what American theologian and cultural critic H. Reinhold Niebuhr calls "Christian realism."[22]

Niebuhr, in effect a prophetic voice to the mainline Church, offers his message of Christian realism to a mainline American Christianity intoxicated with optimism. The liberalism that dominated the denominations at the beginning of the twentieth century resulted in a romantic mood of near utopianism. However, such a mood, Niebuhr argues, runs counter to the biblical message. World War I did much to remove utopianism from European Christianity, but the war had no such effect on the United States, removed as it was from the carnage and rubble. The same thing occurred, it could be argued, after World War II. While France was incubating existentialists, the United States was going wild at sock hops.

Niebuhr points the prophetic finger at this euphoric American Christianity and sounds a wake-up call. Trained at Eden Seminary in St. Louis and at Yale Divinity School in New Haven, Connecticut, Niebuhr's true education came in Detroit, where he served his first pastorate and where he watched firsthand the plight of the working man, a class Cash could well identify with. In fact, much of Cash's music was aimed at giving the working man a voice. Niebuhr desired to do the same but used theology rather than country music to do it.

Through the 1930s, Niebuhr sensed that American Christianity was not up to the challenge of speaking meaningfully to the harsh realities of the twentieth century. By the time he wrote his two-volume work *The Nature and Destiny of Man* in 1941 and 1943, his Christian realism view had fully matured. In short, Niebuhr suggested to his fellow American Christians that they take God, sin, redemption, and heaven seriously. He had seen these concepts become vacuous, which resulted in the church's inability to speak meaningfully to culture and to the harsh realities many of the working class faced.[23]

Throughout his musical career, Cash similarly championed the cause of the marginalized. Serving as an anthem of this emphasis in his music, the song "Why I Wear Black" declares that as long as the marginalized need a voice, he will be up front, wearing black and pleading their cause.

The Christian realism of Cash, however, is more than merely a socioeconomic statement, just as it was more than that for Niebuhr too. For Cash (and Niebuhr), it was a theological statement. It is important to elaborate on what I call Cash's Christian realism. It is not pessimism. Cash had an intense sense of humor. Kristofferson tells the story that while sitting next to Cash at June's funeral, someone approached Kristofferson, saying what a great fan he was of his music. Cash overheard this and, turning to Kristofferson, said, "Well, that's one."[24] Allan Messer, Cash's photographer through the 1980s and beyond, thinks of Cash first as a "happy man, always telling jokes."[25] And this is from the time arguably of the worst decade of Cash's career. But it is not optimism, either. Cash knew all too well the limitations of being human; he knew of the dark side of the human condition. To put it theologically, he knew sin, and he knew what sin did and could do. German theologian and martyr Dietrich Bonhoeffer once spoke of this world as a fallen-falling world. Cash understood the full implications of that. Bonhoeffer also spoke of a redeemed world, or a world being redeemed. And Cash understood the full implications of that as well.

Cash forges a middle way between the two paths of pessimism and optimism that so derail evangelicals as they engage culture. The pessimists see culture as all-bad, resulting in the culture-warrior stance. The optimists lose sight of Christ's warning to his disciples that his kingdom is "not of this world" (John 18:36). The optimists overly accommodate culture, identifying Christ's kingdom and mission with that of political or ideological kingdoms and missions and agendas. Niebuhr forged a middle way between the fundamentalists, who largely abandoned culture, and the liberals, who embraced culture, baptizing it and calling it Christian. Likewise, Cash—even in his death as his legacy continues—points to a path between.

As Niebuhr's Christian realism sounded a prophetic message to mainline Christianity, so too can Cash's Christian realism sound a prophetic call to American evangelicalism. It speaks directly to evangelical naïveté and what sometimes gets called the "happy clappy" culture of evangelicalism. It also speaks directly to those lingering fundamentalist strongholds that seize every opportunity to rail against culture's degradation.

From his stance of Christian realism, Cash took the gospel where it seldom goes. At the end of his life, Cash worked relentlessly on the American Recordings for Rubin, the noted producer of heavy metal and rap—two genres not necessarily known for having an affinity with evangelicalism. Cash recorded in his studio on his home property in the rolling fields of Tennessee; Rubin put the finishing touches on the work in his Los Angeles studios. These were two worlds, two realities. Cash and Rubin had connected more in person when they first started the collaboration. By the end, they relied on long phone conversations. At times, Cash would partake of communion with Rubin. Cash presided as they each, over the few thousand miles that separated them, remembered the body of Christ broken and the blood of Christ poured out on the cross.[26]

It was not just Rubin that Cash connected with or to whom he spoke the gospel. Rapper Kid Rock attended Cash's funeral; they had struck up a friendship at the end of Cash's life. Tom Petty lent his guitar playing to Cash's recording of Petty's popular song "I Won't Back Down." Cash turned Depeche Mode's sardonic "Personal Jesus" into a sincere plea. In Depeche Mode's version, Jesus does not pick up the phone because, in Depeche Mode's world, Jesus is not there. But as Cash sings it, one knows Jesus is on the line. As already noted, Cash turned a song from Nine Inch Nails into a moving personal confession of hope born of sorrow and suffering. Cash was a singer, but maybe in the end he was more of a traveling evangelist.

Cash also made a contribution when it came to politics and American evangelicals. Since the days of Jerry Falwell's Moral Majority and the organization's contribution to the election of Ronald Reagan to the White House, American evangelicals have enjoyed a seat at the table of U.S. political power. When James Dobson, and again Falwell, along with a cast of others, also helped George W. Bush get in office and stay in office, American evangelicals moved even closer to the head of the table. But then evangelicals on the other side of the political aisle shot back, wondering rather loudly how Jesus and his ethics had been hijacked. In the last few decades, American evangelicals have fought rather public battles over public policy and national elections, claiming Jesus for both the right wing and the left wing.[27]

According to writer and cultural critic Rodney Clapp, Cash has something to say to both sides. Clapp sees in Cash someone who is not one committed to political parties or political ideologies, which, as Clapp has it, is precisely the way it should be. Clapp asserts that "God and God's kingdom are bigger and beyond any single public." Cash, too, was beyond party, beyond a political box. Clapp sees in Cash the level of complexity necessary to speak meaningfully as a Christian in the public square.[28]

Cash's most significant contribution to evangelicalism, however, comes in the form of his vocation, the making of music. One of the last songs Cash wrote is "1 Corinthians 15:55," released posthumously on *American VI: Ain't No Grave* (2010). In his aged voice, vocals gently lifting over the acoustic guitar and the soft keys of the piano, he speaks of death being stripped of its sting, of the grave's empty victory. Cash was clinging to the resurrection and with quiet but solid resignation affirmed hope eternal. His hope comes from the fact that Cash was awaiting his Redeemer, the one who stands, beckoning Cash to come home. In the end, for Cash, there is music. There is the song of redemption.

Conclusion

Because Cash was unable to attend the MTV video awards in 2003, MTV went to him, dispatching Kurt Loder for an interview with Cash in his home. Loder's questions ranged freely over Cash's career from Cash's relationship to Rubin and the American Recordings of the last decade of his stardom back to the days of the Louisiana Hayride and touring with Jerry Lee Lewis, Orbison, and Carl Perkins in the first decade of his stardom. Very few musicians can boast of putting out hit records in six successive decades. However, the most penetrating of Loder's questions concerned Cash's faith. Facing death, Cash could speak of "unshakeable faith" in God; he could speak of God's forgiveness. Cash could also speak in that same interview, however, of his songs of "death, hell, and drugs."

As an evangelical speaking to culture, Cash is likely without peer. Not only did he land an interview on MTV at the age of 71, but he also comfortably moved between heaven, hell, and drugs and his unwavering faith in God. For the new sensibilities of the 1990s and the 2000s and now the 2010s, Cash sets the standard. For those seeking authenticity and reality—warts and all—one needs to look no further than to Cash. He makes no pretensions, no pleas for self-righteousness. Cash stands as an agent of grace precisely because he knew his dire need. He knew he had no hope without grace.

Kristofferson once called his mentor a "walkin' contradiction," a wonderfully ironic mix of part truth and part fiction.[29] While treading lightly in disagreeing with Kristofferson, I would not use the word *contradiction*. *Complex* works well; *complicated* works well, too. Cash was not a contradiction; instead, he was human, all too human. But it is precisely Cash's humanity, his unmitigated, unpolished, uncalculated, undesigned, unairbrushed humanity that sets him apart. It is that full humanity that makes him, this poet from the black dirt of the Arkansas side of the Mississippi Delta, a preacher.

Graham was too ill to attend Cash's funeral on September 15, 2003, dispatching his son Franklin Graham to deliver the eulogy instead. Franklin said John R. Cash was a "friend of the gospel."[30] The elder Graham did offer a statement, mentioning how he mourned the loss of his dear friend but was full of hope, knowing that he would see Cash in heaven, longing for the day to once again sit with his friends Johnny and June.

While Cash is in heaven, his music and legacy are still healthily alive on earth. Those who listen closely, even humbly, may hear in that music the song of redemption.

Notes

1. "Billy Graham Mourns Johnny Cash," September 1, 2003, http://www.christianitytoday.com/ct/2003/septemberweb-only/9-8-52.0.html. Press release used by permission of *Christianity Today* magazine, copyright 2003 by *Christianity Today*.

2. See Marshall Grant, *I Was There When It Happened: My Life with Johnny Cash* (Nashville, TN: Cumberland, 2006).

3. Ibid., and Marshall Grant, interview by author, October 18, 2008.

4. Johnny Cash, *My Mother's Hymn Book* (American Recordings/Lost Highway Records, 2004).

5. Steve Turner, *The Man Called Cash: The Life, Love and Faith of an American Legend* (Nashville, TN: W Publishing, 2004), 145–146.

6. Ibid., 145.

7. See Stephen J. Nichols, *Jesus Made in America: A Cultural History from the Puritans to "The Passion of the Christ"* (Downers Grove, IL: InterVarsity, 2008); see especially "Jesus on Vinyl: From the Jesus People to Contemporary Christian Music," 122–145.

8. During his performance, frustrated by a cantankerous public-address system, Kristofferson stunned the audience, mostly churchgoing teens and their parents, with a string of expletives, punctuated with the crown jewel of expletives.

9. Turner, *The Man Called Cash*, 163.

10. Marshall Grant, "Remembering Johnny Cash," presentation at the Johnny Cash Flower Pickin' Festival, Starkville, MS, October 18, 2008.

11. Johnny Cash, *The Man in White: A Novel about the Apostle Paul* (1986; repr., Nashville, TN: Westbow, 2006), xix.

12. Ibid., xix.

13. Grant, *I Was There When It Happened*, 305–307.

14. Quoted in Michael Streissguth, *Johnny Cash: The Biography* (Cambridge, MA: De Capo, 2006), 178.

15. Quoted in Turner, *The Man Called Cash*, 242.

16. David Bebbington, *Evangelicalism in Modern Britain: A History from the 1730s to the 1980s* (London: Routledge, 1989).

17. Quoted in Anthony DeCurtis, "Johnny Cash Won't Back Down," *Rolling Stone*, October 26, 2000, 60.

18. Russell D. Moore, "Real Hard Cash," *Touchstone*, December 2005.

19. Rob Bell, *Sex God: Exploring the Endless Connections between Sexuality and Spirituality* (Grand Rapids, MI: Zondervan, 2008). Bell devotes chap. 8 to the marriage, titling it "Johnny and June."

20. This emphasis on cultural engagement within evangelicalism, especially as it differentiates it from fundamentalism, can be seen as far back as 1947 with the publication of Carl F. H. Henry's *The Uneasy Conscience of Modern Fundamentalism* (Grand Rapids, MI: Eerdmans, 1947).

21. See Turner, *The Man in Black*, 213–214; and Streissguth, *Johnny Cash*, 277–278.

22. See H. Reinhold Neibuhr, *Moral Man and Immoral Society: A Study of Ethics and Politics* (New York: Scribners, 1932).

23. See Robin W. Lovin, *Reinhold Niebuhr and Christian Realism* (Cambridge, UK: Cambridge University Press, 1995).

24. Kris Kristofferson, foreword to Turner, *The Man Called Cash*, xi.

25. Allan Messer, "Remembering Johnny Cash," unpublished paper, Johnny Cash Flower Pickin' Festival, Starkville, MS, October 18, 2008.

26. Rick Rubin, interview by Stephen Evans, "The Song Doctor," BBC Radio 4, July 31, 2007.

27. See Nichols, *Jesus Made in America*, 198–221, for a discussion of Jesus and politics.

28. Rodney Clapp, *Johnny Cash and the Great American Contradiction: Christianity and the Battle for the Soul of a Nation* (Louisville, KY: Westminster/John Knox, 2008), 131.

29. Kris Kristofferson, "The Pilgrim: Chapter 33," *The Essential Kris Kristofferson* [2 discs] (Sony Records, 2004).

30. Franklin Graham, quoted in Morris Abernathy, "Franklin Graham: Cash Was 'Friend of the Gospel,'" *Baptist Press*, September 16, 2003.

Chapter 6

Navigating the Treacherous Waters of Celebrity Culture: A New Challenge for Evangelicals

Benson P. Fraser and William J. Brown

"You shall not make an idol for yourself." (Exod. 20:4)

"You are my idol." (American Idol *contestant to judge Jennifer Lopez*)

During the past several decades, scholars have taken interest in the rise of celebrity culture in the United States and its impact on evangelical church culture. In this chapter, we explore the nature of celebrity culture, the processes by which celebrities wield social influence, and the way in which evangelical Christians are affected by American celebrity culture. We also consider implications of the evangelical community's susceptibility to celebrity influence and provide recommendations for evangelical Christian leaders for avoiding the seduction of celebrity status.

Defining Celebrity Culture

Scholars provide multiple definitions of *celebrity*, a word loaded with meaning and "slippery and varied in its connotations."[1] In film studies, many scholars prefer to use the term *star* as synonymous with *celebrity*. In most fields of study, *celebrity* refers to those who are famous. Some scholars include notoriety and renown in their conceptions of celebrity, and most focus on "the impact on public consciousness" of well-known people within a society.[2]

American historian and professor Daniel J. Boorstin traces the word *celebrity* to the Latin word *celebritas*, meaning "famous," suggesting a "condition of being much talked about."[3] Boorstin elaborates on the subject by providing a useful and much quoted definition of celebrity: "a person who is known for his well-knownness."[4] More recently, celebrities are seen as more than just well-known people; they have become "myth bearers; carriers of the divine force of good, evil, lust and redemption."[5] For many media consumers, celebrities take on transcendent or sacred qualities that contribute to their sense of self-importance and influence. Although no one seriously thinks about celebrities as deities, audiences often treat them as such—as it is the public who confers celebrity status. "What generally unites the work on stardom and celebrity is the agreement that celebrity or fame does not reside in the individual: it is constituted discursively," usually through clever public relations firms and agents.[6]

A secularized culture that rejects being organized around belief in God is more likely to organize around celebrities.[7] When celebrities take on the persona of "gods in human form or simulacra of departed deities,"[8] then celebrity culture becomes the functional equivalent of religion, with its own set of beliefs, practices, and artifacts. In the religious forms of celebrity culture, the sermon is replaced by the celebrity interview, the holy embrace or greeting is replaced by the celebrity autograph, physical presence is replaced by illusions of intimacy created by visual media, the small group or prayer meeting is replaced by the fan club, and the crucifix, holy scriptures, and pictures or statues of saints are replaced by celebrity shrines, biographies of celebrities, and slick pictures from celebrity magazines. Like religious saints, celebrities provide ways for us to organize our world and become models for our behavior. Many celebrities distract fans from the difficulties of their own lives or transport their fans into another time when life was more manageable, predictable, and easier to understand.

In addition to possessing religious elements, celebrity culture also is an economic enterprise anchored in consumerism. Celebrities embody the message that "enjoying novelty, change, excitement, and every possible stimulant" can be purchased at a shop counter, on a toll-free telephone number, or at the click of a mouse.[9] Consumers, of course, are coconspirators in this venture, allowing celebrities to become commodities or objects to be consumed within capitalistic systems.

Characteristics of Celebrity Culture

There are a number of characteristics of celebrity culture that need to be considered in order to understand its pervasiveness and influence in American society. First, celebrities have replaced traditional heroes.

Historically, the hero was given the highest status in democratic societies. Heroes are known for great acts of courage or outstanding accomplishments requiring exceptional skill and fortitude. As Boorstin notes in his comparison of heroes and celebrities, "The hero was distinguished by his achievement; the celebrity by his image or trademark. The hero created himself; the celebrity is created by the media. The hero was a big man; the celebrity a big name."[10]

In contrast to traditional heroes, celebrities become known for their self-promotion and media exposure, often relishing the public spotlight. The status of traditional heroes usually develops slowly and is enduring, but celebrities achieve status very rapidly, although it is usually short lived. In today's highly mediated culture, achieving fame is separated from acts of moral courage or heroism.[11] True heroism requires self-sacrifice on behalf of others,[12] yet many celebrities have not sacrificed for others.

"To be a celebrity is widely regarded as the most exalted state of human existence,"[13] but this high status is a more recent phenomenon. The proliferation of entertainment enables us to impose on celebrities the same characteristics we attribute to heroes.[14] One possible danger of the religious practice of exalting celebrities to hero status is the blurring of important differences between the two terms—a difference that confuses fame and entertainment for moral or spiritual sacrifice. It may be that the alternative reality and comfortable vision of life inspired by celebrity status has thrust entertainment ever closer to new secular theology.

Celebrity is essentially a media production—with hype as its clearest example—rather than an admirable acknowledgment of greatness. Hype by itself has no intrinsic value. Hype simply indicates that the object of the hype can be made to appear valuable.[15] The root for *hype* is *hyperbole*, which is Greek for "excess." The characterization of celebrities as exhibiting hype and drawing attention to themselves is diametrically opposed to the concept of a traditional hero.

A second characteristic of celebrity culture is the commoditization of celebrities. The ascent of celebrity culture is directly linked to the rise of industrialization, technological development, and the growth of large urban populations. Thought of in this way, the celebrity is regarded as a commodity and valued as such.[16] Some see celebrity as "a system of valorizing meaning and communication," linking success with celebrity status.[17] The development of celebrity endorsements in product marketing is a clear example of how celebrities have became an essential component of our economy. For many, the world is increasingly constituted as an event or spectacle, framed around the capitalistic notion that everything becomes a product to be gazed upon and consumed, including people.[18] "The machinery of image production is so pervasive that consumers begin to confuse image and reality."[19]

American culture embraces the logic of consumption, and celebrities promote the idea that anything desired, both tangible items and emotional experiences, can be purchased. For their part, consumers gain social status and define themselves through the products they possess and in this way become willing accomplices in this enterprise. Placing one's identity in one's possessions replaces traditional religious attitudes with consumerism, so that humankind's "longings for transcendence, justice, and self-transformation" is searched for in commodities.[20]

Obviously, celebrity culture is associated with one's craving for wealth; however, the accumulation of money and material possessions alone cannot fully explain the pervasive presence of celebrity in modern culture. Celebrities are "symbols of belonging and recognition that distract us... from the terrifying meaninglessness of life in a post-God world"; these desires for distraction make us "particularly vulnerable to shamanism [an animist religion with magic practices]."[21] Thus the central place of celebrities in the United States's culture of consumerism competes with devotion to God.

A third characteristic of celebrity culture identifies psychological and emotional involvement as one of the most enduring, complex, and investigated concepts in communication research.[22] Three distinct processes of involvement are closely associated with how audiences respond to celebrities: parasocial interaction, identification, and worship.

Parasocial interaction is a type of cognitive and emotional involvement that occurs when television viewers form an imaginary relationship with a television personality or persona.[23] Through repeated exposure to television personalities, audiences experience a sense of friendship, connection, or intimacy with them.[24] Parasocial relationships with television newscasters, talk-show hosts, and soap-opera stars have been studied extensively.[25] Television and other visual media create pseudo-relationships when audiences see and hear other people and share in their experiences without being physically present.

Parasocial interaction occurs through other forms of media consumption, including film viewing,[26] music and attendance at music performances,[27] and sports events.[28] A number of studies show audiences have experienced strong parasocial interaction with many different kinds of celebrities, including American basketball great Earvin "Magic" Johnson;[29] Diana, Princess of Wales;[30] Argentinian soccer star Diego Maradona;[31] Australian wildlife conservationist and *Crocodile Hunter* host Steve Irwin;[32] NASCAR racing legend Dale Earnhardt;[33] and talk-show host, producer, and actor Oprah Winfrey.[34]

The concept of *identification* occurs when an individual adopts the attitudes, values, beliefs, or behavior of another individual or group based on a "self-defining" relationship.[35] The object of identification may be completely unaware of this process. The concept of identification as a form of social influence[36] is especially applicable to studying audiences' involvement with media personas because people regularly identify with media personas without ever having face-to-face interaction with them.[37]

American literacy theorist and philosopher Kenneth Burke theorizes that "identification occurs when one individual shares the interests of another individual or believes that he or she shares the interests of another."[38] From a Burkean perspective, media consumers search out personas with whom to identify, and when they find them, they adopt their attitudes, values, beliefs, and practices that are already similar to their own or that they are already predisposed to adopt.

The third and most intense level of involvement with media celebrities considered here is conceptualized as *worship*. Researchers explain how audiences tend to idolize celebrities to a degree that simulates the practice of worship.[39] The concept of celebrity worship is important to scholars who seek to understand the psychological and emotional bonds that audiences form with celebrities. In some studies, celebrity worship is conceptualized as relegating to celebrities the attention and status normally given to God or some other form of deity.[40] This phenomenon is described as "an abnormal type of parasocial relationship, driven by absorption and addictive elements and which potentially has significant clinical sequelae [or pathological condition]."[41] As these definitions indicate, celebrity worship is regarded as an extreme and unhealthy type of parasocial interaction.

The word *worship* comes from the Old English word *weorthescipe*, meaning "worthy," and thus "to worship someone or something means to show respect or acknowledge merit."[42] It is not too much of a leap to think that those who follow celebrities may do so with a zeal that in fact resembles religious enthusiasm. Some scholars also equate devotion to a celebrity with devotion to God.[43] It may be that celebrity culture is secular society's response to the waning of religion in our culture, so that commodities and celebrity emerge as the counterfeits for belonging, recognition, and spiritual life.

Celebrity culture has clear parallels with religious worship, which are reinforced by their fans' belief in the extraordinary power or divine-like qualities of the celebrity. The rites, myths, symbols, divine forms, sacred and venerated objects, sacred places, and priests of religious societies are replaced by the sacred vestiges of mass-media celebrities who turn into objects of cult worship.⁴⁴ "Stars and other celebrities seem to be much more like devotional objects than royal figures, and they inspired devotional language."⁴⁵ Celebrity worship may be thought of as a union of yearning for the transcendent and a lust for fame.

The rapid multiplication of fans and growth of fandom is a fourth important characteristic of celebrity culture. Americans are attracted to celebrities for a variety of reasons, including physical attraction, admiration of unique skills, and similarity of personal values and beliefs. The word *fan* can be traced to the adjective *fanatic*, derived from the Latin *fanaticus*, meaning "of a temple."⁴⁶ Therefore, a fan is thought to be a person who is excessively enthusiastic or someone who is filled with religious fervor. Audiences become fans of celebrities not by simply consuming media or participating in public events but, rather, by translating that mediated experience into a cultural activity involving other fans with shared interests.⁴⁷ Part of the enigma of celebrity culture is its ability to provide the fan with encounters that are seemingly as meaningful as religious encounters and by so doing make fandom a counterfeit religious community.

It is through community that fans seek validation of the imaginary relationships they have established with celebrities. Fan clubs exist throughout the world for thousands of celebrities, bringing together followers from across the globe, spanning socioeconomic, cultural, geographic, and religious boundaries. A robust fan culture need not even include the presence of the admired celebrity. The largest Elvis Presley fan club, for example, is in London, England, a city Elvis never visited; Elvis never visited Bangalore, India, where an Elvis temple exists.

Clearly, religious communities and celebrity culture share many characteristics with each other, and there seems to be a strong convergence between these two significant social structures. One of these similarities is public gatherings to celebrate their fandom and favorite stars. *Star Trek* fans, for example, meet to share experiences with each other or with people who play their favorite characters in the media. These gatherings are akin to fellowship meetings within religious communities.⁴⁸ Fandom is one way our society organizes itself and at the same time helps us discover a sense of something definite—a community.

Influences of Celebrity Culture on Evangelical Christians

Celebrity culture in the United States has undoubtedly affected evangelical Christians and American evangelical culture. For the last sixty years, evangelical leaders have been on the forefront of using new media and popular trends in the entertainment industry for ministry and evangelism. The influence of capitalism and celebrity culture has taught leaders, including evangelicals, to focus on appearance. In other words, evangelicals are preconditioned to expect their leaders and celebrities to be charismatic, photogenic, engaging, entertaining, and affirming. (Most likely Jesus would not qualify today as having the attributes of a popular evangelical, nor would most of the early apostles.)

Famous pastors, Christian talk-show hosts, television evangelists, and other accomplished religious leaders in the evangelical community market themselves to their followers in ways very similar to those of celebrities, focusing on presentation, style, clothing, appearance, attractiveness, and entertainment appeal. Their followers (who act much like fans) have learned how to relate to celebrities by being fans of sports celebrities, movie stars, and politicians. Much of religious life today is mediated and socially constructed through the processes of our celebrity culture. We may not call religious leaders celebrities but many people treat them with the reverence with which they treat other celebrities.

Religious celebrities and their fans—although they are more likely regarded as leaders and followers—manage their image much like their mainstream counterparts. First, ministry activities often center on media images and visual representations of the primary celebrated leader, who fills the featured role in media productions or events. Second, religious fandom tends to be media focused and organized. Most people interested in a particular religious leader are strong supporters of their own favorite religious radio or television programs. Third, religious followers or fans engage in a variety of communal activities, for example, supporting a ministry project or joining others in praying for a specific need. During these communal activities, they may incorporate religious celebrities into their imaginary social worlds and may selectively integrate what they consider to be important qualities of the religious celebrity's life into their own lives. Therefore, fans of religious celebrities are not necessarily hapless victims mindlessly following a charismatic leader, but instead they strategically use these religious leaders to infuse their lives with attitudes, values, and social practices they both observe and support.

Just like other celebrities, evangelical celebrities want to be loved by their fans or followers. This is why they spend so much time trying to keep their image before their followers. They want people to like them and follow them because it is in their (and their religious organizations') financial or professional interest. The size of the audience that follows popular celebrities is directly related to their economic potential in advertising and the amount of money they can make or raise for their "cause." Leading evangelical celebrities, as all celebrities, feel pressure to expand their efforts to gather a large following and then keep it through a positive image or media presence.

In striving to meet the needs of the mediated flock, religious leaders have adopted the methods of celebrity culture in seeking to establish a strong emotional connection with their audiences. Many celebrated evangelical leaders are charismatic television personalities, pastors of megachurches, conference stars, or best-selling authors who personally know very few of their followers and who are accountable to very few people. Their sermons arrive in people's homes via television, radio, direct mail, or the Internet, reinforcing the parasocial relationships formed with their audiences.

Joel Osteen is a clear example of an evangelical celebrity leader who connects with his audiences emotionally. His messages are simple and uplifting—they provide emotional intimacy and hope. His church services,

Televangelist, pastor, and best-selling author Joel Osteen (right) and his wife, Victoria (left) at Lakewood Church in Houston, Texas, formerly the Compaq Center, the arena that basketball fans once packed to see the NBA's Houston Rockets. (AP Photo/Jessica Kourkounis.)

television programs, books, and other ministry outlets have grown in part because he has been able to share or market a compelling vision to his audience that embodies changing American sensibilities. Osteen and other evangelical celebrities must carefully manage their image in order to keep their celebrity status and large geographical outreaches. They must strive to maintain an engaging presentation style and attractive appearance, appealing to the greatest number of people.

Consequently, it is not surprising that cultural icon and social healer Oprah Winfrey presents guest after guest giving testimony to their growing belief in her priestly role as the hearer of confessions and dispenser of grace. Oprah's show, for instance, is flush with testimonies of endurance and survival that "hinge on an individual's ability to transcend difficulty leading to a state—or partial state—of self-realization,"[49] a substitute for the state of salvation presented by religious broadcasters. The stories of overcoming a significant life challenge or of an amazing story of endurance, survival, or surrender are all regular features on both mainstream programs like Oprah's and on religious programs like Osteen's. Celebrities (both secular and religious) are fortified with dozens of media personnel and marketing departments that work tirelessly to choose the right guests and maintain their public image.

Both Oprah and Osteen focus on providing people with a positive experience rather than challenging them to ponder the perplexities or difficulties of life, which masks an almost passive unquestioning presentation that is more about the celebrity than anything else. The purposes of their programs are not so much to provide knowledge as they are to make people feel better, creating a therapeutic influence buoyed by encouraging testimonials. The merging of celebrity culture and religious experience in U.S. media has a strong appeal to many Americans as evidenced by the high audience ratings of Oprah's and Osteen's television programs. It is not a coincidence that both Oprah and Osteen are seen as highly spiritual people.

Professor and author Vincent Miller identifies several negative influences of consumerism on our culture, including religious beliefs and practices. First, he argues that "beyond the excesses of consumerism lie cultural dynamisms that incline people to engage religious beliefs as if they were consumer commodities."[50] Therefore, consumption becomes the dominant cultural practice, which tends to penetrate many traditional religious practices and moves religious culture towards the dominant culture. Ultimately, commodification downplays the negative consequences of narcissistic consumer behaviors and drives a wedge between belief and practice. Thus, consumerism and the values of celebrity culture conflict with biblical values.

Most evangelical Christians are likely not cognizant of the negative influences of consumerism and celebrity culture on their lives. Just as advertisements are woven into media use in ways that most Americans take for granted, so too has the need to consume become a pattern in American life that is accepted as normal and often unexamined. These consumptive practices are frequently theologically supported (e.g., "God wants you to prosper") and enthusiastically embraced by many evangelicals as part of valued spiritual experiences and practice.

Second, Miller notes that in consumerism culture, "the dominance of the visual accompanies a disconnection between what is represented and what is going on in people's lives."[51] This characteristic is also reflected in celebrity culture, which focuses on appearance (or the external) at the expense of the internal life of the spirit. The gospel, however, is addressed to the whole person (body, mind, and spirit), yet we tend to question or downplay activities that deal primarily with the spirit such as prayer, meditation, and silence and favor things seen or heard such as the spectacle of church attendance, religious broadcasts, and religious music performance. One scholar claims that "celebrity culture is inherently inflationary,"[52] and much of evangelical religion has itself already surrendered to this craze, borrowing from the mainstream media industry's devices to stir up large crowds and create a frenzy of experience.

Despite what most religious leaders say or how hard they try to avoid the trappings of celebrity culture, more often than not the image they choose to present overwhelms their inner life. As their lives become more scripted by the demands of the media-hungry culture, it becomes clear that it is not just the outward life that is controlled by style, entertainment, and the need to be seen; the inner life is also deeply affected. The normal checks on the inner life (encouragement as well as confession and correction) are not peripheral to the Christian life: as German pastor, theologian, and martyr Dietrich Bonhoeffer reminds us, to be a Christian is to live in community,[53] that is, in "the physical presence of other Christians" who have the power to speak into our lives. It is challenging for an evangelical celebrity to meet the demands of an adoring public and still maintain an active life in a healthy community where he or she is accountable to others.

A fixation on image leads away from reality, as images "come to have a life of their own independent of the objects of which they are images."[54]

The result of this separation is that both the celebrity and his or her followers begin to confuse the image with reality, oftentimes leading to the confusion of the celebrity's personal life and his or her public or mediated life. When religious followers confuse the image of the religious celebrity for the person in reality, truth becomes subjective.

A third influence of consumerism as discussed by Miller is how consumer-centered media supplants traditional community structures.[55] This also takes place in celebrity culture, and the mechanisms of celebrity culture influence the Church. In terms of the intrusion of the camera, for example, people cannot have communion with a camera. If we bring the media into our most sacred spaces in our church communities or in our sacred rituals, these communities and rituals will be changed, and worship is subverted by the imaging event. The presence of Christ is interrupted, and our full attention is taken off the sacred rituals. As attention is drawn away from being Christ-centered to celebrity-centered, focus is shifted from the unseen inward bonds of Christ's community to the outward iconic representation or image of things seen—from the real to the artificial. Certainly, icons have their place in the community of faith and in worship, as do ministers and priests, but the undue attention given to celebrities and image making when worshiping is often unhealthy and distracting for the worshiping community.

Moreover, we cannot be assured that the value of depicting religious life outweighs the cost of always recording our religious experiences. People often pass from one religiously mediated "village" to another, striking up relationships—some short lived and some not—with others with whom they communicate.[56] These are not villages in the conventional sense; they are cyber-communities in which people can remain transient yet still interact habitually, perhaps even changing identities as they move from one site to another. As in ancient Roman times when persecuted Christians were made an imperial spectacle, resulting in the rapid growth of Christianity, modern media can both harm the Church and expand the Church.[57]

Fourth, both consumer culture and celebrity culture generate passions for staged events rather than for genuine forms of acknowledgment and community. While the entertainment-driven, celebrity-oriented culture is not necessarily one that devastates all moral value, it is one in which the measure of value is whether or not someone can captivate and then hold the public's interest. Evangelical Christians need be reminded that some of Jesus's followers were not happy that he spent so much time in secluded villages, out of the public spotlight, where he enjoyed the company of common people more than celebrated ones.

In order to address the challenges presented by consumer culture, evangelical Christians "must attend to the structures and practices that connect belief to daily life, attend to the lived, everyday theology of believing communities, and adopt the task of helping communities preserve and sustain their traditions."[58] In facing the constraint and distortion of celebrity culture and global capitalism, evangelical Christians must look to both an ancient and future faith that is free of subservience to the technological interference that is so often embraced. In establishing and maintaining their communities of belief—which are embedded not only in this present time but also belong to the eternal—evangelicals need to carefully think through the consequences of adopting the techniques and instruments of our age. French sociologist and lay theologian Jacques Ellul has warned that the technologies of this age, though comfortable and efficient, cannot be used without exacting an often hidden and costly price.[59]

Despite these pitfalls, there are a few positive influences of celebrity culture on evangelical Christians, for example, the potential of social agency.[60] Evangelicals have greater entrée to cultural material of all kinds (both traditional and popular) with the potential to reach larger numbers of people with artistically creative and socially persuasive messages. As Miller states, "this positive aspect of consumer culture provides the possibility for the tactic of deepening agency. We need not retreat to monasteries to ride out the new dark ages ... The path lies forward, through this explosion of agency, by embracing and forming it."[61] Although this seems to be an optimistic evaluation of the challenge facing the evangelical community, it does suggest the possibility that evangelical Christians may find ways to move forward while avoiding the pitfalls of celebrity culture. Certainly, the ability of a religious celebrity to draw media attention is not in itself depraved.

Conclusion

If evangelical Christians adopt a vigilant posture toward celebrity culture, it will require "a level of attention to cultural processes to which theology is unaccustomed."[62] Furthermore, it will demand more consideration of the development and maintenance of the prophetic voice and a willingness not only to examine but also to break free of embracing every form of comfortable and powerful technology available. Although challenging unbridled consumptive behavior is difficult in the evangelical Church, it is necessary to avoid being seduced by the fleeting pleasures of entertainment—poor counterfeits for the righteousness, peace, and joy promised by God to believers.

Celebrities are part of the culture of distraction, a culture drenched in media and entertainment. Society requires distraction at a great cost to itself and to the church. Celebrity culture clouds our consciousness from both structured inequities and the meaninglessness of existence apart from God. The decline of the Church has been brought about in part by our culture's need to be distracted and entertained.

Celebrity and celebrity culture fill the vacuum left by a religion that is seen as stale and irrelevant. However, "Celebrity culture cannot produce transcendent value because any gesture towards transcendence is ultimately co-opted by commodification."[63] Furthermore, celebrity culture functions to focus our attention on the outward image (the superficial and gaudy) and in so doing distracts us from attention to the real issues confronting us. Celebrity culture functions to mask the true condition of humankind and our disintegrating culture. Real life that embraces the whole of humankind (unmasked) leads us to consider the transcendent work of God in our world and in our own lives.

Notes

1. Su Holmes and Sean Redmond, "A Journal in Celebrity Studies," *Celebrity Studies* 1, no. 1 (March 2010): 4.
2. Chris Rojek, *Celebrity* (London: Reaktion, 2001), 10.
3. Daniel J. Boorstin, *The Image: A Guide to Pseudo-Events in America* (New York: Vintage, 1961), 57.
4. Ibid.
5. Jill Neimark, "The Culture of Celebrity," *Psychology Today*, May–June 1995, 54.
6. Holmes and Redmond, "A Journal in Celebrity Studies," 4.
7. Rojek, *Celebrity*, 58.
8. Ellis Cashmore, *Celebrity/Culture* (New York: Routledge, 2006), 252.
9. Ibid., 266.
10. Boorstin, *The Image*, 61.
11. Mary Loftus, "The Other Side of Fame," *Psychology Today*, May 1995, 48–53, 70–81.
12. Christopher Vogler, *The Writer's Journey: Mythic Structure and Writers*, 3rd ed. (Studio City, CA: Michael Wiese, 1998), 35.
13. Neal Gabler, *Life: The Movie* (New York: Vintage, 1998), 176.
14. Joseph Campbell, *The Hero with a Thousand Faces* (Princeton, NJ: Princeton University Press, 1949), 36–38.
15. Cashmore, *Celebrity/Culture*, 259.
16. Sherryl Wilson, *Oprah, Celebrity and Formations of Self* (New York: Palgrave/Macmillan, 2003), 160.

17. P. David Marshall, *Celebrity and Power: Fame in Contemporary Culture* (Minneapolis: University of Minnesota Press, 1997), x.

18. Nicholas Abercrombie and Brian Longhurst, *Audiences: A Sociological Theory of Performance and Imagination* (Thousand Oaks, CA: Sage, 1998), 78.

19. Ibid., 87.

20. Vincent J. Miller, *Consuming Religion: Christian Faith and Practice in a Consumer Culture* (New York: Continuum International, 2004), 144.

21. Rojek, *Celebrity*, 95.

22. Charles T. Salmon, *Information Campaigns: Balancing Social Values and Social Change* (Newbury Park, CA: Sage, 1989).

23. Donald Horton and R. Richard Wohl, "Mass Communication and Parasocial Interaction: Observations on Intimacy at a Distance," *Psychiatry*, 19 (1956): 215–229.

24. Mark R. Levy, "Watching Television News as Parasocial Interaction," *Journal of Broadcasting*, 23 (1979): 69–80.

25. William J. Brown, "Steve Irwin's Influence on Wildlife Conservation," *Journal of Communication*, 60 (March 2010): 73–93.

26. Deborah K. Buenting and William J. Brown, "Exploring Audience Involvement with Yellow Card and Its Promotion of Sexual Responsibility among African Youth," paper presented to the International and Intercultural Communication Division of the National Communication Association, 95th annual convention, Chicago, November 2009.

27. Benson P. Fraser and William J. Brown, "Media, Celebrities, and Social Influence: Identification with Elvis Presley," *Mass Communication & Society* 5, no. 2 (Spring 2002): 185–208.

28. William J. Brown et al., "The Influence of Famous Athletes on Health Beliefs and Practices: Mark McGwire, Child Abuse Prevention, and Androstenedione," *Journal of Health Communication*, 8 (2003): 41–57.

29. William J. Brown and Michael D. Basil, "Media Celebrities and Public Health: Responses to 'Magic' Johnson's HIV Disclosure and Its Impact on AIDS Risk and High-risk Behaviors," *Journal of Health Communication* 7 (1995): 345–370.

30. William J. Brown et al., "Social Influence of an International Celebrity: Responses to the Death of Princess Diana," *Journal of Communication* 53, no. 4 (December 2003): 587–605.

31. William J. Brown and Marcela deMatviuk, "Sports Celebrities and Public Health: Deigo Maradona's Influence on Drug Use Prevention," *Journal of Health Communication* 15, no. 4 (2010): 358–373.

32. Brown, "Steve Irwin's Influence," 73–93.

33. William J. Brown et al., "The Social Impact of Mediated Celebrities: Cognitive and Emotional Responses to the Death of Dale Earnhardt," paper presented to National Communication Association's Annual Conference, San Diego, CA, November 2008.

34. Wilson, *Oprah, Celebrity and Formations of Self*.

35. Herbert C. Kelman, "Process of Opinion Change," *Public Opinion Quarterly* 25, no. 1 (Spring 1961): 63.

36. Herbert C. Kelman, "Compliance, Identification, and Internalization: Three Processes of Attitude Change," *Journal of Conflict Resolution* 2, no. 1 (March 1958): 51–60.

37. Cynthia A. Hoffner, "Children's Wishful Identification and Parasocial Interaction with Favorite Television Characters," *Journal of Broadcasting & Electronic Media* 40, no. 3 (Summer 1996): 389–402. See also Cynthia A. Hoffner and Martha Buchanan, "Young Adults' Wishful Identification with Television Characters: The Role of Perceived Similarity and Character Attributes," *Media Psychology* 7, no. 4 (2005): 325–351.

38. Kenneth Burke, *A Rhetoric of Motives* (Berkeley: University of California Press, 1969), 180.

39. For example, see David C. Giles and John Maltby, "The Role of Media Figures in Adolescent Development: Relations between Autonomy, Attachment, and Interest in Celebrities," *Personality and Individual Differences* 3, no. 4 (March 2004): 813–822; John Maltby, "Celebrity and Religious Worship: A Refinement," *Journal of Psychology* 138, no. 3 (May 2004): 286–288; John Maltby, James Houran, and Lynn E. McCutcheon, "A Clinical Interpretation of Attitudes and Behaviors Associated with Celebrity Worship," *Journal of Nervous and Mental Disease* 191, no. 1 (January 2003): 25–29; John Maltby et al., "Thou Shalt Worship No Other Gods—Unless They Are Celebrities: The Relationship between Celebrity Worship and Religious Orientation," *Personality and Individual Differences* 32, no. 7 (May 2002): 1157–1172; and Lynn E. McCutcheon et al., "A Cognitive Profile of Individuals Who Intend to Worship Celebrities," *Journal of Psychology* 137, no. 4 (July 2003): 309–322.

40. Giles, *Illusions of Immortality*; Michael Jindra, "Star Trek Fandom as a Religious Phenomenon," *Sociology of Religion* 55, no. 1 (Spring 1994): 27–51; and Maltby et al., "Thou Shalt Worship No Other Gods."

41. Maltby et al., "A Clinical Interpretation of Attitudes," 25.

42. Cashmore, *Celebrity/Culture*, 253.

43. Gabler, *Life: The Movie*, 57–58.

44. Rojek, *Celebrity*, 53.

45. Gabler, *Life: The Movie*, 174.

46. Cashmore, *Celebrity/Culture*, 79.

47. Jonathan Gray et al., *Fandom: Identities and Communities in a Mediated World* (New York: New York University Press, 2007), 305.

48. Jindra, "*Star Trek* Fandom."

49. Wilson, *Oprah, Celebrity and Formations of Self*, 3.

50. Miller, *Consuming Religion*, 225.

51. Ibid., 95–96.

52. Rojek, *Celebrity*, 97.
53. Dietrich Bonhoeffer, *Life Together* (London: SCM, 1954), 9.
54. Abercrombie and Longhurst, *Audiences*, 87.
55. Miller, *Consuming Religion*, 95.
56. Cashmore, *Celebrity/Culture*, 95.
57. Miller, *Consuming Religion*, 95.
58. Ibid., 226.
59. Jacques Ellul, *The Technological Society*, trans. John Wilkinson (Toronto: Vintage, 1964).
60. Miller, *Consuming Religion*, 226.
61. Ibid.
62. Ibid.
63. Rojek, *Celebrity*, 90.

Chapter 7

Scandalous Evangelicals: Sex, Greed, Politics, and the Arts

Judith M. Buddenbaum

In a July 2009 *Christianity Today* editorial, Mark Galli laments that scarcely a year goes by that evangelicals are not rocked by another major scandal: "Governor Mark Sanford (adultery) and Ted Haggard (immorality) and CEO Kenneth Lay (fraud) and evangelist Jim Baker [sic] (licentiousness) —to take but a very few examples!"[1] However, as Galli also notes, "history is a discomforting witness to the truth that church leaders *and* followers are all too easily mesmerized by money, sex, and power—or just plain sloth."[2]

Although most evangelicals are good people, occasionally they commit violent crimes. More often, they lie, cheat, steal, or commit adultery. Each such episode is, in effect, a scandal—an affront to the faith and to cultural notions of propriety and common decency. However, for the behavior to count as a scandal, it must become widely known, and that usually requires attention from mainstream media.

While evangelicals have no monopoly on scandalous behavior,[3] scandals involving people publicly identified as evangelicals have made news throughout U.S. history. Murders, lies, larceny, and illicit sexual acts committed by clergy are the subject of the first three sections in this chapter. Scandals created by evangelical political leaders acting either out of a sense of entitlement or taking liberties with ethical or legal standards in order to promote what they considered godly ends are described in the fourth and final section.

Murder and Mayhem

Although murders committed by people publicly identified by their religion are relatively rare, they happen more often than one might think.[4]

One of the first major evangelical scandals of the twentieth century is among those murders.

On July 11, 1926, the Reverend J. Frank Norris shot and killed D. E. Chipps at First Baptist Church in Fort Worth, Texas, where Norris was pastor. At the time, Norris was well known both for the protests against "modernism" he regularly staged and for his very public anti-Catholicism.[5] When Fort Worth arranged to purchase land from St. Ignatius School, Norris accused Catholic mayor H. C. Meacham and his Catholic allies of concocting a plan to enrich the church at taxpayer expense. As Norris's campaign against what he saw as a Catholic conspiracy escalated, Chipps, a Catholic businessman and Meacham supporter, appeared at the door of Norris's church office. An altercation ensued; Norris shot Chipps and then called the police. At trial, Norris's claim that the murder was self-defense gained support from two telephone operators who had heard Chipps threaten Norris in a phone call to him the morning of the shooting. The jury acquitted Norris, but forever after the mainstream media routinely referred to him as a killer.[6]

Although the Norris case was the only major evangelical murder scandal, he is not the only evangelical to have killed. In 2007, for example, Matthew Murray took out his frustration at being dismissed from a minister-in-training program run by Youth for a Mission by shooting and killing several people in Denver, Colorado, before traveling to New Life Church in Colorado Springs, Colorado, where he shot four people, killing two, before a volunteer security guard at the megachurch killed him.[7] In 2010, fundamentalist Baptist preacher David Love made the Top Ten list on the Bad Clergy website for "ma[king] hash of four commandments [by] bedding Randy Stone's wife, murdering him and sharing warm remembrances of their kinship while presiding over his funeral."[8]

However, cases like those where evangelicals killed in spite of their faith have generally received far less attention than the isolated instances in which people killed because of their faith. Among the most common, and the most heavily covered, have been the murder of abortion providers that the killers have justified as necessary to protect the lives of innocent babies. Of those killings, the June 29, 1994, murder of Dr. John Barrett by the Reverend Paul Jennings Hill, whose own independent Presbyterian congregation had asked him to leave because of his advocacy of violence against abortion providers, was the only one committed by an evangelical clergyman.[9] However, John C. Salvi III, a Roman Catholic, found inspiration for his March 19, 1996, rampage at a Massachusetts Planned Parenthood clinic in brochures distributed by Human Life International and in televangelist Pat Robertson's book *The New World Order*.[10] Other victims had long been targeted by Operation Rescue.[11] After each murder, leaders from mainstream evangelical pro-life groups decried the violence, but their denunciations could not fully counter support for the murderers from fringe antiabortion groups loosely affiliated with the mainstream evangelical prolife movement.[12]

The image of evangelicals as violent, fed by attention to the murders of abortion providers,[13] was not helped by nationwide news stories about Pastor Ken Pagano's 2009 call for parishioners to show support for the Second Amendment by bringing their guns to church[14] or by the public burning of the Qur'an the Reverend Terry Jones scheduled for September 11 in 2010.[15] Neither was that image helped when 2008 Republican vice-presidential nominee Sarah Palin claimed to be the victim of "blood libel" after mainstream media called attention to an image on Palin's website of Arizona congresswoman Gabrielle Giffords's district in the crosshairs of a gun shortly after a lone gunman killed six people and gravely wounded Giffords and thirteen others.[16]

However, the most sensational religiously inspired violent act was the drowning of five children on June 20, 2001, in Clear Lake, Texas, by their mother. Andrea Yates, a disciple of the itinerant evangelist Michael Peter Woroniecki, had become convinced that her inability to devote all of her time to proselytizing as Woroniecki said she should do meant that she was a bad mother. She killed her children, she said, because bad mothers create bad children. Only her state-sanctioned execution would rescue her from Satan's grip.[17] At trial, her lawyers told of the mental illness that ran in her family and of the postpartum depression and paranoia that had repeatedly sent her to mental hospitals after the births of her fourth and fifth children. The jury, however, chose to believe the prosecution's star witness, who told them the crime was a pre-edited copy-cat one that mimicked a murder featured on the television show *Law & Order*. In the end, however, Yates was saved from the death penalty only when a jury accepted the insanity defense at a second trial granted after the court learned there never had been a *Law & Order* story featuring a mother drowning her children.[18]

Lies and Larceny

In her book *Lying*, philosopher and ethicist Sissela Bok makes the case that given the right circumstances, everyone will lie.[19] Whatever else they may have been about, the two twentieth-century evangelical scandals that received the most mainstream media attention featured evangelists who proved themselves to be less than truthful.

In the 1920s, Aimee Semple McPherson—Sister Aimee, as she billed herself—was a media darling first as a traveling evangelist and then as pastor of Angelus Temple in Los Angeles. Thousands flocked there three times each day to hear her preach but also to watch the religious pageants and morality plays she staged.[20] After she disappeared on May 26, 1926, while swimming, both the faithful and the media flocked to Ocean Park Beach on the California coast to watch the search for Sister Aimee. After three weeks, during which her congregation thought her dead, Sister Aimee showed up, saying she had been kidnapped and held hostage in Mexico. When her tale could not be verified and accounts surfaced that she had been spotted at a hotel with the former engineer at her radio station,[21] she was arrested and charged with corruption of public morals, obstruction of justice, and conspiracy to manufacture evidence. The trial became a media circus.[22] But in the end, all charges against Sister Aimee were dismissed. Until her death in 1944, she remained pastor of Angelus Temple and head of the Foursquare Gospel denomination she founded,[23] but sixty years later another deceitful Pentecostal evangelist was not so fortunate.

That scandal, the first of two major televangelist scandals, came to light after church secretary Jessica Hahn accused Jim Bakker of rape. On March 7, 1987, the *Charlotte Observer* broke news of serious problems at Bakker's cable Praise the Lord (PTL) religious television network. Richard Dortch, Bakker's second-in-command at PTL, had known of the adultery for at least three years. To cover up the affair, PTL had authorized paying Hahn $265,000 in hush money. PTL was also footing the bills for Bakker and his wife Tammy Faye Bakker's opulent lifestyle, at least some of the money for which came through the sale of exclusive partnerships at PTL's Heritage USA. Those partnerships entitled investors to a three-night stay at a luxury hotel at the Christian theme park, but there were thousands more partners than available rooms.[24] In December 1987, Jim Bakker was indicted on twenty-four counts of fraud, conspiracy, and income tax evasion. Following trial, he was found guilty and served five years in prison.[25]

Although the Sister Aimee and Bakker scandals were the only major ones involving outright lies, instances of evangelicals withholding material information, cheating, and committing fraud are quite common. In 2010, Dr. Ergun Caner lost his position as dean of Liberty Baptist Theological Seminary for padding his résumé;[26] Anthony Jinwright, pastor of Greater

Former PTL chairman Jim Bakker and his wife Tammy talk to reporters on June 11, 1987. This was Bakker's first appearance in South Carolina after resigning from the PTL ministry. Left to right are Norman Bakker, brother; Jim Bakker; Raleigh Bakker, father; Tammy Bakker; and Jamie Charles Bakker, son. (AP Photo/Pete Jorgenson.)

Salem Church of God in Charlotte, North Carolina, and his wife Harriett were convicted on charges of conspiracy and income tax evasion;[27] and Vaughn Reeves, a former pastor, was found guilty of convincing parishioners to help build churches by investing in a bond fund that turned out to be a Ponzi scheme.[28]

All of these scandals were created by evangelicals whose faith did not prevent them from lying, but highly religious people sometimes engage in "pious frauds" for what they consider God-pleasing reasons.[29] In the 1930s and 1940s, Daddy Grace and Father Divine, black evangelical preachers operating on the fringe of Pentecostalism, were portrayed as "huckster[s] getting rich off the donations of gullible and simpleminded followers."[30] Since then, the huckster label has more often been attached to preachers of a prosperity gospel such as Robert Tilton, whose Success-n-Life ministry drew some national attention as a result of a 1992 *Primetime Live* exposé and Tilton's subsequent libel suit against reporter Diane Sawyer and the ABC network.[31] In court, Tilton failed to win his libel case, but neither could those church members and contributors who sued him prevail in their claims against him.[32] However, allegations of fraud by disgruntled followers who failed to receive the material blessings they believe preachers like Tilton promised them in return for their financial contributions to the ministry became so common that in 2008 Iowa Republican senator Charles Grassley launched an investigation into six ministries. Joyce Meyer Ministries and Benny Hinn's World Healing Ministry fully cooperated with the investigation and were exonerated of any wrong doing. Although no penalties against them were handed down, Creflo Dollar's World Changers Church International, Eddie Long's New Birth Missionary Baptist Church, Kenneth Copeland Ministries, and Randy and Paula White's Without Walls International Church did not cooperate and remain under suspicion.[33]

While Grassley's investigation was still underway, televangelist Robertson created a minor sensation by proclaiming the January 2010 earthquake in Haiti a divine punishment for a nation that gained its independence by making a pact with the devil.[34] However, it was the actions in Haiti of Baptist missionary Laura Silsby that created a scandal with international implications. When the children Silsby tried to bring from Haiti to the United States after the earthquake turned out not to be the orphans she claimed they were, she and eight co-workers from her New Life Children's Refuge were arrested on charges of child abduction and criminal association. According to mainstream media reports, Silsby had a history of "flouting laws."[35] Her legal adviser in Haiti was wanted in El Salvador on charges of sex trafficking.[36] While charges against her co-workers were quickly dropped, on May 17, 2010, Silsby was found guilty but sentenced to just the time she had served. However, continuing support for Silsby from evangelical quarters, including her own Southern Baptist Convention, raised questions about whether evangelicals might be using humanitarian efforts abroad as covers for proselytizing in countries where such activities are unwelcome, if not illegal.[37]

Sex and Sexuality

Since the 1830s when the *New York Herald* began covering stories of clergy sexual improprieties, clergy affairs have proved to be so common in all

116 Evangelical Christians and Popular Culture

religions that only a handful of evangelical ones have ever received enough media attention to turn them into full-blown scandals.

The first of those came to light in 1872 when feminist and free-love advocate Victoria Woodhull told readers of her weekly magazine that the renowned minister Henry Ward Beecher, son of prominent evangelist Lyman Beecher, was having the kind of affair with Elizabeth Tilton that he preached against.[38] For her efforts, Woodhull was convicted for mailing obscene material, but the mainstream media picked up the story and kept it alive for nearly a decade through every twist and turn in the saga as Tilton confessed, recanted, and then confessed again.[39] Beecher steadfastly maintained his innocence. Two church investigations exonerated him, and a jury failed to convict him by a 6–3 vote in a criminal case sought by Tilton's husband, but for the rest of the century newspapers routinely compared each new clergy sex scandal to the Beecher-Tilton case.[40]

In 1933, Minnie Lee Campbell created a sensation when she claimed Daddy Grace raped her.[41] At a trial marred by racism, Grace was convicted

Illustrations of the Henry Ward Beecher-Theodore Tilton scandal. Commercial Lith. Co.; design and drawn by James E. Cook. (Library of Congress.)

under the Mann Act for transporting Campbell across state lines for sexual purposes, but the conviction was overturned when another court ruled he had not fathered Campbell's child.[42] Although that scandal was a major one, it received far less attention than either the Beecher-Tilton affair or the televangelist scandals of 1987 and 1988.

After televangelist Bakker's affair with Hahn became public knowledge in early 1987, his fellow televangelist and Assembly of God minister Jimmy Swaggart pronounced it "a cancer that needs to be excised from the body of Christ" by levying on Bakker at least the denomination's standard one-year ban on public preaching.[43] Swaggart said much the same thing about the Reverend Marvin Gorman, a popular Assembly of God minister headquartered in Louisiana.[44] But just a few months later, on February 18, 1988, Swaggart tearfully told the 8,000 people who packed his Baton Rouge Family Worship Center and the thousands more who watched on television that he had sinned.[45] Although he never named the sin, everyone knew what had happened. Photographs of Swaggart leaving the Travel Inn motel in New Orleans with prostitute Debra Murphree that were taken by a detective hired by Gorman had made their way to denomination headquarters. The denomination first imposed just a three-month preaching ban on Swaggart but swiftly raised it to the standard one year amid protests from the faithful. Instead of accepting the penalty, Swaggart announced his intention to continue preaching. That effectively ended his career as an Assembly of God minister but not his career as a pastor and televangelist.[46]

Since 1988, just three more evangelical sex scandals have received more than passing national attention. Like the Beecher-Tilton and Swaggart affairs, there was a strong element of hypocrisy in these scandals; however, unlike those scandals, these also had strong political overtones.

After admitting to his affair with Monica Lewinsky, President Bill Clinton and his family turned to the Reverend Jesse Jackson, a fellow Baptist, for spiritual counsel. But even as Jackson was telling the media that the president had embarrassed his family and his country, news broke that Jackson had fathered a "love child" with Karin Stanford. Indeed, Jackson and a very pregnant Stanford had visited Clinton in the Oval Office just days before his impeachment trial.[47] Although Jackson confessed to the affair and apologized for it, he was roundly castigated by press and public for not living up to the high moral standards he expected of others.[48]

Ted Haggard was not as well known as Jackson, but as pastor of the 14,000-member New Life Church in Colorado Springs and president of the National Association of Evangelicals he was a powerful figure in evangelical circles. In weekly phone conversations with President George W. Bush, he pressed the president for an amendment to the U.S. Constitution to ban gay marriage; he was the driving force behind Colorado's Amendment 43 that, if passed by popular vote in the November 6, 2006, election, would ban gay marriage in the state.[49] But just a week before the election, male prostitute Mike Jones revealed during an interview on Denver's KHOW radio that for three years Haggard had regularly been paying him for his services. Haggard initially denied even knowing Jones, but audio analysis showed samples of Haggard's voice taken from a television interview matched samples from voicemails from Jones's phone.[50] Although Amendment 43 passed with 52 percent of the vote, Haggard's professional life was in shambles. New Life Church removed him as pastor for "demonstrated immoral conduct." Nine months later, Haggard was asking supporters to make up for his lost earning power by sending contributions directly to him or channeling them to him through Families with a Mission, which, though listed as a charitable organization in good standing in Colorado, shared a Monument, Colorado, address with a man listed in Hawaii as a registered sex offender.[51]

Bishop Eddie Long was also well connected. His 10,000-seat New Birth Baptist Church in suburban Atlanta hosted the 2006 funeral of Coretta Scott King, wife of Martin Luther King Jr.; their daughter, the Reverend Bernice King, is one of the pastors at the church, which counts entertainers, athletes, and political figures among its 25,000 members.[52] Conservative politicians running for election on a family-values platform regularly showed up at the church to court black voters. As an outspoken critic of promiscuity and homosexuality, Long encouraged families to pay $500 to send their sons to his LongFellows Youth Academy for four months' training in fiscal and sexual responsibility.[53] In September 2010, however, three men from the Georgia congregation and one from a satellite church in Charlotte, North Carolina, filed lawsuits claiming Long seduced them with expensive gifts before exerting his authority as bishop to engage them in sexual relationships.[54] Comparing himself to the biblical David in his fight against Goliath, Long denied the charges. The lawsuits, he claimed, were simply extortion attempts.[55] Long and his accusers agreed to mediation in order to avoid a public trial, but Long's ministry, still under a cloud from Senator Grassley's investigation of prosperity gospel ministries, soon found itself facing new problems when an investment scheme he had vetted went awry.[56]

Power and Politics

During the early years of the twenty-first century, the role of Kenneth Lay as Enron CEO in creating the financial mess that led to the collapse of the giant conglomerate was big news, but like other evangelical business leaders, Lay's faith was never really a part of the story.[57] That was also the case with the scandals at Southern Methodist University and at Baylor University that led the National Collegiate Athletic Association (NCAA) to levy its heaviest penalties on record against those respected evangelical institutions for their lack of institutional control over athletic programs that persistently flouted NCAA rules.[58] The situation, however, has been different with scandals created by people in positions of political power who touted their evangelical faith and their support for evangelical interests.

Because of the threat they pose to the First Amendment's religion clauses, the most important of these scandals are ones where evangelicals have tried to create what historian-theologian Martin Marty refers to as "Evangelicaldom"[59] by using their positions to impose their faith on others. The most notorious of these scandals culminated in the 2003 removal by court order of Roy Moore from his position as chief justice of the Alabama Supreme Court for failing to abide by a court order to remove the 5,280-pound granite monument topped with the Ten Commandments he had surreptitiously installed in the rotunda of the state judicial building. The court took that drastic step because Moore, who had reluctantly complied with an earlier order to cease opening court sessions with a Christian prayer, admitted he erected the monument as a way of making public his belief—and that of the many Alabama evangelicals who had elected him—that the Ten Commandments must be acknowledged as the foundation for U.S. law and government.[60]

Just one year after Moore's removal from office, the U.S. Air Force Academy found itself embroiled in scandal after the Yale Divinity School issued a critical report documenting complaints from some cadets that evangelical faculty members, officers, and cadets routinely harassed, intimidated, and retaliated against those at the Academy who did not accept their evangelical faith.[61] When MeLinda Morton, a Lutheran chaplain at the Academy, sided with the complaining cadets and also raised questions about the removal of information about Islam and other world religions from a tolerance training program instituted to address the problem, she was summarily transferred to a military base in Okinawa.[62] A Pentagon investigation into the matter led to a promise by Academy leadership to be more watchful of the religious rights of all cadets; however, problems popped up again in January 2011 when two civilian and three military Air Force Academy faculty sued to stop the school's National Prayer Luncheon, claiming it amounted to "endorsing and promoting" religion in violation of the U.S. Constitution.[63] Although U.S. District Judge Christine Arguello dismissed the case, she also pointed to a need to be more careful in distinguishing between events that are voluntary and ones at which attendance is mandatory.[64]

Scandals created by evangelicals in the military trying to impose their religion on others are not confined to the Air Force Academy,[65] but that kind of scandal is rather rare. More common have been scandals caused by evangelicals who, in failing to distinguish between "discipleship and partisanship," have "seized the language of the faith and made it captive to [a] partisan [political] agenda."[66] In attempting to promote that agenda, evangelical politicians, most notably Newt Gingrich and Tom DeLay, have repeatedly gamed the political system in ways they hoped would further the interests of their conservative Republican base—and also their own political careers.

After the *Wall Street Journal* and the *Los Angeles Times* broke the story in spring 1996 that Democratic vice-presidential candidate Al Gore, a Southern Baptist, had received potentially illegal campaign contributions from foreign contributors and from a California Buddhist temple, Republicans gleefully latched onto the story as evidence of Democratic wrongdoing. However, they quickly backed off when the *Atlanta Constitution* reported that House Speaker Gingrich, a Republican from Georgia and lifelong Baptist until his 2009 conversion to Catholicism, had received much the same kind of benefits.[67] The very next year, the House of Representatives voted 395 to 28 to reprimand Gingrich for providing the House Ethics Committee with inaccurate information about the use of funds that came from his Renewing American Civilization class.[68] Those scandals were, however, quite minor compared to those created by DeLay.

DeLay, a Republican from Texas, was House minority leader from 2003 until 2005 when he resigned after a Travis County, Texas, grand jury indicted him on a felony conspiracy charge to move $190,000 in corporate donations to Republican candidates in the Texas State Legislature.[69] He also faced a federal government investigation for his role in the Abramoff influence-peddling and Indian lobbying scandal,[70] which also caught up Ralph Reed, who had left his position as head of the Christian Coalition to make a bid for election as lieutenant governor of Georgia.[71] Out of office but undeterred, DeLay established a political consulting business in Texas to work for the election of Republicans because, as he said in an interview for a *New Yorker* article, "I listen to God, and what I've heard is that I'm supposed to devote myself to rebuilding the conservative base of the Republican Party."[72] On November 24, 2010, DeLay was found guilty by a Travis County jury in Austin of money laundering and conspiracy to commit money laundering. He was sentenced on January 10, 2011, to three years in prison and ten years of probation.[73]

While still in Congress, however, DeLay was instrumental in the K Street Project, a scheme hatched in 1995 with fellow Republicans to deny lobbying firms who failed to hire a significant number of Republicans access to Republican government officials. Although the House Ethics Committee reprimanded him for pulling a bill off the House floor in retaliation after the Electronics Industries Alliance hired a former Democratic congressman,[74] the scandal of DeLay's K Street Project attracted far less attention than the scandal that swirled around The Fellowship a decade later.

The Fellowship, more commonly known as The Family, includes businessmen, high-ranking government officials, and members of Congress from both political parties. Although the organization sponsors the National Prayer Breakfasts and engages in many behind-the-scenes charitable activities, some evangelicals have criticized The Family for the "obsession with privacy and problems in the areas of discipline, accountability, and theology" that contributed to its becoming embroiled in both fiscal and sexual scandals.[75] Sources quoted in an August 29, 2009, cover story in the evangelical news magazine *World* describe the organization variously as "stealthy" and "opaque" and as a "Christian mafia."[76]

The Family operates a house on C Street that paid no local property tax until 2009 when Washington, D.C., partially revoked its classification as a church because it holds no regularly scheduled public worship services.[77] Members of Congress meet there for private Bible study and prayer and also to discuss politics and plan ways to promote each others' political agendas; some also live there, paying well below market rates for their accommodations,[78] while others have had their international travel paid for by the organization.[79] As a result of those practices, Christian[80] and secular[81] watchdog groups have challenged the organization's status as a tax-exempt non-profit organization. The Office of Congressional Ethics opened a probe to determine whether the subsidized housing and international travel are improper gifts.[82] Although neither the Internal Revenue Service nor Congress had taken any definitive action on the complaints as of April 2011, by then questions of fiscal impropriety became submerged in stories of sexual scandals involving politicians associated with The Family and its C Street "frat house for Jesus."[83]

The extra-marital affairs of Congressman Chip Pickering, a Republican from Mississippi, and Senator John Ensign, a Nevada Republican, took place while they lived at the C Street House. South Carolina governor Mark Sanford, also a Republican, received counseling there after his disappearance while presumably hiking the Appalachian Trail turned out to be a cover-up for a trip to Argentina to visit his mistress. Although the Pickering affair got little attention, those of Ensign and Sanford, both of whom had been prominently mentioned as potential candidates for the presidency in 2012, became front-page news in papers around the country—the Ensign one because it included charges of illegal payments to his lover's husband, who was also one of Ensign's top aides,[84] and the Sanford one because its titillating aspects seemed so neatly to encapsulate both the sense of entitlement and the hypocrisy of evangelical politicians who "talk like traditionalists but live like libertines."[85]

During the Clinton-Lewinsky scandal, Pickering, Ensign, and Sanford voted for impeachment, as did Indiana Republican Mark Souder, whose adultery got some limited media attention in 2010.[86] DeLay and Gingrich also voted for impeachment even though they were engaged in affairs of their own at the time.[87] Gingrich divorced two wives in order to marry a lover. In confessing his sin, Sanford sought to salvage his reputation with evangelicals by comparing himself to the biblical King David, whom God favored in spite of his affair with Bathsheba.[88] Gingrich, too, played the David-Bathsheba card on the Christian Broadcast Network as he prepared to announce a run for the presidency in 2012, but instead of confessing to sin as Sanford had done, Gingrich excused himself by saying he loves his country "so passionately" that at times "he worked too hard and things happened in my life that were not appropriate."[89]

Conclusion

Both their numbers and the active role evangelicals have played in the public arena have made whatever they do a matter of public interest and concern. In response, the mainstream media have for the most part covered them thoroughly. Although evangelicals are no more prone to behave badly than are people of other faiths or ones with no faith, a part of that coverage has always focused on scandal. Over time, however, there have been some changes in the kinds of scandals that evangelicals have created and in their reactions to being caught that have produced subtle changes in mainstream media framing of those scandals. Those changes have created problems for evangelicals and for the evangelical faith more severe than those created by even the most negative scandal coverage of a century ago.

From the Beecher-Tilton affair of the 1870s through the televangelist scandals a century later, evangelicals caught in scandal either professed innocence or confessed their sin. But rarely in confessing did they make excuses for their behavior. However, as evangelicals sought and largely gained political influence after nearly half a century out of the limelight, scandals created by evangelicals acting because of their faith gained prominence over the earlier kind where evangelicals behaved scandalously in spite of their faith. Evangelical politicians in particular seemingly invited and were rewarded with the hypocrite label when they turned to the Bible in an effort to justify their acts or at least try to prove to themselves and their supporters that they were still on God's side. As a result, the acts of a few have, in recent years, tarnished the image of the many.

Notes

1. Mark Galli, "We've Won the Lottery—Now What?" *Christianity Today*, July 2009 (web-only), http://www.christianitytoday.com/ct/2009/julyweb-only/130-41.0.html (accessed September 4, 2009).
2. Ibid.
3. Judith M. Buddenbaum, *Religious Scandals* (Santa Barbara, CA: Greenwood, 2009), ix.
4. Ibid., 59–88.
5. Barry Hankins, *Jesus and Gin: Evangelicalism, The Roaring Twenties, and Today's Culture Wars* (New York: Palgrave/Macmillan, 2010), 135–137.
6. Ibid., 143–147.
7. Buddenbaum, *Religious Scandals*, 17.
8. Chris Parker, "What Wouldn't Jesus Do?: David Love Murders Mistress' Husband, Presides over His Funeral," http://www.truecrimereport.com/bad_clergy/index.php?page=2 (accessed February 2, 2011).
9. Buddenbaum, *Religious Scandals*, 73.
10. Ibid., 73–74.
11. Ibid., 73–75.
12. Andrew Walsh, "Who Killed George Tiller?" *Religion in the News* 12, no. 2 (2009): 5–7, 26.
13. Peter A. Kerr and Patricia Moy, "Newspaper Coverage of Fundamentalist Christians, 1980–2000," *Journalism and Mass Communication Quarterly* 79, no. 1 (2002): 58–59.

14. Katherine Q. Seelye, "Pastor Urges His Flock to Bring Guns to Church," *New York Times*, June 25, 2009, http://www.nytimes.com/2009/06/26/us/26guns.html (accessed March 3, 2011).

15. "Religious Leaders Condemn Plan to Burn Koran on September 11," *Washington Post*, September 8, 2009, A3.

16. Cathy Lynn Grossman, "Rabbis Blast Palin's Use of Phrase," *USA Today*, January 13, 2011, 3.

17. Buddenbaum, *Religious Scandals*, 84.

18. Ibid., 84–85.

19. Sissela Bok, *Lying* (New York: Vintage, 1989).

20. Buddenbaum, *Religious Scandals*, 46–47.

21. Ibid., 47–48.

22. Ibid., 48.

23. Ibid.

24. Ibid., 29.

25. Ibid., 30–31.

26. Ray Reed, "LU Won't Renew Caner's Contract as Dean of Seminary," *News & Advance*, July 1, 2010, http://www2.newsadvance.com/news/2010/jun/25/caner_removed_as_head_of_liberty_university_semina-ar-320882/ (accessed May 22, 2012).

27. Eric Frazier, "Jury Convicts Jinwrights in Fraud, Tax Evasion Case," *Charlotte Observer*, May 4, 2010, 1B.

28. "Jury Convicts Ex-Pastor of Bilking Investors," *Indianapolis Star*, October, 22, 2010, B2.

29. Bok, *Lying*, 7, 165–181.

30. Hankins, *Jesus and Gin*, 157. See also 159, 163, 165–166.

31. Buddenbaum, *Religious Scandals*, 55–57.

32. Ibid.

33. Lillian Kwon, "Grassley Concludes Senate Probe of 'Prosperity' Televangelists," *Christian Post*, January 7, 2011, http://www.christianpost.com/news/grassley-concludes-senate-probe-of-prosperity-televangelists-48383/ (accessed May 22, 2012).

34. Leslie G. Desmangles, "Haiti Laid Low," *Religion in the News* 13, no. 1 (2010): 2.

35. Shannon Smith, "Snatching Babies for Jesus," *Religion in the News* 12, no. 2 (2010): 4.

36. Ibid., 5.

37. Ibid.; see also Dennis R. Hoover, "Missionaries Or Not?" *Religion in the News* 5, no. 1 (2002): 16–18, 31.

38. Buddenbaum, *Religious Scandals*, 7.

39. Ibid., 7.

40. Ibid., 8–9.

41. Hankins, *Jesus and Gin*, 149–155.

42. Ibid., 157.
43. Buddenbaum, *Religious Scandals*, 9–10.
44. Ibid., 9.
45. Ibid., 10.
46. Ibid., 10–11.
47. William R. Piotrowski, "Hide, Jesse, Hide," *Religion in the News* 4, no. 1 (2001): 18, 30.
48. Ibid., 30.
49. Buddenbaum, *Religious Scandals*, 15.
50. Ibid., 16.
51. Ibid., 17.
52. Anthea Butler, "The Fall of Eddie Long," *Religion in the News* 13, no. 2 (2011): 13.
53. Greg Bluestein, "Pastor's Academy Preached Sexual Control," *Indianapolis Star*, September 25, 2010, A11.
54. Butler, "The Fall of Eddie Long," 14.
55. Erin Haines, "Megachurch Pastor Vows a David-like Fight," *Indianapolis Star*, September 27, 2010, A3.
56. Butler, "The Fall of Eddie Long," 15.
57. See, e.g., Sylvia Moreno, "Lay Is Remembered as 'Strait Arrow'; Mourners Denounce Enron Prosecution," *Washington Post*, July 13, 2006, A3.
58. Peter Finley et al., *Sports Scandals* (Santa Barbara, CA: Greenwood, 2008), 17–19, 95–97.
59. Martin E. Marty, "Evangelicaldom," *Sightings*, October 5, 2009, http://divinity.uchicago.edu/martycenter/publications/sightings/archive_2009/1005.shtml.
60. Buddenbaum, *Religious Scandals*, 129–134.
61. Laurie Goodstein, "Religious-Bias Inquiry Is Set at Air Force Academy," *New York Times*, May 5, 2005, A29.
62. Laurie Goodstein, "Air Force Chaplain Says She Was Removed for Being Critical," *New York Times*, May 15, 2005, A22.
63. Bill Vogrin, "Group Sues to Block Prayer Speaker at AFA," *Gazette*, January 31, 2011, http://www.gazette.com/common/printer/view.php?db=colgazette&id=112098 (accessed February 10, 2011).
64. "Judge Dismisses Air Force Academy Prayer Lawsuit," *Gazette*, February 9, 2011, http://www.gazette.com/common/printer/view.php?db=colgazette&id=112586 (accessed February 18, 2011).
65. Amory C. Minot, "The Beat Goes On," *Religion in the News* 11, no. 3 (2009): 16–17; and Buddenbaum, *Religious Scandals*, 156–159.
66. Martin E. Marty, "The Idolatry of America," *Sightings*, June 2, 2008, http://divinity.uchicago.edu/martycenter/publications/sightings/archive_2008/0602.shtml (accessed March 16, 2011).
67. Buddenbaum, *Religious Scandals*, 34–35.

68. John E. Yang, "House Reprimands, Penalizes Speaker," *Washington Post*, January 22, 1997, A1.

69. R. Jeffrey Smith, "DeLay Is Indicted on Two New Charges: Money Laundering Alleged in Texas," *Washington Post*, October 4, 2005, A1.

70. Jonathan Weisman, "Abramoff Probe Turns Focus on DeLay," *Washington Post*, January 8, 2006, A1.

71. David D. Kirkpatrick and Philip Shenon, "Ralph Reed's Zeal for Lobbying Is Shaking His Political Faithful," *New York Times*, April 18, 2005, A1, A16.

72. Jeffrey Goldberg, "Party Unfaithful," *New Yorker*, June 4, 2007, http://www.newyorker.com/library/politics/062199delay-profile.html (accessed May 20, 2010).

73. Juan A. Lozano, "DeLay Gets Prison Term in Political Funding Ruse," *Indianapolis Star*, January 11, 2011, A3.

74. Jeffrey Birnbaum, "Going Left on K Street," *Washington Post*, July 2, 2004, E1.

75. Emily Belz and Edward Lee Pitts, "All in the Family," *World*, August 29, 2009, http://www.worldmag.com/articles/15778 (accessed March 10, 2011).

76. Ibid.

77. "It's Official: The C Street House Is Not a Church," *Washington Post*, November 18, 2009, A3.

78. Belz and Pitts, "All in the Family"; and "Watchdog Calls for Probe Into Lawmakers' Bargain Rent at 'C Street House,'" FOXNews, April 1, 2010, http://www.foxnews.com/politics/2010/04/01/watchdog-calls-probe-lawmakers-bargain-capitol-hill-rent/ (accessed May 22, 2012).

79. Paul Singer, "Group Linked to C Street House Pays for Overseas Excursions," *Roll Call*, June 23, 2010, http://www.rollcall.com/issues/55_152/news/47618-1.html (accessed July 1, 2010).

80. Peter Sevin, "C Street House Is Target of Clergy IRS Complaint," *Washington Post*, February 23, 2010, A3.

81. "Watchdog Calls for Probe."

82. Susan Crabtree, "C St. Lawmakers Hit with Ethics Complaint," *The Hill*, April 1, 2010, http://thehill.com/homenews/senate/90225-c-street-house-lawmakers-hit-with-ethics-complaint (accessed June 17, 2010); and Paul Singer, "Ethics Office Investigates C Street Residence," *Roll Call*, June 9, 2010, http://www.rollcall.com/issues/55_144/news/47140-1.html (accessed June 17, 2010).

83. Belz and Pitts, "All in the Family"; and Peter J. Boyer, "Frat House for Jesus: The Entity behind C Street," *New Yorker*, September 13, 2010, 50.

84. Eric Lichrblau and Eric Lipton, "Report Urges U.S. to Consider Charging Ensign," *New York Times*, May 12, 2011, A1.

85. R. Marie Griffith, "Sanford and Wife," *Religion in the News* 12, no. 2 (2009): 2.

86. Bill Ruthhart, "Why Do They Stray?" *Indianapolis Star*, May 19, 2010, A1, A4.

87. Goldberg, "Party Unfaithful."
88. Griffith, "Sanford and Wife," 2–3.
89. Shannon McCaffrey, "Newt Gingrich Says His Passion for His Country Contributed to His Marital Infidelity," *Chicago Tribune*, March 9, 2011, http://www.chicagotribune.com/news/sns-ap-us-newt-gingrich-2012,0,624356.story (accessed April 5, 2011).

Chapter 8

Evangelical Media Cults

Quentin J. Schultze

When a popular Roman Catholic media priest in Florida announced his conversion to the Episcopal Church in 2009, it strained ecumenical relations between the two churches.[1] Why? Because this was no ordinary priest. He was known as "Father Oprah" because of his media savvy and his devout fans. Presumably, some of his television followers might convert with him and follow him from Rome to the Church of England. Rome was not pleased.

In the contemporary United States, the democratic spirit produces *personality cults* made up of loyal followers led by a trusted, charismatic person.[2] Authority derives from market success, such as best-selling books, large audience ratings, booming congregations, and rising financial contributions. Who can argue with success when the pastor of a megachurch—a congregation with over 2,000 members—becomes a *New York Times* top-selling book author or a nationally syndicated radio show host? Enthusiastic followers have the power to confer authority upon popular leaders in the religious open market of charismatic opportunity. Religious leaders freely compete for audiences' attention, time, money, and membership. Personality leads to popularity and often to power.

In this chapter, I first suggest that well-known, media-visible celebrities are an especially important aspect of American evangelical culture. In spite of hundreds of years of the Protestant Reformation, many American evangelicals still yearn for their own pope-like celebrities. Television evangelists, in particular, embody the American myths of individualism and success. Second, I address how American religious leaders have effectively cultivated their personas on radio and later television. Third, I explain why television became the most powerful medium for evangelicals, especially *charismatics*—evangelicals who believe in exuberant worship that might include the "baptism of the Holy Spirit" as evident in the practice of "speaking in tongues" (glossolalia). Fourth, I explore both the potential and the limits of mediated personality cults, including the difficulty of leadership succession within monarchic media ministries. Finally, I conclude that mediated personality cults are a mixed blessing for evangelicals and are likely to shift from broadcasting to cyberspace.

Personal Authority in the United States

From the beginning, Americans have believed in individuals and individualism. They inherited the concept from the classical Greeks and used it to establish the rights and freedoms found in the Constitution and Declaration of Independence. However, this individualism was always projected into the future as a source of social and economic progress. Individuals would make the United States a great nation. Government was to serve the individual, not the other way around.

From the early days of the American colonies, immigrants linked their individualistic spirit to their hopes for the future. Settlers sought to establish a land where they could freely chart their own destinies, where they could be themselves and define their own identities without external constraints. This New World represented an opportunity for a new start in life. The past would not determine the future, people believed, because America had not been spoiled by some of the undesirable traditions of European society. The country was a new and noble experiment in freedom and individualism.[3]

These founding myths led to a unique culture that glorified the future and stressed the importance of individual personality as well as unfettered religious freedom. The First Amendment of the U.S. Constitution even tied freedoms of assembly and speech to religious convictions—the only type of conviction specifically mentioned. Citizens would be free to hold whatever religious beliefs they wished and could not be excluded from citizenship for those beliefs. Gathering in their own communities, early Americans were sometimes skeptical of various religious groups' beliefs and practices. But Americans were increasingly open to new religious ideas and practices, creating a land of remarkable religious pluralism. Above all, they sought practical religions that worked for individuals—that led to salvation, happiness, and personal as well as communal peace. In short, they wanted the kinds of religious faiths that mirrored their own hopes in the New World and their belief in the ability of individuals to be happy and successful. The Declaration of Independence states that "all men are created equal" and are "endowed by their Creator with certain unalienable Rights, that among these are Life, Liberty and the pursuit of Happiness."

To a large extent, success in the United States has come to mean individual prosperity and fame. Gossip columnist Liz Smith says, "We don't have heroes to believe in anymore. Today, people with money are godlike. Malcolm Forbes and [Donald] Trump are absolute stars."[4] Smith might have added that such celebrities often *seek* fame with their fortunes. Money is great, but it is usually not sufficient for individuals who crave notoriety. Modern stars also want to have their names on the cornerstones of buildings, at the head of corporations, and in the titles of charitable foundations. Such notoriety completes the American image of success. According to these standards, show business produces more successful Americans than any other enterprise. Hollywood is not just in the entertainment business. It also manufactures public personas. So do mass media.

Evangelical Personalities and Media

Most of the approximately 10,000 Christian television ministries are local and congregation-related—hardly national, let alone international, personality cults.[5] Yet the size and power of some media ministries concerns evangelical leaders who worry about the power of such personality-led movements on Christian belief and community. They see that evangelical record companies and book publishers promote popular evangelical celebrities. One significant evangelical pastor and radio personality chastises the Church for failing "to see the pitfalls inherent in modern communications. . . . Most of the new media are better suited to entertainment."[6] Another evangelical broadcaster calls much evangelical media content "Christianity-Lite."[7]

In spite of such contemporary concerns, the fact is that personality-oriented evangelical media have been part of the American evangelical movement since at least the late nineteenth century. By the beginning of the twentieth century, American evangelicals were already contributing remarkable sums to particular mission enterprises and building projects led by well-known religious personalities. Like a popular nineteenth-century circuit rider, a convincing turn-of-the-century preacher with charisma could elicit contributions. A dull and uninspiring evangelist could not. In 1886, the Chicago Evangelization Society raised $250,000 to convince well-known urban revivalist Dwight L. Moody to start a school for training evangelical leaders. Moody did not seek the money. Chicago evangelicals offered it to him as a statement of their desire for him to establish what later became Moody Bible Institute.[8] Eventually, his followers launched one of the first religious radio stations in the nation, WMBI.[9]

Increasingly, the successful preacher was the one who was able not only to evangelize unsaved souls or revive waning ones but also to create visible symbols of success. Unlike old European cathedrals or local American churches, new church buildings in the United States frequently reflected the concepts and personalities of individuals rather than the traditions of denominations. Religious leaders, like their business counterparts, erected large churches partly as public statements of their success. These structures overshadowed traditional Protestant and Roman Catholic churches. Among the first radio evangelists to communicate publicly with a strong, new architectural presence in the United States was Aimee Semple McPherson, who dedicated her Angelus Temple in Los Angeles in 1923. The structure provided both worship and entertainment space, including a stage and studio for live radio broadcasts.[10]

The Magic of Radio Personas

By the 1930s, radio established stronger personality cults than earlier print media by creating the impression of a personal relationship between listener and broadcaster. It often seemed to listeners that a radio personality was like a friend or acquaintance speaking to them personally in the privacy of their homes. The radio persona seemed to be "live" (even if recorded). Popular pre-television radio stars such as Arthur Godfrey depended heavily on the medium's capacity for establishing that kind of intimacy between themselves and individual listeners. So did the early disc jockeys (DJs) on the first rock radio stations in the 1950s.

Radio listeners sometimes felt that well-known radio personalities, whether DJs or actors, were no different from the real persons behind the microphone. They even believed that actors such as those who played in the nightly network comedy *Amos 'n' Andy* were not acting. The real genius of that program, which attracted an estimated 40 million listeners (one-third of all Americans) in the 1930s, was not the comic gags but the characterizations. By changing their vocal inflection, tone, dialect, and phrasing, the two actors were able to establish effective characters that made the actors seem like real people rather than personas.[11]

Early radio evangelists such as Charles E. Fuller similarly established personal connections with listeners. One listener wrote Fuller, "I am a young man ... a commercial traveler by occupation covering a territory from coast to coast.... I have been held by some supernatural power to my room on Sunday evenings and drawn to listen to your broadcast. Why, I do not know, because church has never held any place in my life. I feel you are so sincere in your talks."[12] Fuller's popularity on his *Old Fashioned Revival Hour* resulted significantly from his ability to employ radio effectively to establish a personal ethos with millions of listeners. His folksy broadcasts made him the most popular radio evangelist of all time.[13]

From Radio to Television

American evangelicalism was particularly ripe for personality cults. Compared with those religious groups anchored securely in historical tradition and power-sharing church governance, evangelicals were independent and innovative. Preachers like McPherson were usually not joiners as much as adaptors, revisionists, and innovators, especially with communications media. Every generation of evangelical leaders in the United States reshaped its message for new audiences and emerging media.[14] They were amazingly free and open to novel ways of doing things, including evangelism. Lacking strong religious traditions and enamored with the American version of success, evangelicals imitated personality cults entering mainstream broadcasting. No denominations were free of these trends, as even the Roman Catholic church discovered with highly political radio preacher Father Joseph Coughlin in the 1930s, prime-time television priest Bishop Fulton J. Sheen in the 1950s, and most recently Mother Angelica of the Eternal Word Network. However, evangelicals have always been the personality professionals.

After World War II, evangelicalism became a widely visible expression of Protestant personality cults in the United States. In para-church movements of all kinds, from non-denominational Bible colleges to world mission organizations and especially domestic broadcasting, evangelical leaders mastered people-pleasing abilities and optimistic rhetoric. It seemed that every successful para-church leader had to have his or her own publication with a personal note to the constituency, and that sermon tours (preaching from church to church, somewhat like nineteenth-century circuit-riding preachers who sold Bibles and inspirational books) were becoming public relations vehicles. Television broadcasting soon became the most potent tool for communicating personal authority to large and distant constituencies, equipping evangelical leaders to become major celebrities with national followings.[15]

Beginning in the 1950s with Sheen, Oral Roberts, and Rex Humbard—and continuing in the 1960s through the 1980s with Jerry Falwell, Robert Schuller, M. G. "Pat" Robertson, and Jim Bakker—American television offered a growing display of prominent new media personalities. Each one told a story of personal success. Roberts overcame poor health, poverty, and a stutter to produce the first religiously oriented prime-time variety specials on American television.[16] Falwell succeeded in spite of his rebellious youth and an alcoholic father who died young.[17] Schuller's ministry grew from a kitschy Los Angeles drive-in "church," where he preached to worshippers in their cars from the roof of the concession stand, to the magnificent, Philip Johnson–designed Crystal Cathedral, which served as the setting for his top-rated Sunday-morning *Hour of Power* television broadcast syndicated to hundreds of mainstream stations across the country.[18] In Virginia Beach, Robertson launched his first television station with little more than spending money. Decades later he was one of the most successful cable television network executives in the nation—the Ted Turner of evangelical cable television.[19] Bakker, a short, working-class kid who suffered from intense feelings of inferiority, eventually founded the Praise the Lord (PTL) network and the Heritage U.S.A. theme park, where attendance in the 1980s was third only to the two Disney parks.[20]

The personal stories of such evangelical leaders, especially as portrayed in their autobiographies, form a body of contemporary hagiography—saint-like stories of living persons.[21] These men became modern-day saints whose own lives seemingly displayed the special work of God. Like Moody and many pre-broadcasting evangelical leaders, televangelists used their personal pasts to establish their charismatic authority in the present. In their strongest forms, televangelists' autobiographies function like modern parables—testimonies to the acts of God in history. Televangelists and their publicists interpret these personal narratives for the ministry's followers; the televangelists are both writers and interpreters of their own textual canons. Television becomes the medium for these new, personalized, hagiographic texts, recalling and mirroring the actions of evangelical saints.

Parasocial Televised Intimacy

Why was television so ripe for such persona creation? Television added seemingly real images to radio's intimate voices. As English journalist and author Malcolm Muggeridge argues, televised images invariably appear real.[22] Cameras do not seem to lie. What viewers see on home television sets is what the camera is actually recording with its lens. Even when viewers disagree with a reporter's interpretation of televised news, viewers tend to trust the televised images they see with their own eyes. To the average viewer, television, like the home video camera, simply documents on film what really happens. Just as a radio voice is created by the microphone, a television image is produced by the camera. Viewers naturally assume that voices and photographic images are more personal and real than the printed word.

Moreover, television visually communicates one type of evocative image better than all others: the human face. Facial expressions that convey human emotion are easily gleaned from a television picture. Although large-screen, high-definition television technologies improve the range of images that the medium can communicate effectively, television still best conveys human emotion through human expressions.

Day in and day out—on cable, over the air, and through satellites—the faces of televangelists are delivered electronically to audiences. In the privacy of viewers' homes, television recreates those images on the screens. There the televangelist takes on a persona. The television viewer sees both more (and less) than what someone in the studio audience sees. The television pulpit, auditorium stage, or talk-show set recedes to the visual background while the televangelist's countenance fills the screen. Through this process, the viewing of televangelism becomes an entirely different experience than attending an evangelistic crusade or participating in a local revival. In face-to-face interaction, the audience decides what to see within the limits of the human eye. On television, by comparison, the camera sets the technological limits and the camera operators and film editors determine what the viewer actually sees.

Televangelism's personality cults are made possible only by the viewers' desires for someone to follow; they are then enhanced by the intimate way that the medium communicates. Even if the televangelist does not seek to gain exclusive religious authority over his or her viewers, some will trustingly become followers. Television inherently creates the illusory sense that preacher and viewer are communicating personally. As one critic put it in the early days of the medium, a religious broadcaster can triumph as a personality "without having achieved any essential relatedness at all."[23] The negative side of this is that televangelists can create the "illusion" of personal concern for a "faceless audience" regardless of whether or not they actually have such concern.[24] The image appears to tell the truth—that the televangelist is the viewer's personal friend—while hiding the real truth that there is no relationship whatsoever between the viewer and the televangelist.

Even in situations where television does not give preachers cult-like status, it typically elevates their standing among believers. Televangelists may not have a high official status in the Church, but unofficially many evangelicals look up to them as specially gifted individuals. The medium provides them a privileged place in public life among their followers. Even in denominations with their own subsidized programs, a broadcaster automatically becomes one of the most authoritative voices among their clergy. He or she is typically invited to local churches and keynoted at denominational conventions as a major speaker. He or she will often be quoted or cited in denominational publications and might even address the clergy at denominational business meetings. A denomination's broadcaster becomes a symbol of the strength and visibility of the entire denomination. Radio and television were able to put various denominations "on the map" by giving them a personal media presence in the wider culture.[25]

Television Charismatics

The spectacular growth of the *charismatic movement*—far larger than the earlier Pentecostal and charismatic groups who believed more narrowly in divine healing and especially speaking in tongues—paralleled the growth of television in American society. Even into the 1960s, some denominations were highly critical of television and film, but by the 1970s few religious groups were still trying seriously to keep television out of the homes of their members. Television was ubiquitous, and so was the charismatic movement. Charismatics existed throughout the churches and across the spectrum of religious television. Cable television and satellite dishes helped deliver into millions of homes a new wave of charismatic religious leaders, including Bakker and Robertson. Television may have helped establish a new religious sensibility and a new style of popular worship heavily dependent on personality. In other words, the charismatic movement gave way to a charismatic *style* of religious life strongly characterized by emotion and personality.

The most intriguing aspect of the contemporary charismatic movement is its broad appeal. Historically, Pentecostals, although sharing with charismatics some beliefs and practices (for example, healing and speaking in tongues), were always distinct organizations and movements identified by denominations and to some extent even by social class, educational background, and region of the country. The new charismatics, on the other hand, spanned the scope of American Christianity. *Christianity Today* magazine, which represents mainstream American evangelicalism, commissioned a Gallup poll in 1979 to determine the number of charismatics and Pentecostals in the country. The magazine found that 19 percent of all American adults considered themselves to be Pentecostal or charismatic Christians. Moreover, this charismatic movement stretched across the spectrum of organized American Christianity, from Roman Catholics (18 percent charismatic) to Baptists (20 percent), Methodists (18 percent), and Lutherans (20 percent). However, only a small fraction of those who called themselves Pentecostal-charismatic (17 percent) actually spoke in tongues.[26] Perhaps the charismatic movement was partly the culmination of religious expression in a televisual culture. The movement sought to turn loose the personality of the Christian and the personality of God in the act of worship. It centered worship on *personal* experience, with the song leader or pastor directing participants' emotions. These leaders were like music video directors, orchestrating live performances for the church audience.

The nature of television as a personality-driven, facially expressive medium might explain why charismatic evangelicals and non-charismatic (in doctrine) but charismatically styled (in rhetoric) evangelicals dominated the top-ten weekly syndicated religious-program audiences during the 1980s and 1990s. Roberts led the weekly ratings for years. Then Jimmy Swaggart and Schuller (not a charismatic) competed for the lead, with Swaggart dropping considerably after the scandals of 1986 and 1987. Among the most popular new televangelists during the 1980s was Kenneth Copeland, a Pentecostal who once worked for Roberts. Even though televangelists such as Schuller, Falwell, and D. James Kennedy did not call themselves charismatics, they adapted their television programs to elements of personality-oriented communication. They made themselves symbols of Christian authority on a wide range of social, political, and religious issues. Falwell, for example, formed the Moral Majority in 1979, which attempted to shape U.S. political policies until 1989.[27] Although Falwell never called himself a charismatic, he sought to gain viewers' personal, emotional involvement in his causes.

As a product partly of a televisual culture, *charismatic-styled* Christianity—as opposed to members of the charismatic movement and other charismatic groups who still believed in the baptism of the Holy Spirit and the use of special charismatic gifts (*charisms*) such as healing and prophecy for all believers—was a popular style of religious expression that increasingly transcended historical and doctrinal differences among

Christians. As author and researcher Pierre Babin says, even when the pope goes on television, "he is more symbol than word." On the tube, the pontiff is able "to be everywhere and has an aura of prestige, an affective, sensory influence which puts him in a totally different position to his predecessors."[28] During the 1970s and 1980s, Pope John Paul II became the "charismatic" (in the sense of popular and evoking strong emotional connections with followers) leader of the largest religious organization in the world. Of course, the Vatican had its own public relations department, which orchestrated international television coverage of the pope's many trips.[29] Still, he became the first pope with televisual charisma. The mainline Protestant journal *Christian Century* called him in retrospect the "philosopher pope in a media age."[30]

In addition, most of the popular televangelists have been from the South, where oral culture is a better fit with the charismatic medium: Falwell, Joel Osteen, Robertson, Swaggart, Roberts, Copeland, James Robison, and Charles Stanley. The others have generally adapted the Southern oral tradition. Bakker was an engaging and often humorous storyteller from a small Pentecostal church in a working-class community in Michigan. Schuller established a simple, alliterative, conversational style of preaching that maintains its white, Northern refinement while freeing him to be rather personal and emotional. Stanley of Atlanta, a Southern Baptist, probably has most effectively kept essential elements of both Northern and Southern rhetorical traditions so as to appeal to both. He is practical but propositional, emotional but level-headed, persuasive but inoffensive, animated but controlled, doctrinal but biblical, discursive but narrational. Stanley's meteoric rise in televangelism during the late 1980s was perhaps due as much to his ability to put these styles together as it was to the actual content of his sermons. He was one of the few televangelists who appealed to viewers across the spectrum of American society. Through all these characteristics, he was able to convey a remarkable humility and sincerity. Those were key traits, especially in the late 1980s as televangelism coped with the public skepticism caused by the Swaggart and Bakker scandals.

The Southern, Pentecostal communication style is the most compatible with television. Swaggart—the cousin of rock musician and singer Jerry Lee Lewis—best represented that style on television, and during the 1980s clearly was the most engaging weekly television preacher. Compared with the academic, managerial, or professional styles of Northern preachers, Swaggart's televisual style was leagues ahead of the Northern competition. Given a choice, few viewers would watch the faces or actions of dull, sophisticated, scholarly preachers. Audiences much prefer to see a good storyteller use his or her face and voice to make the Bible come alive. It is no accident that Swaggart had the highest weekly audience ratings among religious broadcasters. Not only were his performances often electrifying, but for most people he conveyed genuine belief in his own messages. Even viewers who disagreed with those messages tended not to question his personal integrity and especially his ability to communicate those messages with power and conviction—at least until the scandals. In fact, Swaggart's 1988 televised confession for having a motel rendezvous with a prostitute was one of the most emotionally moving religious broadcasts of all time. With an agonized look on his face and tears streaming down his cheeks, Swaggart conveyed genuine repentance. His self-loathing seemed real, even to many skeptics of televangelism.[31]

From Charisma to Cult

Like the local church, where gifted preachers attract large congregations, televangelists with personal magnetism will generally build greater audiences than television preachers who cannot communicate effectively. Communication is always dependent on the character of the speaker, which is established partly by a speaker's public personality. The most popular news commentators and talk-show hosts, like the highest-rated televangelists, convey their messages through a particular style. Although some televangelists try to imitate other ones, popularity requires a distinctive persona that attracts an audience.

Gifted evangelical communicators can easily establish pseudo-relationships with their audience members, who sometimes begin to believe that they know their favorite televangelist intimately. Admirers can become so emotionally involved that they feel personally connected to their religious leaders, whom they believe are their direct lines to heaven. These dedicated followers are not always looking for traditional religious messages; they often seek to relate to someone who will help them commune with God. They often want a connection to God more than theology or doctrine about God.

The majority of viewers are not nearly so personally attached to a preacher they meet only on a screen. Nevertheless, the preacher's charismatic style, if not his or her message, can have a spellbinding effect if viewers feel they have lost hope and become estranged from others. The most popular televangelists are sometimes deluged by letters from lonely, stressed, hopeless, and fearful individuals. Many television ministries maintain telephone hotlines or prayer lines for viewers to call any time. Especially when addressing human beings' personal crises is the message, a preacher's televisual style—his or her eloquence, persuasiveness, or personal aura—can set him or her strikingly apart from other voices of authority in society. The television medium seemingly transforms common, sinful preachers—people who are like everyone else—into extraordinary figures.[32] Many viewers place their hope and find their comfort in the apparently authoritative voices and face-to-face images of individuals they have never met and who are sometimes thousands of miles away. A televangelist can become a personal source of wisdom and truth.

The most gifted television preachers, those with the greatest visual charm, inevitably end up with their own groups of cult-like followers. Bakker and his wife Tammy had some of the most committed daily followers among all televangelists in the 1980s. Some viewers were so loyal to the Bakkers that even after Jim went to federal prison in 1989 for fraud they continued to send donations and to disbelieve the media reports about his financial and sexual misconduct.[33] If viewers believe that their favorite televangelist is a personal friend, they will be inclined to place more trust in what he or she says than in what their local pastor preaches or even what their denomination or church officially professes. Such devoted viewers form a televangelist's personality cult—and their faith in his or her integrity and wisdom is sometimes unshakable in spite of contrary evidence.

Within the typical television ministry, there will also be workers who staunchly believe in their leader. Indeed, televangelists tend to attract employees who find more meaning in working for someone they admire than in working for the distant and seemingly uncaring management of a large mainstream business. Employees and volunteers in these ministries are rarely in it for the money. Although salaries are generally low, televangelism's employees are inspired by the televangelist to work hard on behalf of the ministry and to turn their spiritual labor into a meaningful endeavor. Because their work is defined as a mission, there is little room for internal critics or naysayers. Workers must have faith, and that means faith in the televangelist as well as in God.

In local churches, the one-on-one relationship existing between pastors and their congregants largely precludes personality cults. Typically only in the megachurches, where size creates significant anonymity, is the climate conducive to the development of such blind allegiance to a preacher and his or her causes. Not surprisingly, a television ministry may emerge from within a megachurch. Falwell, Swaggart, Schuller, and several other televangelists were pastors of their own large churches, where they had greater authority than the rest of the staff. Aside from televangelism, religious personality cults are most prevalent in large churches where few members know the main pastor well and where other leaders obediently submit to the authority of their main pastor.

Well-intentioned televangelists, like well-meaning politicians, are sometimes corrupted by faithful devotees. If followers project greatness onto their leaders, soon the leaders themselves can believe in their greatness. This is most obvious in the practice of physical healing. When followers hope for healing and express a firm belief in the healer's personal power to cure them, even skeptical preachers eventually can come to believe in their own on-demand ability to conquer diseases and restore wholeness. A "successful" Christian who becomes a celebrity "may begin to believe the publicity that's written about him/her, may come to have a bloated opinion of his importance as a result of being interviewed, having his picture on magazine covers, being adulated by a fan club that hangs on his every word and accepts his every action."[34]

In the mid-1980s, Swaggart's televised sermons suggested that he had become a victim of his own fame. In those years, he preached vigorously against other expressions of the Christian faith. It appeared for a time, as Swaggart increasingly used his broadcasts to respond to critics, that the battle he preached about was no longer between God and Satan but between Swaggart and the rest of Christianity. Later, when Swaggart was disciplined by the Assemblies of God denomination for his sexual misconduct, the televangelist asserted his independence by leaving his denomination. Swaggart apparently believed that his ministry was more important than the ministry of his own denomination—that he was above ecclesiastical law and had more authority than the denomination. Sometimes spiritual arrogance is the ultimate outcome of the psychological pressures imposed on the leader of a personality cult. Personality supplants community and accountability.

Religious Monarchies

Personality cults are so significant in the dynamics of televangelism that the future of a particular ministry depends heavily on the credibility of one person—the celebrity preacher. The result is a potential crisis of authority when this central personality retires, dies, or suffers bad publicity. Unlike most local churches and nearly all denominations, television ministries hang on the ability of one individual to attract audiences and elicit

Evangelical Media Cults 141

contributions. Although many people create the programs, the on-air personality is unquestionably the most important figure, the driving force that energizes the public ministry.

Like saints in some Christian traditions, televangelists are treated as special individuals whom God has used in extraordinary ways. They become the kings of the evangelical world, dispensing their edicts and marshaling the troops for holy wars against secular powers or competing religious groups. Their infectious charisma rallies the followers for skirmishes of all kinds, from fights over bad publicity to struggles for more finances. Swaggart and Bakker, for example, openly fought verbal battles against mainstream publications that wrote critical articles about them. Preachers sent letters to supporters, alerting them to the alleged false charges against them and calling supporters to complain to the offending media and send contributions to the ministry. The kings of televangelism used direct-mail messengers to dispense their decrees.

Televangelists and their households usually try to rule over distant flocks like religious royalty. In fact, the succession of leadership, a significant problem for almost all of the major televangelists, often becomes a family affair. In the United States, however, monarchical transitions are highly suspect as the nation was formed partly in reaction against monarchies; that approach provides no guarantee of popular support for a potential leader. Although monarchies offer orderly and obvious transitions of power and authority, they reject individualism and challenge the sovereignty of the people to decide their own political fate. Not surprisingly, many Americans are especially skeptical of family-led religious kingdoms. After all, the offspring never quite earned their own authority; they inherited the cult.

In addition, few offspring of televangelists have the people-pleasing qualities of their kingly parents.[35] It appears that these strong parents, who spent more time building their ministry than raising their offspring, almost invariably produce children with less charisma than their own. Rather than finding their own place in life, many of these children have been awkwardly thrust into the ministry. Some of them are uncomfortable with their second-class status next to their highly successful, well-respected parents, and they may suffer insecurities about being able to live up to the established standards. When Robertson vacated the television ministry to run for president of the United States in 1988, he left a son, Tim, in charge. A gifted administrator, Tim managed the Christian Broadcasting Network (CBN) organization well, but he was simply not a charismatic *700 Club*

Gordon Robertson (left), with his father Pat Robertson in Virginia Beach, Virginia. In 2007, Pat Robertson turned over his duties as chief executive officer of the Christian Broadcasting Network to his son while remaining chairman. Gordon is the second of Robertson's two sons to serve as host of *The 700 Club*. (AP Photo/Christian Broadcasting Network, File.)

television host like his father. Donations to the ministry dropped (perhaps partly because some supporters contributed instead to Pat's political campaign), and the elder Robertson eventually had to return to the network after his unsuccessful presidential bid in order to bail it out financially. Not long after his return, contributions were up and the future once again looked bright, both for the network and for Robertson's Regent University, a graduate school heavily dependent on network subsidies.

There is not a single case of a successful transition of leadership from father to son in a major television ministry.[36] Organizational and managerial momentum might keep such ministries going after the founding leader dies, but more likely personality-oriented programs will slowly wither and eventually fade away. Reruns are sufficient only for a time, except on radio, where very small constituencies can support broadcasts for years. J. Vernon McGee and Lester Roloff are examples of radio preachers whose recorded programs remained popular long after their deaths. McGee's radio broadcast picked up 300 American radio stations between 1988 and 2002 after McGee's death.[37] By contrast, television viewers have not been so apt to seek out reruns or downloadable video recordings of previously popular television preachers.

The inability of televangelists to create their own successful religious monarchies suggests the tenuousness of their long-term authority. Unlike the saints of some Christian traditions, whose personal charisma extended over centuries in the hearts and minds of hopeful believers, television-created saints suffer the same hardships of popular acclaim as film actors and news anchors. Even though publicists and ghostwriters help televangelists compose contemporary hagiographies, such publications are short lived; used book stores and other resale shops are dumping grounds for once-popular stories about successful televangelists' rise from obscurity and hardship to celebrity and prosperity.

Ironically, the original Christian cult of saints was developed in the Middle Ages and became a major part of Counter-Reformation piety. The Council of Trent (1545–1563) responded to Protestant challenges "by justifying the devotion to saints."[38] Hundreds of years later, Protestant television clergy have sometimes attempted to establish their own sainthood, despite Catholic criticisms.[39] Biblically speaking, sainthood was never envisioned as a power play between competing brands of Christianity or among clergy. In American culture, however, that is what it partly has become, and no degree of attempted monarchical intervention can alter that.

Holy Charisma

In historical perspective, televangelism's disparate cults seem only to be the latest version of personality-based competition among and within religious groups. After all, Christianity has been riddled with personality cults, from the early church at Corinth to contemporary Protestantism. Even Roman Catholicism, which stresses tradition and church law as well as doctrine and sacrament, has had such problems—and not just from critics who fled to the Protestant ranks, like a Martin Luther or a John Calvin. If human personality is not evil, and if the gifts of the Holy Spirit are given to all individuals, it would be naïve for Christians even to attempt to remove all charismatic-styled preaching, worship, and television programming from the Church.

The legitimate role of human charisma—as opposed to charismatic style—in religious communication is primarily a matter of ethics. Religious individuals and institutions use the Spirit's gifts—*charisms*—with selfless as well as selfish intentions. Similarly, they use them to serve as well as manipulate audiences. Augustine of Hippo long ago wrote the first treatise (*De Doctrina Christiana*, 4, 4), defending Christian orators' ethical use of emotional as well as intellectual styles of communication. Yet dangers remain when Christians confuse humanly created communication styles with God-given charisma. Evangelical leader Charles Colson writes, "We seem to think we need a big para-church organization or a well-known celebrity in order to accomplish anything for the kingdom of God. As a result, the church has elevated popular pastors, ministry leaders, and televangelists to the dubious pedestal of fame—only to watch many topple in the winds of power, influence, and adulation."[40]

Most evangelical media stars probably believe that they are humbly and altruistically ministering to their broadcast congregations. Whether or not they are doing so is not for them alone to determine, however, for personal motivation can be clouded and hidden. Just as television can create new show-business stars overnight, it can establish religious authorities in only a few years or even months. Suddenly a televangelist is perceived as a spokesperson for all of Christianity or evangelicalism. Then he or she is quoted by the news media and appears on the talk shows. He or she may establish a political organization to further influence public life and to enhance his or her prestige with the media and supporting church members. These temptations to misuse such public notoriety can be just as strong as the desire to use it to serve others.

Conclusion

American culture and media together promote cults of personality. In American culture, where media are largely show business and people are more interested in the future than the past, television especially provides a favorable climate for religious personality cults. Perhaps American media theorist and cultural critic Neil Postman is correct that God does not play well on television—that God comes out as "second banana."[41] Surely a few talented televangelists do seem to have the kind of authority-winning charisma that many local pastors lack, but this hardly suggests that even the most popular media ministers cannot lead people to God, or that all non-televised ministers will. Moreover, traditional network television is beginning to run its course in American culture. Online media are creating many new venues for religious communicators to build audiences. Cyberspace's combination of media—aural, textual, visual—might be the next venue for the rise of powerful, mediated personal cults. In ancient Rome, some local religious cults remained strong in spite of new cults proclaimed by the Senate. Mass-mediated culture never quite eclipses vernacular culture. There is something genuine about in-person faith communities that withstands scrutiny and probably equips rank-and-file believers to hold evangelical media stars accountable for their excesses and hopeful about their potential to represent the evangelical faith accurately to the Church and to the broader society.

Notes

1. Daniel Burke, "Media Priest's Conversion Strains Ecumenical Ties," *Christian Century*, June 30, 2009, 18.

2. The concept of "cult of personality" or "personality cult" was widely employed by scholars and popular writers in the twentieth century to describe those individuals who use media to create movements of followers. For example, the election of Barack Obama as U.S. president in 2008 elicited many such analyses of his rise to power. One prominent example is Jerome R. Corsi, *The Obama Nation: Leftist Politics and the Cult of Personality* (New York: Threshold, 2008). The academic concept of an individual personality cult as a socioreligious phenomenon probably came originally from Emile Durkheim's works, especially *The Elementary Forms of the Religious Life* (1912; repr., New York: Free Press, 1995).

I am not using the word *cult* to mean a modern religious and especially quasi-Christian personality cult as a close-knit group that recruits unwitting members, employs mind control, and promotes false beliefs. I am using it more sociologically to refer to a group of devoted followers of a particular person whom the group believes has a special relationship with God and is thereby worthy of following. One of the few sources to address this topic directly in the context of modern American evangelicalism is Richard Quebedeaux, *By What Authority: The Rise of Personality Cults in American Christianity* (San Francisco: Harper and Row, 1982). For how American evangelicals have used personality-oriented movements and institutions, see Joel A. Carpenter, *Revive Us Again: The Reawakening of American Fundamentalism* (New York: Oxford University Press, 1997).

3. Quentin J. Schultze, *Christianity and the Mass Media in America: Toward a Democratic Accommodation* (East Lansing, MI: Michigan State University Press, 2003), 54–57.

4. Quoted in Jennet Conant, "Billionaire Bashing," *Newsweek*, May 30, 1988, 67.

5. See "TV Ministry: Not Just for Big-Name Preachers Anymore," *Christian Century*, July 24, 2007, 17.

6. John MacArthur, "A Challenge for Christian Communicators," *Master's Seminary Journal* 17, no. 1 (Spring 2006): 9.

7. Dick Staub, *The Culturally Savvy Christian: A Manifesto for Deepening Faith and Enriching Popular Culture in an Age of Christianity-Lite* (San Francisco: Jossey-Bass, 2008).

8. Safara A. Witmer, *Education with Dimension: The Bible College Story* (Manhasset, NY: Channel, 1962), 36.

9. Carpenter, *Revive Us Again*, 129.

10. David L. Clark, "Miracles for a Dime: From Chautauqua Tent to Radio Station with Sister Aimee," *California History* 57 (1978–1979): 354–363. See also Matthew Avery Sutton, *Aimee Semple McPherson and the Resurrection of Christian America* (Cambridge, MA: Harvard University Press, 2007).

11. Robert C. Toll, *The Entertainment Machine: American Show Business in the Twentieth Century* (New York: Oxford University Press, 1982), 54–55.

12. Quoted in J. Elwin Wright, *The Old Fashioned Revival Hour* (Boston: Fellowship, 1940), 196.

13. Schultze, *Christianity and the Mass Media in America*, 142–155.

14. Nathan O. Hatch, *The Democratization of American Christianity* (New Haven, CT: Yale University Press, 1988). See also Quentin J. Schultze, "Keeping the Faith: American Evangelicals and the Mass Media," in *American Evangelicals and the Mass Media*, ed. Quentin J. Schultze (Grand Rapids, MI: Zondervan, 1990), 23–45.

15. Quebedeaux, *By What Authority*.

16. David Edwin Harrell Jr., *Oral Roberts: An American Life* (San Francisco: Harper and Row, 1985). See also Oral Roberts, *The Call* (New York: Avon, 1971).

17. Jerry Falwell, *Strength for the Journey* (New York: Simon and Schuster, 1987).

18. Dennis Voskuil, *Mountains into Goldmines: Robert Schuller and the Gospel of Success* (Grand Rapids, MI: Eerdmans, 1983).

19. David Edwin Harrell Jr., *Pat Robertson: A Personal, Political and Religious Portrait* (San Francisco: Harper and Row, 1987). Also see Pat Robertson, *Shout It from the Housetops* (South Plainfield, NJ: Bridge, 1972).

20. Charles E. Shepard, *Forgiven: The Rise and Fall of Jim Bakker and the PTL Ministry* (New York: Atlantic Monthly, 1989). Also see Jim Bakker, *You Can Make It!* (Charlotte, NC: PTL Enterprises, 1983).

21. Some media have reported over the years that Robert Schuller is not an evangelical. Although his televised sermons and books do not appear adequately evangelical to some observers, he is officially a pastor of the Reformed Church in America, which certainly has evangelical roots. Therefore, I include him as an evangelical leader. Clearly he appeals to far more than evangelical viewers, but so do many other televangelists. Norman Vincent Peale, Schuller's mentor, was a member of the same denomination.

22. Malcolm Muggeridge, *Christ and the Media* (Grand Rapids, MI: Eerdmans, 1971). See also Virginia Stem Owens, *The Total Image: Or Selling Jesus in the Modern Age* (Grand Rapids, MI: Eerdmans, 1980).

23. Malcolm Boyd, "Communicating the Gospel through Commercial Media," *Encounter* 18 (Autumn 1957): 409.

24. John S. Kater Jr., *Christians on the Right* (New York: Seabury, 1982), 106.

25. Quentin J. Schultze, "Evangelical Radio and the Rise of the Electronic Church 1921–1948," *Journal of Broadcasting & Electronic Media* 32, no. 3 (1988): 294. See also Stewart M. Hoover, *Mass Media Religion* (Beverly Hills, CA: Sage, 1988).

26. Kenneth S. Kantzer, "The Charismatics among Us," *Christianity Today*, February 22, 1980, 25–26.

27. See William Martin, *With God on Our Side: The Rise of the Religious Right in America* (New York: Broadway, 1996).

28. Pierre Babin, "The Spirituality of Media People," *The Way*, Supplement 57 (August 1986): 47.

29. Joseph Ferullo, "Flacking in the Fields of the Lord," *Channels*, March 1987, 45–48.

30. Robin Lovin, "Papal Witness: A Philosopher Pope in a Media Age," *Christian Century*, August 16, 2005, 45.

31. A different interpretation of the importance of the South in contemporary evangelicalism and televangelism is offered in Grant Wacker, "Uneasy in Zion: Evangelicals in Postmodern Society," in *Evangelicalism and Modern America*, ed. George Marsden (Grand Rapids, MI: Eerdmans, 1984), 17–28.

32. Todd V. Lewis, "Charisma and Media Evangelists: An Explication and Model of Communication Influence," *Southern Communication Journal* 54 (Fall 1988): 97.

33. Christine McCarthy McMorris, "People Who Loved Tammy Faye," *Religion in the News* 10 (Summer–Fall 2007): 17–18.

34. Joseph Bayly, "The Nouveaux Famous," *Eternity*, September 1985, 88.

35. Kenneth L. Woodward, "Following Dad to the Pulpit," *Newsweek*, February 8, 1988, 62–63.

36. One possible exception is Joel Osteen, who "inherited" a 5,000-member church when his minister father died. However, the father's ministry was not well established as a media ministry. Son Joel himself turned the local church into a major media ministry while simultaneously increasing the size of the congregation to about 40,000. See Julia Duin, "Osteen Still the Name Leaders Know: Picking Up Where His Father Left Off, Minister Spreads Faith," *Washington Times*, September 5, 2008, A5. In the case of *Day of Discovery*, the television ministry of Radio Bible Class (now RBC Ministries), son Martin De Haan became the principal replacement for his father, Richard. But the overall ministry is so oriented toward literature as well as the electronic media that the succession to Martin was not really a test of a television ministry.

37. Anna Wilde Mathews, "Eternally Popular, This Radio Preacher Actually Died in '88," *Wall Street Journal*, December 19, 2002, A1.

38. Richard Kieckhefer, "The Cult of Saints as Popular Religion," *Explor* 7 (Fall 1984): 42.

39. See, for example, James Breig, "Catholics Should Boycott TV Preachers," *U.S. Catholic*, May 1984, 12–17.

40. Charles Colson, "The Celebrity Illusion," *Christianity Today*, December 11, 1987, 72.

41. Neil Postman, *Amusing Ourselves to Death: Public Discourse in the Age of Show Business* (New York: Viking, 1985), 117.

Chapter 9

How Evangelicals Are Covered in the News: From Curiosity through Obscurity to the Mainstream

Judith M. Buddenbaum

In a survey of top officials from American Christian denominations, all were equally harsh in their evaluations of news media performance. The average grade for news coverage was a D; for religion news, the average grade was even lower, D–.[1] However, leaders from mainline churches and from evangelical churches gave significantly different reasons for such low grades. For mainline churches, the primary problem was with a lack of substantive, hard news about religion. Among evangelical leaders the desire was for a softer kind of news promoting faith and good works.[2]

Indeed, evangelicals over the past half-century see themselves at war with a secular media whose areligious and anti-Christian journalists "hide the truth" by engaging in "censorship of Christian principles and ideas."[3] For their opinion of how news should be, many evangelicals cite or allude to Marvin Olasky's *Prodigal Press*.[4]

Although the image of today's news media as wholly secular and journalists as anti-religion is something of a myth,[5] Olasky is correct in saying that mainstream media, which by design serve a religiously diverse audience, no longer report news from a Christian perspective as once was the norm. Evangelicals have sometimes suffered as a result of the way the news media have described them, but that was as true in colonial America as it is today. The review in this chapter of almost 300 years of news coverage of evangelicals shows that the media have, on balance, been more evangelicals' friend than their foe.

Evangelicals Become News (Eighteenth Century)

In the United States, evangelicalism, as a distinct form of Protestant Christianity, got its start during the era of revivalism and religious fervor known as the Great Awakening. George Whitefield made it news.[6]

While still in England, Whitefield had learned from the Church of England's hostile reaction to his extemporaneous preaching style and his emphasis on an experiential, emotional commitment over doctrine and the sacraments that even negative attention "built audiences as effectively as word of mouth."[7] Therefore, in London in 1737, while awaiting clearance for a mission trip to the colonies, he capitalized on the controversy he had stirred up by rushing into print "everything he had."[8] Announcements for the new publications made their way into American newspapers, where they piqued curiosity. En route to the New World, he kept a journal filled with accounts of divine providence and successful evangelization onboard the ship and made arrangements for its publication. Benjamin Franklin published his books; news of their availability made their way from Franklin's *Pennsylvania Gazette* to newspapers throughout the colonies.[9]

By the time Whitefield began preaching in Georgia and South Carolina, he was already news. According to Isaiah Thomas, the United States' first journalism historian and one-time printer-editor of the *Massachusetts Spy*, "newspapers were filled with paragraphs of information respecting him [Whitefield], or with pieces of animated disputation pro or con."[10]

Franklin published Whitefield's sermons, sometimes on the front page of his newspaper. He also accepted letters and commentaries from both Whitefield's supporters and his opponents,[11] which was uncommon. In colonial America, most editors saw their papers as fulfilling a religious function. Therefore, they practiced a kind of religious journalism through which they interpreted news as signs of God's favor or disfavor. In commentaries and letters, they gave favorable attention to religious and political issues that they found God-pleasing; positions with which they disagreed were mentioned in their papers only as an excuse to rebut them. In Boston, the quintessential multi-media town, that kind of one-sided coverage was intense and sometimes nasty. While papers such as the *New England Weekly Journal* praised Whitefield for his message of hope and salvation, the *Boston Evening Post* labeled Whitefield and his followers fanatics, disturbers of the peace, and a threat to true religion.[12]

Both the publicity and the notoriety Whitefield created for himself with the help of the media spilled over to others associated with him and the revival movement. Papers from South Carolina to Boston portrayed Methodists as buffoons and their converts as insane; they routinely accused Methodists of everything from "ruining the wool trade" to "killing and maiming people because of their beliefs."[13]

Whitefield did not help matters any when in April 1741 he accused faculty and students at Harvard and Yale of heresy. The outcry from even his supporters was so fierce that Whitefield, who had already set sail for England, found himself compelled to issue an apology, which the *Boston Gazette & Weekly Journal* published on March 16, 1742, but the controversy continued in the Boston media.[14] Upon Whitefield's return to Boston in 1745, controversy again flared up but quickly died down as area papers turned their attention to news of French and Indian activity in the area.[15]

Although there was a brief flurry of coverage of Whitefield's 1770 death in Newburyport, Massachusetts,[16] news of evangelicalism as a religion largely disappeared from newspapers until after the War of 1812. Evangelical views did, however, appear in newspapers, most notably when letters and essays in strong support of religious freedom from Baptist Rhode Island became part of the media discourse on adoption of the First Amendment.[17]

Evangelicalism's Golden Age (Nineteenth Century)

After the War of 1812, evangelicals, responding to the perceived threats posed by a seemingly lawless frontier and the industrialization that lured Irish Catholic immigrants to the United States's burgeoning industrial cities, formed missionary, Bible, and tract societies in an effort to make a Christian nation in their own image. Their efforts to place a Bible and a regular supply of religious reading material in every American home did create a Protestant Christian culture, but the religious material they distributed could not satisfy the appetite for reading their strategy fostered.[18]

To satisfy that appetite, a new kind of newspaper emerged on the scene in 1835.[19] In contrast to the existing, subscription-only mainstream papers that provided a relatively educated and affluent audience with a steady stream of views in the form of letters and essays, these new newspapers initially catered to a working-class and immigrant audience by giving them stories of everyday life developed through active news gathering for just one penny an issue. When James Gordon Bennett Sr. added religion to the mix of stories of everyday life in his *New York Herald*, he made news of religion quite different from what it had been.[20]

As a Scottish Catholic in a predominantly Protestant United States, Bennett covered religion from the standpoint of an interested outside observer. Instead of writing to promote a religion or a religious viewpoint, Bennett wrote about religious behaviors and their likely impact on Christians and non-Christians alike. Bennett covered and sometimes skewered his own Catholic Church, Protestant churches, and their clergy for their excesses, their ethical lapses, political meddling, and outright criminal behavior.[21]

In shedding a spotlight on evangelicals, Bennett named clergy caught up in adulterous affairs and told readers about a revival where "a little backsliding" by "one of the most immediate brothers, with a dearly beloved sister" left her "burthened with a little responsibility."[22] Bennett kept a wary eye on the temperance movement, which he suspected of being inspired less by religious zeal than by anti-Catholic and anti-immigrant sentiments. He decried the mixing of religion and politics, aiming some of his harshest criticism at Protestants who used the stridently anti-Catholic sermons of the Reverend Lyman Beecher and other Protestant clergy to justify arson at a convent in Massachusetts and the anti-Catholic riots in Philadelphia that gave rise to the Know Nothing movement.[23]

With Bennett at the helm, religion news in the *Herald* was always a mixture of the bad and the good.[24] Along with the sometimes quite biting criticism he leveled at all religions, Bennett provided at least as many neutral-to-favorable accounts of their religious activities. His May 23, 1836, report filled with scene-setting description and fact-laden details about the anniversary meeting of the Bible Society became a model for subsequent coverage about all the anniversary meetings of Bible, tract, and missionary organizations. By 1838 Bennett had also begun sending his reporters out to report on Sunday sermons. In between those regularly occurring features, Bennett reported on evangelists such as Charles Finney, told readers of new clergy in the area, and gave them colorful descriptions of Millerites awaiting the end of the world, of Baptist revivals, and of Methodist camp meetings.[25]

Although none of Bennett's contemporaries in the newspaper business considered him a role model, they quickly recognized the appeal religion news had for many readers. By the 1850s, Horace Greeley was priding himself on giving readers of his *New York Tribune* the kind of timely, complete, and colorful stories about revivals that Bennett pioneered. Around the same time, the *New York Times* began setting aside space in its Monday edition for stories about Sunday sermons at major Protestant churches. By the end of the century, weekly church pages for stories about local and usually Protestant religious events and people became standard. Although most nineteenth-century newspapers would cover evangelical scandals as the occasion demanded, few chose to raise the kind of questions Bennett raised about their involvement in politics or their positions on burning issues of the day. Both on and off the church pages, nineteenth-century newspapers were generally quite deferential to and supportive of evangelical interests.[26]

During the first two decades of the twentieth century, newspapers found and labeled Pentecostalism a "weird babel of tongues."[27] They gave generally favorable coverage to the social gospel movement,[28] but they paid far more attention to evangelicals and evangelical causes.[29] When, in March 1900, the *Topeka (Kansas) Daily Capital* gave the Reverend Charles M. Sheldon freedom to produce a newspaper "as Jesus would do," some papers mocked his efforts, but other papers from coast to coast gave the experiment front-page coverage. Although most ultimately described the "Jesus newspaper" a failure, coverage turned it into a cultural phenomenon[30] in much the same way newspapers made celebrities of evangelists Dwight L. Moody[31] and Billy Sunday.[32]

Evangelicalism's Loss of Influence (1918–1975)

By the time Congress passed the Eighteenth Amendment, some evangelicals had come to accept the teachings of "modernist" clergy who argued for taking into account findings from science when interpreting scripture. Others embraced "fundamentalism" with its insistence on a literal reading of the Bible.[33] Complaints from fundamentalist evangelicals about the appointment in 1918 of Harry Emerson Fosdick (a Baptist and leading voice in the modernist camp) as preaching pastor at First Presbyterian Church in New York City initiated what fundamentalists proclaimed a "battle for the Bible."

With controversy and conflict now standard news values, New York City newspapers found it impossible to ignore the battle brewing in their midst. Regional papers picked up the story as national conventions of Presbyterians and Baptists in their cities debated the question of whether modernists, fundamentalists, or both should be credentialed as ministers.[34] The story went nationwide when, in the context of the meeting of the General Assembly of the Presbyterian Church, the new *Time* magazine devoted the religion page in its first issue to the growing fundamentalist-modernist divide. Although that May 19, 1923, religion page clearly spelled out each side's position, the presentation seemingly agreed with Fosdick's own negative response to the question he raised in his "Shall the Fundamentalists Win?" sermon. In the June 4 issue, *Time* told readers the Presbyterian Church condemned Fosdick but also rejected William Jennings Bryan's anti-evolution platform. Under the headline "Science Serves God," the magazine quoted extensively from what it called "A great and glorious manifesto of liberalism" signed by "Secretaries Hoover and Davis, and by 40 other distinguished Americans of various denominations."[35]

However, evangelicals were apparently not among those signatories. Amid growing evangelical sentiment that science and religion were incompatible, the Baptist State Mission Board in Kentucky passed a resolution calling for a ban on teaching evolution in public schools. With passage of the Butler Act in 1925, Tennessee became one of the first states to ban that teaching.[36]

A May 11, 1925, front-page story in the *Nashville (Tennessee) Banner* told readers of John Thomas Scopes's arrest for teaching evolution in his biology class at the Dayton, Tennessee, high school and American Civil Liberties Union plans to challenge the law on constitutional grounds. Newspapers in Tennessee both defended the law and castigated Dayton for staging a publicity stunt. From there, the Associated Press picked up and spread the word. When Clarence Darrow signed on as lead attorney for the defendant—and for the modernist position—and Bryan agreed to argue for the state—and the fundamentalists—newspaper reporters, radiomen, and newsreel crews descended on the tiny town of Dayton. Chicago radio station WGN ("World's Greatest News") transmitted live broadcasts from the courthouse via special telephone lines to Chicago.[37]

Although editorially the *New York Times* favored the modernists, it routinely published the full text of Bryan's courtroom speeches alongside those by the defense.[38] The *Times* and other northern papers picked up columns from the *Arkansas Gazette* in which Tennessee legislator John W. Butler explained the rationale behind the law that gave rise to the court case.[39] The *Baltimore Sun* carried stories by Frank R. Kent which, though marred with some stereotypical language, created a generally favorable image of a religious and social culture alien to his Northern, urban audience.[40]

However, in spite of some efforts at balance, media coverage was generally biased against fundamentalists and their cause.[41] Over time, H. L. Mencken's columns for the *Baltimore Sun*, characterizing fundamentalists as backward hicks too uneducated to understand science, had the most impact.[42] Even though Bryan and the fundamentalists won their battle in court, conventional wisdom has it that the media proclaimed the trial the "fundamentalists' last stand" and lost interest in them.[43]

As the fundamentalist-modernist controversy played out in the media, newspapers and magazines gave Pentecostal evangelist Aimee Semple McPherson the kind of sympathetic coverage she courted. In 1926, her tale of having been kidnapped and held hostage in Mexico vied for front-page newspaper coverage with stories about the trial for murder of the Reverend J. Frank Norris, a nationally known Southern fundamentalist leader and pastor of the 5,000-seat First Baptist Church in Fort Worth, Texas.[44]

Two years later, evangelicals were again in the news, this time for their opposition to the Democratic Party's decision to nominate Alfred E. Smith for president. Both during the nominating convention and the election campaign, the *New York Times* and other Northern papers carried stories saying that Baptists throughout the South opposed Smith, partly because of his opposition to prohibition but mostly because of his Roman Catholic faith. But so widespread was anti-Catholic sentiment then that there was little negative commentary directed at Baptists. With newspapers now striving for balanced coverage, newspapers sometimes included in the same story both favorable comments from Smith's supporters about his "admirable" record as New York's governor and evangelical contentions that a Catholic president would use the power of the presidency to impose the Vatican's agenda on Americans.[45]

Over the next half-century (1928–1976), evangelicals always got their share of coverage on church pages,[46] but serious attention to them by mainstream media was, at best, sporadic. To some extent that lack of attention can be attributed to media bias; however, it was also a case of "out of sight, out of mind." By the 1920s, many evangelicals had made a principled decision based on their end-times beliefs to devote their time to saving souls before it was too late rather than waste resources trying to fix an unfixable, sinful society.[47] With their withdrawal from the public arena, mainstream reporters turned to the Federal Council of Churches (FCC), the forerunner of today's National Council of Churches in Christ, and its member churches as the most readily available sources for religion news and commentary. Reliance on Federal Council members as news sources made it both easy and quite logical to accept the FCC view that it and its member churches were the mainline while evangelicals were a disruptive, schismatic offshoot.

Over time, both the FCC self-image and Mencken's stereotypical portrayals of fundamentalists found their way into occasional media profiles of evangelicalism. Evangelicals' religious enthusiasm became equated with neurosis, their Biblical literalism with authoritarianism of the fascist-communist ilk.[48] Time-Life publications portrayed fundamentalists as "doomsday-preaching sects;" *Newsweek* lumped them together with "California cults."[49]

With evangelicals neither actively defending themselves from attack nor publicly promoting their own interests, it became easy for the media to treat the deep theological divide between them and the modernists as a relic from the past. In the media, the half-century of relative evangelical absence from the public arena became portrayed as one of ever-increasing ecumenism. In this era of consensus religion during which mainstream media began describing the United States as a Judeo-Christian nation,[50] evangelicals got a boost after William Randolph Hearst met Billy Graham, found him impressive, and ordered his reporters at the *Los Angeles Examiner* to "puff Graham." *Examiner* reporters responded with lavish attention to Graham's 1949 Los Angeles revival. The Associated Press picked up the story from Hearst's paper; *Life* magazine featured Graham's Los Angeles crusade in its November 21, 1949, issue.[51]

Although neither the positive attention that made Graham the benign face of evangelicalism nor the occasional negative, stereotypical story were the result of evangelical efforts to garner attention, the mainstream media quite willingly covered them whenever they made news. In 1960, for example, when Baptist hostility toward a Catholic for president resurfaced, the media reported that most evangelicals, including Graham, opposed John F. Kennedy out of concern that a Catholic president's allegiance to the Vatican would undermine the wall of separation between church and state that guaranteed their religious freedom.[52] With voters showing willingness to entertain the possibility of a Catholic president, evangelicals found their position no longer had the firm support of mainline denominations. Neither could evangelicals count on the kind of uncritical media attention to their arguments they had enjoyed in 1928. When the Reverend Norman Vincent Peale, a popular television personality and syndicated columnist, voiced his opposition to Kennedy on religious grounds, the *Philadelphia Inquirer* cancelled his column.[53]

During the tumultuous decade following Kennedy's assassination, television networks and Northern newspapers generally supported Southern black evangelicals, their Baptist clergy leaders Martin Luther King Jr. and Ralph Abernathy, and the Northern Jews and mainline Protestants who joined them in their fight for civil rights.[54] The overwhelmingly hostile views of many Southern white evangelicals toward the civil rights movement[55] were conspicuously absent from network television newcasts and Northern newspapers. Also below the media radar were their equally hostile views about the counterculture movement, Vietnam War protesters, and women's rights, especially after opposition to the Equal Rights Amendment got mixed in with views on abortion following the U.S. Supreme Court's *Roe v. Wade* decision.[56]

Evangelicalism's Return to Prominence (1976–Present)

Having mistaken evangelicals' relative inactivity in the public arena for acceptance of the kind of consensus religion touted through media coverage of ecumenism, the mainstream media were caught off guard when a religion they assumed was dormant, if not dead, suddenly became news during the 1976 presidential election campaign. That race between Republican Gerald Ford and Democrat Jimmy Carter was the first presidential election to pit two evangelicals against each other, but it was Carter's references to his faith that sent journalists scrambling, with mixed results, to explain what he meant when he unabashedly identified himself as a "born-again Christian."

During the initial flurry of coverage, NBC anchorman John Chancellor faced criticism from evangelicals for rather ineloquently attempting to reassure the approximately two-thirds of all Americans for whom being "born again" had no real meaning: "By the way, we've checked this out. Being 'born again' is not a bizarre mountaintop experience. It's something common to many millions of Americans—particularly if you're Baptist."[57] The media sometimes treated evangelicalism as if it were exotic, but by the end of the campaign, most had come to see it as a real and genuinely American kind of Christianity. An October 25 *Newsweek* cover story proclaiming 1976 "The Year of the Evangelicals" told readers, "Evangelicalism is the religion you get when you 'get' religion."[58] A month later, however, both Carter and the mainstream media again took heat from evangelicals—Carter for agreeing to an interview with *Playboy* in which he both used some rather salty language and admitted to having committed "lust in my heart," and the media for picking up, trivializing, and sensationalizing the story.[59] Once Carter became president, his faith generally merited media attention only on those occasions when he chose to teach a Sunday School class. However, evangelicalism as a religion remained in the news throughout his presidency.

During the Carter years, the media produced a flurry of stories about the budding televangelism ministries of Jim Bakker, Rex Humbard, Robert Schuler, and Jimmy Swaggart. Attention to M. G. "Pat" Robertson, both as a personality and as the driving force behind the creation of a religious cable network, was particularly heavy.[60] While some stories told about evangelical worship and ministry, many more focused on concerns raised by clergy from both mainline and evangelical churches about the effect of the so-called "electronic church" on Sunday worship attendance.[61] As both personal experience and research evidence quieted those fears, coverage dwindled, flaring up locally only when a new television ministry entered the scene or when an established televangelist did or said something deemed outrageous.[62]

The media also revisited the fundamentalist-modernist debate in 1976 and again in 1980, but this time the battle between the two camps played out within the Southern Baptist Convention (SBC). When the fundamentalist Bailey Smith emerged victorious as the denomination's president in 1980, coverage was particularly intense.[63] The media reported both Smith's comments that Jews have "funny-looking noses" and that God does not hear the prayers of Jews, alongside allegations of voter irregularities at the SBC convention in Houston.[64] At the same time, mainstream media downplayed the contention of SBC moderates that fundamentalists' insistence that all Southern Baptists accept a belief in an inerrant and literally true Bible subverted the traditional, historic Baptist faith that emphasized individual and congregational autonomy in matters of faith and doctrine. Instead, they framed the issue in fundamentalist terms as a "battle for the Bible" just as they had done during the Scopes trial. In the mainstream media, biblical literalism became the orthodox position.[65]

That SBC battle over the theological direction the denomination would take became the most frequently covered story by religion writers at the *New York Times*.[66] However, there were two other evangelical stories among the most frequently reported religion stories in the 1980s: an attempted boycott of television for airing "unwholesome" content engineered by the conservative Methodist minister Donald Wildmon and his Coalition for Better Television and the arrival on the political scene of the Jerry Falwell–led Moral Majority.[67]

The media first paid attention to Falwell in April 1979 when he staged an I Love America rally.[68] Falwell chastised the media for underestimating attendance at that Washington rally and a subsequent Washington for Jesus rally and also for covering the demonstrations as political events instead of

Rev. Jerry Falwell (front left), and Phyllis Schlafly (to his right), head of Stop ERA, stand during the singing of patriotic songs on Tuesday, May 6, 1980, at an "I Love America" rally organized by Rev. Falwell. (AP Photo.)

as outpourings of religious fervor.[69] By then evangelicals had already created a network of para-church organizations intent on undoing the political and cultural developments of the 1960s.[70] The most visible of those organizations, which collectively became known as the New Christian Right, were the Religious Roundtable, Christian Voice, and the Moral Majority.[71]

In the earliest and still one of the most thorough examinations of media coverage of evangelical activism during the 1980 presidential election campaign, Echo Ellen Fields found the media covered the New Christian Right the same way they previously had covered the left-wing Students for a Democratic Society.[72] The media marginalized the New Christian Right by labeling it as "extremist" and by portraying its evangelical supporters as comprising a small, fringe religious subculture: homogeneous, uniformly white, mostly rural or working class.[73] In reporting on evangelicals' issue concerns, the media trivialized them by using leaders' most absurd, militant, and extreme statements such as those by Bailey Smith concerning Jews.[74] Although coverage was balanced in the technical sense of giving voice to both evangelicals and their opponents, it rendered evangelicals suspect by presenting issue concerns in simplistic, black-and-white terms: *against* abortion, homosexuality, drugs, pornography, affirmative action and school busing, big government, sex education, and welfare spending; *for* family values, morality, Israel, and defense spending.[75] Hypocrisy became a common theme in the coverage through the use of quotes provided by Catholic and mainline Protestant leaders who speculated that evangelicals were more driven by desire for political power than by true religious zeal. Their comments pointed out the irony that evangelicals, who had opposed a Catholic for president out of fear he would use government power for church purposes, now seemed to want a president and legislators who would use the government for evangelical purposes.[76]

Although that kind of coverage delegitimized the New Christian Right, Fields found the media also made the movement appear powerful, first by turning Falwell into a celebrity spokesperson for it and then by treating him as king-maker through coverage of his appearance at the Republican National Convention and his meetings with would-be presidential candidate Ronald Reagan.[77] Later, coverage of Reagan's appearance at a meeting of the Religious Roundtable cemented the image of the movement as a viable political force. As the election neared, the media increasingly accepted Falwell's representation of his movement as "mainstream."[78] With polling showing that Southern white evangelicals would for the first time vote solidly Republican, the mainstream media framed the evangelical vote for Reagan as symbolic of a broad "rightward shift" in U.S. politics.[79]

A slight post-election decline in media attention to the New Christian Right led Fields to speculate that the media career of the New Christian Right had run its course.[80] Within a few years, the organizations of the New Christian Right disappeared, only to be replaced by other evangelical para-church organizations. With evangelicals remaining politically active, network television newscasts continued to mention them twice as often as mainline Protestants,[81] and media coverage of them steadily increased.[82]

Outside the political arena, the media devoted far more attention to the 1987–1988 televangelism scandals involving Bakker and Swaggart than they did to the more long-standing and widespread pedophile priest scandal that rocked the Roman Catholic Church at the end of the century.[83] Apart from coverage of other televangelists and prominent clergy caught committing sexual or fiscal improprieties, there were also slight increases in mentions of evangelicals in 1993 during the confrontation between the government and the Branch Davidians at Waco, Texas, as reporters mixed Branch Davidians' Adventist religion with "evangelicalism" and "fundamentalism," and again in 1999 when Y2K coverage mixed evangelical end-time beliefs together with those of doomsday cults and Christian Identity survivalists.[84]

As a general rule, however, coverage was always higher in election years as Republicans sought endorsement from evangelical leaders by touting their faith and their support for the issue positions that evangelicals established as "Christian" during the 1980 election campaign.[85] It was highest in 1988 when televangelist Robertson made a bid for the Republican presidential nomination and Jesse Jackson, a Baptist minister, entered the race on the Democrat side, and again in 1992 when President Bill Clinton's apparent support for gays in the military led to an outpouring of evangelical opposition.[86]

For the most part, political coverage followed the pattern set during the 1980 presidential election. The media sometimes marginalized evangelicals through stereotyping, as in a February 6, 1993, story in which the *Washington Post* described television evangelists' followers as "largely poor, uneducated, and easy to command."[87] The media also continued to trivialize them by using extreme quotes from evangelicals, most notably 2008 Republican vice-presidential candidate Sarah Palin.[88] Reports of sex scandals involving both evangelical politicians and clergy reinforced and expanded the hypocrisy theme developed during the 1980 presidential election campaign.[89]

Across all media and all regions of the country, media coverage of evangelicals consistently skewed slightly negative,[90] especially on some topics such as the teaching of Creation Science in public schools.[91] Unfavorable coverage of evangelicals was always higher in opinion columns and letters to the editor than in news reports and feature stories; it was also higher in Western newspapers than in those in the South and Midwest, where evangelicalism is strong.[92] However, there were also some developments in news coverage that worked to evangelicals' advantage.

In response to evangelical complaints that *fundamentalist* is a derogatory term, reporters from all beats began avoiding that label as much as possible.[93] However, instead of replacing it with more precise denominational identifiers, as recommended by the Associated Press stylebook, they began referring even to those who had once proudly called themselves "fundamentalists" as "conservative Christians." Just as often, they used the "orthodox Christian" label evangelicals had began using as a self-identifier in the 1920s or referred to them simply as "Christian."[94]

Amid growing awareness of the importance of faith in American life, interview subjects were increasingly allowed to tell, without explanation or comment, about "walking with Jesus," "turning their lives over to Him," or about being "born again" in ways that made evangelicals appear ubiquitous. Television newscasts began showing athletes and survivors of accidents and disasters thanking God for their good fortune so often as to become almost a cliché.[95]

Much the same thing happened in newspapers as the old religion page, with its emphasis on local Protestant people and events, gave way to expanded multi-page sections devoted to religion, broadly understood to include all manner of faiths, spirituality, values, and ethics. Although evangelicals now found themselves competing for space not just against other Christians and the occasional Jew but with other world and alternative religions, the change made room for depth stories about all aspects of evangelical culture.[96] At the same time, the new emphasis on inclusivity in these expanded religion sections sometimes produced stories so lacking in specific religious labels that they could easily have appeared in some other section of the paper.[97] In fact, journalists from all mass media found and reported stories about evangelicals whom they referred to simply as Christian in ways that sometimes suggested all Americans are or should be Christian, and that all Christians are or should be evangelicals. Though no single media outlet covered everything and few provided sustained coverage of anything, collectively they brought to public attention all aspects of evangelical religion, culture, and practice.[98]

Stories produced by reporters from all beats about the faith life of evangelical entertainers, business leaders, athletes, and politicians created an aura of prominence and power that also infused political coverage. *Time* magazine, for example, devoted its February 7, 2005, cover story to the "25 most influential evangelicals." In the political arena, researchers found that during the 2004 presidential election campaign, elite newspapers' focus on political activism by white evangelicals caused them to miss the

Catholic activism that secured George W. Bush's re-election through its impact in key states such as Ohio. By focusing on evangelicals as "values voters" and abortion as the only "real" values issue, they also ignored or downplayed divisions within evangelicalism on issues and candidate positions as well as the extent to which "values-voters" across the religious and political spectrum were making faith-based voting decisions on a host of other issues.[99]

More narrowly focused studies of media coverage of issues closely associated with evangelicalism lend support to the assessment that media coverage has made it appear that evangelicals are the only true Christians, or at least the only ones whose views matter. In the decade following the U.S. Supreme Court's *Roe v. Wade* decision, news stories routinely included pro-choice comments from mainline Protestants and occasionally from spokespersons for other religions. However, over time secular organizations, most notably the National Organization for Women and Planned Parenthood, replaced religious voices on the pro-choice side in a way that lent support to evangelical contentions that their position is the only truly religious one.[100] That same pattern occurred in coverage of homosexuality and gay marriage. Opposition came from evangelicals; support for homosexuals came from gay-rights organizations or the American Civil Liberties Union. Religious rationales for inclusiveness were generally missing even in coverage of debates about homosexuality within mainline churches. On questions of cause and effect, the media gave as much or more credence to statements from the evangelical-allied Family Research Council and Focus on the Family as to ones from the medical profession.[101] Similarly, in covering the international push for religious freedom in all countries, the mainstream media relied on evangelical spokespersons and emphasized evangelical involvement while downplaying and sometimes ignoring equal activity by Jews and mainline Protestants.[102]

Conclusion

During the nearly three centuries evangelicalism has been a part of the American religious landscape, media coverage of evangelicals shifted from their beliefs to their behaviors as reporting from an outsider's perspective replaced religious insiders' letters and essays promoting their faith and beliefs. But whether the media practiced religious journalism as in the past or religion journalism as they do today, coverage has always been a mix of the negative and the positive. It has also been cyclical.

The periods of intense, seemingly hostile coverage of evangelicals that occurred both in colonial times and during the fundamentalist-modernist divide of the 1920s gave way to decades of relative inattention. Away from the limelight, evangelicals banded together to form para-church organizations whose activities once again returned them to the spotlight.

The shift from passive newsgathering to active reporting from an outsider's perspective that occurred in the 1830s when Bennett began covering religion news in his *New York Herald* meant evangelicals could no longer count on friendly editors to carry reports written from their perspective. However, the change to active reporting also created what was the one true golden age of media attention to evangelicals. In spite of some negative coverage of instances of sexual and fiscal improprieties and some harsh criticism of their forays into the politic arena, the media publicity given to evangelicals' Bible, missionary, and tract societies helped make evangelicalism the face of American religion for more than a century.

Similarly, in the late twentieth century it was evangelicals banding together in para-church organizations intent on changing the political and social landscape that again made them news after nearly half a century of media inattention, and that has kept them in the news. Attention to evangelicals during this modern era has skewed more negative than it did during their golden age, but as Whitefield realized nearly three centuries ago, even negative attention from the secular media is useful. The overwhelming amount of attention given to evangelicals and their interests relative to that afforded mainline Protestants and Roman Catholics has again created a media image of them as the dominant form of Christianity.

Notes

1. Judith M. Buddenbaum, *Reporting News about Religion: An Introduction for Journalists* (Ames: Iowa State University Press, 1998), xiii, 109–111.

2. For a comparison of the news preferences of conservative and more liberal Protestants, see Judith M. Buddenbaum, "News about Religion: A Readership Study," *Newspaper Research Journal* 3, no. 2 (1982): 7–17; Judith M. Buddenbaum and Stewart M. Hoover, "The Role of Religion in Public Attitudes toward Mass Media," in *Religion and Mass Media: Audiences and Adaptations*, eds. Daniel A. Stout and Judith M. Buddenbaum (Thousand Oaks, CA: Sage, 1996), 141–145.

3. Tim LaHaye, quoted in James Davison Hunter, *Culture Wars: The Struggle to Define America* (New York: Basic Books, 1991), 227.

4. Marvin Olasky, *The Prodigal Press: The Anti-Christian Bias of the American News Media* (Wheaton, IL: Crossway, 1988).

5. For an analysis of surveys assessing the religiosity of journalists, see Stewart M. Hoover, *Religion in the News: Faith and Journalism in American Public Discourse* (Thousand Oaks, CA: Sage, 1998), 56, 59–62.

6. David Copeland, "Religion and Colonial Newspapers," in *Media and Religion in American History*, ed. William David Sloan (Northport, AL: Vision, 2000), 62–66.

7. Harry S. Stout, "Religion, Communication and George Whitefield," in *Communication and Change in American Religious History*, ed. Leonard I. Sweet (Grand Rapids, MI: Eerdmans, 1993), 113.

8. Ibid.

9. Ibid., 116–117.

10. Isaiah Thomas, *The History of Printing in America* (1810, repr., New York: Weathervane, 1970), 568; see also Copeland, "Religion and Colonial Newspapers," 63.

11. Stout, "Religion, Communication and George Whitefield," 113.

12. Copeland, "Religion and Colonial Newspapers," 63–65.

13. Ibid., 65.

14. Judith M. Buddenbaum and Debra L. Mason, eds., *Readings on Religion as News* (Ames: Iowa State University Press, 2000), 32–36, 39.

15. Copeland, "Religion and Colonial Newspapers," 63.

16. Buddenbaum and Mason, *Readings on Religion as News*, 33.

17. Ibid., 44, 56, 63–65.

18. David Paul Nord, "The Evangelical Origins of Mass Media in America," in *Media and Religion in American History*, ed. William. David Sloan (Northport, AL: Vision, 2000), 68–70.

19. Judith M. Buddenbaum, "The Penny Press and the Birth of Modern Religion Journalism," in *Handbook of Religion and the News Media*, ed. Diane Winston (New York: Oxford University Press, forthcoming).

20. Ibid.

21. See also Judith M. Buddenbaum, " 'Judge . . . What Their Acts Will Justify': The Religion Journalism of James Gordon Bennett," *Journalism History* 14, nos. 2–3 (1987): 64–65.

22. "A Revival in Saratoga," *New York Herald*, May 15, 1840, 2, quoted in Buddenbaum and Mason, *Readings on Religion as News*, 98–100.

23. Buddenbaum, "The Penny Press," forthcoming.

24. Buddenbaum, " 'Judge . . . What Their Acts Will Justify,' " 56, 60–61, 63–65.

25. Buddenbaum, "The Penny Press," forthcoming.

26. Ibid.

27. "Weird Babel of Tongues," *Los Angeles Daily Times*, April 18, 1906, quoted in Buddenbaum and Mason, *Readings on Religion as News*, 175–176.

28. Ibid., 177–180.

29. Ibid., 161–174, 189–195.

30. Ibid., 149–160; Ron Rodgers, "'Goodness Isn't News': The Sheldon Edition and the National Conversation Defining Journalism's Responsibility to Society," *Journalism History* 34, no. 4 (Winter 2009): 204–215.

31. Bruce J. Evensen, *God's Man for the Gilded Age: Dwight L. Moody and the Rise of Modern Mass Evangelism* (New York: Oxford University Press, 2003), 72–188.

32. Barry Hankins, *Jesus and Gin: Evangelicalism, The Roaring Twenties, and Today's Culture Wars* (New York: Palgrave/Macmillan, 2010), 50–62.

33. Ibid., 64–67.

34. Ibid., 66–78.

35. "Science Serves God," *Time*, June 4, 1923, quoted in Buddenbaum and Mason, *Readings on Religion as News*, 201–203.

36. Hankins, *Jesus and Gin*, 90.

37. Edward J. Larson, *Summer for the Gods: The Scopes Trial and America's Continuing Debate over Science and Religion* (Cambridge, MA: Harvard University Press, 1997), 142.

38. Ibid., 180.

39. Buddenbaum and Mason, *Readings on Religion as News*, 198–199, 203–207.

40. Ibid., 198, 207–210.

41. See Edward Caudill, "The Roots of Bias: An Empiricist Press and Coverage of the Scopes Trial," *Journalism Monographs* 114 (July 1989): 1–37; and Olasky, "Journalists and the Great Monkey Trial," in *Media and Religion in American History*, ed. William David Sloan (Northport, AL: Vision, 2000), 223–229.

42. Buddenbaum and Mason, *Readings on Religion as News*, 198–199; Hankins, *Jesus and Gin*, 94–95, 101.

43. Larson, *Summer for the Gods*, 244.

44. Hankins, *Jesus and Gin*, 107–147.

45. Ibid., 187–211; Buddenbaum and Mason, *Readings on Religion as News*, 251–254.

46. Debra L. Mason, "God in the Ghetto: A Study of Religion News from 1944–1988," PhD dissertation, Ohio University, 1995, 99, 168.

47. Garry Wills, *Head and Heart: American Christianities* (New York: Penguin, 2007), 453.

48. Sean McCloud, *Making the American Religious Fringe: Exotics, Subversives and Journalists, 1955–1993* (Chapel Hill: The University of North Carolina Press, 2004), 25.

49. Ibid.

50. Buddenbaum and Mason, *Readings on Religion as News*, 225, 229–230.

51. Ibid., 230–233.

52. Edward J. Richter and Berton Dulce, *Religion and the Presidency: A Recurring Problem* (New York: Macmillan, 1962), 158–163.

53. Ibid., 167.

54. Wills, *Head and Heart*, 467–471.

55. Ibid., 469.

56. Ibid., 480–482.

57. Quoted in John Dart and Jimmy Allen, *Bridging the Gap: Religion and the News Media* (Nashville, TN: The Freedom Forum First Amendment Center at Vanderbilt University, 1993), 47.

58. Kenneth L. Woodward with John Barnes and Laurie Lisle, "Born Again!" *Newsweek*, October 25, 1976, 68.

59. Buddenbaum, *Religious Scandals*, 102–105. For the *Playboy* interview, see Robert Scheer, "*Playboy* Interview with Jimmy Carter," *Playboy*, November 1976, 63–86.

60. Echo Ellen Fields, "Preachers, Press, and Politics: The Media Career of a Conservative Social Movement," PhD dissertation, University of Oregon, Eugene, 1984, 123; Peter G. Horsfield, *Religious Television: The American Experience* (New York: Longman, 1984), 25–26.

61. Buddenbaum and Mason, *Readings on Religion as News*, 299–315.

62. Ibid., 300–302, 308–315.

63. Mark G. Borchert, "The Southern Baptist Controversy and the Press," in *Practicing Religion in the Age of the Media: Explorations in Media, Religion, and Culture*, eds. Stewart M. Hoover and Lynn Schofield Clark (New York: Columbia University Press, 2002), 190, 193–194.

64. Borchert, "The Southern Baptist Controversy and the Press," 189, 193.

65. Ibid., 191–195.

66. Buddenbaum, *Religion in the News*, 222, 231.

67. Ibid.

68. Fields, *Preachers, Press, and Politics*, 122.

69. Ibid., 127, 272–273.

70. Ibid., 127.

71. Ibid.

72. Ibid., 4. Fields adapted the methodology developed by Todd Gitlin in his study of Students for a Democratic Society in *The Whole World Is Watching* (Berkeley: University of California Press, 1980).

73. Ibid., 128–129, 205.

74. Ibid., 272.

75. Ibid., 205–218.

76. Ibid., 164–175.

77. Ibid., 124, 252–255, 273–275, 280.

78. Ibid., 274–275.

79. Ibid., 121.

80. Ibid., 124.

81. Judith M. Buddenbaum, "Network News Coverage of Religion," in *Channels of Belief: Religion and American Commercial Television*, ed. John P. Ferré (Ames: Iowa State University Press, 1990), 65.

82. Peter A. Kerr and Patricia Moy, "Newspaper Coverage of Fundamentalist Christians, 1980–2000," *Journalism and Mass Communication Quarterly* 79, no. 1 (2002): 58–59.

83. Buddenbaum, *Religious Scandals*, 30.

84. Kerr and Moy, "Newspaper Coverage of Fundamentalist Christians, 1980–2000," 57.

85. Ibid., 59; Mason, *God in the Ghetto*, 153, 155.

86. Ibid.

87. Quoted in Dart and Allen, *Bridging the Gap*, 20.

88. Melissa Proctor, "Picturing Palin's Faith," *Religion in the News* 11, no. 3 (2009): 8–9, 28.

89. Buddenbaum, *Religious Scandals*, 15–17.

90. Kerr and Moy, "Newspaper Coverage of Fundamentalist Christians, 1980–2000," 58, 60–61.

91. Justin D. Martin et al., "Journalism and the Debate over Origins: Newspaper Coverage of Intelligent Design," *Journal of Media and Religion* 5, no. 1 (2006): 49–62. See also Edward Caudill, "Intelligently Designed: Creationism's News Appeal," *Journalism and Mass Communication Quarterly* 87, no. 1 (2010): 84–89.

92. Kerr and Moy, 59–60, 62; Peter A. Kerr, "The Framing of Fundamentalist Christians: Network Television News, 1980–2000," *Journal of Media and Religion* 2, no. 4 (2003): 203–206.

93. Dart and Allen, *Bridging the Gap*, 29.

94. Ibid., See also Fred Vultee et al., "Faith and Values: Journalism and the Critique of Religion Coverage of the 1990s," *Journal of Media and Religion* 9, no. 3 (2010): 157.

95. Dart and Allen, *Bridging the Gap*, 33; Vultee et al., "Faith and Values," 159–162.

96. Buddenbaum and Mason, *Readings on Religion as News*, 345–350.

97. Vultee et al., 153–154.

98. For analyses of some stories of this kind, see Dart and Allen, *Bridging the Gap*, 20–21; Thomas Hambrick-Stowe, "Left Behind at the Box Office," *Religion in the News* 4, no. 1 (2001): 23–24; Christine McMorris, "What Would Jesus Drive?" *Religion in the News* 6, no. 1 (2003): 19–21; Andrew Walsh, "Men in Green," *Religion in the News* 6, no. 3 (2003): 2–5; and Christine McMorris, "Praise God and Pass the Diapers," *Religion in the News* 12, no. 1 (2009): 19–20, 24.

99. C. Danielle Vinson and James L. Guth, "'Misunderestimating' Religion in the 2004 Presidential Campaign," in *Blind Spot: When Journalists Don't Get Religion*, eds. Paul Marshall et al. (New York: Oxford University Press, 2009), 97–104.

100. Kirsten Isgro, "Conservative Christian Spokespeople in Mainstream US News Media," in *Fundamentalism and the Media*, eds. Stewart M. Hoover and Nadia Kaneva (London: Continuum International, 2009), 101–104.

101. Ibid.

102. Allen D. Herzke, "The Faith-Based Human Rights Quest: Missing the Story," in *Blind Spot: When Journalists Don't Get Religion*, eds. Paul Marshall et al. (New York: Oxford University Press, 2009), 70–71, 81.

Chapter 10

Daring to Believe: Evangelical News and Journalism

Michael A. Longinow

The man is pushing a wheelbarrow. Broad shoulders slightly hunched, his mouth is open in a shout of anger or desperation. But he looks tired—as if this has happened before. On the wheelbarrow, sideways, is an unpainted wooden casket. Half its lid is open, and the body inside, draped in a sheet, has one stiff, cocked arm stretched toward the sky. Mindy Belz, an editor of *World* magazine, a Christian news publication, writes in a brief opening to that photo that despite the horrors of death and pain in places like Port-au-Prince, God was not absent. His people were there, huddled in makeshift tents to pray and sing even as the ground trembled under their feet in aftershocks. The story was part of *World*'s recap of top stories in 2010.[1]

Time magazine's list of top stories in 2010 also led with Haiti. But there is no mention of God showing up in the devastation. Indeed, there is in *Time*'s description a chilly detachment in the statistics and description, along with a sense of the absurdity of providing help in a place where helplessness is such a norm. *Time*'s news-headline list is one of fifty such lists, on varying topics, available on its website.[2]

Bad news is evident in *World*'s and *Time*'s accounts of Haiti's 7.0 magnitude earthquake. However, what sets apart the evangelical version is the sense that to believe that God sees, that he cares, is permitted in grasping the enormity of such brokenness.

This chapter examines evangelical Christian approaches to news in the twenty-first century, noting ways that what evangelicals do with news is similar to, yet very different from, what mainstream media do with it. The chapter will trace the roots of evangelical news to this country's colonial era, arguing that news for and about people who claim a relationship with Jesus Christ is by no means a recent phenomenon. Rather, news

January 2011 cover of *World* magazine. (© *World* magazine. Used by permission.)

reported by those who know Christ intimately serves a crucial role in this nation's marketplace of ideas. It is a role that will become all the more vital as the nation's mainstream majority media, and audiences of all kinds, lose touch with the vernacular of evangelical faith amid the pursuit of balanced, truth-driven news gathering.

Evangelicals and Mainstream News

An unspoken reality of the mainstream news marketplace in the United States since at least the 1920s is that evangelical Christians have fled it in droves.[3] Evangelicals tend not to seek out work in mainstream newsrooms and tend not to follow mainstream news as closely as their non-Christian neighbors.[4]

The perception among many evangelicals, with some justification, is that mainstream news media, particularly media headquartered in the ten largest cities, are led by people who do not "get religion": evangelical Christianity, in particular, seems the most baffling to them. Or maybe, say many evangelical critics, the problem is that these journalists would prefer not to really understand.[5] For Christians whose grandparents enjoyed public rhetoric and media filled with references to faith and the role of God in everyday life, it has been a vexing problem.[6]

But Christians in the United States have a long history of finding ways to get their own news when the powers-that-be cut it off or made it difficult to publish. The steady exit of evangelicals from mainstream newsrooms over the decades has made for growth and development of many Christian alternatives.[7]

A chief spokesman for one of those alternatives in evangelical media has been Marvin Olasky. Soft-spoken and satirical, not one for hype, Olasky is one of the twenty-first century's most aggressive publishers of news among evangelicals in any medium. He brings a reporter's heart and an archivist's brain to his claims that evangelicals have made some of the best reporters in the news business for centuries.

Olaksy is not alone in this belief. Doug Underwood, in a bold piece of twenty-first-century research, claimed that most news journalists, tracing from the eighteenth-century printers through Mark Twain, Henry Luce, and into the post-Watergate era, have been believers in something—using language that ranges from subtle reference to outright preaching.[8]

Since 1992, Olasky has served in leadership of *World* magazine, a news publication with an explicit evangelical perspective and a bulldog reputation for news reporting and commentary. In his speaking tours, writing, and interactions with students as lecturer at (and for a time, provost of) King's College in New York, Olasky has called mainstream journalism "the wayward son of Christianity."[9]

Generations of tradition in mainstream journalism would insist that the word *Christian*, let alone *evangelical*, should not be in the same sentence with the words *news* or *reporting*. But to Olasky, this is a criticism born of the myth of objectivity.[10] News by its very nature is subjective, Olasky argues, pointing out the partisan press that surrounded our nation's birth and that is the norm today across much of the developed world. When an evangelical journalist comes out from behind his or her claim to objectivity, there comes a freedom to be thoroughly Christian. But along with this freedom comes an even greater urgency for fairness, balance, and accuracy.[11]

Olasky's claim that those most fervent in following Christ must inform themselves about the world around them is not new. Prominent theologian Karl Barth said Christians should pray with the Bible in one hand and the newspaper in the other.[12]

Barth's admonition might be easy or difficult to follow depending on what newspaper one reads. Olasky's indictment of sidewalk-level news in the nation's largest cities is that mainstream journalism is a post-modern, post-Christian assault on people of faith. His claims are, with some exceptions, supportable.[13]

Christian Newspapers: Old Model, New Approaches

An alternative, the Christian newspaper, is a special breed of news publication (now with increasingly sophisticated Web versions) that carries news and commentary sympathetic to the views of believers, highlighting national and regional leaders of churches, ministries, and missions agencies. It is mostly good news—positive stories with happy endings. Where bad news appears, it comes with the view that God or his people will generally find a way to remedy the problem. Evangelicals have been looking to this kind of news for centuries.

Christian newspapers in the United States, though now a niche market in an ideologically diverse American publishing landscape, have a history that traces back to the first newspaper in the colonies.[14] As evangelists and church-planters landed on the eastern shores of the North American continent, they brought not just the spoken word but media.[15] Elias Smith, a Jefferson-era reform preacher, launched the *Herald of Gospel Liberty*, possibly the first distinctly Christian newspaper in the United States. This preacher-editor drew criticism from more established clergy for singing in public places, confronting people about their souls, and leaving piles of printed materials behind him.[16] Preachers, whether circuit-riders or those living in town, were generally some of the most educated of any in the boroughs scattered across the American frontier of the eighteenth century. Methodists in particular were known for their publishing in the early American republic and, as one historian has put it, turned every circuit-rider into a distributor of religious books; within a generation of the nation's founding they had built a 15,000-name subscription list for the *Western Christian Advocate*, a weekly publication.[17]

By the late 1800s, a rising middle class and professionalism in American life had led clergy to hand off much of their news promulgation and efforts for moral reform to what had become a reform-minded press.[18] Christian newspapers were part of that mix, though they tended to come by way of mail rather than on street corners. Charles Sheldon, an author best known for his novel *In His Steps*, made history by launching a short-lived newspaper in Topeka, Kansas, devoted only to news gathering procedures that held to the operational motto, "What would Jesus do?"[19]

Today, Christian newspapers are as likely to be read online as they are in a print version. One of the more prominent is the *Christian Post*. On the weekend after Thanksgiving in 2010, the *Post*'s website carried a main-page story with the headline, "Don't Do Christmas on Credit, Debt Charity Warns." Just above it was a story about a campaign aimed at young people to make theirs a "more purposeful Christmas" by shopping at socially responsible stores. The collection fits the pattern of what evangelicals have sought out for decades in print media: news they trust, opinion with which they agree, products that speak to a culture of faith in which they live.[20]

Other regionally prominent evangelical newspapers include the *Christian Examiner* (part of a news group serving southern California, the Seattle/Tacoma area, and Minneapolis, Minnesota); *Christian News Northwest* (Oregon, Washington, and Vancouver); *Minnesota Christian Chronicle* (Minneapolis, St. Paul); and *Mennonite Weekly Review* (a national publication).[21]

Much of the news that serves evangelicals is provided by funding, staffing, or office space within evangelical denominations. Among the largest and most aggressive of such news operations is Baptist Press, run by the Southern Baptist Convention, with a Washington, D.C., bureau and network of well-connected national and international bureaus.[22] Associated Baptist Press, founded in 1990 and separate from Baptist Press, claims to be the "only independent news service by and for Baptists."[23] The Assemblies of God, the Churches of God, the Churches of Christ, and evangelical Lutherans provide systematic news operations as well. Many of the websites for the thirty-nine groups on the National Association of Evangelicals membership webpage contain a news link with varying detail in feature articles, headline news, or listings of linked articles.[24]

Why the varying attention to news by these denominational groups? At least part of it can be attributed to decisions about media economics in each organization. News is not cheap to produce as original, fresh inquiry—with costs mounting the longer and deeper one's reporting goes. Thus, news gathering by evangelicals is subject to the same pressures as news in any other context in the U.S. media marketplace.[25]

Evangelicals, Good News, and a Place in the Media Discussions

As the twenty-first century unfolds, news for evangelicals is more difficult than it appears to produce, promote, and maintain as a media niche. Whether one looks to them as benefactors or not, evangelicals today who do news reporting with a biblical world view owe much to two key figures of the last generation: Billy Graham and Pat Robertson.

Graham is credited with being formative in a circle of leaders who, in the mid-1950s, launched *Christianity Today* (*CT*). Veteran journalist and theologian Carl F. H. Henry was *CT*'s first editor.[26] Today, *CT* is one of several nationally circulated magazines under the umbrella of Christianity Today International (CTI).[27]

Robertson, son of a prominent Virginia senator, became a pioneer of multicultural approaches to Christian media and satellite television news in the post–World War II media era, creating the Christian Broadcasting Network (CBN) in 1961. He followed it up years later with the *700 Club*. That program, named for the number of pledges aimed at the ministry his programming pursued, was originally a prayer-and-talk program. Later, it became a Christian-focused magazine-style news segment patterned after national news on such networks as NBC, ABC, CBS, and public broadcasting channels.[28]

News on CBN follows conventions of broadcast news found on national networks: anchors introduce video clips with graphics, reporters appear live on location, and state-of-the-art graphics illustrate stories. Its editing and depth of reporting are competitive with industry standards, although it has been compared to Al Jazeera in its approach to news by sociologists of communication.[29] By the end of the twenty-first century, CBN had gained respectability on Capitol Hill and became a factor in the election race leading to the Obama presidency.[30]

Bad News: Best Avoided by Good Evangelicals

What is largely missing from news in Christian newspapers, news magazines, broadcast media, or the Web is investigative reporting. Where there is injustice in public life, in the corporate world, or in church leadership, evangelicals are not the ones breaking the story, though they will link to it if someone else does the research.

A classic example was the investigative work into abuses underlying Jim and Tammy Faye Bakker's PTL Network television ministry in the late 1980s. It was not Christian media that brought an in-depth look at the story but the *Charlotte Observer* (later joined by news media from New York to Miami and from other Western nations).[31]

The obvious questions arise: How much did evangelical leaders know? When did they know it? And if they knew, why did they fail to break the story as a cautionary tale to believers the world over? Could it be that evangelical editors just do not have the fortitude, or maybe the training, for in-depth reporting? Olasky thinks so. "The rarity of good Christian news publications represents both a crisis of entrepreneurship and a faltering of applied faith," he observed in the 1990s, having served as a category judge for the annual contest of the Evangelical Press Association, a coalition of magazines and newspapers run by evangelicals. "Judging from their publications, many editors do not know how to develop stories that pile up specific detail gained through journalistic pavement pounding."[32]

It should be noted that evangelicals have done better about covering news about their own since Olasky's harsh observation. Nearly a generation after the Bakker scandal, the 2006 revelation that Ted Haggard, pastor of a large church in Colorado Springs, had been visiting a male prostitute got plenty of early and ongoing coverage in *Christianity Today*, *Charisma*, and other evangelical publications.[33] At the time, Haggard was also president of the National Association of Evangelicals and had drawn mainstream media attention as a spokesman for the evangelical movement.

If the lapse in investigative impulse at the end of the twentieth century stemmed from lack of training, part of the blame might be put on inadequate preparation provided by evangelical colleges and universities.[34] Until the 1990s, few institutions in the Council of Christian Colleges and Universities (CCCU), a nationwide evangelical coalition, offered much in the way of practical training in news reporting. Today dozens of evangelical Christian colleges and universities in the CCCU offer undergraduate or graduate studies in journalism and news-related media, many of them serving as feeder institutions for Christian (and mainstream) media in print, radio, and video and on the Web.[35]

The challenge for evangelicals crafting curriculum aimed at producing top-notch news reporters is that news is not packaged, certainly not monetized, as it used to be. News gathering in the twenty-first century is aligning itself to entrepreneurial thinking in ways unseen since the Industrial Revolution. Olasky wrote that in the 1990s, when an eager evangelical would contact him for advice on how to launch a news publication, he would "ask about management expertise: rarely have those with particular vision put together or even heard of a publication business plan."[36]

But where should the business plan aim? What will become of evangelical print media as we know it? Will news by evangelicals in the middle of the twenty-first century be reported entirely on hand held devices, digital tablets, and laptop computers? Will television and radio in 2050 be entirely Web-driven media? Will photojournalism be a media voice with any credibility in an age where digital manipulation can cause the most challenging types of news storytelling to be mistaken for special effects?[37]

Unfortunately, discussions that have led to the most innovation in media since the first quarter of the twentieth century have not been funded or hosted by evangelical organizations.[38] Indeed, an ongoing argument from some evangelical scholars has been that given a choice between pursuit of news and pursuit of theological insights, the latter should win out.[39]

Persuading New Generations of Evangelicals That News Matters

Research on Americans' motivation to pursue news shows they seek out news for many reasons, some of them related to how they feel at a given moment. And what they take away can depend on their mood as well—a function perhaps related not just to their age but also their gender, personal economics, education level, and profession or occupation.[40]

Age really does matter when measuring audience tendency to care about news—in print, broadcast, or Web formats. Audience studies of Americans suggest that those born since 1990 read, watch, or listen to news much less than their parents—markedly less than their grandparents—or even their older siblings. Evangelicals, who by anecdotal observation appear to consume even less news than their mainstream neighbors, fit this description. To these teens and twenty-somethings, all but the most carefully targeted niche news reports are boring or irrelevant.[41]

One media organization that grasps the realities of a tuned-out younger generation of potential news consumers is *Relevant* magazine and its website Relevant.com. The media group's tag-line is "God. Life. Progressive Culture." One can find news on the site, but it requires some navigation and appears under the "Life" tab. There, one of two interior pages that contain news is called "Reject Apathy." It has links, among others, titled, "Haiti Relief," "Unjust War," and "Loss of Innocence."[42]

It is still uncertain whether *Relevant*'s approach to news will lure younger evangelical audiences into a deeper concern for news. Another open question is how evangelicals will cope in their approach to news with the growing diversity among those who claim Christ as their savior.

Evangelicals whose first language and culture draw from Latino cultures or who are from Korean, Chinese, Japanese, Indian, Pakistani, Filipino, or Arabic backgrounds are a growing demographic in the United States. One example of a publication that is seeking to bridge the gap is the *Gospel Herald*, calling itself a global Chinese Christian news service. It carries reporting by the *Christian Post*.[43]

Another example of this kind of cross-cultural news gathering comes from Compass Direct, a subscription news service that specializes in the latest about Christians being persecuted for their faith.[44] Such news, consumed with urgency by those who care about those in harm's way, is increasingly migrating to YouTube, Twitter, and Facebook—all news engines that evangelicals who do journalism ignore at their peril.

Conclusion

News that is reported, written, illustrated, and blogged by evangelicals follows a centuries-long tradition of applying biblical insight to popular culture and public life. From the time of John Wesley and George Whitefield, American evangelicals have looked to their clergy as those who can brandish both the scriptures and the front pages of news publications. The news produced by evangelicals is niche media. It depends for its readers and viewers on those who understand evangelical vernacular, cultural rituals, and the personalities of evangelical life in ministry, entertainment media, and, where appropriate, the public sphere. Evangelical news media are not investigative or antagonistic to ruling authorities as compared to mainstream media. Evangelical news media's main attention is to what is good, wholesome, and successful in the lives of Christians. Where there is reporting about disaster or tragedy, including the lapses of human will or morality, evangelicals' main focus is on the good and more often than not will come to a happy ending.

News for evangelicals, like news in the mainstream press, is in a time of self-assessment. It has no alternative: readers and viewers of news are a diminishing audience demographic. The future of news appears to be something that is tied to the fortunes of social media, interactive Web storytelling, and the niche interests of those who see news as valuable only as it relates to their immediate experience. Can evangelicals produce news effectively in such an on-demand world? Time will tell. But if history is any indication, it will be evangelicals, among Christians of any description, who make a successful leap.

Notes

1. Mindy Belz, "2010 News of the Year," *World*, January 1, 2011, http://www.worldmag.com/articles/17424 (accessed December 19, 2010).

2. "Top 10 of Everything in 2010: Top 10 World News Stories," *Time*, http://www.time.com/time/specials/packages/article/0,28804,2035319_2035311,00.html (accessed December 19, 2010).

3. John Dart and Jimmy R. Allen, *Bridging the Gap: Religion and the News Media* (Nashville, TN: First Amendment Center, 2000).

4. Rose French, "Evangelicals Are in the News, But Not in Newsrooms," Pew Forum on Religion and Public Life, October 17, 2008, http://www.pewforum.org/Religion-News/Evangelicals-are-in-the-news-but-not-in-newsrooms.aspx (accessed May 24, 2012).

5. Paul Marshall et al., *Blind Spot: When Journalists Don't Get Religion* (New York: Oxford University Press, 2008).

6. Bob Briner, *Roaring Lambs: A Gentle Plan to Radically Change Your World* (1993; paperback, Grand Rapids, MI: Zondervan, 2000), 23.

7. Stewart M. Hoover, *Religion in the News: Faith and Journalism in American Public Discourse* (Thousand Oaks, CA: Sage, 1998), 33.

8. Marvin Olasky, *Compassionate Conservatism: What It Is, What It Does, and How It Can Transform America* (New York: Free Press, 2000), 3–5. See also Olasky, *Renewing American Compassion: How Compassion for the Needy Can Turn Ordinary Citizens into Heroes* (Washington, DC: Regnery, 1999), and Olasky, *The Tragedy of American Compassion* (Wheaton, IL: Crossway, 1992).

9. Marvin Olasky, *Telling the Truth: How to Revitalize Christian Journalism* (Wheaton, IL: Crossway, 1996), xi.

10. Evan Thomas and Suzanne Smalley, "The Myth of Objectivity," *Newsweek*, March 10, 2008, 36–38. See also Jeremy Iggers, *Good News, Bad News: Journalism Ethics and the Public Interest* (Boulder, CO: Westview, 1999), chap. 6.

11. Olasky, *Telling the Truth*, 1–27, 232–244.

12. "Theologians: Barth in Retirement," *Time*, May 31, 1963, http://www.time.com/time/magazine/article/0,9171,896838,00.html (accessed November 19, 2010). See also "The Bible in One Hand and the Newspaper in the Other," *Nacreous Kingdom*, http://www.nacreouskingdom.com/2010/10/bible-in-one-hand-and-newspaper-in.html (accessed November 19, 2010). The quote from Barth is commonly agreed to have reflected a consistent pattern in Barth's worldview and theology.

13. Gloria Shur Bilchik, "Is Predicting the Return of Christ Front-Page News?" *St. Louis Journalism Review* 30, no. 221 (November 1999), 1–2; Joseph M. Valenzano III and Lisa Menegatos, "Benedict the Bifurcated: Secular and Sacred Framing of the Pope and Turkey," *Journal of Media & Religion* 7, no. 4 (2008): 207–230.

14. Judith L. Buddenbaum and Debra L. Mason, eds., *Readings on Religion as News* (Ames: Iowa State University Press, 2000), 3–4.

15. Ibid., 1–2.

16. Nathan O. Hatch, *The Democratization of American Christianity* (New Haven, CT: Yale University Press, 1989), 70, 73.

17. Ibid., 126. See also Richard D. Brown, "Spreading the Word: Rural Clergymen and the Communication Network of 18th Century New England," *Proceedings of the Massachusetts Historical Society* 94 (1982): 1–14; and Larzer Ziff, *Writing in the New Nation: Prose, Print and Politics in the Early United States* (New Haven, CT: Yale University Press, 1991).

18. Ronald R. Rodgers, "The Press, Pulpit and Public Opinion: The Clergy's Conferral of Power and the Concomitant Call for Journalism Advocacy in an Age of Reform," *Journal of Media & Religion* 9, no. 1 (January–March, 2010), 1–18.

19. Timothy L. Smith, *Revivalism & Social Reform: American Protestantism on the Eve of the Civil War* (Nashville, TN: Abingdon, 1957; repr., Baltimore: Johns Hopkins University Press, 1980), 15. See also Michael A. Longinow, "Mysterious and Spontaneous Power: Shaping of an Evangelical Social Culture for Revivalist Higher Education in Henry Clay Morrison's *Pentecostal Herald*, 1910–1942," PhD dissertation, University of Kentucky, 1996; and Michael Ray Smith, *The Jesus Newspaper: The Christian Experiment of 1900 and Its Lessons for Today* (Lanham, MD: University Press of America, 2002).

20. *The Christian Post*, November 27, 2010.

21. See *Christian Examiner* media group, http://www.christianexaminer.com/ (accessed December 19, 2010); *Christian News Northwest*, http://www.cnnw.com/, whose website has, as an icon on its nameplate, the profile of a circuit-riding preacher reading a book (accessed December 19, 2010); and *Mennonite Weekly*, http://www.mennoweekly.org/ (accessed December 19, 2010).

22. Baptist Press, http://www.bpnews.net/ (accessed December 20, 2010).

23. "About Us," Associated Baptist Press, http://www.abpnews.com/about (accessed May 24, 2012).

24. "Current Denominational Members," National Association of Evangelicals, http://www.nae.net/membership/current-members (accessed December19, 2010).

25. See Jill Drew, "Time the Conqueror: Three Newspapers in Thirty-Nine Minutes. Uh, Oh," *Columbia Journalism Review*, January–February 2010, http://www.cjr.org/feature/time_the_conquerer.php?page=all (accessed January 21, 2010); and Jennifer Saba, "More Readers Skimming Google Headlines Than Going Directly to the Newspaper Web Sites?" *Editor & Publisher*, January 19, 2010, http://mediaworkers.org/index.php?ID=7177 (accessed June 25, 2012).

26. Carl F. H. Henry, *Confessions of a Theologian* (Waco, TX: Word, 1986), 158–163.

27. Sarah Pulliam, "Billy Graham Turns 90," *Christianity Today*, November 28, 2010, http://www.christianitytoday.com/ct/special/graham.html (accessed November 27, 2010); and "God's World Publications, Inc.," MinistryWatch.com, http://www.ministrywatch.com/profile/Gods-World-Publications.aspx (accessed December 19, 2010).

180 Evangelical Christians and Popular Culture

28. Daniel Roth and Martin Schoeller, "Pat Robertson's Quest for Eternal Life," *Fortune*, June 10, 2002, 132–140.

29. Sam Cherribi, "From Baghdad to Paris: Al-Jazeera and the Veil," *Harvard International Journal of Press/Politics* 11, no. 2 (Spring 2006): 121–138.

30. Walter Ganz and Paul Kowalewski, "Religious Broadcasting as an Alternative to TV: An Initial Assessment of Potential Utilization of the Christian Broadcasting Network Alternative," paper presented at the 62nd Convention of the Association for Education in Journalism, Houston, TX, August 5–8, 1979. See also Robert Abelman, "News on the *700 Club:* The Cycle of Religious Activism," *Journalism Quarterly* 71, no. 4 (Winter 1994): 887; David Brody et al., "What Place Do Christians Have in the Tea Party Movement?" *Christianity Today*, October 2010, 54–55; and Stuart Miller, "A New Wing and a Prayer," *Broadcasting and Cable*, February 9, 2009, 20–22.

31. Charles E. Shepard, *Forgiven: The Rise and Fall of the PTL Ministry* (New York: Atlantic Monthly, 1989). See also other writings by Shepard: "PTL Paid Bakkers Millions, Source Says," *Charlotte Observer*, April 18, 1987; "PTL Cash Used to Hush Up Secretary, Falwell Says Ministry Board in Dark as Contractor Arranged Secret Deal," *Charlotte Observer*, April 30, 1987; and "Minister Gives Up PTL Post, Falwell Named to Head Board," *Charlotte Observer*, March 20, 1987.

32. Olasky, *Telling the Truth*, xiii–xiv.

33. See Ted Olsen, "'I Am Guilty of Sexual Immorality . . . a Deceiver and a Liar,' Haggard Confesses," *Christianity Today*, November 5, 2006, http://www.christianitytoday.com/ct/2006/novemberweb-only/144-58.0.html (accessed December 8, 2010); J. Lee Grady, "A Hero Has Fallen," *Charisma and Christian Life*, December 31, 2006, http://www.charismamag.com/index.php/blogs/520-fire-in-my-bones/14287-a-hero-has-fallen (accessed December 8, 2010); and Lillian Kwon, "Ted Haggard Begins 'Restoration,'" *Christian Post*, December 8, 2006, http://www.christianpost.com/article/20061208/ted-haggard-begins-restoration/ (accessed December 8, 2010).

34. Not all evangelical leaders are trained at such schools—they are among the priciest in the nation. Many evangelical young people attend state and private nonsectarian institutions, relying on para-church organizations such as InterVarsity Christian Fellowship, Campus Crusade for Christ, and the Navigators for spiritual sustenance.

35. Marc Fisher, "Pat Robertson's J-School," *American Journalism Review* (March 1998), http://www.ajr.org/article.asp?id=1326 (accessed November 20, 2010). For programs mixing theory with hands-on approaches to journalism preparation for secular news outlets nationally, see the Washington Journalism Center, http://bestsemester.com, and the World Journalism Institute, http://wji.org.

36. Olasky, *Telling the Truth*, xiv.

37. Chris Connell, *A Way Forward: Solving the Challenges of the News Frontier: A Report of the Carnegie Corporation of New York* (New York: Carnegie Corporation of New York, 2011), 50.

38. Albert Van Den Heuvel, "Faith, Hope, Love and New Technologies," *Media Development* 53, no. 12 (2006): 11–17.

39. Christo Lombard, "Fleetingness and Media-ted Existence: From Kierkegaard on the Newspaper to Broderick on the Internet," *Communication: South African Journal for Communication Theory & Research* 35, no. 1 (2009): 17–29.

40. David Z. T. Mindich, *Tuned Out: Why Americans under 40 Don't Follow the News* (New York: Oxford University Press, 2005), 61–73, 76; and Vlad Tarko, "Why Do You Read the News? The Other Side of the Story," softpedia, March 29, 2006, http://news.softpedia.com/news/Why-Do-You-Read-News-The-Other-Side-of-the-Story-20511.shtml (accessed October 27, 2010).

41. "Stop the Presses? Many Americans Wouldn't Care a Lot If Local Papers Folded," *Pew Research Center Publications*, March 12, 2009, http://pewresearch.org/pubs/1147/newspapers-struggle-public-not-concerned (accessed January 21, 2010). See also Mindich, *Tuned Out*, 9–12.

42. Haley Bodine, "Freedom 4/24," Relevant.com, http://www.relevantmagazine.com/loss-of-innocents/spotlights/22931-freedom-424 (accessed December 19, 2010).

43. *The Gospel Herald*, http://www.gospelherald.net/ (accessed December 19, 2010).

44. Compass Direct News (accessed December 20, 2010).

Chapter 11

Charles M. Sheldon's Jesus Newspaper and the Reformist Impulse in Evangelical Publications

Michael Ray Smith

Where do Christians go for their news? For television, some use FamilyNet.[1] Others subscribe to *World* magazine for its biblically centered approach to news gathering. Then there is *Christianity Today*, which remains the gold standard for evangelical magazines. A plethora of online sites exist including the popular Crosswalk.com, which has an ample supply of news with a Christian focus, not to mention GetReligion.org, pioneered by syndicated columnist Terry Mattingly, who says between 3,000 and 8,000 readers, including Christians, visit this blog daily. However, he is quick to point out that identifying the concept of the Christian news seeker is slippery: "It depends on the believer's politics. *The New York Times* is for the old line; Fox [TV] is for the great evangelical world."[2]

Evangelicals sometimes charge the mainstream press with practicing the sin of omission and neglecting content that has more eternal value than an update on a school board conflict or some other volatile issue. Nevertheless, while online news continues to siphon off readers from the printed edition, old-style daily newspapers still command authority in the world of current events. Enter the Christian press and its rich tradition of providing news, often as an advocate for reform.

This chapter explores an episode in American journalism history where a clergyman, weary of a mainstream press that left God out of the newsroom, pioneered an experiment to help readers think about news in the context of evangelism and Christian outreach. The Reverend Dr. Charles

M. Sheldon treated the newspaper, the mass medium of his day, as an evangelist would a non-Christian. Sheldon wanted to "redeem" the newspaper by transforming it through the power of the social gospel where Christian ethics are applied to vexing social problems. In the process of mixing the idea of an objective press with an advocacy press, Sheldon failed to usher in the journalistic breakthrough that he had hoped to achieve.

While Sheldon did not succeed in his quest to remake mainstream journalism in the image of something sacred as well as newsworthy, his efforts are helpful in exploring and understanding how an evangelical critique can be brought to bear on mainstream culture and how an evangelical made use of mainstream culture for spiritual and religious purposes.

The Religious Roots of American Journalism

In the early history of the press in the United States, newspapers possessed many identities. Some publishers, who willingly sought permission to print from government authorities, depended on political subsidies to spread a partisan message. Others included religious content as a matter of standard practice. Religious expression in the American press can be found in the first newspaper published in the colonies, Benjamin Harris's *Publick Occurrences Both Forreign and Domestick*. In his first (and only) issue, September 25, 1690, Harris wrote that he intended to publish regularly so that "Memorable occurrents of Divine Providence may not be neglected or forgotten, as they too often are."[3] By the 1730s, Benjamin Franklin and Thomas Whitmarsh, founders of the *South-Carolina Gazette*, used their periodical to highlight spiritual conversion to promote the good of society.[4] However, by the time of the Civil War, the mainstream press lost much of its tendency for partisan causes in both religion and politics. Today the modern press tends to retain its reformist tendencies and regularly points out crime and hypocrisy while maintaining a modest respect for the values associated with religion.[5] On the other hand, more than 100 varieties of Christian religions are now active, and these voluntary organizations often use some form of press to share a message with members.[6] In the case of religious and evangelical periodicals, the niche is one where the adherents use the content to stay informed as well as reinforce existing beliefs and predispositions.

A Novel Experiment in Mainstream Press

Criticism of the mainstream press throughout the decades is common, but rarely has anyone come up with a suitable replacement for a press that emphasizes providing both sides of a controversy as well as attention to sports, government, entertainment, and all the other issues readers believe are newsworthy. One clergyman may have gained the most traction in trying to do this with his experiment in 1900. He may be the best example of an evangelical working to shape the American press into a new product in which evangelical Christianity is the organizing principle for what ordinary readers consider a mainstream, general-circulation newspaper. The novel experiment was called the "Jesus newspaper," published by Sheldon in 1900.

Sheldon (1857–1946) was a Congregational minister whose book *In His Steps* (1897) eventually sold millions of copies.[7] At the heart of this bestselling sensation was the question, "What would Jesus do?" (WWJD). Sheldon urged readers to ask the WWJD question in seeking God's will in all of life's activities, including the operation of a mainstream newspaper.

Sheldon had long advocated a new vision for a newspaper. In 1891, his first reference to a Christian newspaper was in a sermon story, *Richard Bruce, or The Life That Now Is*, published in 1893.[8] Sheldon lectured about the idea of a Christian daily newspaper throughout 1895. He wrote about the concept in the *Topeka Daily Capital* in Kansas on April 23 of that year and in the *Kingdom* in Minneapolis, Minnesota, on June 28 and July 5.[9] On October 11, 1895, newspaper publisher Arthur Capper had Sheldon edit his *Topeka Mail and Breeze* as a guest editor,[10] and this experiment proved to be a good warm-up for the main event of Sheldon's work almost five years later at the *Topeka Daily Capital* in late March 1900.

Between 1896 and 1897, as he was writing *In His Steps*, Shedon read his book in installments on Sunday evenings to the Central Congregational Church in Topeka, Kansas (which he pastored from 1889 to 1912). The WWJD question captured readers' attention then and continues to inspire readers today.[11] The novel tells the melodramatic story of clergyman Henry Maxwell, who convinces Edward Norman of the *Raymond Daily News* to ask himself "What would Jesus do" when deciding the news. While not a literary success[12] and often lacking in literary style,[13] Sheldon's work inspired readers.

By 1899, Sheldon found traction for his idea of a daily newspaper with a Christian identity in an interview with George T. B. Davis of *Our Day*. Sheldon explained that the proposed newspaper would recruit a Christian news gathering team to write news while asking themselves, "What would Jesus do?"[14] The idea stuck, and in 1900 the owner of the *Topeka Daily Capital*, Frederick O. Popenoe, made Sheldon an offer.[15] Sheldon accepted

Popenoe's offer because he wanted "to demonstrate to the public in general and to the skeptical American press in particular the practicability of publishing a [daily paper] as he thought Jesus would."[16] Popenoe turned over the editorial leadership to Sheldon from March 13 to March 17, 1900. Sheldon published six issues, two on Saturday to avoid printing on Sunday, and the experiment became a marvel of promotion and novelty.

The Overlap of *In His Steps* and the Newspaper

Sheldon's novel *In His Steps* gives a fictional blueprint for a Christian daily newspaper. Editor Norman reviews all potential content by asking the WWJD question. When Norman, for example, tries to explain his decision not to publish an article on a professional boxing match, he invokes the Jesus question and asks,

> "Do you honestly think He [Jesus] would print three columns and a half of a prize fight?"
> "No, I don't suppose He would."
> "Well, that's my only reason for shutting this account out of the *News*. I have decided not to do anything in connection with the paper for a whole year that I honestly believe Jesus would not do."[17]

When Sheldon edited the six issues of the *Topeka Daily Capital*, he implemented many of the policies and initiatives that his fictional editor puts into practice. With each issue, he reviewed the content by asking the WWJD question, using a principle that relied on a personal sense of ethics rather than a systematic or well-defined approach. Sheldon borrowed from his own novel, behaving like the fictional editor Norman and instituting rules for news and advertising. In fact, because some in the *Topeka Daily Capital* newsroom may have been hostile to Sheldon's approach, he posted a set of rules that banned swearing, smoking, or coarse behavior. He reviewed advertisements and banned illustrations of women's underwear and stockings. He offered no rationale for all these decisions except the WWJD question. By asking the WWJD question, people could answer from their personal perspective. The question relies on assumptions about Christ and his approach, which means that people who pose the question will be permitted some built-in flexibility as they seek to answer the question. Because no one can know for sure what Christ would do, the person who poses the question and answers it creates a dynamic that no one else could challenge. Who can know what Christ would do? Nonetheless,

Charles M. Sheldon, pastor of Central Congregational Church in Topeka, Kansas, and editor of the *Topeka Daily Capital* for a short time in March 1900. Sheldon is best known for his novel *In His Steps*. (Photo courtesy of Kansas State Historical Society.)

Sheldon attempted to give his readers an answer to his question: "What would Jesus do?"

In terms of acceptable content, Sheldon made a point of publishing temperance news[18] and editorials that condemned alcohol.[19] He also endorsed other social issues he thought were worthwhile. Sheldon transformed a mainstream newspaper into an advocacy newspaper because he believed it to be a superior form of journalism. This advocacy approach stood in contrast to most other newspapers at the time, which would not advocate political or ideological positions but practiced the journalism of verification, relying instead on accuracy and attribution. Most mainstream editors, therefore, rejected Sheldon's partisan approach that filtered all news through the lens of faith. While the experiment proved popular, the idea of a personal God who is involved in people's day-to-day lives left some readers puzzled. Breaking with tradition, Sheldon's work makes a useful case study in how an idea that is at odds with traditional journalism gained a hearing.[20] Although his work did little to challenge the news conventions of his day, he did anticipate the rumblings of the citizen journalism movement of the late twentieth century with its emphasis on reporting that depends on active involvement of reporters and ordinary people in the problem solving of the community.[21]

Sheldon used his first editorial, "The *Topeka Capital* This Week," in the six-issue series to define "news":

> The word "news" will be defined as anything in the way of daily events that the public ought to know for its development and power for a life of righteousness. Of necessity the editor of this paper, or of any other with this definition of "news," will determine not only the kind, but also the quantity of any particular events that ought to be printed. The importance of one kind of "news" compared with another kind will also determine the place in the paper where matter will be printed. . . . The first page of the *Capital* this week will contain what seems to the editor to be the most vital issues that affect humanity as a whole.[22]

In effect, Sheldon was redefining news away from being communication about events, changes in laws, government action, and so on to expressing a concern about personal behavior and social ills such as the use of liquor. To succeed in inspiring personal reform, Sheldon wanted the newspaper to retrain its burgeoning readership while providing advocacy content. The idea that readers gravitated to general-circulation newspapers because those publications avoided undue bias did not seem to affect Sheldon.

Sheldon believed that for this type of newspaper to be successful, it had to have a general circulation and be read by a diverse audience. The circulation of the *Topeka Daily Capital*, despite its attention to faith with sermons dominating page one, soared to more than 360,000 copies during an era when the nation's premier newspaper—the *New York World*—published about 250,000 copies on Sunday.[23] For Sheldon, the circulation success validated the advocacy approach that he was using and seemed to suggest that readers wanted this kind of radical reform in which editors would evaluate newsworthiness using the WWJD question.

Following the Sheldon experiment, the newspaper attempted to sustain the artificial circulation, but it could not.[24] Today that newspaper remains an ordinary daily that mirrors the features of other mainstream newspapers with detached reporting and opinion and columns prominently labeled.

Sheldon's assumption that financial rewards would follow the spiritual discipline of taming the mainstream newspaper was shortsighted. However, Sheldon believed that the reformed newspaper would work like an effective sermon and lead readers to salvation. Sheldon thought his work could accelerate the Second Coming, which would end the kind of visible sin such as drinking that so distressed him. In his third editorial, "The World's Greatest Need," Sheldon identified the world's greatest need as its need for spiritual reform.

Sheldon's dream for a redeemed world was a middle-class haven where people would not only avoid sinful behavior such as drinking and smoking but would also express selflessness and sacrifice for others. For instance, on March 13, Sheldon featured a report of a great famine in India.[25] "No paper in the United States had featured that item or given it any prominence," Sheldon later wrote in his autobiography.[26] "It seemed to me to be the most important piece of world news, and it went in on the front page of the first number of the paper, at the left-hand column which was the regular position the *Capital* had always given to feature news."[27] Sheldon used the experiment to promote hunger relief for India in both news stories and editorials, which he considered novel but not dramatically different from newspapers of the period. He believed that this kind of content helped. "If editorials are written to be read why not put them where the reader will read them?" asked Sheldon.[28] By the next issue, the newspaper noted that a system had been organized to accept contributions through organizations such as the Christian Endeavor World in Boston.[29]

More than any other feature of the Sheldon editions, the response to the East Indian famine appeal prompted Sheldon to consider his newspaper a success. "Sometimes when people have asked me if the paper were not a failure, as the press reports for the most part said it was, I have replied that if it accomplished nothing more than saving several thousand children from starvation I would always feel as if the paper was a success, if it did nothing else."[30]

However, Sheldon's idea of publishing a news article side by side with an editorial was not a new feature of superior journalism. Blending news and opinion is a very old tradition in the United States and can be seen as early as 1721 in the *New England Courant* when editor James Franklin urged readers to oppose a smallpox inoculation.[31]

Sheldon considered his advocacy approach using the blend of editorial and news that highlighted the same message as a persuasive tool to gain support. Individuals would read of the need and respond to the need. However, in communication in general, a uniform response is rare—and even more so with a general-circulation newspaper and its diverse audience that may not share the same cultural or religious values. Readers who sense a need may offer a variety of responses beyond the one suggested by the press.

According to the standards of the day, newspapers did their duty to provide news that suggested action, and readers did their duty to institute the social change. Little attempt at reform by individuals was made. Typically newspapers that use the traditional model of reporting and then editorializing on the news ushered in reform by readers who took on the call to action independently. Sheldon's approach emphasized the collaborative nature of an editorial voice that skipped the step of allowing readers to think for themselves and insisted that the decision could not be debated. Sheldon believed the response would come naturally and, once one community acted, it would not be long before the work of individuals influenced a nation.[32]

Sheldon worked toward reform in institutions marked by greed and selfishness, such as business[33] and politics.[34] Sheldon called for public policy reform in these institutions in four of his six editorials.[35] For Sheldon, all areas of life were fallen and could have genuine reform only when people asked and answered, "What would Jesus do?"

Despite support from many corners, Sheldon did not persuade all of the leaders of the *Topeka Daily Capital* of his approach. J. K. Hudson, the editor before and after the Sheldon experiment, refused to participate.[36] In the February 6, 1900, edition of the *Topeka Daily Capital*, he wrote that he would not participate in the Sheldon editions and defended the press of his day:

> The modern secular daily newspaper must be published every day, give all the news of the entire world, and be made for all the people who read. This does not prevent the tone, politics and policy of the paper from being clean, honest and courageous in all questions affecting the rights and interests of

the people, the state and the union. While the American daily press is no higher intellectually and morally than the people it is made for, it stands today as the most powerful protector of communities against crime, tyranny and corruption of officials, and as the greatest promoter of all public enterprises, and in my judgment making it conform to certain restrictions and limitations in order to bring it within the idea of a Christian daily would detract from, rather than add to, its influence and usefulness.[37]

After being editor for six issues of the *Topeka Daily Capital* in March 1900, Sheldon went on to do many other things, but his experiment was over.[38]

Evangelical News Practices after Sheldon

Others have attempted a Sheldon-like model. In 1975, Logos Books began the *National Courier* as a national newspaper for the Church, primarily evangelical Christians.[39] While Christians said they wanted this kind of periodical, however, they did not subscribe enough to make the periodical economically viable.

Today the Christian subculture has its own publications, including the output of the 400-member Evangelical Press Association and the vigorous online voices with an evangelical worldview. For example, one can point to the success of the Christian news magazine *World*. In addition to the denominational press and Christian magazines that focus on spiritual issues, *World* magazine has become an important source of news and information for weekly church attendees in the United States during the past decade. It had a circulation of 130,000 in 2009 (the most recent year available from Ulrich's Periodical Directory). Each week it competes with the nation's leading opinion magazines. According to the figures from 2009, circulation is as follows: *Time*, 3.1 million; *Newsweek*, 3.1 million; and *U.S. News & World Report*, 2.3 million. While *World*'s circulation is not as high as that of these periodicals, a 2004 study found that the amount of coverage *World* gave to specific issues did not differ significantly from that of *Time, Newsweek*, and *U.S. News and World Report*.[40] Although the readers of *World* represent a diversity of religious affiliations, they are strongly evangelical, with an estimated 92 percent going to church at least once a week.[41] The 2004 study categorized news into six major categories: (1) domestic news, (2) international news, (3) arts and media, (4) commentaries, (5) letters to the editor, and (6) advertising. This study also found that *World* magazine did not devote more space to religious issues than did *Time*, *Newsweek*, and *U.S. News & World Report*. All four news magazines, for example, provided about the same amount of coverage of family and children's issues. In addition, *World* magazine did not devote more of its international news coverage to the nation of Israel than *Time*, *Newsweek*, or *U.S. News & World Report*. These findings suggest that the content may differ but the topic selection is the same. *World* provides news and insight on issues from a conservative Christian point of view[42] and, in that way, it is similar to Sheldon's "Jesus newspaper."

Conclusion

Sheldon measured the press of his day and found it wanting for leaving the power of the divine out of the news mix. His idea of a newspaper that routinely sought solutions based on the social gospel did not catch on, yet Sheldon helped journalists and readers rethink the idea of interpreting events that relied on three socially shared narrations suggested by his bestselling book *In His Steps:* (1) the idea that the Christian deity could empower each person who has a relationship with him; (2) the idea that the mainstream general-circulation newspaper could be redeemed and be a tool to advance the idea of eternal salvation by grace; and (3) the theological assumptions of the social gospel movement that said it could advance heaven on earth through public policy reforms using the dominant communication tool of the day, the daily newspaper. For Sheldon and his followers, the idealized state where everyone would practice temperance in a middle-class utopia would lead to heaven on earth.

So where did Sheldon go wrong? Sheldon's model may have confused readers and critics. Newspapers of his day, like now, use Enlightenment ideas of knowing reality through scientific means as the best way to report information. When Sheldon's newspaper used metaphysical ideas of God intervening, readers were surprised. Although Sheldon readily admitted to this approach in all that he did, readers and critics found it to be too severe a departure from the usual approach of neutrality that most expect in a mainstream newspaper. Today critics continue to question a press that is resistant to criticism and operates in a cloud of self-denial about its subtle support of political goals that represent the dominant worldview. While European readers demand that the press explain while they report, the American press makes a point of separating the functions of opinion writing from news reporting. Nonetheless, room may yet exist for a Sheldon-like model where news can be reported while exploring a divine viewpoint reminiscent of the question, "What would Jesus do?"

Notes

1. Collen McCain Nelson, "Christians Flocking to Religious Media Turned Off by Bad News, Faithful Find Salvation in Alternative Stations," *Dallas Morning News*, June 5, 2005, 1A.

2. Quoted in ibid.

3. Benjamin Harris, *Publick Occurrences, Both Forreign and Domestick*, September 25, 1690, 1. Newspapers of this period did not use headlines as is the convention in modern newspaper design.

4. See David P. Nord, "Teleology and the News: The Religious Roots of American Journalism, 1630–1730," *Journal of American History* 77, no. 2 (June 1990): 9–38.

5. Mark Silk, *Unsecular Media: Making News of Religion in America* (Chicago: University of Illinois Press, 1995).

6. Judith M. Buddenbaum and Debra L. Mason, eds., *Readings on Religion as News* (Ames: Iowa State University Press, 2000), xviii–xix.

7. Michael Ray Smith, *The Jesus Newspaper: The Christian Experiment of 1900 and Its Lessons for Today* (Lanham, MD: University Press of America, 2002), 8. See also Cara L. Burnidge, "Charles M. Sheldon and the Heart of the Social Gospel Movement," master's thesis, Florida State University, 2009.

8. See Timothy Miller, *Following in His Steps: A Biography of Charles M. Sheldon* (Knoxville: University of Tennessee Press, 1987), 103.

9. John W. Ripley, "Another Look at the Rev. Mr. Charles M. Sheldon's Christian Daily Newspaper," *Kansas Historical Quarterly* 31, no. 1 (Spring 1965): 7.

10. Miller, *Following in His Steps*, 107.

11. In the late 1990s, "What Would Jesus Do?" became a merchandising phenomenon, particularly as WWJD bracelets. See Michael Ray Smith, "The Jesus Bracelet Fad: Is It Merchandising or Ministry?" *World*, January 10, 1998, 17.

12. Frank Luther Mott, *American Journalism: A History of Newspapers in the United States through 250 Years, 1690 to 1940* (New York: Macmillan, 1947), 195.

13. See Ripley, "Another Look," 3.

14. R. L. Woodworth, "The Life and Writings of Charles M. Sheldon (1857–1946), with Special Reference to His Relations with the Press," PhD dissertation, Southern Illinois University, Carbondale, 1983, 127.

15. The project was a trial and did not attain the enduring prestige of newspaper experiments such as the *Deseret News* (Church of Jesus Christ of Latter-day Saints), the *Christian Science Monitor* (Christian Scientists), or the *National Courier* (a failed attempt by evangelical Christians at a daily newspaper).

16. Ripley, "Another Look," 2.

17. Charles M. Sheldon, *In His Steps* (1897; repr., Grand Rapids, MI: Fleming H. Revell, 1994), 31.

18. "Prohibition Tested," *Topeka Daily Capital*, March 13, 1900, 1; and "The Cry for Work," *Topeka Daily Capital*, March 13, 1900, 1.

19. Charles M. Sheldon, "The *Topeka Capital* This Week," *Topeka Daily Capital*, March 13, 1900, 2. See also Sheldon's "The World's Greatest Need," *Topeka Daily Capital*, March 15, 1900, 2; "Moral Issues," *Topeka Daily Capital*, March 16, 1900, 2; and "Four Open Letters," *Topeka Daily Capital*, March, 17, 1900, 2.

20. Michael Ray Smith, "Fantasy Theme Analysis in the Interplay of Charles M. Sheldon," *Journal of Media and Religion* 3, no. 1 (Spring 2004): 57–72.

21. Smith, *The Jesus Newspaper*. See also David Merritt, *Public Journalism and Public Life: Why Telling the News Is Not Enough* (Mahwah, NJ: Lawrence Erlbaum, 1995), 113–115; and James W. Carey, "Afterword: The Culture in Question," in *James Carey: A Critical Reader*, eds. Eve Stryker Munson and Catherine A. Warren (Minneapolis: University of Minnesota Press, 1997), 308–345.

22. Sheldon, "The *Topeka Capital* This Week."

23. Mitchell Stephens, *A History of News* (Fort Worth, TX: Harcourt Brace College, 1997), 200.

24. Auguste C. Babize, *Fifty Years After, The Class of 1885* (Williamstown, MA: Private printing, 1935), 39, 73.

25. Charles M. Sheldon, "Starving India," *Topeka Daily Capital*, March 13, 1900, 1.

26. Charles M. Sheldon, *Charles M. Sheldon: His Life Story* (New York: George H. Doran, 1925), 125.

27. Ibid.

28. Sheldon, *Charles M. Sheldon*, 126.

29. Harold T. Chase, "Funds for India," *Topeka Daily Capital*, March 14, 1900, 1.

30. Sheldon, *Charles M. Sheldon*, 127.

31. See Daniel Webster Hollis III, *The ABC-CLIO Companion to the Media in America* (Santa Barbara, CA: ABC-CLIO, 1995), 76.

32. "Rev. Mr. Sheldon's Sermon," *Topeka Daily Capital*, March 20, 1900, 5.

33. "Standard Oil Dividends," *Topeka Daily Capital*, March 16, 1900, 1.

34. "A Fair Suffrage," *Topeka Daily Capital*, March 15, 1900, 1.

35. See "The *Topeka Capital* This Week," "The World's Greatest Need," "Moral Issues," and "Four Open Letters." Sheldon used his editorials on page two to denounce the liquor industry and called for public policy reform by outlawing this trade.

36. Ripley, "Another Look," 5.

37. J. K. Hudson, "How the Saviour Would Conduct a Modern Newspaper," *Topeka Daily Capital*, February 6, 1900, 6.

38. After editing the *Topeka Daily Capital* in March 1900, Sheldon traveled to Great Britain, Australia, New Zealand, and France to lobby for prohibition, one of his pet issues. From 1920 to 1924, he was editor-in-chief of the *Christian Herald* in New York. Sheldon edited the *Everyday Bible* in 1924 and spent his remaining

years speaking and writing. When he died in 1946, prohibition had passed from the law of the land. The 1920 law was repealed in 1933 because it was thought to contribute to, rather than reduce, crime.

39. Ken Waters, "Pursuing New Periodicals in Print and Online," in *Understanding Evangelical Media: The Changing Face of Christian Communication*, eds. Quentin J. Schultze and Robert H. Woods Jr. (Downers Grove, IL: InterVarsity, 2008), 71–84; and J. D. Keeler et al., "The National Courier, News and Religious Ideology," in *Media and Religion in American History*, ed. William David Sloan (Northport, IL: Vision, 2000), 275–290.

40. Michael Ray Smith and William J. Brown, "*World* Magazine's News Coverage and News Agenda Setting," in *Selected Proceedings of the 2004 Conference of Faith and Communication*, ed. Edward A. Johnson (Buies Creek, NC: Faith and Communication Conference, 2004), 87–93. The reader should note that in 2010, *U.S. News and World Report* became an online publication. The publication will continue to print special issues, such as their college and graduate guides, among others.

41. Ibid., 89.

42. Marvin Olasky, "Depressing, Yes—But at Least Some Editors Acknowledge Bias," *World*, December 27, 2003–January 3, 2004, 84.

Chapter 12

Evangelical Magazines

Kenneth E. Waters

World magazine called the 2010 blockbuster film *Inception* a work with "stupefying" graphics and a "classic heist plot," resulting in a "boldly philosophical exploration of truth."[1] Another evangelical periodical, however, said the film was below average and dealt with "the nationalistic, sometimes pagan and sometimes humanist question of what is dream and what is reality."[2] *Plugged-in* magazine said of the film's main characters, "They're intellectual rapists, ravishing and despoiling the very thing that makes us."[3]

Such a varied reception to a controversial film is expected among mainstream cultural critics. But the writers of the reviews mentioned above are evangelicals; they speak to a readership that holds many theological tenets in common, yet they do not share similar viewpoints. In their relationship with mainstream culture, evangelicals are just as diverse as they are in their patterns of worship, church organization, and doctrines. The conversation these publications engage in with their readers—and thus their indirect influence on mainstream culture—is powerful. The targeted, small-circulation publications like those quoted above are a lifeline of conversation helping evangelicals create, maintain, repair, and transform their identity as a coculture.[4] The power of these publications, which are almost invisible on the United States's newsstands, arises from their sheer numbers. There are more than 300 such publications. While most are circulated to a few thousand readers, when one multiplies the number of publications by the number of readers, the aggregate total readership is in the millions.

The first part of this chapter focuses on the history of evangelical periodicals and their influence on mainstream culture. The second part of this chapter focuses on three evangelical publications—*Christianity Today*, *Sojourners*, and *World*—that present readers with news analysis of world events from a Christian perspective, coupled with news about religious events not found in mainstream publications. These periodicals were chosen because they are independent of para-church or denominational control, and the editors are free to report and comment on any news event. Their worldview reflects that of evangelicals, but their content is not so narrowly defined to a particular ideology or denominational viewpoint as to render them powerless to affect the attitudes and behaviors of large numbers of evangelical believers. These are also the publications most likely to be quoted in the mainstream press as exemplifying the doctrinal and cultural viewpoints of evangelicals.

As I argue throughout, first, the existence of religious magazines is the result of the unique historical occurrences that formed American politics and culture; second, evangelicals are serial entrepreneurs who embrace new technology to reach even more people with the message of salvation through Jesus Christ; and third, because evangelical periodicals are products of the uniquely American culture, they often criticize the very culture and the social, political, and church leaders who created the legal framework and culture of religious toleration in which they operate and thrive.

Evangelical Periodicals and American Culture

Newspapers and magazines presenting an evangelical view of the world date to the earliest days of the American colonies. Editorial content assumed God's dominion over every aspect of life. As the ideas of individual freedom grew in the colonies and early republic, citizens assumed that it was their right—free from government control—to choose allegiance to any of the many Christian traditions available for their loyalty.[5]

The first explicitly Christian magazine was *Christian History*, published from 1743 to 1745. Its editors printed evangelical messages from leaders of the Great Awakening movement sweeping Europe and the colonies. Preachers like Increase Mather, George Whitefield, and Jonathan Edwards wrote for the magazine, and it, in turn, chronicled their evangelical ministries. The German American *Ein Geistliches Magazien* ("A Religious Magazine"), published from 1764 to 1773 in Germantown, Pennsylvania, helped non-English-speaking newcomers adapt to their new home while helping them preserve parts of their unique religious history and ethnic identity. *Christian Scholars and Farmers Magazine* claimed a three-part editorial focus: "to promote religion, to diffuse useful knowledge, and to help farmers in their work."[6]

The battle to define the parameters of evangelical Christian belief occupied early publications. For instance, the *Arminian*, published by Methodist Church founders John and Charles Wesley and first appearing in the United States in 1789, defended the doctrine of free will: each person is free to choose whether to accept or reject the message of Christ. The *Arminian* also printed testimonies of faith from Methodist believers, many of them women who were strong followers of the movement.

A second Great Awakening challenged the spiritual beliefs of Americans during the early portion of the nineteenth century. As circuit preachers spread Christianity by horseback through the new territories to the west, denominational strife escalated from dialogue to division. The strife prompted several Baptist and Presbyterian ministers to call for an end to continual denominational divisions. Thomas Campbell and his son Alexander began publishing a small newspaper called the *Christian Baptist*. The paper set forth a plan for a fellowship of Bible-believing Christians, regardless of their denominational affiliation.[7]

Millennial Harbinger and *Gospel Advocate* (which is still published today) exerted influence on the creation of the identity of this uniquely American religious movement. As the issue of slavery divided the nation, Alexander Campbell, who freed his own slaves, counseled others on how to preserve unity while disagreeing on social and political issues such as slavery.[8] Despite his attempt to push for unity, Campbell and his successors could not keep their movement unified.

Evangelical periodicals reached their height of influence during the first half of the nineteenth century. Pioneering women editors first appeared as leaders of evangelical publications promoting missions and weighing in on the most important cultural issues of the day, including prohibition and opposition to slavery.[9] In 1852, the African Methodist Episcopal Church began *Christian Recorder* (still published today), which was seen by proslavery advocates as a dangerous publication that was eventually banned in many of the slave states.[10] It was the American Bible Society's creation and distribution of evangelical tracts that ushered in the era of mass media in the United States.[11]

The number of evangelical publications grew during the first three-quarters of the nineteenth century but began to decline a few decades after the Civil War. The decline in popularity resulted from a number of gradual changes in culture. An influx of immigrants from non–Western European countries—people who were more likely to embrace Catholicism or non-Christian religions—came to the United States fleeing poverty and injustice. The rise of near-universal literacy, the mass movements of people to cities where "penny papers" proliferated, and the growth of scientific explanations for the origins of life increased to a point where the narrow worldview of conservative evangelicals lost credibility with progressive Christians and mainstream society. Gradually, evangelicals dropped their subscriptions to their own publications in favor of new nationally circulated magazines.

Rejection and Rebirth

Historians consider the 1923 trial of John Scopes, who taught evolution in defiance of Tennessee state law, as the turning point for evangelicals and their publications. Although Scopes was convicted, mainstream media ridiculed the faith of those who backed the Tennessee law, many of whom had chosen for themselves the name "fundamentalists." This name was chosen by conservative evangelicals to refer to their insistence on making the fundamentals of the faith the litmus test of whether a person was a Christian or not. It was the fundamentalists who had passed and defended the Tennessee anti-evolution law in the first place. Secular and liberal religious press depicted conservative Christians "as southern hillbillies, even though leadership came from northern urbanites. They were also just as readily dismissed as desiccated, fossilized relics in an age of science, reason and progress."[12]

Thus dismissed by mainstream culture, these fundamentalists seemingly disappeared from the American cultural landscape, turning inward and focusing on ideology and doctrine rather than on concern for the larger political and social events occupying other Americans.[13] "By 1925, Christians were often voiceless, except in publications that largely preached to the choir."[14] Because society had become so morally compromised, fundamentalist leaders advocated winning souls to Christ with an assumption that if more Christians populated the United States, then more of the nation's culture would reflect conservative biblical values. In turning inward, "[F]undamentalism did not die. To the contrary, it attracted an ever-increasing number of adherents nourished on a steady diet of antievolution books, articles and tracts published by conservative Christian presses."[15] What emerged was a dynamic subculture lurking just below the surface of mainstream awareness. Periodicals such as *Christian Fundamentalist* (1927–1932), *King's Business* (1910–1970), *Christian Beacon* (1936–present), and *Sword of the Lord* (1934–present) used their news and commentary pages to create a common bond of unity based on opposition to religious and cultural figures attempting to modernize Christianity. *Sword of the Lord* exhorted its 150,000 readers to have minimal contact with the unsaved.[16] Even though he was wary of Christians imbibing the joys of the emerging culture of the times, editor John Rice also encouraged believers to vote a strongly conservative and anti-Catholic ticket in presidential elections.

Even as fundamentalists carried on an internal dialogue aimed at strengthening their insular worldview and faith, their younger members undertook evangelism efforts in response to the horrors of World War II.[17] Groups like Youth for Christ, employing firebrand speakers like Billy Graham, used mass crusades and varied media to spread a confident message that salvation leading to eternal life was possible only through a faith in Jesus Christ. Graham and his young fundamentalist peers began to embrace a larger gospel that included evangelism and social action, and they advocated a holistic gospel that included outreach and good works. *Moody Monthly*, another popular fundamentalist publication, spoke favorably of this burgeoning youth movement. "This new evangelistic thrust prompted moderate Fundamentalists to restore the movement's public image."[18] (This approach was much to the dismay of some of the more conservative readers and editors of publications like *Sword of the Lord*.)

The ensuing controversy among existing fundamentalist publications and the new fundamentalists represented by Graham eventually led to a differentiation between the groups. The newer fundamentalists became known as neo-evangelicals or just evangelicals by the beginning of the 1950s. During this revival of evangelicalism, the number of post-war publications increased, and so did their goals. *Youth for Christ* magazine (later called *Campus Life*) and a family-oriented publication called *Christian Life* began as a means of furthering the re-emergence of evangelicals into dialogue with mainstream culture. Family-oriented publications such as *Moody Monthly* (1891–2003), *Eternity* (1950–1989), and *Christian Herald* (1878–1992) gained greater visibility through their features and commentary that helped readers better define themselves as post–World War II evangelicals. Billy Graham started *Christianity Today* in 1956 as a counter-balance to the liberal *Christian Century* (1884–present), then recognized by mainstream journalists as the only legitimate spokes-magazine on behalf of Protestantism. Graham also began *Decision* in 1960 to reinforce the commitment made by millions of people who accepted Christ at his evangelistic crusades around the world. *World Vision*, named after a growing humanitarian organization of the same name, started in 1952 and at one time distributed more than 400,000 copies per month before scaling back its printing and mailing costs during the early part of the twenty-first century. The *Post American*, later called *Sojourners*, began in 1971 as the voice of evangelical students opposed to the Vietnam War. The magazine's writers also criticized evangelicals for not speaking out forcefully enough, or doing enough, to fight poverty and oppression in the United States.[19] Another publication emerging during that time was *World*, which began in 1986. Its editor, Marvin Olasky, stressed a return to nineteenth-century reporting standards in which the Christian worldview was infused into news articles about world and national events. Considered politically conservative, it has nonetheless avoided being categorized as an unquestioning advocate for the Religious Right.[20]

The latter part of the twentieth century ushered in an era of dialogue between evangelicals and Pentecostals, who early in the century rarely fellowshipped together because of their differences over belief in modern-day miracles, speaking in tongues, and healing. Among evangelicals, *Charisma & Christian Life* helped readers from a variety of Pentecostal denominations and churches better define what it means to be a charismatic believer who is fully engaged in mainstream culture and politics.

The advent of desktop publishing and the national trend toward creating specialized magazines encouraged pastors and lay editors to start more publications during the latter part of the twentieth century, even as several venerated publications lost readership. Evangelical general-interest publications that tried to copy mainstream publications such as *Life* and *Look*—specifically *Christian Herald*, *Christian Life*, *Eternity*, and *Moody Monthly*—succumbed to the same fate in the 1980s and 1990s as those they mimicked. Even with a slight dip in the number of magazines, the international dialogue among evangelicals fostered by their publications is dynamic, varied, and vigorous.

Examples of Dialogue and Dissent

Now I turn my attention to the three evangelical magazines I listed in the introduction of this chapter—*Christianity Today*, *Sojourners*, and *World*—to help illuminate the vigorous discussions and influence of evangelical magazines on the Christian Church and mainstream culture. Several issues showcase the discussion and influence of these evangelical magazines: the stealth Bible, AIDS in Africa, and the election of 2008.

The Stealth Bible

The Bible is the best-selling book of all time, and publishing companies today still reap millions of dollars of profit each year. Since the fundamentalist controversies of the early twentieth century, conservative Christians have debated with their fellow believers the nature of God's word. The issue arose again in a multimagazine dialogue in 1997, when *World* attacked the publisher of the popular New International Version of the Bible (NIV). Since its release in 1978, NIV's publisher Zondervan claims sales exceeding 200 million copies, resulting in hundreds of millions of dollars in revenue. The economic power of Zondervan and its large Christian magazine advertising budget did not deter *World* when NIV translators attempted to eliminate certain wording such as "He" and "His" from passages referring to God, inserting words and phrases that were more gender neutral. In April of 1997, a *World* article claimed that "the feminist seduction of the evangelical church" was being foisted on believers by the Committee of Bible Translators (CBT), the International Bible Society (IBS), and Zondervan, which owns the license to sell the translation. The author asserted that the "stealth Bible" could "transform understandings of how God views the sexes he created," adding, "The result of the shift to unisex language may be to cloud the uniqueness of men and women. And that reflects gains made by feminists over the past decades. It also underscores the uphill nature of the battle being fought by those who seek to preserve a 'complementarian' view—that, for example, women can be leaders in many spheres but must not be pastors."[21] Zondervan's corporate affairs director Jonathan Petersen responded: "Terms such as 'inclusive language,' 'unisex language,' and 'gender-neutral' can be seen as negative and politically charged. We object to being put in these camps in the *WORLD* article; we intend in no way to advance a particular social agenda or stray from the original biblical texts. We have never identified with these phrases nor will we ever."[22] *Christianity Today* picked up the topic of the new translation, reporting on the ethical issues surrounding *World*'s coverage. In one of those articles, a translator told *Christianity Today* that he would never consent to another interview with *World*: "They have simply done too much unwarranted damage to the NIV, the CBT, Zondervan and IBS."[23]

A few issues later, *World* editor Olasky charged that other Christian magazines could have also acted with a prophetic voice and uncovered the story but did not because they feared upsetting feminists and jeopardizing advertising revenue from Zondervan and other publishers.[24] Stirred by the *World* articles, Christian leaders such James Dobson, president of Focus on the Family, and Albert Moehler, president of the Southern Baptist Seminary, met with the translation team executives who announced after the meeting that the translation was being shelved. The decision by the translators was seen as either a "major victory for conservative Southern Baptists" at the urging of *World* or as a selling out to capitalist interests—a reference to the damage that could have occurred to Zondervan's overall profit if evangelicals decided to boycott the company's wide offering of Bible translations and books.[25] Zondervan did eventually publish a gender-neutral Bible once the spotlight brought about by *World*'s reporting had dimmed.

For many evangelicals, this issue struck at the heart of what it meant to be an evangelical. *World*'s articles alerted evangelicals to pressure from groups calling for a translation that reflected changing cultural norms. Olasky and his editorial team seemed to channel a no-compromise approach of a nineteenth-century evangelical editor and spoke up to maintain traditional evangelical beliefs about the nature of God, the historic accuracy of the Bible, and God's roles for men and women as seen in the male-dominated language in the Bible. Mainstream newspapers and magazines reported on the implications of this Bible fight, and *Christianity Today* entered the fray as a voice of reason, in keeping with its historic role as an evangelical magazine attempting to create a moderate evangelical identity. In an opinion piece, *Christianity Today* editor David Neff was more circumspect than *World*, preferring to assume that believers were people capable of showing respect and caring for one another in a spirit of loving discussion. Calling for a more measured consideration of the issue, Neff noted that the debate over Bible translation, gender, and evangelical identity was a positive sign: "Lively argument based on careful study can bring light and can promote both our conservationist and missionary goals. Demonization, however, failing to acknowledge the faithful commitments of those whose priorities and emphases differ from our own, can only delight the Devil and split the church."[26] While not stated directly, there is little doubt Neff's latter comments were directed at *World*.

Using its editorial influence, *World* rallied enough readers and Christian leaders to force a multi-million dollar mainstream publishing conglomerate to delay plans to release a new version of the Bible. As it did so, it continued a debate within Christianity and mainstream culture about the infallibility and inerrancy of the most sacred book in the Christian religion.

AIDS in Africa

Evangelical publications have had a checkered history of pushing readers to embrace civil rights and issues of social justice. These include not only the civil rights movement in the United States but also debates over abortion, euthanasia, and homosexuality. In recent years, the magazines have covered a variety of important cultural issues including how the church should respond to the AIDS epidemic. A search of *World*'s website database finds 582 articles mentioning AIDS since the magazine's founding. *Sojourners*'s website lists more than 100 articles on the subject since 1994, and Academic Search Elite (a popular research database) lists 246 AIDS-related stories in the print edition of *Christianity Today* since 1985. As public consciousness about AIDS was in its infancy, many evangelicals struggled to understand the virus and its scourge. Mainstream media, meanwhile, picked up on the few remarks of televangelists asserting that AIDS was God's punishment on homosexuals. This framing of remarks from a small group of evangelical leaders sparked cultural discussion that necessitated a reply from evangelical magazines. A *Christianity Today* article noted, "Initially, many Christian leaders called AIDS 'God's judgment' against homosexuals. In recent months, many of these leaders have softened their rhetoric with statements of compassion and forgiveness. Often such changes in attitude come when a close friend or family member has AIDS."[27] Because of evangelicalism's long history of sending missionaries to Africa, evangelical magazines found it easier to educate readers about AIDS by focusing attention on the death toll in Africa, where most of the victims were heterosexuals. *Sojourners* noted, "Of the 14 million people worldwide who have died of AIDS, more than 11 million have been Africans."[28]

Evangelical magazines also critiqued U.S. government policies regarding AIDS in Africa. Reporting on the lobbying of conservative Protestants, *World* said, "Abstinence is becoming the preferred AIDS preventative, even as condoms remain the most touted."[29] A commentary by *Sojourners* assistant editor Molly Marsh encouraged concerned Christians to continue to pressure Congress. The centerpiece of her argument was a recent statement from Bread for the World president David Beckmann: "In the end, these are politicians who really depend on what Americans say is important to us. So if people back home say to their members of Congress, 'Doing the right thing by Africa is important to me. What's going on?' that'll move this in a flash."[30] Nearly a decade later, in the midst of a possible decline in funding for AIDS prevention and treatment programs in Africa, *Christianity Today* alerted readers that funding fatigue might be setting in. While warning that the cutback in funds would cost lives, church leaders vowed to continue their ministries regardless of government funding.

While victims in the developing world increasingly gained access to expensive new drugs to stay alive longer, a cover article in *Christianity Today* brushed off a scientific or technological solution for Africa. The magazine noted that such interventions were too expensive for the average African to afford and likely would not work anyway. "Health experts see churches and their community networks as unrivaled in their potential to fight AIDS through community awareness, care for the sick, and encouraging either sexual fidelity or abstinence."[31]

The educational efforts of evangelical publications seem to have had an effect. A poll commissioned by World Vision in 2001 found evangelicals were most likely to make donations to help alleviate the international AIDS crisis, and mainline Protestants were least likely to donate. The percentages of each group's willingness to give were dismal, though, at about 8 percent for "born-again" Christians, a term used to denote evangelicals. By 2005, though, the number of evangelicals willing to give to AIDS victims had jumped to 14 percent.[32] As more believers became concerned about the HIV crisis in Africa, evangelical publications began focusing less on advocacy and coverage of the political process and more on the valuable work of African Christians, American churches, and other Christian groups to care for AIDs victims and the millions of orphans who lost both parents to the disease. Still, their role in educating their readers gradually changed the dialogue among evangelicals regarding their responsibility to people with AIDS, leading to an increase in Christian involvement in reaching out to its victims. By keeping the issue of AIDS alive in the minds of evangelicals, the magazines played an important role in reminding Congress that millions of religious voters cared about this issue and were watching the actions of their politicians.

Election of 2008

The presidential election of 2008 presented evangelicals with a dilemma their publications discussed for several years leading up to the election. Neither candidate fit the evangelical political expectation like President George W. Bush, his father, or the conservative icon Ronald Reagan. Thus they presented a fairly even-handed treatment of the position of both candidates—Democrat Barack Obama and Republican John McCain— although ultimately most evangelicals voted for McCain. A reading of key articles in evangelical publications shows that they did not resort to using manipulative or biased reporting to push readers to vote for the ticket espoused by the Religious Right. *World* criticized Republican candidate

McCain's positions as a U.S. senator, provoking an outcry from national columnists such as William Safire.[33] In its build-up to the 2008 presidential election, *World* showed only tepid support for McCain's candidacy. Once a staunch supporter of Republican causes, *Christianity Today*'s articles and editorials about Obama were even-keeled, often interviewing prominent evangelicals asked to consult with the Obama camp; the analysis of the McCain campaign indicates that the Arizona senator was playing catch-up in terms of articulating his Baptist faith and energizing evangelical leaders he had criticized at times in the past.[34] Writing in an October 2008 analysis of the election, John W. Kennedy noted, "Rather than criticizing his Republican opponent for pandering to the Religious Right, Obama hopes to siphon off sufficient evangelical votes to put him over the top in November. It helps that he speaks the language of faith comfortably."[35] Noted evangelical activist Ron Sider is quoted as claiming that Obama "understands evangelicals better than any Democrat since Carter."[36] *Sojourners* stopped just short of endorsing Obama for president, and its coverage painted the candidate as a person struggling daily with how to integrate faith and politics. Editor Jim Wallis participated in hosting debates about the role of religion in society and helped formulate portions of the Democratic Party platform. While his publication maintained a fairly small circulation of 40,000 to 60,000, his staunch activism and prolific book writing on themes of God and politics gave him credibility with Democrats seeking evangelical input and support. A *Christianity Today* editorial decried the assumption that all evangelicals would vote for McCain.[37]

While Obama ultimately won the vote, the coverage of each candidate in the major evangelical publications undercuts any stereotypical assumption that these publications assumed a cheerleading function for the Religious Right and the Republican Party. Overall the articles analyzed each candidate's platform from the standpoint of a Christian worldview, providing a valuable service lacking in most mainstream media.

Looking toward the Future

The varied content, opinions, and advocacy of evangelical magazines face an uncertain future. As the twenty-first century began, the growth of the Internet and wireless communication led to a loss of readers and advertisers for mainstream media and the religious press. Given their entrepreneurial culture, evangelical publications have adapted well thus far. *Christianity Today*, *Sojourners*, and *World* have active websites that include abundant opportunities for reader commentary, blogging, and daily updated reports and commentary that complement their print products. The key to their future success will be the ability to begin to charge readers for access to online content and to migrate more and more of their advertisers to the websites. How well these multi-platform presences will increase readership among younger believers is yet to be determined.

The Internet also affords the opportunity for new models of how evangelicals can continue their dialogue over cultural issues. Internet-only sites called ezines abound. Few have the credibility or readership yet to attract the attention of evangelical leaders seeking information and insight, but it is only a matter of time before an enterprising evangelical entrepreneur learns how to attract a critical mass of readers and financial resources.

One successful venture, *Relevant*, might point the way to new models of evangelical magazine publishing. Begun in 2003, the magazine is targeted to a group of evangelicals least likely to read traditional magazines, those between the ages of 18 and 35. In a fairly short time, the bi-monthly, 100-page printed magazine has reached a circulation of 80,000 while the dynamic website includes thriving communities that discuss a variety of news and cultural content. *Relevant* is the brainchild of Cameron Strang, whose parents own Strang Communications, which publishes *Charisma* and other Christian magazines. *Relevant* began as a modest website created while Strang and some fellow Oral Roberts University (ORU) graduates ran a marketing and communication company by day. While Strang's parents did not fund the start-up, they did ask valuable questions about marketing, distribution, advertising, and fulfillment—issues that are the bane of any traditional magazine trying to reach its core audience. After initial success with the website and a book-publishing venture, Strang and his partners asked their Web readers for $10 annual subscriptions for a print magazine focused on culture and God. As its website, Relevant.com, notes, "*Relevant*'s niche, our voice, is our ability to look at mainstream culture from a God-centered perspective." Today the print edition is part of a multi-faceted strategy to encourage younger believers to discuss their faith, their disillusionment with organized religion, and the interaction of their faith with culture. Relevant.com attracts more than 400,000 unique visitors a month. The site also includes blogs by editors and guest editors, a weekly newsletter, videos, and a streaming Christian radio station. Covers feature musicians (John Mayer, Kings of Leon, Switchfoot), and actors and actresses (Zac Levi, Zooey Deschanel, Zach Galifianakis, Mickey Rourke).

The content is "edgy," and non-Christian culture makers are afforded the opportunity to talk about their art and craft and its effect on culture. They also talk about their spiritual journey, even if they are not evangelicals.[38] Strang told *USA Today* that the first printed issue of *Relevant* contained a tongue-in-cheek story on Jesus action figures that was considered too racy for the magazine to be displayed in the ORU bookstore.[39] The magazine and website heavily market *Relevant*'s "Reject Apathy" theme with articles profiling young believers active in political, social, and cultural causes around the world. Befitting a magazine dedicated to culture, most of the magazine pages are devoted to profiles on known and unknown bands, authors, and musicians.

March–April cover of *Relevant* magazine, celebrating the publication's fiftieth issue. *Relevant* represents a new model of evangelical magazine publishing. (© *Relevant Magazine*. Used by permission.)

Political issues are also discussed. The tone is more moderate, in keeping with the growing number of young evangelicals who consider themselves political independents. Strang told *USA Today* that while *Relevant* adheres to the same biblical interpretations as its evangelical elders, its editors question "whether we need the government to enforce our beliefs, our religion, on people who don't adhere to the same faith."[40] In keeping with its outreach to evangelicals during the run-up to the 2008 presidential election, the Democratic National Committee asked Strang to deliver an opening prayer at its national nominating convention. A registered Republican, Strang originally said yes, then backed out. "I want to vote because of values and convictions, not party affiliations. To me, that's an important part of a thinking, values-minded Christian."[41]

Challenges and Conclusions

As *Relevant*'s story shows, evangelicals have remained entrepreneurial in their approach to spreading the word and using new technologies to leverage that message. While some have moved their print editions to an online-only format because of financial pressures, others are starting online and hoping to copy *Relevant*'s success. Younger evangelicals are less likely to support printed publications in the future, a fact that has already led the most influential magazines of the late twentieth century to launch rich, multi-media websites to complement their magazine brands. An additional challenge to evangelical periodicals, the changing demographics of religion itself, poses a greater challenge to the publications' future. As North America becomes even more multi-cultural, white evangelicals will face challenges to growing both their number of adherents and readers for their publications. In the future, news publications such as those mentioned here will have to adapt not only to changing technology but also to changing preferences by their readers. Not only will the tone of the conversation need to change to accommodate new generations of consumers familiar with interactive news and entertainment media, but the range of issues that the publications cover must also change to include more items of interest to people from a variety of ethnic backgrounds. Nevertheless, if history is a guide, existing evangelical publications and newer non-print communication vehicles will live side by side. Throughout American history evangelical magazines have played an important moderating role in educating readers about issues of theology and doctrine while facilitating discussions with them and mainstream culture about the Christian's role in impacting society and culture. The role these publications play in helping evangelicals define and redefine their identity within mainstream culture is too valuable for evangelicals to lose. Thus while the technological delivery system might morph from print to the Internet, journals of opinion and news for evangelical audiences should continue to play an important, if largely unknown, role in the American way of life.

Notes

1. Megan Basham, "Truth & Consequences," *World*, July 31, 2010, http://www.worldmag.com/articles/16949 (accessed December 3, 2010).

2. "*Inception*," Movieguide.org, http://www.movieguide.org/reviews/movie/inception.html (accessed November 25, 2010).

3. Paul Asay, "*Inception*," *Plugged In*, http://www.pluggedin.com/videos/2010/q4/inception.aspx (accessed June 26, 2012).

4. James W. Carey, *Communication as Culture: Essays on Media and Society* (Boston: Unwin Hyman, 1989), 23.

5. Nathan O. Hatch, *The Democratization of American Christianity* (New Haven, CT: Yale University Press, 1989).

6. Quoted in ibid., 8.

7. See James DeForest Murch, *Christians Only* (Cincinnati, OH: Standard, 1962), 70.

8. Ibid., 194–195.

9. Teresa Lueck, "Women's Moral Reform Periodicals of the 19th Century: A Cultural Feminist Analysis of the Advocate," *American Journalism* 16 (1999): 37–52.

10. Frederick Detweiler, *The Negro Press in America* (Chicago: University of Chicago Press, 1922), 43.

11. Paul David Nord, "The Evangelical Origins of the Mass Media in America, 1815–1835," *Journalism Monographs* 88 (1984): 6–37.

12. Martin E. Marty, *Modern American Religion: The Noise of Conflict, 1919–1941* (Chicago: University of Chicago Press, 1991), 161.

13. James Davison Hunter, *American Evangelicalism: Conservative Religion and the Quandary of Modernity* (New Brunswick, NJ: Rutgers University Press 1983), 35–41.

14. Marvin Olasky, *Telling the Truth: How to Revitalize Christian Journalism* (Wheaton, IL: Crossway, 1996), 272.

15. Edward J. Larson, *Summer for the Gods: The Scopes Trial and America's Continuing Debate over Science and Religion* (Cambridge, MA: Harvard University Press, 1997), 231.

16. Warren L. Vinz, "Sword of the Lord," in *The Conservative Press in the Twentieth-Century America*, eds. Ronald Lora and William Henry Longton (Westport, CT: Greenwood, 1999), 132.

17. George Marsden, *Religion and American Culture* (Orlando, FL: Harcourt Brace College, 1990), 208.

18. Joel A. Carpenter, "*Moody Monthly*," in *The Conservative Press in Twentieth-Century America*, eds. Ronald Lora and William Henry Longton (Westport, CT: Greenwood, 1999), 107.

19. John Oliver, "A Failure of the Evangelical Conscience," *Post American*, May 1975, 26–30.

20. See Marvin Olasky, ed., *Salt [Not Sugar]: Twenty Years of World-Class Reporting* (Asheville, NC: World, 2006); and Olasky, *Telling the Truth*.

21. Susan Olasky, "The Battle for the Bible," *World*, March 29, 1997, http://www.worldmag.com/articles/424 (accessed May 24, 2012).

22. The Editors, "Zondervan's View: Not Serving the Feminist Agenda," *World*, April 19, 1997, http://www.worldmag.com/articles/428 (accessed May 24, 2012).

23. Quoted in Doug LeBlanc, "Bible Publishing: Hands Off My NIV!" *Christianity Today*, June 16, 1997, 52.

24. Marvin Olasky, "Philosophical Doubleheader," *World*, July 26–August 2, 1997, http://www.worldmag.com/articles/1070 (accessed May 24, 2012).

25. Yonat Shimron, "Plans for Gender-Neutral NTV Bible Are Shelved," *Minneapolis Star Tribune*, May 31 1997, 9B; and Bill Tammeus, "Stopping a Bible Translation," *Kansas City Star*, May 30, 1997, C8.

26. David Neff, "The Great Translation Debate," *Christianity Today*, October 27, 1997, 16.

27. "One of Our Own: One Man's Struggle with AIDS," *Christianity Today*, February 3, 1989, 56.

28. Laura Dely, "Aiding and Abetting an Epidemic," *Sojourners*, November–December 1999, 38.

29. Priya Abraham, "The ABCs of AIDS," *World*, May 10, 2003, http://www.worldmag.com/articles/7178 (accessed May 24, 2012).

30. Quoted in Molly Marsh, "Keeping Promises," *Sojourners*, 32, no. 6 (November–December 2003): 20.

31. Timothy Morgan, "Have We Become Too Busy with Death?" *Christianity Today*, February 7, 2000, 37.

32. Tim Stafford, "The Colossus of Care," *Christianity Today*, March 2005, http://www.christianitytoday.com/ct/2005/march/18.50.html?start=6 (accessed February 17, 2011).

33. William Safire, "Bush Campaign Stoops to Sleaze," *Ventura County Star*, February 20, 2000, B-11.

34. See Tony Carnes, "Talking the Walk," *Christianity Today*, October 2008, 32–36; and Sarah Pulliam, "The Party of Faith," *Christianity Today*, September 2008, 17.

35. John W. Kennedy, "Preach and Reach," *Christianity Today*, October 2008, 28.

36. Quoted in ibid.

37. "What We Really Want," *Christianity Today*, January 6 2008, 23.

38. See the April 2009 issue of *Relevant*, for instance.

39. Quoted in Cathy Lynn Grossman, "A New Generation Spreads the Word," *USA Today*, June 24, 2004, 1-D.

40. Quoted in ibid.

41. Quoted in Sarah Pulliam, "Evangelical Moderates," *Christianity Today*, November 2008, 17.

Chapter 13

Christianity Today: Uniting Evangelicals, Changing the Culture

Phyllis E. Alsdurf

One night in the fall of 1953, the Reverend Billy Graham awoke with a vision for a Christian magazine that was so vivid that he got up and wrote down what had come to him. Convinced that these were ideas "the Lord had given me," Graham outlined a magazine that would articulate an evangelical worldview just as the *Christian Century* had been doing for the liberal Protestant perspective since the late 1800s.[1] As Graham wrote years later, he had been thinking for some time about ways to reach a broader audience than he was able to do through his crusades. What was needed, he was convinced, was a magazine for American clergy and church members with a different message than the "progressive, inclusive, optimistic, and relatively humanistic" philosophy espoused by the *Christian Century*.[2]

During those early morning hours, Graham sketched out a detailed concept for a new magazine:

> I thought its name should be *Christianity Today*. I worked out descriptions of the various departments, editorial policies, even an estimated budget. I wrote everything I could think of, both about the magazine's organization and about its purpose. I stated that it should have the best news coverage of any religious magazine and even specified that it should be located in Washington, D.C., which might give it a measure of authority in the minds of some; that crucial location would also keep its editors and staff in contact with the latest news. I wanted it also to be a focal point for the best in evangelical scholarship.... My idea that night was for a magazine, aimed primarily at ministers, that would restore intellectual respectability and spiritual

impact to evangelical Christianity; it would reaffirm the power of the Word of God to redeem and transform men and women.[3]

With the launching of *Christianity Today* (*CT*) magazine in 1956, Graham's dream became a reality. His notes from that night in 1953 served as the template for what emerged: a magazine that some believe forever changed the shape of the modern evangelical movement. Graham claims that *CT* helped "change the profile of the American church"[4] and "bring about an evangelical revolution in America" by giving intellectual respectability to evangelicalism.[5] "It has gone far beyond anything that I ... or any of us ever envisioned," he said.[6]

From the beginning, *Christianity Today*'s purpose was understood in relationship to the wider American culture. An editorial in the first issue stated one goal was to transform American culture through the impact of conservative evangelicalism.[7] The founders wanted to help move evangelical Christianity from a position of misrepresentation and neglect to one of influence within American culture; they were convinced that the publication of this magazine would solidify evangelicals into a unified force that one day would influence the wider culture. While to some degree that vision did become reality, a consequence of evangelicalism's growth in strength and numbers was that rallying this cumbersome movement for collective action became increasingly more difficult. And its diversification over the past fifty years has necessitated a shift in focus such that today *CT* sees its mission as speaking less to a "them" out in the mainstream culture than it does to the many strands of an "us" that fit within evangelicalism.

The Emergence of Neo-Evangelicals

The decade preceding *CT*'s launching was a time of foment and change within conservative Protestantism and a period that set the stage for the emergence of a national magazine for evangelicals. In the 1940s, Graham was among a coalition of "neo-evangelicals" that chafed at the anti-intellectual bent and cultural withdrawal of the fundamentalists who dominated conservative Protestantism after the Scopes trial of 1925. These neo-evangelicals were instrumental in establishing a number of evangelical institutions, including the National Association of Evangelicals (NAE) in 1942, a group that opened its membership to a wide network of evangelical groups and organizations. They also put their energies behind the establishment in 1947 of Fuller Theological Seminary in Pasadena, California, a school with a mission to represent a moderate brand of evangelicalism and showcase the best in evangelical scholarship. Both the NAE and Fuller Seminary were presided over by Harold John Ockenga, pastor of Boston's prestigious Park Street Church and a well-respected theological moderate whom Graham would eventually invite to join the *CT* board.

Graham reports that around this time he was "attacked from both the Left and the Right," but his crusades were showing "that a great number of clergy in the so-called mainline denominations throughout the country were evangelical in their convictions. To the amazement of most fundamentalists, they were cooperating with us." Graham was convinced that a publication for evangelicals was needed to fill what he considered "a tremendous vacuum in religious publishing. I thought the articles should appeal especially to men who were open to the biblical faith in the mainline denominations, but the magazine had to be thoroughly evangelical," Graham stated in 1981 on the twenty-fifth anniversary of *CT*'s founding.[8]

Another pivotal moment for neo-evangelicals occurred in 1947 with the publication of *The Uneasy Conscience of Modern Fundamentalism* by theologian and Fuller Seminary professor Carl F. H. Henry. The book took both modernists and fundamentalists to task, but its most pointed message was directed at fundamentalists for their cultural isolationism, denominational separatism, and silence on social reform. It has been called "the manifesto of evangelical Christians serious about bringing the fundamentals of the Christian faith to bear in contemporary culture."[9] The challenge raised by Henry would be reflected in many of *CT*'s editorial positions nine years later when the magazine was launched with Henry as editor-in-chief.

During this era, Graham was gaining national prominence for his crusades and his bridge-building across denominational and theological lines. As he met with presidents, popes, and other world leaders, he became the public face of the new evangelicalism. Graham was convinced that evangelical ministers and other Christian leaders needed an alternative both to theological and political liberalism and to reactionary fundamentalism. By interjecting a well-reasoned evangelical perspective into the national dialogue, the magazine's founders hoped to incorporate an evangelical worldview into a culture where it was largely absent.[10]

The Launching of the New Magazine

Graham had shared his vision for the new magazine with his father-in-law, L. Nelson Bell, a surgeon and former medical missionary to China who had helped found the *Presbyterian Journal* and had extensive contacts in conservative Presbyterian circles. As plans for the new magazine took shape,

Bell came on as executive editor, and Henry eventually took a leave of absence from his duties at Fuller Seminary to join as editor. To this day, Henry is regarded as one of the most important shapers of evangelicalism through his writing, the direction he gave to *CT* at its founding, and the leadership he provided for evangelical conferences and training schools worldwide.[11]

Graham also solicited key men for the *CT* board, many with connections to the Billy Graham Evangelistic Association, which subsidized the magazine for many years. Among the original board members was J. Howard Pew, chairman of the board of Sun Oil Company and a political and theological conservative whose initial investment of $400,000 in *CT*'s launching was critical to the success of the magazine. On October 10, 1956, 285,000 copies of the first issue came off the press, most sent out in the form of a free one-year subscription given to all U.S. clergy, seminary students, and professors, just as Graham's founding vision had dictated.

Evangelist Billy Graham, shown here in New York, 1955, as he prepares to leave on a European preaching tour. The first issue of *Christianity Today* was published one year later in October 1956. (AP Photo/John Lent.)

Over the past fifty years, *CT* has moved from being a fledgling magazine that advocated for neo-evangelical outsiders to being a well-established media system and something of a cultural icon for evangelicals who to a large degree represent American culture. The international communications ministry called Christianity Today International (CTI), which includes *CT*, produces seven print publications and over twenty media services. Through its various outreaches, CTI claims 634,000 magazine readers, 5 million monthly online page impressions, 1.4 million unique monthly online visitors, and 657,000 opt-in e-newsletter subscribers.[12]

February 2011 cover of *Christianity Today*. (Cover illustrated for *Christianity Today* by Rob Day. Cover image used by permission of Christianity Today magazine, copyright 2011 by *Christianity Today*.)

Today *CT*'s circulation is 130,000, and its readership an estimated 260,000. However, its influence as the flagship publication of evangelicalism is far greater than those numbers might indicate. CTI describes the typical *CT* subscriber as "a decision maker and leader in his church" who is "comfortably affluent, travels for pleasure, and gives generously to nonchurch ministries." CTI's market research reveals that this subscriber has a median age of 55 and earns more than $80,000 annually. The majority of *CT* readers are male (80 percent), with 94 percent having attended college.[13]

Reaching Evangelical Opinion Shapers

According to CTI president and CEO Harold Smith, his organization aims to reach women and men of influence who "give shape to whatever cultures they find themselves in." CTI's audience is not "the entire spectrum of Protestantism in America," but evangelical opinion shapers. "Evangelicalism is in need of a place to go where various voices can come together and talk—theologically, socially, politically, culturally." Smith sees evangelicalism moving away from the "attack mentality" that characterized much of the rhetoric in the 1980s and 1990s and returning to the cooperative spirit of Graham and other neo-evangelical founders in the 1950s. "CT is in a unique position to communicate who evangelicals are, what evangelicalism is, and the orthodoxies of our faith. We are in a unique role to get voices together and then disseminate that in our desire to work for change—not politically, but through the power of the gospel."[14]

CTI editors say they are less interested in challenging evangelicals to "redeem" the culture than they are in helping them engage with the various cultures in which they find themselves. *CT*, and CTI more broadly, shapes the culture by addressing what its readers are seeing, reading, and listening to, said Smith. "The meat of *CT* is the truth of Jesus Christ as lived out by women and men of influence. Our stories tell readers that this Jesus thing is real and it does transform lives. And in the transforming of lives comes the transforming of communities and cultures at large."[15]

CT editor Mark Galli agrees: "If we are trying to shape anything, we're trying to shape evangelical culture so as a movement we become more faithful to what Jesus calls us to be. That will inevitably have an impact on culture." But, he adds, *CT*'s job is no longer "to tell the rest of the movement what to think and what to do" as it was in the early years of *CT*. "Now we are a magazine that wants to reflect the movement and be a gathering place for evangelicals to talk about important issues. We still have a leadership responsibility to keep prodding and pushing evangelicals on to the next level."[16]

Citing the *Economist, Atlantic Monthly*, and the *New Yorker* as magazines he admires "for their journalistic excellence," Galli says *CT* tries to imitate publications that provide deep reporting and thoughtful analysis.[17] With layout and design elements that rival those of the most sophisticated magazines published today, issues of *CT* exemplify high standards of journalistic excellence in the content they offer: thoughtful features, essays, and articles by leading evangelical figures; pages of book and entertainment reviews; crisply written editorials and views pieces; and a compact "Briefing" section filled with updates, columns, data charts, and news stories about religion news worldwide.

Shifts in evangelical values and trends over time have been reflected in *CT*'s content, and what it means to be an evangelical has been constructed and reconstructed throughout *CT*'s history in response to fluctuations in cultural norms and values. While in the early 1950s evangelicals largely were considered a fringe religious group on the margins of significant religious thought and dialogue, and those within evangelicalism saw themselves as an oppressed and beleaguered minority, evangelicals today are much more likely to be part of the mainstream in terms of lifestyle and outlook. Church historian Barry Hankins links the complexity and diversity among evangelicals to the fact that they are "quite at home in the culture, even as some of them insist that the culture is hostile to them."[18]

Called to Transform Culture

In the 1950s, theologian H. Richard Niebuhr offered a typology of five general responses by Christians to the culture in which they find themselves: Christ against culture, Christ of culture, Christ above culture, Christ and culture in paradox, and Christ the transformer of culture.[19] As *CT*'s editor-in-chief and arguably the chief spokesperson of modern evangelicalism, Henry urged evangelicals to unite in order to bring biblical truth to bear on contemporary culture so that it might be transformed through the power of the gospel.

That was the same message Henry had laid out in his popular book, *The Uneasy Conscience of Modern Fundamentalism*: "Though the modern crisis is not basically political, economic or social—fundamentally it is religious—yet evangelicalism must be armed to declare the implications of its proposed religious solution for the politico-economic and sociological context for modern life."[20] Throughout his twelve-year tenure as editor of *CT*,

Henry stressed the importance of evangelical involvement with the wider culture. "What threatens our evangelical witness today is not lack of enduring doctrine and principle," stated an unsigned 1961 *CT* editorial, no doubt written by Henry. "What threatens our witness is lack of spiritual power, reliance on past achievement that stifles creative concern, and lethargy and inertia in applying our sacred convictions."[21] In 1963, another editorial asked, "Do we really understand that the whole of culture soon glides into the service of anti-christ, and in our century glides swiftly into enslavement by anti-christ, when the dominant cultural forces are no longer effectively challenged and confronted by the claims of Christ?"[22] *CT* emphasized that the Christian had "a mandatory responsibility for unflagging interest in public affairs and for informed participation in them."[23] It was a message that was repeatedly stressed during Henry's years at the helm of *CT*.

Today, regardless of the section of the magazine, concern about the Christian's place in the wider culture is frequently addressed. As a case in point, the May 2010 "Briefing" section spotlighted the faith commitments of *American Idol* contestants and noted that media outlets such as *Newsweek* and Fox News had questioned whether the "Christian viewer vote" on *American Idol* had become too powerful. The article also featured the following drop-in quote from Beliefnet blogger Joanne Brokaw: "There was a time when a worship leader performing on a show like *American Idol* would have caused Christians to question his faith. But with the culture of celebrity becoming more common in the Christian community, the idea of a Christian making it big in the mainstream isn't so distasteful anymore."[24] Perhaps the evangelical presence on programs such as *American Idol* serves as a barometer of how far evangelicals have gone in accommodating the values of popular culture that would have been offensive to a previous generation of evangelicals.

Influencing Evangelicalism and the Mainstream

CT has not only influenced cultural perceptions of evangelicals in the wider culture, but it has also transmitted norms of accepted behavior within the evangelical world through coverage of certain views and the exclusion or marginalizing of others. It illustrates how a publication can be instrumental in transforming a social movement—in this case evangelicalism—from a marginal role outside of mainstream culture to a position within it. The changes in evangelicalism's relationship to culture exemplify what has been identified as "the changes of ideologies from systems of resistance to systems of domination."[25]

Among the ways in which *CT* has attempted to exert influence on mainstream culture is through the endorsement of various evangelical declarations as well as content about and sponsorship of important conferences and corollary events for evangelical leaders. For example, current editor-in-chief David Neff acknowledges that *CT*'s behind-the-scenes networking with government leaders on issues such as global religious freedom or with individuals involved in evangelical-Jewish dialogue illustrates aspects of the magazine's influence. "It's big-tent evangelicalism that Graham envisioned and that we want to carry on," said Neff. "Networking is extremely important. Like every classic journalistic enterprise, we have our editorial pages, our features, and our news. But there is an agenda-setting function. It doesn't happen often, but we do on occasion get people who disagree together in a room to talk."[26]

CT is in a unique position, adds CEO Smith, "to get voices together and then disseminate that in our desire to work for change, not politically, but through the power of the gospel." *CT*'s role is not necessarily to redeem culture, he said, but to influence it. "Obviously there are evangelicals who are the power brokers across many disciplines. Our call is to help them understand the dynamism of their faith, what they believe, why they believe, and how they can manifest that belief in the outworking of the gifts God has given them."[27] Smith predicts that one of *CT*'s key roles in the future will be to serve as "a convener," bringing divergent voices together and then disseminating their message to the Church globally.

CT's current mission of influencing, rather than trying to change, the wider culture is a shift from its founding vision under Henry. He saw *CT*'s purpose as "infiltrating and transforming American culture rather than separating from it," according to church historian Douglas Sweeney.[28] Early content of the magazine reveals that the publication sought to influence national political leadership both through its location in Washington, D.C., and through articles that represented a thoughtful evangelical perspective on current affairs.

CT was to be a means of restoring evangelical Protestantism to what early evangelical leaders considered its rightful place of spiritual impact and cultural significance. Its content was to be conciliatory in tone and deliberately avoid the belligerence characteristic of fundamentalism. "Instead of using the stick of denunciation and criticism," said Graham, "we would present a positive and constructive program. We would attempt to lead and love rather than vilify, criticize, and beat."[29] While seeking to be tolerant of differing viewpoints, *CT*'s editors were determined to avoid intellectual compromise and sought to communicate the best of evangelical thinking in order to convince those outside evangelical circles of the historic and intellectual validity of their message.

Henry's Departure and a New Model for *CT*

Henry stayed at the *CT* helm for a dozen years, then left abruptly for less-than-transparent reasons. Following in Henry's footsteps as editors of the magazine were Harold Lindsell (1968–1978); Kenneth Kantzer (1978–1982); Gilbert Beers (1982–1985); George Brushaber and Terry Muck (1985–1991); and Neff (1990–present).

In 1975, seven years after Henry's departure and two years before the end of Lindsell's editorship, 35-year-old Harold Myra became president and publisher of the struggling magazine. Lindsell, the author of *The Battle for the Bible* and an advocate of biblical inerrancy as the litmus test of true evangelicalism, earned a reputation as being combative during his tenure at *CT*. The number of paid subscribers had steadily decreased and the end of Pew subsidies to the magazine was approaching.

Shortly after coming to *CT*, Myra took radical steps to save the magazine from financial disaster, including moving the magazine from a high-priced Washington, DC, office building that overlooked the White House lawn (and was symbolically important to Henry and other early evangelical leaders) to a modest suburban Chicago setting. That move, accompanied by considerable downsizing of staff, the doubling of *CT*'s subscription price, and the gradual reduction in the number of issues published per year, helped put *CT* on a stronger financial footing.[30] Myra faced considerable criticism for his no-nonsense business approach to running the magazine, but he kept *CT* solvent and put it on a break-even basis within five years. Still, detractors charged that he had turned a well-respected thought journal into a popular magazine for lay Christians, one that lacked the intellectual weight it had displayed under Henry's direction.

In the years that transpired between *CT*'s founding and Myra's arrival, the evangelicalism that *CT* had helped construct and the business of magazine publishing had changed considerably. Evangelicals were no longer seen as the "neglected, slighted, misrepresented" outsiders described in the magazine's first editorial.[31] A year after Myra joined *CT*, a cover story in *Newsweek* would declare 1976 "The Year of the Evangelicals," indicating that in many regards evangelicals were no longer cultural outsiders.[32] In an era of increasing postal rates, production costs, and media competition, publishing a magazine without considerable expertise in the business of publishing was no longer possible regardless of the importance of its ideological message.

From Single Magazine to a Family of Publications

By 1979, *CT* had doubled its circulation in four years to a reported 200,000 subscribers, and the board announced the launching of *CT*'s first sister publication, *Leadership*, a journal for pastors that, Myra said, would help stabilize *CT*'s programs, spread its overhead, and expand its ministry. *Leadership* broke even before the first issue was printed due to "intense interest" and high response to mailings.[33] The next year, *CT* was involved in a "rescue operation" of *Campus Life* magazine, the Youth for Christ publication for which Myra once had served as editor.[34] Eventually CTI would include a family of publications, like *Marriage Partnership, Today's Christian Woman, Christian History*, and *Books and Culture*, that at one point grew to fourteen.

By the mid-1980s, *CT* moved to a team of senior editors who, according to Myra, would take works in progress and shape them "strategically and theologically" in order to "promote evangelical unity and clarity."[35] Under Myra's watch, *CT* did constant research on additional products, publications, and ministry options such as newsletters, magazines, seminars, books, and online offerings. Many ideas were developed into products; several were launched and discontinued when they failed to thrive. Calling magazines "living, breathing entities," Myra noted that just as *CT* had grown and changed throughout its history, so, too, had evangelicalism.[36] Since *CT*'s founding, evangelicals had become better educated, more upwardly mobile, and more politically involved—socio-economic changes that Myra regarded as necessitating adaptations in *CT* if it were to continue to reach its evangelical audience. Aware of the "shifting terrain" of evangelicalism and the sharp contrasts in the milieu of the 1990s compared with that of the 1950s, Myra identified a growing pluralism and fragmentation within the evangelical movement that he doubted could ever be unified.[37]

Myra headed CTI for thirty-two years before retiring in 2007, having served most of that time as part of a leadership team with Paul Robbins. Myra held the position of executive chairman and CEO, and Robbins was president and publisher, but Myra was the public face of the organization. Jack Modesett Jr., chairman of CTI, said in 2005 that Myra "sets the tone at CTI by leading from in front with integrity and from within by example.... His example of hard work and dedication to excellence causes those around him to hold themselves to high standards that would be considered exceptional at another organization but are the norm at *Christianity Today*."[38]

In 2007, Smith, who had joined the *CT* staff in 1984, was appointed editor-in-chief and CEO by the CTI board. At the time of Smith's appointment, CTI was publishing thirteen print magazines as well as "an award-winning website with more than 30 channels," according to a company press release.[39] Within two years, dropping advertising revenues and shrinking circulation numbers forced CTI to sell one magazine, shut down another six, and lay off thirty-one workers, reducing its staff by 22 percent to 108 employees. "We find ourselves—as does our industry—in the midst of a perfect publishing storm," Smith said in a written statement released on May 22, 2009.[40] Since those difficult days, CTI has rebounded somewhat but continues to take a fiscally conservative approach to the business of magazine publishing.

Giving Direction to Evangelicals

Among *CT*'s many journalistic functions is to serve as a mirror that reflects back to evangelicals just who they are and to set an agenda that gives direction to evangelicals about issues of concern to them, says *CT* deputy managing editor Tim Morgan. He considers it paramount for the magazine to offer direction to it readers. "As editors we are always evaluating ideas," he said. "We're asking ourselves, sometimes implicitly and sometimes explicitly, why do people need that information now? And what are they supposed to do with it? We're always making judgments. The gatekeeper function for Christian media is still very much evident."[41]

Telling the truth about the Christian world is one of *CT*'s important responsibilities, notes Neff. In the May 2010 issue of the magazine, he writes, "I've tried to make the way we handle little-t truth reflect the Truth himself, as 'grace and truth came through Jesus Christ.' But even when it is spoken with grace, the truth can lead to tension." That issue of *CT* featured a cover story by Wess Stafford, president of Compassion International, telling of his childhood abuse in a missionary boarding school. "A community's health depends on having an accurate picture of itself," Neff added, "and American Christians need journalists like those at *CT* to hold up the mirror of truth."[42] *CT*'s willingness to "embrace the negative or talk about what is wrong with the world" is an example of what communication scholars have identified as cultivating a prophetic voice that cuts through "comfortable numbness."[43]

Ted Olsen, managing editor for news and online journalism, sees *CT* as set apart from other Christian magazines that cover entertainment and media because it is "an ideas magazine, not a consumer magazine." For most of its history, *CT* has done arts *coverage* rather than reviews, he noted. "At its best, *CT* is less concerned with telling readers how to be relevant, how to be current, and is more ideas-driven. What does this say about the world we live in? What does this say about what it means to be human or Christian?"[44]

In its music coverage, for instance, *CT* tries to connect to the kind of music its readers listen to—whether Christian or not, said Olsen—and produce intelligently and provocatively written articles that prompt readers to thoughtful reflection about the significance of an artist's work. "We want to cover people you may know about in the way the *New Yorker* or the *Atlantic* or those kinds of publications would write about them, but not in the way that *People* magazine or *Entertainment Weekly* would do. We are not into celebrity journalism. We are not a buyer's guide. We are not a gossip magazine. We are definitely an ideas-driven publication."[45]

In his book *To Change theWorld*, professor and author James Davison Hunter challenges evangelicals to replace their mission of redeeming the culture and changing the world with a commitment to serve as a "faithful presence" that works for the common good within "the center-most institutions of cultural production."[46] Hunter concludes that the cultural influence of evangelical Christians has been negligible and peripheral within the arenas of greatest cultural influence because of their emphasis on personal pietism and focus on political power. A publication such as *Christianity Today*, with its commitment to personal piety and goal of speaking to and for the "peripheral" evangelical world, clearly is not the kind of "center-most" institution about which Hunter speaks. Nonetheless, *CT* has been a "faithful presence" within the evangelical subculture, and the ripple effects of its influence have moved out into the wider world of American culture.

Conclusion: *CT*'s Role in an Evangelical Resurgence

CT's original mission was to change American culture through its theological, social, and political influence. Its founding leaders intended the magazine to be a vehicle for restoring evangelical Protestantism to what they considered its rightful place of spiritual impact and cultural significance in the United States and the world. Aimed at an audience of evangelical and non-evangelical leaders, *CT* was to be a vehicle for articulating historic Christianity and its contemporary relevance. With Henry as the chief architect of that vision at *CT*'s founding and in its earliest years, the magazine promoted a definition of evangelicalism as a Christian orthodoxy that stressed evangelicals' responsibility for engagement with the culture.[47]

As Myra stated in the 1990s and as Graham seems to have anticipated in the 1950s, *CT*'s launching gave direction to a largely voiceless and directionless group of conservative Protestants. The overlap in *CT*'s leadership and that of several major evangelical organizations resulted in a cross-fertilization of ideas among evangelicals and reinforced the idea of *CT* as the voice of the evangelical movement. Equally important as *CT*'s role in shaping evangelicalism has been its ability to reflect back to evangelicals the changing character of their movement.

Through the pages of *CT*, evangelicals began to see themselves collectively as a powerful force and to understand who they were within the wider community of faith and the culture more broadly. That sense of self was a byproduct of the mediated form of *CT* and the magazine's role of acculturating a generation of evangelicals into a shared view of themselves and their world. While major mass media outlets such as television networks have the power to mold society through consistent and systematic messages, the same can be seen on a much smaller scale in *CT*.

Since the 1960s, the flourishing of huge para-church organizations—such as Focus on the Family, Campus Crusade for Christ, and Prison Fellowship (each supporting publications of their own)—and the growth of evangelical colleges, seminaries, and book publishing enterprises have decentralized evangelicalism's power in such a way that *CT*'s role was weakened. *CT* had earlier been just one expression of the evangelical impulse among many others—publications such as *Christian Life*, *Moody Monthly*, and *Eternity*, for instance—but it soon became the gold standard and ultimate vehicle through which evangelical distinctives were communicated. However, by the mid-1970s, one magazine could no longer speak for all of evangelicalism as *CT* did in the 1950s and 1960s. Even though much of the 1970s evangelical infrastructure resulted in the vision for cultural engagement that Henry and other early evangelical leaders had articulated, *CT*'s role under Myra's leadership shifted to uniting the many constituencies within evangelicalism in a way that respected their doctrinal differences while highlighting their commonalities.

In its fifty-plus years, *CT* has performed many functions: pulling evangelicals together into an identifiable whole, providing leadership for development of their ideological positions, creating a space for the exchange of evangelical ideas and dialogue, speaking as the conscience of evangelicalism, and providing information about all things evangelical to insiders and those outside the subculture. *CT* is an example of a publication that has, as sociologist Michael Schudson notes, declared "things to be" as well as provided "the forms in which the declarations appear."[48] Having long since eclipsed the *Christian Century* in readership and perhaps influence, *CT* exists as a symbol of the adaptability of evangelical ideology and its successful accommodation to mainstream culture.

Graham and the leaders he recruited to launch *CT* believed that the magazine would serve as an important gateway for cultural impact by evangelicals. *CT*'s founders wanted to see evangelical Christianity develop into a unified force that could transform American culture. But however audacious that goal may have seemed in the mid-1950s, it proved to be less bold than imagining the explosive growth and diversification that would occur within evangelicalism itself. The latter was a transformation that ultimately necessitated decreased emphasis in the magazine on those outside the evangelical fold and made coverage of evangelical culture the more compelling story.

Notes

1. "In the Beginning: Billy Graham Recounts the Origins of *Christianity Today*," *Christianity Today*, July 17, 1981, 27.
2. Billy Graham, *Just as I Am* (San Francisco: HarperCollins, 1997), 285.
3. Ibid., 286.
4. Ibid., 287.
5. "In the Beginning," 27.
6. Ibid.
7. "Why '*Christianity Today*'?" *Christianity Today*, October 15, 1956, 20.
8. "In the Beginning," 26.
9. Carl F. H. Henry, *The Uneasy Conscience of Modern Fundamentalism* (1947; repr., Grand Rapids, MI: Eerdmans, 2003), back cover.
10. See Billy Graham, "Standing Firm, Moving Forward: *CT* Founder Billy Graham Charts the Course for Evangelicalism's Future," *Christianity Today*, September 16, 1996, 14.
11. "In the Beginning," 27.
12. Christianity Today International Advertising, "Reach Your Audience," http://www.christianitytodayads.com/reach-your-audience/ (accessed June 22,

2012); see also "2012 Media Kit," page 3, http://www.christianitytodayads.com/reach-your-audience/2010-media-kit/ (accessed June 22, 2012).

13. Christianity Today International Advertising, "2012 Media Kit," page 5, http://www.christianitytodayads.com/reach-your-audience/2010-media-kit/ (accessed June 22, 2012).

14. Harold Smith, interview by author, July 2010.

15. Ibid.

16. Mark Galli, interview by author, July 2010.

17. Ibid.

18. Barry Hankins, *American Evangelicals: A Contemporary History of a Mainstream Religious Movement* (Lanham, MD: Rowman and Littlefield, 2008), ix.

19. H. Richard Niebuhr, *Christ and Culture* (New York: Harper and Row, 1951). For a more recent exploration of Christian responses to the culture and the media, see William Strom, *More Than Talk: Communication Studies and the Christian Faith*, 3rd ed. (Dubuque, IA: Kendall/Hunt, 2009), chapter 11.

20. Henry, *The Uneasy Conscience of Modern Fundamentalism*, 83.

21. "Where Is Evangelical Initiative?" *Christianity Today*, May 22, 1961, 20.

22. "The Power of the Truth," *Christianity Today*, September 13, 1963, 24.

23. "Evangelicals and Public Affairs," *Christianity Today*, January 17, 1964, 24.

24. Quoted in "Spotlight: American Idols and Saints," *Christianity Today*, May 2010, 11.

25. Teun A. van Dijk, *Ideology: A Multidisciplinary Approach* (Thousand Oaks, CA: Sage, 1998), 11.

26. David Neff, interview by author, July 2010.

27. Smith, interview by author, July 2010.

28. Douglas Sweeney, "*Christianity Today*," in *Popular Religious Magazines of the United States*, eds. Mark Fackler and Charles Lippy (Westport, CT: Greenwood, 1995), 144.

29. Graham, *Just as I Am*, 291.

30. Harold Myra, "President's Report to the CTI Board," June 10, 1980.

31. "Why *Christianity Today*?" 20.

32. See Kenneth Woodward, "Born Again!" *Newsweek*, October 25, 1976. The cover of that issue declares 1976 as "The Year of the Evangelicals."

33. Harold Myra, "President's Report to the CTI Board," January 27, 1981.

34. Harold Myra, "President's Report to the CTI Board," January 4, 1982.

35. Harold Myra, "President's Report to the CTI Board," June 24, 1998.

36. Harold Myra, "President's Report to the CTI Board," January 26, 1989.

37. Harold Myra, "President's Report to the CTI Board," January 23, 1991.

38. "Harold Myra: Leader of the Month for July 2005," LeaderNetwork.org, http://www.leadernetwork.org/harold_myra_july_05.htm (accessed May 24, 2012).

39. "Christianity Today International Names New Editor-in-Chief Following Retirement of Team Leaders after 30 Years," press release, March 15, 2007, http://

www.christianitytoday.com/help/media/pr_ctisuccession.html (accessed July 12, 2011).

40. Quoted in "*Christianity Today* to Close Four Publications, Lay Off 31," *Presbyterian Outlook*, June 21, 2009, http://www.pres-outlook.com/news-and-analysis/1-news-a-analysis/8898-christianity-today-to-close-four-publications-lay-off-31.html (accessed July 12, 2011).

41. Tim Morgan, interview by author, July 2010.

42. David Neff, "The Mirror of Truth," *Christianity Today*, May 2010, 6.

43. Robert H. Woods Jr. and Paul D. Patton, *Prophetically Incorrect: A Christian Introduction to Media Criticism* (Grand Rapids, MI: Brazos, 2010), 41.

44. Ted Olsen, interview by author, July 2010.

45. Ibid.

46. James Davison Hunter, *To Change the World: The Irony, Tragedy, and Possibility of Christianity in the Late Modern World* (New York: Oxford University Press, 2010), 238.

47. Henry, *The Uneasy Conscience of Modern Fundamentalism*. That theme was revisited often in unsigned *CT* editorials, probably written by Henry. For example, see "Step Up the Evangelical Thrust," October 13, 1961; "The Evangelical Thrust," February 2, 1962; and "A Proposal for Evangelical Advance," May 13, 1966.

48. Michael Schudson, "The Politics of Narrative Form: The Emergence of News Conventions in Print and Television," *Daedalus* 111 (Fall 1982): 98.

Chapter 14

Evangelical Film Festivals

Terrence R. Wandtke

"So you're a Christian professor at a Christian college, and you think your film festival will therefore be a Christian film festival? Is that so different from a Christian farmer who expects Christian milk from his Christian cows?"

"Well, yeah. It's a very different situation because what I'm doing is intentional in all ways. I can't believe you're using that old stereotypical question on me. And furthermore . . . "

Of course, with a professor, there almost always is a "furthermore." The above is a fragment from one of many conversations that preceded the organization and founding of the Imago Film Festival, a five-day Christian event that identifies itself as a celebration of independent films exploring issues of faith. In the interests of full disclosure, I am that professor and I co-founded the festival in 2004. I will keep the identity of my dear friend on the other side of the conversation a secret to all but him. Nevertheless, friends like him were instrumental in the development of the identity of a festival that I wanted to be somewhat distinctive in the midst of a rapidly proliferating landscape of Christian film festivals. I thought the venture would undoubtedly fill a festival-shaped hole in the heart of Christians everywhere. Even with that naïve notion firmly in place, I realized that *Christian* could not be used as an adjective to describe a film festival unless I clearly understood what that would mean for filmmakers and filmgoers.

Do we call our film festival Christian because it is organized by Christians? Because the festival is based on Christian principles? Because the festival is designed to showcase Christian film? Depending on whom we asked, Christian film was the dogmatic missionary film made by Christians, or the period-piece film featuring biblical characters (usually Jesus) with low production values or uninspired storytelling. If our festival was to showcase Christian film, I asserted that we certainly were not going to seek out those types of films. Luckily, there was no need to reinvent the wheel as other Christian film festivals had preceded us and undoubtedly dealt with these issues. I was vaguely aware of the Damah Film Festival, in Seattle, because several friends had submitted their films to it, and knew the City of the Angels Film Festival that was somehow connected with Fuller Theological Seminary.

Unfortunately, when I sought a formal history of Christian film festivals, I found that scholars tended to approach Christian film in a similar way to how scholars had approached mainstream film: focus on film and ignore cultural events like festivals that shape film appreciation. After a few well-placed emails to certain Christian film festival directors, I proceeded with the Imago Film Festival in 2004—but still regretting not having a fuller picture of the Christian film festival landscape. As no one has since described that missing bit of Christian cultural history, this chapter is the product of that continuing regret. I am not a historian but rather an academic who teaches media studies and directs a film festival at an evangelical university. As a consequence, this chapter has a historical framework but not a strictly historical goal. With information that I gathered primarily through interviews with people directly involved in the Christian film festival movement of the past two decades, I have identified trends that seem to be connected with ideas central to evangelicalism. In order to represent those ideas better, I will begin with a brief historical overview that brings together evangelical history, film history, and film festival history in the twentieth-century United States. Next, I will showcase the various Christian festivals as they occurred, with comments from their directors. I will argue that the festivals fall into two distinct categories depending on their emphases in the evangelical world: the first is based primarily on personal conversion and sharing the gospel, and the second on well-founded interpretation and the centrality of Jesus (wherein film functions as a dynamic art form beyond the confines of doctrine).

History: Evangelicalism and Film

Because this chapter appears in a collection on evangelicals and popular culture, there is no need to explain how complex and wide-ranging the term *evangelical* is or to provide an extensive history of evangelicalism. Nevertheless, I do intend to highlight several aspects of evangelical history and theology that lead to certain distinctive ideas pertinent to the Christian film festival scene in the late twentieth and early twenty-first centuries.

At a very basic level, Charles Finney's revivalism in the nineteenth century forms a foundation for the social activism of early evangelicalism and the political movements for and against film in the early twentieth century. The means of evangelizing groups considered to be non-Christian, secular, and unchurched were often determined by the technology at hand. The more accessible and affordable printing presses of the nineteenth century allowed the mass printing of tracts, magazines, and Bibles put in service of the desire to convert.

Due to the well-known Christian opposition to the controversial content of certain new media of the twentieth century, it is often assumed that the evangelical love of media technology ended with the printing press. However, as theologian and Columbia University professor Randall Balmer clarifies, "In the 20th century, radio preachers and televangelists used electronic media long before Franklin Roosevelt and Ronald Reagan discovered their value as political tools... With regard to modernity, then, the issue for evangelicals has never been a skittishness about innovation or technology. Rather they have been suspicious of assaults on 'traditional morality,' however variously defined."[1] Consequently, with little anxiety about technology itself, the real debate within evangelical "tribes" has been a Christ-and-culture question: "How should Christians live in the world without being fully of the world?... Should they restrict the media that they consume or produce?"[2] Christians answered these questions variously in the early twentieth century with the advent of film. Early Christian protests of film led to standards for classic Hollywood films represented in the production code. As twentieth-century evangelicalism developed subcultures that were interested in new media but worked against "liberal" theology, many Christians took stands against media like film on the basis of content.[3]

Of course, with the claim that content might be problematic, the related notion is that the medium is not a problem in and of itself and therefore may be a vessel for the good news. In *Sanctuary Cinema*, Virginia Wesleyan professor and author Terry Lindvall identifies several things that stood in the way of evangelicals readily accepting film (such as biases against visual representation of the divine and basic questions about the theater as connected with modernism).[4] However, evangelicals' general engagement with modern culture and optimism for their causes tended to move them past many of the anxieties about visual art developed in the course of Protestant Church history. Lindvall represents this idea of cultural engagement in the words of the Reverend Herbert A. Jump. Arguing persuasively for the positive impact of figurative and literal illustrations to

Bible stories, Jump set up the idea that films may be a more-than-appropriate vessel for the gospel message: "Because the motion picture carefully selected will tell to the eye more truths with vigor of illustration and an eloquence of impression that the most enthusiastic orator cannot command, it has a proper place in the equipment of any church trying to reach the masses."[5] Although Jump is the foremost advocate of film in American Christian culture, this led to other positive conversations about exhibiting film in church and considering the film theater a holy place.[6] Subsequently, many films were independently produced by church organizations as missionary films and corporately produced by studios with explicit and implicit religious content to the satisfaction of many churchgoing Christians.

History: Evangelicalism and Film Festivals

As Hollywood grew into the era of the classic studio system (1930s–1950s), Christians continued to interact with film culture, expressing a certain level of control over studio production and continuing to develop independent films more specifically tailored to evangelical purposes. Festival culture, as it would eventually be known in the United States, emerged in Europe as an alternative to the limitations of national cinemas (in particular Hollywood cinema). Film festivals were short-term events that showcased films rarely seen in local venues available to most people.

While film festivals began to make their appearance in different parts of the world, they were slow to take hold in the United States (San Francisco in 1957, New York in 1963, and Seattle in 1976). The reasons for this slow build to festival culture had much to do with the dominance of Hollywood cinema through the 1960s; on the whole, Americans had little awareness of or interest in other cinematic traditions, either international or independent. As independent films became the new challenge to the old and now inefficient Hollywood system in the 1970s, the desire to showcase them began with the Sundance Film Festival in 1978.[7] Initially, this change in the market did not affect Christian attitudes toward film, but it did change Hollywood's strategy with a turn toward the blockbuster. Christian film festivals became an appealing alternative for Christians looking for a venue driven less by the popular audience and more by a uniquely Christian perspective.

As noted by Calvin College professor and author William D. Romanowski in *Eyes Wide Open*, Christians during the "golden age" of Hollywood entertainment assumed that films with offensive content succeeded because sinful people wanted to see sinful things. As the production code was replaced by a rating system and Hollywood committed to making fewer films with more sensational content, most Christians reached a different conclusion: "Beginning in the 1980's, ... Christian reformers began to assert the opposite of their historical counterparts—they said the majority of people want clean and decent entertainment ... The problem, according to these critics, is that the entertainment industry lost touch with the hopes and attitudes of the 'family values' audience."[8]

However, film culture was changing; the American independent films of the 1970s and 1980s represented a counter-culture potentially at odds with mainline Christianity, and Christian independent filmmaking no longer seemed to have a strong base of support. As a consequence, the film festival became a more appealing alternative to Christians looking for films made outside the production, distribution, and exhibition model mandated by the cineplex.

Many film scholars have been critical of mainstream film festivals like Sundance, which seem to offer lip-service support of independent film but in essence exist as another Hollywood industry event. Regardless, the impact of Sundance in the United States is undeniable: "Festivals are popping up like Starbucks franchises, in terms of numbers—every major city now has one—and in terms of the products they offer."[9] The number of film festivals in the United States has exponentially increased in recent years and not necessarily with a positive effect as the line between cineplex and festival offerings becomes less distinct. Nevertheless, film festivals seem less daunting to plan than before, and the audience for them is more of a given with the popularity of the so-called independent film. In addition to the presence of film festivals in even small-town venues, recent years have seen a rapid increase in a specialized type of film festival: the thematic festival. Perhaps traced back to the exhibition of Third World cinema,[10] recent thematic festivals often focus on filmmakers, subject matter, or genre.

Types of Evangelical Film Festivals

My primary area of interest is the way that festivals seem to grow from different sorts of evangelical sensibilities. In an effort to highlight how that happens, I am adapting David Bebbington's description of evangelical beliefs, which include four ideological points: conversionism as personal conversion (stressing the born-again experience), activism as communication of the gospel (making a vessel to carry the message), biblicalism as well-founded interpretation (understanding art as God-breathed), and crucicentrism as the centrality of Jesus (knowing Christ as reconciliation and the embrace of the other).[11] Using these four ideological points, I argue that there are two categories in evangelical film festivals. The first category emphasizes personal conversion and sharing the gospel. The second category emphasizes well-founded interpretation and the centrality of Jesus. Of course, these two categories are related. While some festivals fit more comfortably than others in the two categories, the festivals are complex events and should be understood in ways that allow them to exist in more than one category.

Film Festivals: Personal Conversion and Sharing the Gospel

Although they do not organize a film festival in the traditional sense of the term, International Christian Video Media (ICVM) is a good starting point for several reasons. The organization dates back to the early 1970s, when it was first called the Christian Films Distributors Association (CFDA), and consisted of about seventy film libraries across the country that rented 16mm films to churches. This connects that organization to the missionary film tradition. It began as a distribution system that worked outside the monolithic influence of Hollywood and the cineplex. In 1993 the name, the fundamental structure, and the goal of the organization were changed. The film library cooperative largely disbanded, and ICVM became an organization that networks Christian producers, distributors, directors, writers, and actors, holding an annual conference at various locations around the United States. Involved with ICVM throughout its history, executive director Brice Fennig describes the goal of the organization: "At the beginning of CFDA, I viewed it as an arm of the Church, that is, to provide them with a film to enhance their ministry. Now because of the advance in technology, I see it as an opportunity to get the Christian message into homes ... We view film as a cultural influence and entertainment. We attempt to have the 'good news of the gospel' as the main emphasis of each production."[12] The conference consists of a series of events featuring well-known speakers in Christian filmmaking with three distinctive tracks: creation, production, and distribution. Like other festivals in this category, the emphasis has remained clearly on an activist orientation to film: independent Christian filmmakers finding more effective ways to share the gospel. On occasion, ICVM has worked with larger Christian organizations like Zondervan and Focus on the Family, but the consistent focus has been on independent filmmaking such as *Facing the Giants* by the Kendrick brothers.

While having a more traditional open-exhibition format, the 168 Hour Film Project similarly keeps the focus on film production with a format designed to bring together filmmakers who will make a film to be exhibited in a week. Founded in 2003 in Burbank, California, director John Ware extended work he was doing with an arts and entertainment group at Bel Air Christian Church. Many people involved with film production at the church wanted to work together to develop films that would encapsulate a Christian worldview. Ware designed a film festival that required filmmakers to gather about one week in advance of film exhibition to make a film based on a Bible verse. When it comes to the films themselves, the 168 Hour Film Project may begin with an obvious verse, but Ware encourages subtlety: "I think the best way to go is to be subtle . . . If all films made were gospel films, no one would go to the movies because it would be one big sermon. My philosophy is that we need the whole spectrum of gospel films to good films with good story and a Christian worldview."[13] This modifies the stated goal of the ICVM with a different sense of what makes a film "Christian"; nevertheless, the idea of a Christian worldview still suggests the centrality of the Christian message within the film. In regard to

The 168 Hour Film Project in 2009. Filmmakers work to produce *Abel's Wheels*, a film to be screened at the week's end. (Photo courtesy of Terrence R. Wandtke.)

the filmmakers, Ware states, "We're trying to give them a better appreciation of the scripture and get them to trust that the spirit will move... And we've had numerous success stories with 168. We're hoping to change the world."[14] The successes Ware refers to include festival filmmakers who continue to make films that counter dominant trends of selling through sex and salaciousness, and filmmakers who have found their spiritual way and become Christians during the one-week process of filmmaking.

In 2004, the San Antonio Independent Christian Film Festival debuted as an outreach of the Vision Forum Ministry and was "dedicated to the reformation of Christian family culture."[15] Doug Phillips, the director of the ministry and film festival, suggests that the festival is a necessary outgrowth of the ministry goal with film as "the decisive media communicator of our generation. From a strategic perspective, film is absolutely critical, and it is in the area of film that many battles are being waged right now."[16] As Phillips describes, the war is between Hollywood's worldview and the Christian worldview as Hollywood develops projects that are "incredibly antagonistic to the family and biblical Christianity."[17] Phillips identifies the type of content he finds unacceptable even in artfully rendered films with high production value. He argues that the gospel message need not be obvious but that evil things must be called evil and cannot be used even as metaphor. In this way, he understands the San Antonio Independent Christian Film Festival as an answer to a problem: "We believe that it is not enough to curse the darkness. In fact, we don't believe you should curse the darkness. We believe that you should light candles. And the way that you light candles is to do things. We decided to honor excellence by giving an award. The world does that."[18] The top award at the festival is $101,000, a significant amount for a festival without major corporate sponsors or connections to Hollywood. The festival itself is designed primarily to support the Christian Filmmakers Academy. Bringing together seasoned Christian filmmakers with novices, the academy tries to encourage independent Christian filmmaking and circumvent Hollywood, which Phillips finds unlikely to be reformed in any meaningful way.

In 2007, the Gideon Media Arts conference was established in Ridgecrest, North Carolina, in association with LifeWay Ministries (and the Southern Baptist Association). Dealing with a variety of new media, Gideon continues to focus on film more than other media. With attention split between helping Christian filmmakers to network with one another, improve their skill set, and exhibit their work, Gideon synthesizes several of the ideas espoused by ICVM, 168, and San Antonio. Gideon Media Arts director Rodney Marett explains: "We wanted our conference to erase the negative connotation associated with 'Christian film.'... Our mission is to promote Christ through media. You can do this overtly or covertly where the Bible is not thrown in your face... We take in both [approaches] and don't discriminate against either one."[19]

One of the foremost ideas shared among the festivals described in this category is that film functions primarily as a popular vehicle that conveys a message; at these festivals, the central goals are to showcase films that share the gospel and to teach filmmaking that aspires to this goal. The second category of evangelical film festivals does not work in opposition to these goals but has points of focus that make it distinctive from the first.

Film Festivals: Well-Founded Interpretation and Centrality of Jesus

The City of the Angels Film Festival is a good starting point in the second category. When campus minister Scott Young was invited to be part of the pilot faculty for the Los Angeles Film Studies Center in 1991, he expanded his notion of film beyond being merely "a means to open up great discussions."[20] Study led him to more academic appreciation of film and informed a conversation at Fuller Theological Seminary between Young, Richard Mouw (subsequently president at Fuller), and several evangelical Christians working in the filmmaking community of Los Angeles. As they developed the idea of a film festival in 1993, Young argued that the festival should serve the city of Los Angeles, at that time dealing with the Rodney King riots. Young states,

> We wanted to pick films from a century of filmmaking that raised questions about the city and spirituality and pushed forward the aesthetics of film... We tried to have someone to speak about the religious aspects of the film, the aesthetics, and someone to speak about the city. We selected a lot of films that were controversial... I really wanted the community speaking about a wide variety of issues and saw film as a means to create a conversation.[21]

Film was understood as a matrix that represented the intersection of faith, culture, and art and required an informed perspective to appreciate the medium. Filling a previously unrecognized need for retrospective programming, the festival was well received by the mainstream media in Los Angeles that approved of its goals of studying the Los Angeles experience. The controversial films to which Young refers were *American Gigolo*, *Blade*

Runner, and *El Norte;* his commitment to "edgy" films continued in years to come with *Breaking the Waves* and *Mulholland Drive*. Young identified these films as pushing artistic boundaries in a way that disoriented viewers but ironically encouraged more genuine conversation about spiritual issues. As for the festival's identity, Young states, "I deliberately did not ever call our film festival a Christian film festival. I was more likely to say that our film festival explored the spiritual and religious dimensions of film."[22] In years to come, retrospective festivals became more prevalent, and after 2005 the festival began showing recent independent film and more discretely targeting a Christian audience.

Along similar lines, the Flickerings Film Festival grew slowly, beginning in 1995 with the Imaginarium, a speaker venue at the Cornerstone Festival (a music and arts festival organized by Jesus People USA). When Mike Hertenstein, the director of programming, was contacted by many long time festival attendees who were filmmakers interested in seeing a venue devoted exclusively to film, the result was the Flickerings Film Festival. In establishing it in 2001 as another venue at Cornerstone, Hertenstein tried "to create a community of filmmakers and film-watchers, who looked to Flickerings as more than just a one-time event but an ongoing conversation and growing core group."[23] Hertenstein initially regarded the venue as he would a serious international film festival but quickly recognized that its Christian context and small size limited it in that regard. Nevertheless, this vision was pursued. Hertenstein describes the reason he tried to avoid the influence of most other Christian film festivals:

> "Christian" in this context [of film festivals] typically functions as code language for the identity politics of popular culture: it denotes culturally-approved products, which fulfill expectations (e.g., "family friendly," evangelistic, and didactic) . . . [However,] as C. S. Lewis notes, . . . art—including film—offers an opportunity to see with other eyes. . . . Some of the most powerfully contemplative and/or moral or human films have been made from within Islamic or Taoist, Buddhist or Confucian traditions—films many Christians would find spiritually edifying.[24]

Programs have included the exhibition of original films but also of thematic, retrospective programming. Film discussion is an essential part of the festival, and those discussions have regularly been led by Christian academics interested in the way films work in dialogue with culture.

In 2002, W. David O. Taylor expanded his arts festival at Austin's Hope Chapel to include film, soon to be called the Ragamuffin Film Festival, a short but well-remembered festival (lasting until 2005 with a reappearance in 2007). His basic idea differed slightly from the ideas associated with the City of Angels and Flickerings in that "there was an aesthetic discipleship... On the artistic side, we wanted to feature the best film possible... [However,] in relation to production value, we often felt that what filmmakers did with the limited budget they had was quite good."[25] When establishing the film festival within the Austin arts community, Taylor wanted to impress the purveyors of culture but not at the expense of his identity as a Christian:

> We wanted to be known as Christians as we were attached to a church but wanted to be known through our work and develop personal relationships that went beyond stereotypes. There were other film festivals that very much wanted to be known as Christian and we didn't want that because we believed it would be too difficult to qualify what a Christian film or Christian film festival might look like... We were trying to navigate a middle way.[26]

Taylor looked at film as something potentially conceptual and abstract that moves beyond standard narrative films. As the festival grew and festival staff moved on, Taylor decided to end the festival before it became less than it had been. However, he came to the conclusion that a film festival and Hollywood could never be described as uniform entities that fit into some sort of sacred/secular paradigm: "Every film festival was governed by politics, and acceptance/rejection had as much to do with those complex politics as whether the festival was Christian or not."[27]

In consultation with fairly objective colleagues, I find my festival, the Imago Film Festival in the Chicago area, falling roughly into the category of evangelical film festivals that stress well-founded interpretation of film and the centrality of Jesus. Founded in 2005 and hosted by Judson University, the festival features original independent films and a few theatrically released films that explore the intersections between faith and film. This general description is not intended to hide the Christian identity of the school or film festival but to attract a wide audience that extends beyond the church community. Two commitments further shape the festival. The independent nature of independent film is based on the film's concept as much as the film's production, and Imago has made a special commitment to experimental film. My bias as an evangelical educator leads to activities such as discussions led by filmmakers and film critics meant to explore the dynamic presence of faith in film.

One more festival needs mention: the Damah Film Festival, founded in Seattle in 2001. Because it is identified as a film festival put together by people from a variety of spiritual backgrounds to showcase spiritual films, it cannot be classified as a Christian film festival per se. At the same time, many of the other above-mentioned festivals avoid a Christian nomenclature for a variety of reasons, and Damah's refusal to engage in typical Christian debates (such as the sacred/secular debate) has been used as a basis for the shape of other Christian film festivals.

For festivals in this second category, the directives of well-founded interpretation and the centrality of Jesus are applied in abstract fashion to the experience of film. Within this framework, film is a dynamic and living art form that potentially embodies the person, teachings, and body of Christ but requires a discerning mind to interpret effectively. As opposed to film festivals in the first category, these film festivals would regard classic moralistic Hollywood films less favorably and see the independent films of the 1970s and 1980s as more liberating than threatening. One of the foremost ideas shared between these festivals is that film functions as a dynamic art form that enables a connection with the ethical and spiritual presence of our savior; at these festivals, the central goal is to increase an understanding of film that recognizes the creative spirit of the Word beyond the confines of doctrine.

Conclusion: Christian Film Festivals and Culture

In my estimation, the driving forces behind most of these festivals are evangelical in nature. Although admittedly complex and somewhat varied historical forces are at work, what can be seen on the festival landscape of the last two decades is a new strategy utilized by Christians in the United States to address a lack of certain types of films and film criticism in current filmmaking. As previously noted, most of these festivals are part of a basic evangelical sensibility despite the fact that various festivals fit more conveniently within one of the two significant categories. However, there can be overlap. Just as the first category in Christian film festivals—stressing personal conversion and sharing the gospel—expressly seeks to encourage Christian filmmakers, its desire for independent filmmaking seems to be at least an implicit purpose of the second category of film festivals. Just as the second category in Christian film festivals—stressing well-founded interpretation and the centrality of Jesus—intentionally works to educate Christian filmgoers, its critical viewing seems to be at least a subtle part of the first category of film festivals.

It is also important to note the variety within each of the two categories that I have established. In the first category we see the message-centered goal of ICVM, the call for subtlety at the 168 Hour Film Project, and the question of content with the San Antonio Independent Christian Film Festival. In the second category we see the past retrospective programming at City of the Angels, the emphasis on world cinema at Flickerings, and strong interest in experimental film with Imago.

While I would argue that this brief overview of Christian film festivals covers the most important festivals in recent history, I acknowledge that it is not a complete history. Other festivals include Kingdomwood Christian (founded in 2006), Projecting Hope (2008), Doorpost Film Project (2008), Moonlight (2009), The Attic (2010), Phoenix International Christian (2010), and San Diego Christian (2010), among others. However, aside from the innovative design of Doorpost as an online film festival, these film festivals seem to be following in paths established by other Christian film festivals in terms of design and purpose: Doorpost is much like the Damah Film Festival; Projecting Hope is similar to the distinctly Christian Heartland; and San Diego Christian is less restrictive but still worldview-minded like San Antonio Independent Christian.

In any case, after identifying common links between Christian film festivals that are tied to evangelicalism, it seems important to raise the question of audience. If these film festivals are the new way in which (evangelical) Christianity is expressing itself, who is listening? The audience for the San Antonio Independent Christian Film Festival has been largely churchgoing Christians from the start, and even the City of the Angels Film Festival has transitioned from targeting a mainstream audience to a much more specific college-age Christian audience. Of course, there is nothing wrong with this. However, do the festivals serve the purpose of evangelizing mainstream culture by creating influential Christian filmmaking and filmgoing communities, or are they in danger of becoming institutions that unintentionally serve themselves? I ask this question because my own festival, the Imago Film Festival, has been not entirely effective at extending its audience beyond college students and churchgoers as we had intended from the start; I ask this question as I see Christian film festival programs become more homogenous and the Christian Film Festivals of America organization become a franchise planner for such festival events. The recent group of Christian film festivals may have evangelical roots, but will they continue to maintain distinctly evangelical goals of being independent from and yet influential on culture? In his essay "The Festival Viewed as a

Religious Order," French film critic and theorist André Bazin critiqued the early, important festivals of his day (like Venice and Cannes) as supplanting the church with its spectacle but having no higher purpose than its self-serving celebration.[28] Hopefully, Christian film festivals are not currently moving in that direction. Nevertheless, it will take careful and continuing introspection on the part of their organizers to ensure that Christian film festivals do not become an obsolete strategy in the history of evangelical Christianity's attempt to influence U.S. culture.

Notes

1. Randall Balmer, *Blessed Assurance: A History of Evangelism in America* (Boston: Beacon, 1999), 10.

2. Quentin J. Schulze and Robert H. Woods Jr., "Getting the Conversation Going about Media and Culture," in *Understanding Evangelical Media*, eds. Quentin J. Schultze and Robert H. Woods Jr. (Downers Grove, IL: InterVarsity, 2008), 22.

3. William D. Romanowski, *Pop Culture Wars: Religion and the Role of Entertainment in American Life* (Downers Grove, IL: InterVarsity, 1996), 39–40.

4. Terry Lindvall, *Sanctuary Cinema: Origins of the Christian Film Industry* (New York: New York University Press, 2007), 20–24, 28–36.

5. Quoted in Lindvall, *Sanctuary Cinema*, 62.

6. John Belton, *American Cinema/American Culture* (Boston: McGraw Hill, 2009), 3.

7. Kenneth Turan, *Sundance to Sarajevo: Film Festivals and the World They Made* (Berkeley: University of California Press, 2002), 36.

8. William D. Romanowski, *Eyes Wide Open: Looking for God in Popular Culture* (Grand Rapids, MI: Brazos, 2001), 24.

9. Mark Peranson, "First You Get the Power, Then You Get the Money: Two Models of Film Festivals," in *Dekalog 3: On Film Festivals*, ed. Richard Porton (London: Wallflower, 2009), 23.

10. Marijke De Valck, *Film Festivals: From European Geopolitics to Global Cinephilia* (Amsterdam: Amsterdam University Press, 2007), 166–167.

11. David Bebbington, *Evangelism in Modern Britain: A History from the 1730s to the 1980s* (Grand Rapids, MI: Baker, 1989), 3. I rename the four points slightly from Begginton's original not to fundamentally change their meaning but to refine each so that they better relate to an understanding of the role of art (particularly film) in culture.

12. Brice Fennig, email message to author, September 20, 2010.

13. John Ware, interview by author, September 17, 2010.

14. Ibid.

15. Doug Phillips, interview by author, September 8, 2010.

16. Ibid.
17. Ibid.
18. Ibid.
19. Rodney Marett, interview by author, September 14, 2010.
20. Scott Young, interview by author, October 15, 2010.
21. Ibid.
22. Ibid.
23. Mike Hertenstein, email message to author, August 21, 2010.
24. Ibid.
25. W. David O. Taylor, interview by author, October 28, 2010.
26. Ibid.
27. Ibid.
28. André Bazin, "The Festival Viewed as a Religious Order," in *Dekalog 3: On Film Festivals*, ed. Richard Porton (London: Wallflower, 2009), 15–18.

Chapter 15

Themed Destinations, Museums, and Evangelicals

Annalee R. Ward

By the end of a typical day, Les Chevaldayoff, the actor who plays Jesus at the Holy Land Experience (HLE) in Orlando, Florida, will have sung, danced, acted, given communion, been flogged, hoisted up on a cross, cleaned up, and emerged from the fog in gleaming white—or, in evangelical language, will have suffered and been crucified and resurrected, twice. A committed Christian evangelical, Chevaldayoff passionately proclaims his belief that this work serves the hurting and lost people by bringing them the love of Jesus—in 3D.

From the HLE to the Creation Museum and beyond, multi-media spectacles of entertainment are drawing increased attention from the broader culture, often as the easy target of jokes. Nevertheless, evangelicals are producing more of this non-traditional popular culture as a form of evangelical tourism. The growing critical attention shows these venues are emerging from the margins to be seen and heard by the mainstream culture.

What kind of evangelical tourist destinations are there, and how do they express their faith? Why are they drawing attention, and are they viable tourist destinations? To answer these questions, I set out to visit sites from Florida to Arkansas, Missouri to Ohio, observing and interviewing managers, employees, and visitors at various Christian tourist destinations in the United States.[1] I found variety in purpose, means, and messages but unity in a mindset of entertainment. From themed destinations reflecting historical precedence to museums, these attractions entertain and inspire but also raise issues of how evangelicals faithfully engage popular culture.

Les Cheveldayoff as Jesus at Holy Land Experience, Orlando, Florida, after being flogged as tourists look on. (Photo courtesy of Annalee R. Ward.)

Themed Destinations

The Holy Land Experience (HLE)

Situated just off I-4 and down the road from Universal Studios in Orlando, Florida, is HLE. With my return visit to the park, I wondered if the new ownership would make much of a difference. As I walked toward the entrance, I encountered Adam and Eve—at the HLE. Founded by Baptist minister and converted Jew Marvin J. Rosenthal and his ministry, Zion's Hope, HLE opened in 2001 more as a living history experience than a theme park. He wanted to establish "a wholesome, family oriented, educational and entertainment facility, where people can come to be encouraged, instructed, and reinforced in their faith."[2] Financially struggling over the years, HLE was acquired by Trinity Broadcasting Network (TBN) in 2007 for $37 million. TBN promptly fired about one-fourth of the employees and proceeded to brand the park with a flashier, baroque style.[3] Now as I approached the gray block entrance of the Damascus Gate, the walkway was lined by a faux Garden of Eden with plastic figures—a sign of things to come?

HLE's space evokes the themed environment of the *Ten Commandments* movie set.[4] A fake reality washed over me, from the plastic smiles of the greeters to the fake flowers and fruit filling the marketplace. An old Hebrew woman assured visitors, "You'll be so blessed that you've come out of the world and into the kingdom." The very statement belies an odd worldview, to say the least.

This passageway shuttled us into the first stage area where a Jesus look-alike in the Anglo-Saxon style was singing, "You raise me up to be more than I can be . . ." He ends with "You guys have a blessed day." The words ruined my image of a Jesus who speaks with authority. Most of the audience, more women than men, are older than the performer. I feared that the casual contemporary address did not fit the setting but was proved wrong with the main act's bridging of old and modern worlds. In it some women in sparkly Hebrew garb delivered a show based on the story of Jesus's encounter with the woman at the well (John 4:7–26), but their language also reflected today's casual vernacular. It was a biblically based story interpreted through twenty-first-century eyes.

Schedules are distributed to visitors upon entry, and while some shows are repeated, the set-up is structured in such a way as to move the visitor on past this central stage toward other shows, often described as "worship." Options include the Wilderness Tabernacle where there is a priestly reenactment of a "typical" sacrifice at the Ark of the Covenant of the Israelites; a small children's area with a climbing wall; the Temple Plaza with a variety of shows including one or two of Jesus's miracles; the Theatre of Life showing a TBN film; the Dead Sea Qumran Caves where communion is served ten times a day by Jesus and a disciple; a scaled Jerusalem Model, AD 66; various gardens; the Scriptorium, which houses the Van Kampen Collection of Scriptures; and the centerpiece show, which is performed twice, once outdoors and once inside on stage—the death, crucifixion, and resurrection of Jesus.

A key change under TBN's ownership of HLE is more intentional evangelism and what they call "ministry." The park encourages people to fill out color-coded slips of paper and post them on a cross. This provides TBN with more names for its contact list and hope for prayer support from these visitors. More overt evangelical efforts are evident in programming. For example, during the crucifixion, the character of the centurion breaks the fourth wall and challenges the audience to commit to Christ. It is more of a command than an invitation as he then leads everyone in a "repeat after me" sinner's prayer and acceptance of Christ. Standing in the hot sun, wishing the program would end, I felt coerced and wondered about the ethics of this kind of demand for group prayer. The day ended with an indoor repeat of the crucifixion story and then a call to come to Calvary's Garden Tomb for ministering prayer from the staff. During this intensely emotional time, with music swelling in the background, Cheveldayoff (the actor who played Jesus), encouraged people to come to various areas for specific kinds of prayer led by the staff. Chevaldayoff, however, had confirmed in an interview that not all actors are Christians, which raises questions of authenticity.

The question of authenticity is a prominent one when applied to the physical space of the park. Calvary, Gethsemane, and the burial tomb (three separate locations in reality) are collapsed into a single space. Moreover, HLE chooses bits and pieces of biblical life as it mixes the reality of the serious Church sacrament of communion with the entertainment environment and function of a themed park. But with the largest Christian television network of TBN promoting and supporting it, HLE just may continue to be a destination for the faithful viewers and those who long for the emotional engagement that music, image, and presence evoke.

Other Holy Lands

While HLE gets the most press, it is not the only Holy Land park. Tierra Santa in Buenos Aires claims to be the world's first religious theme park. Housing more than 600 figures illustrating biblical times, musical shows with singers and dancers, artisans, and diverse religious venues from a temple to a mosque, the park director says it "recreates the experience of being there [the Holy Land]" and is an important place of evangelism. During high season, it gets more than 30,000 visitors a week and is a significant tourist destination.[5]

Because of the seeming success of HLE, discussions for a similar park in Mallorca, Spain, are occurring.[6] Other smaller Holy Land parks have not done as well. For example, Holy Land USA in Bedford, Virginia, was a 200-acre site of biblical scenes staged to point to Christ, but because of high operating costs it was auctioned off in 2009.[7] Another Holy Land USA in Waterbury, Connecticut, operated from 1957 until the mid-1980s. Built on the side of a hill, it commanded attention and was a popular tourist destination, but it now lies in ruins.[8]

248   Evangelical Christians and Popular Culture

Changing patterns of vacationing and more sophisticated multi-media sites mean the quirkier, less mainstream expressions of Christian destinations disappear. Those that survive have the support of a church or organization behind them. For example, not quite as elaborate a destination, Ave Maria Grotto in Cullman, Alabama, claims to be known as "Jerusalem in Miniature." Dedicated in 1934, it has replicas of significant historical buildings as well as a Jerusalem hillside, but it survives today because of the St. Bernard Abbey's support.[9] Another smaller destination supported by the Church of God of Prophecy is the Field of the Woods Bible Park in Murphy, North Carolina, which boasts of a Golgotha and a Ten Commandments mountain.[10] These sites passively engage the visitor, unlike the HLE with its variety of shows and passion play.

Eureka Springs

One site that combines the older style of engagement with a total site experience is found in Eureka Springs, Arkansas, at the New Great Passion Play. Above the winding road, far up on a hillside, a white statue with stiff, outspread arms welcomed me. "Stumpy Jesus—that's what the locals call him," a friend told me in reference to the proportions of the Christ of the Ozarks statue. Erected in 1966 on the side of a hill, the statue rises seven stories and was meant to be both an inspiration and a reminder of God's providence.[11] An outdoor amphitheater seating 3,500 soon followed, and a passion play reenacting Jesus's last week on earth has been produced there since 1968, attracting over 7 million people.[12] At times the cast includes over 200 actors working with a recorded dialogue. The executive director acknowledged that the site struggles financially and has had to make cutbacks.[13]

Other activities on the grounds grew up around the statue and the play. At one point they added a New Holy Land Tour via tram, but a bad storm destroyed most of their sets. Making cutbacks, they now offer a Living Bible tour where visitors walk to various stations to see and hear biblical characters describe their lives. The actors tend to be retirees passionate about the opportunity to share the biblical stories. From a stable keeper to a Hebrew woman, a priest or the apostle Peter, the oral storytelling tradition lives on here.

Evangelical commitment continues in a pre–passion play show given by a potter who, through metaphor, shares his work and the gospel. The site also hosts a Sacred Arts Museum, a Bible Exhibit, a section of the Berlin Wall, and a small chapel. Over the years, the Eureka Springs Passion Play organization contributed significantly to a tourism industry in a town that has proudly participated in the play and supported an environment welcoming to Christians. It fosters a tourist industry created, in part, around Christian symbols and stories, including the architecturally significant Thorncrown Chapel, all designed as entertaining evangelism.[14] From the HLE in Orlando to the Passion Play in Eureka Springs, these tourist sites derive some of their attraction from their adjacency to similar tourist sites.

Branson, Missouri

For the Passion Play, a key selling point is that it is within a comfortable drive's distance from Branson, Missouri, a town described by many residents as "Christian." Driving into town, I was accosted by signage galore and obvious tourist traps. Known for its many musical revues and celebrity musician theaters, Branson, a town of only 7,500 residents, attracts almost 8 million visitors a year.[15] Aimed at those who seek family-friendly, "God and country" entertainment, most of the shows include Christian references, songs, and themes.[16] One of the earliest shows in town, the *Shepherd of the Hills*, now a park and play based on Harold Bell Wright's book, features a character based on the life of a preacher who learns about forgiveness and redemption experientially. A family-run business, the Shepherd of the Hills holds a deep reverence for the traditions there and assumes a working knowledge of Christianity but does not actively promote it.[17]

One of the newest additions to Branson, the Sight and Sound Theatre, declares it is a place "where the Bible comes to life!"[18] Staging biblical stories in a new, almost 2,100-seat auditorium in Branson, its mission is a focal point for all of its employees.[19] The mission statement is printed on the behind-the-scenes tour pass: "Our purpose is to present the Gospel of Jesus Christ and sow the Word of God into the lives of our customers, guests, and fellow workers by visualizing and dramatizing the scriptures, through inspirational productions, encouraging others and seeking always to be dedicated and wise stewards of our God-given talents and resources."[20]

This single-mindedness evidences itself in the backstage tour, which ends with an old-fashioned prayer circle where the guides ask for prayer concerns and present a quick gospel message. It also appears in the gift shop merchandise of Bible-themed puzzles, books, and music, and, of course, in the show itself. This particular show, *Noah*, based on the life of Noah and his family, ends with a dramatic reference to Christ and an offer to pray after the show with any guests who would like to know more about

Christianity. While the three-sided stage and live animals create impressive spectacle, the script, acting, and inconsistent set design detract from an overall impression of a quality production.

I next headed to Silver Dollar City on the edge of Branson, a more traditional theme park owned by the Herschend Corporation and operating under a mission statement that concludes with the phrase, "all in a manner consistent with Christian values and ethics."[21] Sitting in the shaded log chapel on the grounds of the theme park, I heard the excited voices of children and adults rushing to rides, water attractions, and bluegrass shows and found the atmosphere both peaceful and exciting. With a focus on family and service, the Herschend Corporation, which also owns a number of other parks, including Dollywood,[22] believes in practicing its faith rather than proclaiming it but does not require that its employees be Christians. Brad Thomas, the general manager, observes, "Our guests come to our theme park to be entertained: that's our business. Though we don't have preachers on street corners, we hope that through our shows, our actions, our visitors can sense a special family atmosphere that would be pleasing to God."[23]

Many other attractions and shows in Branson reference their commitment to Christ or openly proclaim the gospel. Sunday services are even held in several of the theaters, where the mixture of religion and patriotism abounds. As I walked down the main street past miniature golf, hotels, restaurants, and neon signs, the discount ticket offices and trinket stores seemed to reproduce themselves in each new block and reminded me of pictures I had seen of the booths at medieval pilgrimage sites.

Historical Roots

Western drama traces its roots to the Greeks who, beginning around 700 BC, produced mythical or historical plays acknowledging the gods.[24] Later, the Romans enhanced the dramatic with more varied forms of entertainment and spectacle, some of which began to mock Christianity. By the fifth century AD, Christians rejected games and spectacles partly because people attended these pagan rituals instead of church.[25]

While an early form of a passion play, albeit celebrating the Egyptian god Osiris, can be traced to 2500 BC, strong evidence of the Church's involvement in producing spectacle appears in the Middle Ages. Mystery plays and morality plays staged by traveling troupes brought the Bible to life for people who did not have much access to the scriptures. Specialized ropes and pulleys added the always-entertaining special effects of the day.[26] Passion plays performed as parts of religious festivals soon came to stand on their own in places like Oberammergau in Bavaria, Germany, where a play has been performed regularly since 1634.

A "cult of the martyrs" also developed in the early church, and by the fourth century, places that held relics became significant attractions for pilgrims.[27] That miracles often occurred in these places only increased the popularity of the pilgrimage. The journeys then grew more pleasurable as hotels and services developed to serve the pilgrims.[28]

World fairs popularized in the nineteenth century contributed to today's theme park development with their rich exoticism of otherness and opportunities for entertainment and education,[29] and the religious worldview appeared in several of these fairs in the form of Holy Land representations. While international travel may not have been widely available to the masses, virtual travel in the form of "stereopticons, slide shows, scale models, museum displays, [and] world's fair expositions" was.[30] A "pilgrimage" to the Holy Land attracts the faithful, even if it is a simulation. Thus, the Vienna Fair in 1873 displayed a scale model of Jerusalem. The 1904 St. Louis Fair went beyond the model to create a full-sized Jerusalem that covered 11 acres with scenes from Bethlehem, Jesus's tomb, the Tabernacle, and the Temple. Unfortunately, it also demonstrated some of the problems with contemporary attractions as low attendance led to financial difficulties.[31]

The self-improvement movement in the late nineteenth century gave rise to another related attraction in the form of summer camp experiences called the Chautauqua (named after the New York location). Initiated as a Sunday school assembly, the focus began with improving biblical knowledge but quickly expanded to include a variety of lectures on arts and sciences as well as being a venue for music. To enhance biblical literacy, teachers employed drama and reenactments, photos, paintings, ritual ceremonies, models, and lectures.[32] They even created a three-dimensional relief map of the Holy Land called Palestine Park.[33] This movement again provides evidence of people's longing to engage "material piety."[34]

A more modern forerunner to the religious tourist destinations of today began with televangelists Jim and Tammy Bakker's vision. A religious theme park, Heritage USA saw over 6 million visitors by 1986 as the third largest park in the United States. It combined recreation, a water park, a petting zoo, shopping, and gourmet food with a 5,000 seat church and twenty-four-hour prayer room, but it took $3 million a week to run.

After Jim Bakker's scandal, the park went bankrupt and closed in 1997, but not before people lost millions of dollars.[35]

Museums

Religious tourist attractions, rooted in history in various shapes, include one more category—the museum. Quirky or mainstream, mundane or extravagant, museums exist in a variety of forms to preserve human memories and educate the next generation.[36] The contemporary Christian museums include an interesting mix of memorializing and moral argument.

Precious Moments Chapel

A couple of hours outside of Branson, an unusual place mixes commercialism, the sacred, and public memorializing: Precious Moments Chapel. Located in the geographical heart of the country near Carthage, Missouri, this represents a mecca for the collectors of Precious Moments figurines, the big-headed children with teardrop eyes. Sam Butcher built his park in the mid-1980s out of gratitude to God. It houses a collector's headquarters, a museum for Precious Moments drawings and figurines, and a chapel patterned loosely after the Sistine Chapel. The peaceful grounds dotted with Precious Moment angel statues encourage a reverent quiet. The chapel's paintings and stained glass windows, with biblical stories illustrated by Precious Moments characters, reinforces the solemnity. As the guide tells it, children do not cry when they come into the chapel, implying its sacred power.[37]

Over the years, the chapel has also become a place of memorializing, in particular, dead children. In response to letters he had received, Butcher often painted characters representing a dead child's story on his central mural, "Hallelujah Square," a picture of heaven seen through the eyes of children. Then, when his 30-year-old son died in a car accident, he added on a smaller "Phillip's Chapel," which honors his son but also includes a room of heavy bound books where people enter notes to or about a lost loved one. Butcher responded to their words of sorrow with more messages about God painted in murals and embedded in glass windows. One pointed mural in the hallway includes a picture of Jesus in the clouds with the title "Will you be ready when he comes again?" Is it manipulative or sensitive to provide a place for mourning? Given the number of visitors and the well over 100 filled books, it seems to be meeting a need, but it also provides an easy target for accusations of "kitsch."[38]

Billy Graham Library

A more obvious memorializing museum is the Billy Graham Library in Charlotte, North Carolina, opened in 2007.[39] Created by the same theme park designers as HLE, it even includes an animatronic talking cow and shuttles visitors through various rooms that unpack the narrative of Graham's life and ministry. A walkway through a crystal cross concludes the tour and leads into a small auditorium where a short film of Graham presents the gospel and an altar call. Naturally, there are people available to pray with the willing visitor. In a crass mixture of contemporary religion and culture, the tour ends in the gift shop and snack shop.

Creation Museum

On the Kentucky border near Cincinnati, Ohio, I pulled up to a sleek building that opened out to inviting picnic grounds and dinosaurs. As I entered the Creation Museum, which opened in May 2007, I encountered a professional and mainstream culture atmosphere with a more traditional museum approach. It differed, however, in its obvious argument for a literal interpretation of Genesis, demanding belief in a 6,000-year-old earth created in six literal twenty-four-hour days.[40]

Supported by Answers in Genesis (AIG), the $27 million high-tech site counters natural history museum arguments. With a sophisticated 3D special effects theater, virtual planetarium, multiple dinosaur animatronics, media screens, and exhibits all with a carefully controlled message, the museum makes it very clear what truth it stands for.[41] The controlling spatial design that moves people in one direction from room to room, experience to exhibit, concludes with a brief gospel presentation.

AIG's expensive investment has brought the museum extensive publicity, fans, and critics. Initially they hoped to attract 200,000 visitors a year but have greatly surpassed that. In April 2010, they announced they had had their 1 millionth guest.[42] Visitors come from all over, but judging from the textbooks in the gift shop and the people I spoke with, it is particularly popular with homeschoolers. Fans of the museum appreciate having a high-quality place in the public square that puts forth an alternative view to the evolutionary one presented in mainstream museums.

Critics take issue with how it abuses science to support its perspective as well as with its patriarchal, authoritative tone.[43] This approach lends itself to an objectifying gaze that enhances the perceived authority of the museum.⁴⁴ This museum in Kentucky is not the first Creation Museum but is certainly the most sophisticated to date.⁴⁵

Other Museums

Traditional art museums that focus on scriptural art are also growing in popularity but are not always evangelical in purpose. The Museum of Biblical Arts in Dallas, rebuilt in 2005 after a fire, hopes to use biblical themes to foster "tolerance and understanding" through its focus on classical art.⁴⁶ With a less religious focus, the Museum of Biblical Art (MOBiA) in New York opened in 2005 to promote education on the "role of the Bible in literature and art" as a part of "cultural literacy."⁴⁷

The parks and museums discussed here focus on education, ministry, and inspiration. But leaders in the amusement industry believe that "Biblical projects are the wave of the future."⁴⁸ AIG announced plans to build Ark Encounter, a "historically themed experience" with "live performances" and family fun 45 miles down the road from the Creation Museum in Kentucky.⁴⁹ Will we soon see a Biblical amusement park with holy roller coasters and Noah's Ark water rides? That was the vision of Bible Park USA in Tennessee, but that project ultimately failed from lack of community support.⁵⁰ The interest in religious tourist sites that cater to family entertainment grows, and one scholar believes "the church will continue to seek in tourism all that makes it possible for it to have a stronger influence on believers."⁵¹

Issues of Cultural Engagement

After visiting these attractions, I found the need for critical reflection imperative. So many people I encountered worked out of noble motives, making sacrifices to be a part of an evangelical organization and eager to be pursuing new formats for spreading the gospel. On the other hand, embedded in these kind of attractions are questions regarding the mixing of the sacred and secular, the appropriateness of the entertainment focus, the degree of quality, and stewardship of resources.

Blurring the Sacred and Secular

Popular culture is a key site of secularizing the sacred and sacralizing the secular.⁵² When evangelicals engage stories that have historically belonged to the Church and locate them in tourist sites, the holiness of God and the sacred nature of the narratives may get lost. Sorting out the content added for entertainment value from that which originates in scripture is not always easy. Perhaps this is one reason Silver Dollar City focuses on providing a quality theme park of rides and entertainment rather than mixing in evangelism. Mixing the two is difficult to do with integrity to both.

Concerns over a sacred/secular mix are not new to the Church. Even Saint Augustine (354–430) lamented the blurring of boundaries between the pagan festivals, celebrations, and theater and those of the Church as converts to Christianity brought those practices with them to the Church.[53] The rising popularity, however, of the HLE and the Creation Museum, sites supported by highly organized and well-funded groups that exist outside of traditional Church structures, is something new. These sites in particular have blurred boundaries, especially when HLE, for example, offers the sacrament of Communion and "ministry" without the benefit of any individual church involvement or oversight.

Focusing on Entertainment

A concern closely related to the blurring of the sacred involves popularizing the gospel message by focusing on entertainment. Sam Rey, the executive director of the Great Passion Play, argues for both the need and the legitimacy of using entertainment as a means of evangelism, echoing many evangelists' approaches.[54]

Taking a contrary position in a challenge to Christians to be faithful to their calling, Christian theologian, author, and educator Marva J. Dawn asks, "How do we reconcile the spectacle of media presentations, for example, with the character of the God we are worshiping—an unpretentious Jesus who eschewed the temptation to indulge in spectacle for the sake of winning the crowds . . . ?"[55] The performative emphasis calls for visual spectacle. The Reformation believed there was heresy in the idolatry of iconography, or the making and worshipping of religious images. Is today's impulse to build museums, theme parks, roadside stops, and other attractions a legitimized form of Protestant iconography? Taken out of the formal worship setting and placed in the realm of entertainment, the images, sounds, and multi-media forms encourage religious devotion, in some cases educate, but above all entertain.

Maintaining Quality

How these attractions communicate their message raises questions of quality. Criticized by some for being kitschy, that is, full of cheap sentimentalism, places like the Precious Moments Chapel do not hold up to standards of high art, but I could not deny the role it served to comfort grieving parents with the hope of God's love. Even places that may not appeal to educated tastes hold important functions: "the chapel really does look very different to different people, depending on one's point of view—including one's theology, experience, and aesthetic taste."[56] Humility may require appreciation for the context, the makers, and those who enjoy it.

As evangelicals navigate these tensions, they must also consider the question of resources. High-quality attractions require significant monetary investments and raise questions of stewardship. With investments like TBN's purchase of HLE for $37 million, the building of the Creation Museum for $27 million, the planned Ark Experience to be built for over $125 million added to operating expenses, I can only wonder where the money comes from and if God is pleased with the way it is used.

Conclusion

Leisure entertainment and education combined with faith commitments have long involved travel. Historically, pilgrimages captured that longing for the sacred combined with the curiosity for what was "out there." Today, pilgrim and tourist distinctions matter little as the faithful visit sites that engage belief, entertainment, education, and emotion and do so as part of the over "$4 billion a year religious entertainment industry."[57]

I began my travels with questions of what evangelical destinations existed, how they expressed faith commitments, why they are popular, and if they are viable. All engaged evangelical impulses, some more overtly than others. With growing sophistication, many of them are proving they can attract audiences, but concerns about the sacred/secular divide, uses of entertainment, and quality of production along with the high demand for operating costs will continue to raise questions of viability.

My travels to Christian attractions leave me conflicted: inspired by the faithful commitments of evangelicals to reach their culture but emotionally manipulated by forced sinners' prayers and sentimentality; encouraged by high-quality production values and sophisticated technology but discouraged by outdated language and acting; hopeful that new formats of gospel presentations will reach new audiences but disillusioned that it might be more about monetary gain. Would Jesus be honored by these places that profess to serve him, or would he be offended?

Whether theme park or museum, evangelical tourist sites continue to emerge as destinations for those Christians who long for safe, family entertainment that supports their values. When scholars point out that Disney has become a religious site offering symbolic and mythic power,[58] evangelicals are rightly concerned. Popular culture sites, such as Disney or natural history museums, often present worldviews at odds with that of evangelicals and inspire them to counter with alternative sites. By using the same media, evangelicals hope to speak truth to a culture steeped in mainstream values. One scholar questions the effectiveness of that approach, concerned that popular culture is having more influence on evangelicals than vice versa: "I see them not as shapers of American culture, I see popular culture shaping them."[59] Seeking to be "salt and light" in the culture, evangelicals are increasingly employing the methods, resources, and high financial investments that the surrounding culture uses, but they may be losing their flavor in the process.

Notes

1. Thank you to Trinity Christian College for giving me a Summer Research Grant that made most of my travels possible.

2. Quoted in Mark I. Pinsky, "Six Flags over Israel," *Christianity Today*, March 5, 2001, 102.

3. Mark I. Pinsky, "Scores Lose Jobs as Holy Land Undergoes Extreme Makeover," *Orlando Sentinel*, October 21, 2007, http://articles.orlandosentinel.com/2007-10-21/news/holyland21_1_trinity-broadcasting-holy-land-prosperity-gospel (accessed January 4, 2010).

4. HLE was designed by ITEC Entertainment Corporation, known for its work at Universal's Islands of Adventure. Pinsky, "Six Flags," 101–103.

5. Anil Mundra, "Welcome to Argentina's Holy Land," *Global Post*, October 15, 2009, http://www.globalpost.com/dispatch/general/091015/holy-land-theme-park (accessed January 13, 2011).

6. Giles Tremlett, "Welcome to Holy Land—Europe's First Christian Theme Park," *Guardian*, September 12, 2010, http://www.guardian.co.uk/world/2010/sep/12/holy-land-christian-theme-park (accessed November 3, 2010).

7. Rex Bowman, "Holy Land USA Up for Auction," *Roanoke Times*, November 25, 2009, http://www.roanoke.com/news/roanoke/wb/227555 (accessed January 19, 2011). For a detailed description of the place, see Timothy K. Beal, *Roadside Religion: In Search of the Sacred, the Strange, and the Substance of Faith* (Boston: Beacon, 2005), 25–48.

8. "Holy Land USA," Roadside America, http://roadsideamerica.com/holy/index.html (accessed January 19, 2011).

9. "Ave Maria Grotto," http://www.avemariagrotto.com/ (accessed January 13, 2011).

10. Field of the Woods Bible Park in Murphy, North Carolina, http://fieldsofthewoodbiblepark.com/ (accessed January 19, 2011).

11. Timothy M. Kovalcik, *The Great Passion Play: Images of America* (Charleston, SC: Arcadia, 2008), 9.

12. The New Great Passion Play, "The Play," http://www.greatpassionplay.com/passionplay.asp (accessed January 20, 2011).

13. Sam Rey, interview by author, May 28, 2010.

14. Chris Branam, "Christ of Ozarks Marks 40 Years atop Mountain," *Arkansas Democrat-Gazette*, June 4, 2006, LexisNexis (accessed January 20, 2011).

15. City of Branson, "Branson Profile," http://www.cityofbranson.org/profile/index.htm (accessed January 27, 2011).

16. See Aaron K. Ketchell, *Holy Hills of the Ozarks: Religion and Tourism in Branson, Missouri* (Baltimore, MD: Johns Hopkins University Press, 2007).

17. Sharena Naugher, marketing director, interview by author, May 26, 2010; and Keith Thurman, director, interview by author, May 27, 2010.

18. Sight and Sound Theatres, 2010 Season Brochure.

19. Maria-Jose Tennison, director of marketing and services, Sight and Sound Theatres, interview by author, May 24, 2010.

20. Sight and Sound Theatre, "About Us, Name and Mission," http://www.sight-sound.com/WebSiteSS/getpage.do?id=51 (accessed May 8, 2011). The statement appears on backstage passes, business cards, and advertising brochures.

21. Herschend Family Entertainment, "Our Commitment," http://www.hfecorp.com/commitment/index.php (accessed January 25, 2011).

22. Dollywood is located in Gatlinberg, Tennessee. Nearby is the Christ in the Smokies Museum and Gardens, formerly known as Christus Gardens. See http://www.christinthesmokies.com/ (accessed February 10, 2011).

23. Brad Thomas, interview by author, May 27, 2010.

24. Oscar G. Brockett with Franklin J. Hildy, *History of the Theatre*, 8th ed. (Boston: Allyn and Bacon, 1999), 13–48.

25. Carol Harrison, *Augustine: Christian Truth and Fractured Humanity* (Oxford, UK: Oxford University Press, 2000), 136–139.

26. Brockett and Hildy, *History of the Theatre*, 8–9, 81–120.

27. Harrison, *Augustine*, 141–142.

28. Luigi Tomasi, "Homo Viator: From Pilgrimage to Religious Tourism Via the Journey," in *From Medieval Pilgrimage to Religious Tourism: The Social and Cultural Economics of Piety*, eds. William H. Swatos Jr. and Luigi Tomasi, *Religion in the Age of Transformation* (Westport, CT: Praeger, 2002), 1–24.

29. Salvador Anton Clavé, *The Global Theme Park Industry* (Cambridge, MA: CABI, 2007), 8–12.

30. "Holy Land," *Modiya*, New York University, Center for Religion and Media, http://modiya.nyu.edu/handle/1964/54 (accessed February 2, 2011).

31. Burke O. Long, *Imagining the Holy Land: Maps, Models, and Fantasy Travels* (Bloomington: Indiana University Press, 2003), 43–87.

32. Marilyn Mathews Bendiksen, "The Endless Summers of Chautauqua," *New York Archives Magazine*, Chautauqua Institution, http://www.archives.nysed.gov/apt/magazine/archivesmag_summer02.shtml (accessed February 2, 2011).

33. "Palestine Park," Chautauqua, New York, BiblePlaces.com http://blog.bibleplaces.com/2010/08/palestine-park-chautauqua-new-york.html (accessed June 26, 2012).

34. Long, *Imagining the Holy Land*, 39.

35. James A. Albert, *Jim Bakker: Miscarriage of Justice?* (Chicago: Carus, 1998), 19–30.

36. Campbell B. Gray, "Museums," in *Encyclopedia of Religion, Communication, and Media*, ed. Daniel A. Stout (New York: Routledge, 2006), 271, 273; and Bob Mondello, "A History of Museums, 'The Memory of Mankind,'" *NPR*, November 24, 2008, http://www.npr.org/templates/story/story.php?storyId=97377145 (accessed February 2, 2011).

37. For general information see Precious Moments, "About Us," http://www.preciousmoments.com/content.cfm/about (accessed February 5, 2011). A new website (http://preciousmomentschapel.org/node/1) dedicated to the chapel went up in 2009.

38. See Frank Burch Brown, *Good Taste, Bad Taste, and Christian Taste: Aesthetics in Religious Life* (New York: Oxford University Press, 2000), 138–147.

39. This is not to be confused with the Billy Graham Center Museum in Wheaton, Illinois, which houses his letters and papers, http://www.billygrahamcenter.com/museum/ (accessed February 5, 2011).

40. Chris Kenning, "Science and Religion: Creation Museum Opens," *Courier-Journal, USA*, Religion News Blog, May 30, 2007, http://www.religionnewsblog.com/18374/creation-museum-2, (accessed February 11, 2011).

41. Mark Looy, Chief Communications Officer of AIG and cofounder of the Creation Museum, interview by author, May 24, 2007.

42. Answers in Genesis, "Millionth Guest Visits Creation Museum," http://www.answersingenesis.org/articles/2010/04/26/millionth-guest-creation-museum (accessed February 2011).

43. Stephen T. Asma, "Dinosaurs on the Ark: The Creation Museum," *Chronicle Review*, May 18, 2007, B13; and Bethany Keeler-Jonker, "Rhetorics of Affirmation in the Creation Museum," National Communication Association Conference, San Francisco, CA, November 2010.

44. Gray, "Museums," 271, 273.

45. See the Creation and Earth History Museum in Sanee, CA. One dated website lists multiple creation museums: "Creation Museums," http://www.nwcreation.net/museums.html (accessed February 10, 2011).

46. Museum of Biblical Art, "About Us," http://www.biblicalarts.org/ (accessed February 28, 2011). Smaller places like the Museum of Religious Arts outside of Missouri Valley, Iowa, while aiming for education, also tend to have evangelical impulses; see "The Vision," http://www.mrarts.org/vision.html (accessed February 28, 2011).

47. Museum of Biblical Art (MOBiA), "About, History," http://mobia.org/about/history/ (accessed February 28, 2011).

48. Getahn Ward and Bob Smietana, "Bible Park USA Update (and FBAA Quote)," Faith Based Amusement Association, February 12, 2008, http://faithbasedfun.blogspot.com/2008/02/bible-park-usa-update-and-fbaa-quote.html (accessed February 10, 2011).

49. "Ark Encounter," http://arkencounter.com/faq/#admission (accessed February 10, 2011).

50. Jayne Clark, "Are Religion and Theme Parks a Good Mix?" *USA Today*, December 14, 2010, http://travel.usatoday.com/destinations/dispatches/post/2010/12/should-religion-and-theme-parks-mix/134780/1 (accessed February 10, 2011).

51. Boris Vukonić, *Tourism and Religion*, trans. Sanja Matešić (Oxford, England: Pergamon, 1996), 186. See also Tomasi, "Homo Viator," 1–24.

52. Conrad Ostwalt, *Secular Steeples: Popular Culture and the Religious Imagination* (Harrisburg, PA: Trinity Press International, 2003), 201.

53. Harrison, *Augustine*, 132–134.

54. Rey, interview by author. Bill Jones of HLE similarly advocated for any approach that was ethically sound or any approach that was consistent with scripture, including entertainment, interview by author, January 18, 2007. See also Walt Kallestad, *Entertainment Evangelism: Taking the Church Public* (Nashville, TN: Abingdon, 1996).

55. Marva J. Dawn, *Unfettered Hope: A Call to Faithful Living in an Affluent Society* (Louisville, KY: Westminster/John Knox, 2003), 96.

56. Brown, *Good Taste, Bad Taste*, 144.

57. Dahleen Glanton, "Showbiz Has a Star in Jesus," *Chicago Tribune*, November 12, 2006, http://articles.chicagotribune.com/2006-11-12/news/0611120418_1_evangelicals-popular-culture-theme-park/4 (accessed February 25, 2011).

58. See Eric Michael Mazur and Tara K. Koda, "The Happiest Place on Earth: Disney's America and the Commodification of Religion," in *God in the Details: American Religion in Popular Culture*, eds. Eric Michael Mazur and Kate McCarthy (New York: Routledge, 2001), 313.

59. Alan Wolfe, quoted in Glanton, "Showbiz Has a Star in Jesus."

Chapter 16

Evangelical Theater in a New Century: Redefining the Redemptive Theatrical Event

Paul D. Patton

In the early 1980s, I was the associate pastor of a small Baptist church in suburban Detroit, Michigan, increasingly frustrated by traditional methods of Christian training and education. Several of the people working with me had heard the invitation to "give their lives to God," but they were having a difficult time giving the next moment to anything but their next distraction. The traditional strategies of weekly Bible study and prayer were not working.

I had an idea. Why not exchange the poorly attended weekly meetings with a play production schedule of six to eight weeks and rehearsals several times per week? Getting together would be tied to a tangible mandate of telling a story well.

Thus was born Trinity House Theater. The first play, a musical several of us had written, ended after three weekends. The audiences seemed generally pleased with the new performance venue, though some were surprised that the protagonist did not get "saved" (or convert to Christianity) in the end. More significantly, at least for me as the pastor and founder of the theater, the performers—untrained, raw-edged actors and technicians—experienced a new identity, refined and strengthened by the pressures of the production process.

During the 1980s throughout North America, other Christian artists and ministers were launching new theaters, gathering willing thespians, building audiences, and writing plays. This was not just a case of churches experimenting with new ways to minister to their flocks as I did. These experiments in theater were also the result of a growing evangelical interest

Trinity House Theater, Livonia, Michigan, one of the earliest evangelical playhouses in the country, founded in the early 1980s and still in operation today. (© 2007 Ann Horn. All rights reserved.)

in the faithful integration of the Christian faith and the more traditionally sacred categories of life, including the ancient collaborative art form called theater.[1]

There has been an explosion of interest in the theater arts among evangelical Christians over the last generation.[2] The expansion of interest and involvement was birthed in and sustained by a variety of cultural and ecclesiastical factors. The development has occurred in both corporate worship settings—chancel dramas or "sermon starters"—as well as what Christian theater scholar Peter Lucas Senkbeil calls "dual-loyalty organizations,"[3] which strive to participate both in local art worlds within a popular culture landscape and in local Christian communities.

However, the explosion of interest and involvement in theater is also characterized by a unique tension between a concern for Christian witness and a perceived competing loyalty to artistic excellence. For some evangelicals, the tension remains nearly untenable, resulting in a *separatist* approach to the world,[4] which perceives artistic expressions as unnecessary luxuries unfit for faithful service to Christ. For other evangelicals the tension creates a *transformationist* approach, a "Christ the Transformer of Culture" mentality, which is more conducive to artistic production. It is the tension of these two aesthetic approaches that provides a significant context for understanding how and why evangelicals create theater art in a contemporary setting.

This chapter will provide a brief overview of Christian theater as informed by both aesthetic approaches, the effects of the dominant separatist approach of the past, and the tensions that remain for evangelicals operating within a transformationist approach. The chapter will also touch on some of the popular cultural trends that contributed to the expansion of theater within the evangelical church.

The Separatist and Transformationist Approaches

As mentioned earlier, the tension between faithful, evangelistic witness and passionate commitment to excellent theater for many evangelicals is represented in two ways, each informed by different aesthetic approaches. First, in the *separatist* approach, Christian theater participants "emphasize their religious identity and their separation from local art worlds, doing work informed by a utilitarian, rhetorical aesthetic which regards art primarily as a medium for communicating a religious message."[5] This rhetorical aesthetic is often considered an "art as evangelism" approach commonly associated with conservative, Protestant Christian traditions.

Second, in a *transformationist* approach, theater participants emphasize their identity as artists and operate within their local art worlds, doing work informed by a new Christian aesthetic, a more "poetical aesthetic,"[6] that regards "art primarily as a divinely-given means of expression with inherent worth."[7] This second approach has grown out of a combination of Catholic "natural theology" traditions and Dutch Reformed Protestant traditions.

Senkbeil asserted in an interview in 2010 that the rhetorical (separationist) and poetic (transformationist) tensions are still present, though lessened, and manifest in any media form in which evangelicals are involved—whether television, film, direct video, or live stage. The rhetorical aesthetic, primarily concerned with executing the message to the audience, desires to get a message across with great clarity. This desire leads to aesthetic choices that lessen all ambiguity and, thereby, lose the aesthetic richness of the message. The rhetorical aesthetic of the separationist approach pushes for the clarity of the message at the expense of poetic complexity and nuance. The church, as incubator and steward of gospel truth, has typically preferred the directness of sermons to the ambiguously rich possibilities of narrative.[8] Its playwrights tend to be constrained by a utilitarian urge to preach a sermon rather than unfold a story.

This urge to preach a sermon, in a nutshell, is the general cause of the scarceness of accomplished Protestant evangelical playwrights. Sermons are generally more efficient in garnishing audience effect and assuring clarity. In the process, the rhetorical aesthetic reduces the media message and medium to utilitarian ends: assuring clarity and, often, even quantifiable results (like how many people made "decisions for Christ" after the communication event). Suspicion of the more nuanced poetic aesthetic approach perpetuates an art *versus* evangelism dichotomy and perceives art as a minnow to catch bass, and thus reduces the depth and satisfaction of metaphor, illustrations, and art. The rhetorical aesthetic concerns itself with whether or not the gospel has been articulated with sufficient clarity and is suspicious of artistic expressions that may draw people away from the straightforward sensibilities of the Christian message.

The transformatist approach, known as the Christ the Transformer of Culture[9] approach among some evangelicals, has challenged excessive tendencies of the separatist (rhetorical) approach. Transformationists assert that evangelicals will have no part in helping to shape culture unless they are engaged with it. This approach to culture, perhaps best understood as even a paradigm shift among some evangelicals, was birthed in the philosophical workings of the Dutch Reformed Protestants of the late Victorian era: Dutch writers like Abraham Kuyper and Herman Dooyeweerd[10] set the stage for the transformationist shift that would spill over into the Baptist, Methodist, and Pentecostal assemblies nearly a century later. Popular books in the 1970s and 1980s, like Francis Schaeffer's *Art and the Bible*, Franky Schaeffer's *Addicted to Mediocrity*, Calvin Seerveld's *Rainbows for a Fallen World*, Hans Rookmaker's *Art Needs No Justification*, and Nicholas Wolterstorff's *Art in Action*[11] convinced many evangelicals to be responsible participants in the arts and to resist the temptation to withdraw from the world into a separatist ghetto.

Contributing Factors to Evangelicals' Theatrical Engagements

Shifts in approaches to art and culture among evangelicals were not just attributed to the theological thrust of transformationists. To begin, the more practical reality of television, soon to be cemented as a pop cultural habit (if not addiction) broke through the separatists' barricade. More and more evangelicals were purchasing television sets and, in most cases, unthinkingly giving them a place of prominence in their living rooms to dominate their entertainment focus. Movies and moviegoing, once off limits as "worldly" activities—a condemnation extended from the general disapproval of live theater attendance—was now more easily accessed in the comfort of one's living room. This simply made the demands of "separation from worldliness" a near-impossible act of obedience. As playwright and cultural analyst Ron Reed notes, once the "square-eyed Trojan horses infiltrated evangelical living rooms, the mighty fortress of cultural separationism was breached."[12] It was too tempting to turn on the television and view the same movies condemned a few years earlier.

Some of the renewed interest in a tranformationist approach to all of the arts, and popular culture in general, was inadvertently fueled by the inconsistency of condemning a new Hollywood movie at theaters only to watch the same movie in the privacy of one's home a few years later. Reed notes that it was only a matter of time before evangelical youth were going to the movies and auditioning for school plays without any help on how to integrate their faith with their artistic interests. The children of evangelicals were "signing up for actor training and playwriting workshops" with little awareness that their grandparents never set foot in the theater (or went to movies).[13]

Another factor that contributed to the explosion of evangelical engagement in the theater was the emergence in the mid-1960s of a counter-culture phenomenon dubbed the Jesus Movement that won many to a seemingly more relevant faith in Jesus Christ. The movement remained strident in its faithfulness to the significance of the person and work of Jesus Christ, the importance of the Church, and commitment to Christian evangelism. However, many of the "old-time" traditions linked to "old-time gospel"—Victorian hymns, organ and piano accompaniment—were jettisoned as "old wine skins" unable to steward the passions of the gospel's "new wine."[14] The removal of certain worship traditions helped to pave the way for new possibilities of worship formats that went well beyond the expectations and imaginations of the traditional anti-art Christian sentiments.

In addition to cultural shifts in the evangelical worship of the late 1960s and 1970s, mainstream theater had been diversifying since the 1950s.[15] It became increasingly decentralized, evolving from New York City's Broadway to off-Broadway, off-off Broadway, and other vibrant theater capitals in North America. Theater included alternative performances by and about marginalized ethnic and political groups. Socially marginalized communities—such as African American, Hispanic, feminist, and gay—"celebrated their existence, illustrated their concerns, and challenged the larger culture."[16] In short, the theater movement in general became multidenominational and even more acceptably and unapologetically pro-active about bringing the previously marginalized into the mainstream consciousness.

The diversification of North American theater was also a factor that contributed to the development of the Applied Theater movement. Applied Theater is characterized by a growing focus on community and educational theater and a potentially significant context for evangelical contribution to the cultural landscape.[17] Applied Theater is specifically designed to be written, produced, and performed in the "applied" settings of communities most desperate for narrative representation. In other words, it is an approach to community performance that seeks to bring the theater's "transformative" powers to marginalized, broken, or forgotten communities. It is a theater vision that has brought the reconciling power of enacted story to fractured communities, in which artists "generate scenarios and create opportunities for the community to respond to their pain."[18]

While evangelical congregations were slowly introducing theater in worship and Applied Theater approaches were growing in influence, para-church organizations also contributed significantly to evangelical engagement in the theater. Rather than battling with seemingly overconcerned anti-art critics within the local church, more progressive evangelicals formed theater groups without direct connection to specific church congregations and denominations.

Some evangelicals found "new ways to organize what they do, including theater."[19] For example, Covenant Players, a para-church organization founded in 1963, trained and sent thousands of actors around the world.[20] Evangelical playwright Colin Harbinson's partnership with Youth with a Mission also significantly contributed to the vision of theatrical possibilities for evangelicals. His play *Toymaker and Son* toured several continents for many years.[21] Christians in Theater Arts (CITA), founded in 1990 at evangelical Malone College, organized an annual National Networking

Conference as well as regional gatherings.[22] Its forums cultivated intellectual and aesthetic frameworks for faithfulness and productivity in the arts. Para-church publisher Lillenas Press published scripts for chancel dramas and provided theater-training resources as well as hosting an annual church drama convention.[23]

Another major evangelical movement toward worship-based theater emerged out of Willow Creek Church's model of "seeker-friendly" outreach. As a newer church housed in a theatrically styled building and attempting to get beyond traditional worship styles, Willow Creek demonstrated how to integrate drama into worship. The church's order of service included a live, sermon-prompting "sketch."[24] Willow Creek avoided under-rehearsed and ineffectively directed, lighted, and performed scenes that would detract from the delight as well as the instructional value of the sketches in the context of worship. The church's professional performance standards, as well as its drama-included worship model, spread across the country and demonstrated the possibilities of evangelical excellence and training in theater arts.[25] In so doing, it offered models of refinement in the arts as an expression of synthesis in the tension between rhetorical (separationist) and poetic (transformationist) approaches.

Another significant trend contributing to evangelicals' engagement in theater has been the growing popularity of "art-in-education" as a performance medium, which pre-dates the emergence of an interest in Applied Theater in North America. Gillette Elvgren, with thousands of productions of his plays throughout the country, became a prolific, pioneering playwright within this genre. SaltWorks Theater in Pittsburgh, founded in the early 1980s by Elvgren and other colleagues, contracted with the public schools to present "issue" plays for elementary, middle school, and high school students. Its entertaining short plays have never been explicitly evangelistic but are values friendly: instructional stories that sensitively address issues such as bullying, addiction, and personal character. While some might complain that such plays are moralistic and emphasize a rhetorical approach, the performances have typically been well produced and are an effective means of engaging the audience in generating discussion about issues that are important for society, not just the Church.[26]

Finally, evangelicals have engaged in theater for several decades through regional professional theater (which has at least one full-time staff member) and community theater (where no one is paid). Typically such theaters are, as Senkbeil describes, "dual-loyalty organizations,"[27] which strive to participate in local art worlds in mainstream popular culture and in local Christian communities. Such theaters have been significant contributors to evangelical participation in the arts. These have included Lamb's Players in San Diego; A.D. Players in Houston; Acacia Theater in Milwaukee; Taproot Theater in Seattle; Pacific Theater in Vancouver, Canada; and Master Arts in Grand Rapids, Michigan. Such regional theater reflects the diversification of North American drama that includes various subcultures both to understand each group's own culture and to consider what all groups have in common. The influence of these theaters is partially traced to their sustained presence as dependable artistic venues; they have expanded the size of their audiences for over thirty years, thereby reinforcing and building upon a new subcultural habit of live theater attendance.[28]

Views of the Theater from Church History

Evangelical concerns about theater—in what I have in part presented as a tension between rhetorical (separationist) and poetic (transformationist) aesthetic approaches—echo the early Church's moral criticisms of ancient Roman theater with its gladiator battles, chariot races, circuses, and Greek theatrical fare. Tertullian (AD 155–220) could not imagine theater that would teach, delight, and persuade in a holy manner. His treatise *On the Spectacles* (c. AD 197–202) outlines early Christian defenses of the Roman theater and his critical responses, rigorously arguing from a rhetorical (separationist) perspective. While some early Christian advocates of theater said the art used people and materials created by God, Tertullian countered, "We must not, then, consider merely by whom all things were made, but by whom they have been perverted."[29] He offered Psalm 1:1 to support abstinence from theater: "Blessed is the man who does not walk in the counsel of the wicked or stand in the way of sinners or sit in the seat of mockers."[30]

Tertullian further argued that both Greek and Roman theater evolved from pagan religious holidays and rituals. The characters Venus and Bacchus, for instance, were "two evil spirits" in "sworn confederacy with each other, as the patrons of drunkenness and lust ... That immodesty of gesture and attire which so specially and peculiarly characterizes the stage is consecrated to them."[31] He railed against the vulgar language used in drama, warning Christians that "licentiousness of speech, nay, every idle word, is condemned by God."[32]

To demonstrate the extent of the early Church's rejection of Roman theater, in the middle of the fourth century, when a young, North African thespian on the Roman stage converted to Christ, he created controversy in his church. Church leaders demanded that he sever ties with the profession. To maintain his calling faithfully, he started an acting school in spite of his pastor's disapproval. Unsure exactly how to respond, the pastor wrote to the bishop; the bishop explained that the actor should give up teaching theater, but he also said that the local congregation should assist him financially during his unemployment. The bishop further offered to employ him if the local church could not afford to do so; the newly converted actor would have to give up practicing and teaching a worldly trade.[33]

Coming from a similar mindset, Augustine (AD 354–430) criticized "theatrical exhibitions" that glorified the shameful acts of the ancient poets and gods.[34] He admitted that such acted-out fiction could "carry him away" and add to his personal "miseries" by "fueling his passions and lusts."[35] Essentially agreeing with Plato, Augustine even questioned the usefulness of empathizing with the sufferings of a fictionalized hero, concerned that such empathy might distort the ability to identify and respond to real tragedy. Like Tertullian, he recommended that Roman Christians abstain from the theater.

This kind of prohibition dominated the Church until the middle of the tenth century when the Church's change of heart occurred because of a rhetorical aesthetic very similar to that of evangelical arguments today: drama could be "redeemed" through performances and reenactments of Bible stories or other stories with biblical themes, as long as these productions taught the faith to parishioners. By the thirteenth century, the Roman Catholic Church permitted theater performances, chancel dramas (again, focusing on Bible stories and biblical themes), to be performed outdoors, beyond the constraints of the sanctuary. This move to an outdoor venue provided the intellectual threshold for perceiving the sacredness of natural life and, with the progression of subsequent centuries, the holiness of ordinary things that could be addressed by the theater.[36]

By the fourteenth century, "mystery" and "morality" plays became prominent forms of theatrical expression. "Mystery" plays enacted scenes from the Bible; "morality" plays demonstrated the consequences of sin and the irrationality of sinful choices.[37] The Church permitted but did not sponsor these plays that occurred regularly throughout Europe. Community guilds dedicated their talents to presenting religiously themed plays, thus reinforcing and celebrating the narratives central to the Christians' worldview.

Some would argue that the fiercest critics of the theater were seventeenth- and eighteenth-century Puritans. It was important to them that their light would not be dulled and their affections not sullied by the competing distractions of theater.[38] The stridency of Puritan belief in the impiety of entertainments such as theater was so intense that a riot broke out in New York in 1766 as Puritans protested the attempt of a band of traveling actors to open a theater.[39]

Some evangelical critics today repeat these ancient and Puritan arguments. A seminary president asserts that much of evangelicals' current enthusiasm for stage and screen drama results from their ignorance of the Church's historical prohibition. He says that engagement with theatrical culture is the result of Baby Boomers' unholy embrace of a worldly system that is naïve about "how theater communicates and how it shapes the sensibilities."[40] He agrees that the uniform and uncritical acceptance of television by Christians into living rooms as a dominant source of entertainment focus has significantly altered the abilities of the Church to separate itself from worldly influences.

Evangelicals and Religious Themes Enter the Mainstream Stage

Because the historic Church generally rejected secular or "pagan" theater, today's evangelical presence in mainstream theater is greater than it has been in centuries. In addition to individual Christian actors, directors, and producers serving faithfully in the mainstream theater, some evangelical believers have formed professional groups that stage public plays with both explicit and implicit religious themes. In addition, the evolution away from a more rigid rhetorical (separatist) approach to the arts has opened a vista of new opportunities. This, combined with a greater openness of the mainstream culture to spiritual themes, might make possible an even more significant time "ripe for Christian artists wanting to tell the truth and portray the world in its brokenness and warts."[41]

Examples of a vibrant evangelical presence in mainstream theater dot the North American landscape. Theater 315 has pursued a vital theatrical presence in New York City as part of the Time Square Ministries owned and operated by the Salvation Army. Hosting and producing a variety of cogent and accessible plays and musicals, it has offered *The Great Divorce*, a musical adaptation of C. S. Lewis's book, and most recently Paul Enger's play *In the Air*.[42] Also in the nation's theater capitol, Lamb's Theater Company has produced biblically themed plays and musicals, including the premieres of the musicals *Cotton Patch Gospel* and *Johnny Pye*.[43] San Diego's Lamb's Players Theatre became a multi-staffed, professional, nonprofit performing arts theater with a mission "to tell good stories well."[44]

The front entrance to Lamb's Player's Theatre, San Diego, California. (Courtesy of Lamb's Player's Theatre. Used by permission.)

Evolved from a 1970s touring company, Lamb's Players has one of the largest production budgets of any Christian-affiliated theater in the country.

In Seattle, Taproot Theater provides a full-production schedule of plays and musicals that have delighted audiences for decades. Taproot has maintained a theater-in-education portion of its company, working in schools and community groups in ways similar to Pittsburgh's Saltworks. Houston's A.D. Players produces "plays and programs that uphold human value, offer creativity and promote literacy and education." Its full-length season housed in Grace Theater has hosted more than 40,000 theater guests annually, while the touring company has performed before more than 70,000 annually.[45]

Newer theaters have also been launched across the continent. Firebone Theatre seeks to act "as a lighthouse to New York City audiences by producing quality theatre experiences that confront the timeless questions of human mortality [bone] and divine immortality [fire]." Firebone is committed to cultivating new work and talent and using both to "engage our community in open dialogue."[46] Firebone Theatre is also committed to positively impacting New York City through service and theater-in-education programs aimed at empowering young people through the theatrical arts. Rosebud Theatre, in Alberta, Canada, is a "professional theatre committed to the discovery and mentoring of new young talent and a theatre company whose productions consistently embrace stories that are uplifting to the human spirit."[47]

Although many of these theater groups, composed largely of evangelicals, have enjoyed over twenty years of community service, none of them would identify their primary mission as explicitly evangelistic or instructional and, thus, are poetic (transformationalist) in their orientation. As Lamb's Players puts it, the purpose of their theater is "tell good stories well," to delight more than to persuade. These theaters ensure that mainstream audiences will not be evangelistically assaulted with an altar call and will not have their intelligences insulted by formulaic conversion stories or unrealistically happy endings. In addition, audiences will not confuse the theatrical experience with a heavy-handed lecture, a play possessed by a "message" that crushes the nuance and imaginativeness of story under the weight of propositional conviction. In short, these kinds of evangelical excursions into mainstream theater might suggest a growing aesthetic sophistication. There is hope that evangelicals today more fully comprehend the delicate and complex nature of persuading, informing, *and* delighting audiences.

At the same time, some evangelicals are reviving the biblical reenactment play or passion play. For example, Rocky Hock Playhouse has hosted over 200,000 guests since its founding in 1997. Located in Washington, North Carolina, its thousand-seat theater specializes in premiering musicals based upon biblical characters and themes.[48] Pennsylvania's Sight and Sound Theatre hosts over 800,000 guests each year with vast, elaborate sets and dizzying detail. Reenacting epic Bible tales with large casts and professional lighting and costuming, the Sight and Sound Theatre has seen people come daily from all over the country to witness the dramatic spectacles. Embracing the instructional and persuasive goals of medieval morality plays, Sight and Sound seeks "to present the

Gospel of Jesus Christ and sow the Word of God into the lives of [their] customers, guests, and fellow workers," by "visualizing and dramatizing the scriptures."[49] Sight and Sound's spectacles do not appeal to everyone, let alone to all evangelicals, but audiences know beforehand the nature and purpose of its productions because the group boldly proclaims its goals.

A Hopeful Future

Despite all these positive developments, it appears that some of the evangelical theater offerings are saddled with much of the same rhetorical aesthetic pressures.[50] So far, the evangelicals have only begun to take faith-driven artistic risks in storytelling and imaginative development. Evangelicals will have to continue to learn to embrace the poetic (transformationalist) aesthetic that "allows for the complex ambiguities of real life."[51] In doing so, evangelicals can wean themselves from the restrictions of a rhetorical aesthetic that requires the reinforcement of a moral or doctrinal point in their storytelling. The rhetorical aesthetic best serves the sanctuary pulpit, the courtroom, and the legislative halls of congressional gatherings, not the mainstream theater. Quality mainstream theater is pre-evangelistic at best—that is, it helps its audiences to be pondering life's most significant questions—and not a replacement for the Christian Church's evangelistic efforts and instructional responsibilities.

Significant signs of encouragement have dotted the evangelical landscape. In 1995, Bryan Coley founded Art Within, an arts development organization, to address the need for developing playwrights and screenwriters.[52] In New York City, Threads New Works Series, associated with Redeemer Presbyterian Church, has committed itself to cultivating promising new scripts.[53] At Regent University's graduate school, Elvgren, a writer, director, and teacher—and recipient of Christian in Theater Arts' Lifetime Achievement Award—has been training evangelical playwrights since the early 1990s. In an overview of the engagement of evangelicals in theater at the beginning of the twenty-first century, it appears that a synthesis between the two aesthetic approaches toward the arts—poetic and rhetorical—has garnished sufficient traction to allow a flourishing not seen in centuries.

Conclusion

Trinity House Theater, which I founded along with several friends in 1981, remains an entertainment option for residents of southeastern Michigan and continues to evolve in its poetic (transformationist) orientation. Thirty years later, its season is dominated by a musical lineup of folk and Americana songsters that consistently enchant audiences in its unforgettably intimate setting. The live theater performances are rarer; the veritable army of volunteers necessary to continue the full season of mostly premiered productions has marched on to other posts. But the spirit of Applied Theater remains—the vision of the live theater experience as an institutional invitation to transformation quietly rolls on.

The evangelical presence in drama and theater has increased significantly throughout mainstream culture. Evangelical Christian theater artists have been freed to serve the dramatic text, their fellow performers, and their audiences with a poetic (transformationist) vision of the arts that takes seriously both their Christian commitment and alertness to aesthetic sensibilities. There has never been a better time for evangelical Christians in the theater arts.

Notes

1. For an early pre-television era look at the integration of faith and theater, see Alma Newell Atkins, *Drama Goes to Church* (St. Louis: Bethany, 1931).

2. A highly recommended book that provides a theoretical overview of the major thrust of this chapter is Todd E. Johnson and Dale Savitch, *Performing the Sacred: Theology and Theater in Dialogue* (Grand Rapids, MI: Baker Academic, 2009).

3. Peter Lucas Senkbeil, "Faith in Theatre: Professional Theatres Run by Christians in the United States and Canada and Their Strategies for Faith-Art Integration," PhD dissertation, Northwestern University, 1995, iii.

4. For a helpful historical overview of various Christian approaches to culture, see H. Richard Niebuhr's seminal work, *Christ and Culture* (New York: Harper and Row, 1956).

5. Senkbeil, "Faith in Theatre," iii.

6. The phrases "rhetorical aesthetic" and "poetic aesthetic" are attributed to Stuart Scadron-Wattles, quoted in Peter Lucas Senkbeil, "Why Christian Theatre Is Exploding," *Christianity and the Arts* (February–April 1997), 7; and Ron Reed, "Redeeming the Time: Life Theatre," *Oblations, Writings and Readings*, March 28, 2007, http://oblations.blogspot.com/2007/03/ron-reed-redeeming-time-live-theatre.html.

7. Senkbeil, "Faith in Theatre," iii.

8. Peter Lucas Senkbeil (associate provost, Concordia University, Irvine, CA), interview with the author, October 8, 2010.

9. See Niebuhr, *Christ and Culture*.

10. "The Dooyeweerd Pages," http://www.dooy.salford.ac.uk/ (accessed December 13, 2010).

11. Francis Schaeffer, *Art and the Bible: Two Essays* (Downers Grove, IL: InterVarsity, 1973); Franky Schaeffer, *Addicted to Mediocrity: 20th Century Christians and the Arts* (Westchester, IL: Crossway, 1981); Calvin Seerveld, *Rainbows for a Fallen World: Aesthetic Life and Artistic Task* (Beaver Falls, PA: Tuppence, 1980); Hans Rookmaker, *Art Needs No Justification* (Downers Grove, IL: InterVarsity, 1978); Nicholas Wolterstorff, *Art in Action: Toward a Christian Aesthetic* (Grand Rapids, MI: Eerdmans, 1980). Though influential to evangelical thespians, all of these books primarily addressed visual art, music, and literature, rarely addressing the concerns unique to the theater.

12. Reed, "Redeeming the Time."

13. Ibid.

14. A helpful book in understanding the necessities of this shift in traditional expression of evangelical belief is Howard Snyder, *The Problem of Wineskins* (Downers Grove, IL: InterVarsity, 1975).

15. Interestingly, the diversification of theater intensified with the advent of television. It would appear that television's early success in dominating American culture pressed the live theater into experimenting with new ways to win audiences.

16. Senkbeil, "Why Christian Theater Is Exploding," 4.

17. Christians in Theater Arts (CITA), a national networking organization, is planning to sponsor their first Applied Theater conference in the spring of 2011.

18. Philip Taylor, *Applied Theatre: Creating Transformative Encounters in the Community* (Portsmouth, NH: Heinemann, 2003), xviii.

19. Ibid. Senkbeil, "Why Christian Theatre Is Exploding," is of seminal importance in understanding the growth of theater involvement among evangelicals.

20. Covenant Players, http://www.covenantplayers.org/ (accessed December 15, 2010).

21. Colin Harbinson/Toymaker and Son website, http://www.colinharbinson.com/toymakerandson/training.html (accessed December 15, 2010).

22. Christians in Theater Arts, http://www.cita.org (accessed December 15, 2010).

23. Lillenas, http://www.lillenas.com (accessed December 15, 2010).

24. Senkbeil thinks that the practice of live, theater-sketch "sermon-starters" has waned: "We've seen a wave of interest in live theater in worship sort of come and go, I think. You know the Willow Creek model and the use of live theater as a sort of sermon-introduction sketch, I think, had its time when it was very popular in the late 80s, early 90s. My perception is that it's peaked and it's on the decline. And it's being replaced actually by video, so that fifteen years ago you might see a church using live actors to do some kind of sketch that sets up the message. Today you're more likely to see a video clip." Senkbeil, interview with the author.

276 Evangelical Christians and Popular Culture

25. A very helpful book for an introduction to drama ministry and training principles is Steve Pederson (Willow Creek's drama director), *Drama Ministry* (Grand Rapids, MI: Zondervan, 1999).

26. SaltWorks, http://www.saltworks.org (accessed December 15, 2010). "Theater-in-education" is a performance medium employed by several regional, professional theaters run by Christians. It almost has become a standard arm of the theater's community outreach and a very steady source of income for the theater.

27. See Senkbeil, "Faith in Theatre."

28. The reasons why evangelicals did not attend live theater performance are plentiful, some addressed in this chapter. Yet another, perhaps secondary, reason was that they did not see themselves in the protagonist on stage, namely, few plays were written *about* evangelicals and *for* evangelicals. The new evangelical habit of theater attendance would be spurred by the regional theaters' incremental willingness to stage plays pertinent to the evangelical experience.

29. Quoted in Bernard F. Dukore, *Dramatic Theory and Criticsm: Greeks to Grotowski* (Fort Worth, TX: Harcourt Brace Jovanovich College, 1974), 85.

30. Ibid., 86.

31. Quoted in ibid., 89.

32. Quoted in ibid., 90–91. But then, Tertullian even prohibited a Christian from being a school teacher "because such teaching involved using textbooks that told the ancient stories of the gods and called for observing the religious festivals of the pagan year." Quoted in Bruce L. Shelley, *Church History in Plain Language*, 2nd ed. (Nashville, TN: Nelson, 1995), 39–40.

33. Joseph H. Hellerman, *The Ancient Church as Family* (Minneapolis, MN: Augsburg Fortress, 2001), 184–186. Of course, the fear of idolatry in the early Christian Church led to more than just the rejection of theater as a heathen practice; it prevented Christian participation in a variety of industries and trades.

34. Ibid., 94.

35. Augustine, *The Confessions of Saint Augustine*, 3rd ed., trans. D. D. Pusey (New York: Pocket Books, 1959), 31–32.

36. Oscar G. Brockett and Franklin J. Hiddy, "European Theatre in the Middle Ages," in *History of the Theater*, 9th ed. (Boston: Allyn and Bacon, 2003), 72.

37. For an excellent overview of the history of Christian narrative drama and the aesthetics of the image, see Terry Lindvall, *Sanctuary Cinema: Origins of the Christian Film Industry* (New York: New York University Press, 2007), 28–36.

38. See Edmund S. Morgan, "Puritan Hostility to the Theater," in *Proceedings of the American Philosophical Society* 110, no. 3 (October 27, 1966): 340–347. The Quakers also had an "anti-theatrical prejudice." See Michael P. Graves, "The Anti-Theatrical Prejudice and the Quakers: A Late Twentieth-Century Perspective," in *Truth's Bright Embrace: Essays and Poems in Honor of Arthur O. Roberts*, eds. Paul N. Anderson and Howard R. Macy (Newberg, OR: George Fox University Press, 1996), 239–255.

39. Morgan, "Puritan Hostility to Theater." Morgan also points out that hostility to the theater was not exclusively the attitude of Puritans. Several other explanations for the riot are posited, one being the art form's distraction of the pre-revolutionary audience away from the focus of the rebellion against England.

40. Kevin T. Bauder, president of Central Baptist Seminary in Plymouth, Minnesota, has written a compelling challenge from a fundamentalist-separatist perspective in "Fundamentalism and Theater: Act One, Whatever Happened?" http://www.sharperiron.org/2006/12/05/fundamentalists-and-theater-act-one-whatever-happened/ (accessed December 15, 2010).

41. Reed, "Redeeming the Time," quotes Scott Nolte who sees two significant groups, "believers who are less reactionary and non-believers who are spiritually open," as creating a "crossroads that's more genuine and free to approach life and questions with biblically based options."

42. Theater 315, http://www.theatermania.com/content/theater.cfm?intTheaterID=3632 (accessed August 9, 2007). See their production of Enger's new play, *In the Air*, http://www.playbill.com/news/article/95571-In-the-Air-Premieres-Off-Broadway-at-Theatre-315 (accessed December 13, 2010).

43. Lamb's Theatre, http://www.lambstheatre.org/History.html (accessed December 14, 2010).

44. Lamb's Players Theatre, http://www.lambsplayers.org/ (accessed August 25, 2007).

45. A.D. Players, http://www.adplayers.org/ (accessed December 15, 2010).

46. Firebone Theatre, http://firebonetheatre.com/ (accessed December 11, 2010).

47. Rosebud Theatre, http://www.rosebudtheatre.com/Home/tabid/55/language/en-US/Default.aspx (accessed December 11, 2010).

48. Rocky Hock Playhouse, http://www.rockyhockplayhouse.com/theatre_history.html (accessed December 4, 2010).

49. Sight and Sound, http://www.sight-sound.com/WebSiteSS/getlanguages.do (accessed December 15, 2010).

50. Some of the rhetorical restrictions within evangelical theater are similar in tone to restrictions of much of communist theater offerings in the United States during the Great Depression and World War II, when playwrights were weighed down by Marxist dogma and feared offending the party bosses. With rare exceptions, Marxist plays became elaborate, acted-out tracts lambasting the bourgeois—uninteresting propaganda disguised as stories heavy on persuasion and instruction and weak on narrative delight. See Malcomb Goldstein's *The Political Stage: American Drama and Theater of the Great Depression* (New York: Oxford University Press, 1974), 82–85.

51. Senkbeil, "Why Christian Theatre Is Exploding," 7.

52. Art Within, http://www.artwithin.org/ (accessed December 15, 2010).

53. Threads New Works, http://www.faithandwork.org/new_works_series_page732.php (accessed December 15, 2010).

Chapter 17

Jesus People: The Forgotten Evangelical Offspring of the Counterculture

Larry Eskridge

Saturday morning, June 17, 1972, dawned sunny and hot in Dallas, Texas. Far away in Washington, D.C., a furtive group of political operatives was planning a break-in later that night at the Democratic National Committee's headquarters in the Watergate office complex. However, that morning the nation's attention was focused elsewhere, and in Dallas a crowd estimated at 180,000 gathered together for a Jesus Music Festival, the grand finale of EXPLO '72, a conference sponsored by Campus Crusade for Christ (CCC). "Godstock," as the national media dubbed it, brought together 85,000 youth "delegates" for a series of seminars and night-time rallies at the Cotton Bowl. EXPLO, although designed originally as a student evangelism conference, had instead become the largest event associated with the Jesus People movement, a stunning merger of the hippie counter-culture with traditional evangelical Christianity that had first appeared on the West Coast in the late 1960s and had erupted nationwide in the early 1970s.[1] The closing Saturday gathering was a testimony to both the movement's curious make-up and its tremendous strength. Long-haired, ex-druggie "Jesus freaks" sat beside middle-class teenage churchgoers and their youth group sponsors to listen to Johnny Cash and "Jesus" artists like Larry Norman, Randy Matthews, and Love Song. At the close of the meeting, evangelist Billy Graham exhorted the throng, "Put your hand in the hand of the man from Galilee. When you do you'll have a supernatural power to put your hand in the hand of a person of another race. You have a new love in your heart that will drive you to do something about poverty, the ecology question, the racial tension, the family problems and, most of all to do something about your own life."[2] Then Graham, CCC founder Bill Bright, and the musicians gathered on stage, flashing the "One Way" sign (the Jesus People salute, consisting of an index finger pointing skyward), and led the multitude in the chorus "We Are One in the Spirit."[3]

EXPLO '72 splashed the Jesus People across the national media, earning coverage on the network news and claiming the front page of the *New York Times* and the cover of *Life* magazine.[4] In the weeks and months that followed, the media lost interest in the by-now "old" story of the Jesus freaks, so they largely disappeared from the headlines. By the late 1970s, with the exception of a few lonely communes and coffeehouses, the Jesus People movement had faded into oblivion.

Despite a lifespan of perhaps a decade, the now largely forgotten Jesus People movement exerted a tremendous shaping influence on the nature and future direction of the evangelical subculture. What began with a handful of converted hippies and their church-based mentors eventually became a movement that profoundly altered the nature of evangelicals' interaction with both youth culture and the larger popular culture. Far from an insignificant youth fad that came and went, the Jesus People movement left an indelible imprint upon the life of the American evangelical subculture.

Origins and Growth of the Jesus People Movement

The first identifiable beginnings of the Jesus People can be traced back to the epicenter of the counter-culture: San Francisco's legendary "Summer of Love" in 1967. There, amid the shops, communes, and droves of dropouts and runaways that cluttered the city's Haight-Ashbury district, the first outpost of an evangelical/hippie hybrid appeared in the form of the "Living Room" mission. The Living Room was the fruit of a two-year-old relationship between a straight-laced, suburban Baptist pastor named John MacDonald and a former dope-smoking, LSD-imbibing, bohemian sail maker from Sausalito, California, named Ted Wise.[5] With the backing of a group of mostly Baptist pastors, MacDonald put together a non-profit group called Evangelical Concerns, Inc., that helped Wise and friends begin the Living Room in the Haight and concurrently start a Christian commune (referred to as the House of Acts or, more frequently, as just the House) in suburban Novato, California. Over a period of about a year and a half, Wise and friends would come into contact with literally thousands of hippies and young runaways, spreading their gospel message and the possibility of a hipper, more counter-culture-friendly understanding of traditional evangelical Christianity.[6]

Although it began in the Bay Area, it was in Southern California that an actual Jesus People "movement" truly emerged during 1968 and 1969. One of the key early players in this regard was Arthur Blessitt, a handsome, hiply dressed young Southern Baptist evangelist who opened His Place in Hollywood in early 1968. Combining the ambience of an old gospel mission with a psychedelic nightclub, Blessitt provided peanut-butter sandwiches and Kool-Aid to individuals on Sunset Strip and urged the youth to start "dropping Matthew, Mark, Luke, and John" and get "loaded on Jesus; 24 hours a day you can be naturally stoned on Jesus!"[7]

By late 1968, other examples of evangelism with youth culture appeal had appeared in the Los Angeles area. In Huntington Beach, David "Moses" Berg, an ineffectual former Christian and Missionary Alliance pastor, took over a mission called the Lighthouse Club and attracted a small but dedicated group of hippies and idealistic evangelical youth he dubbed Teens for Christ (known later as the Children of God).[8] Husband and wife Pentecostal evangelists Tony and Susan Alamo emphasized a "turn-or-burn" hellfire-heavy message as they worked the sidewalks of Hollywood and took tired, hungry hippies and potential converts to their desert compound in Saugus.[9] And at the affluent Hollywood Presbyterian Church, youth pastor Don Williams looked around and "began to feel the full weight of the cultural revolution" in the music of Bob Dylan and realized the "great secret" that "the key to this generation" was "music ... he one place in the mass media where kids editorialize to kids."[10] In response, he opened up the Salt Company nightclub that attracted a mixture of church youth and Los Angeles hippies.

The most important single example of the emerging Jesus People movement appeared in conservative Orange County at Calvary Chapel, a medium-sized independent congregation in Costa Mesa, California. The church's pastor, Chuck Smith, had begun to consider the possibility of reaching out to area hippies when his daughter introduced him to Lonnie Frisbee, a Costa Mesa native and former member of the Living Room/House of Acts group. Impressed with his Christian commitment, Smith saw Frisbee and another young member of his church, John Higgins, as the perfect point men for working with the counter-culture.[11]

In mid-May 1968, Calvary Chapel helped subsidize the opening of the House of Miracles communal house. Within a matter of a few weeks, nearly fifty young people were crowding into the bungalow, and several other houses in the area—with names like Mansion Messiah—were soon open. Drawn by the twin team of Smith and Frisbee, the church was transformed almost overnight; casually dressed hippies and local teenagers plopped down in front of the pulpit and crowded the aisles on Sundays and weeknight Bible studies.[12] Soon, the church began holding mass ocean baptismal services at nearby Corona del Mar State Park.[13] As the young Jesus look-alike, Frisbee evangelized his peers, and Smith worked through expositional studies of the Bible—particularly prophecy—to give the teens a foundation in basic evangelical beliefs.

Another important element of Calvary Chapel's success was the church's openness to music with a folk and pop flavor that resonated with its new youthful demographic. The music was often elementary. "I knew each line even before it was sung," recalled Tommy Coomes, a member of the band Love Song, "I wasn't used to simple music like this, but it blew me away! It was a music which drew people into the Lord's presence!"[14] Increasingly, the church gave wider berth to a growing number of musical acts that emerged from within the church, and performers like Debby Kerner, Children of the Day, Mustard Seed Faith, and—most influentially—Love Song heightened the appeal of Calvary Chapel and spread the message and the music of the Jesus People.[15] By the beginning of 1970, a Jesus People movement and "scene" had emerged in Southern California. From Santa Barbara in the north to San Diego in the south, there were well over a hundred churches, coffeehouses, and ministries that identified with the Jesus People.

While Southern California became the early center of the Jesus People movement, it was hardly the only area that possessed the cultural tinder necessary to produce the flames of the Jesus People revival. Anywhere that the counter-culture might bump up against the presence of evangelical Christianity, innovative pastors and hippie converts seemed to spring forth. Between late 1968 and 1970, the new cultural phenomenon cropped up all across the country. In Oregon, former Calvary Chapel leader Higgins and a dozen followers established the Shiloh Youth Revival Center commune near Eugene in the spring of 1969. Eventually, the group would establish nearly 200 communal houses scattered across the country, becoming perhaps the largest communal group to emerge from the counter-culture.[16]

While Shiloh was the largest single organized Jesus People group, dozens of smaller, but regionally influential, groups of Jesus freaks surfaced around North America. In Washington state, Linda Meissner, a former worker with David Wilkerson's Teen Challenge in New York City, established the Seattle-based Jesus People Army (JPA) and established links with leaders like Carl Parks in Spokane and Russell Griggs in Vancouver, British Columbia. By 1971, these loosely affiliated units could claim several hundred full-time members scattered across the Pacific Northwest.[17] Near Ithaca, New York, a former New York City disc jockey named Scott Ross parlayed a radio show on an FM station owned by Pat Robertson's fledgling Christian Broadcasting Network into a coffeehouse and commune group at the Love Inn in rural Freeville.[18] By the beginning of 1971, these various groups—and others like them in Kansas City, Wichita, Milwaukee, Detroit, Fort Wayne, Cincinnati, New Jersey, Atlanta, and Norfolk—had spread the Jesus People movement across the continent.[19]

The "Jesus Revolution" Discovered

Despite its unique combination of the hippie counter-culture and old-time religion, there was surprisingly little media coverage of the Jesus People movement.[20] That all began to change in 1971. Much publicity was generated on the very first day of the new year when Graham served as the grand marshall of the Rose Parade in Pasadena and encountered hundreds of sign-bearing, One-Way-signifying youth gathered along the parade route. At the end of the parade, Graham commented that he and wife Ruth felt as if they had "been in a revival meeting."[21] The event caught Graham's attention, and he began to talk up the new youth revival that was "sweeping the country." Soon, a book was in the works, and he and his staff were solidifying plans to incorporate the Jesus People as the theme for that summer's scheduled crusades.[22]

In the next few months, there was a deluge of coverage in both the mainstream and evangelical press. Major articles on the movement appeared in *Look*, *Newsweek*, the *New York Times*, and the *Wall Street Journal*.[23] NBC aired a two-hour documentary on the Jesus People (particularly the Children of God),[24] and the *Today Show* devoted an entire morning to the phenomenon.[25] Wire-service stories carried news of the Jesus People across the nation, and local reporters excitedly hunted for evidence of the movement in their area.[26] By June, "The Jesus Revolution" had earned the cover of *Time*.[27] Meanwhile, the evangelical press trumpeted the news that the United States's wayward youth were turning to Christ and covered the phenomenon in depth.[28]

The book trade was also soon swimming with titles on, from, or addressed to, the Jesus freaks. Books by Jesus People figures such as Blessitt, Duane Pederson, Don Williams were popular,[29] as were journalistic accounts pitched to evangelicals and non-evangelicals. Several academics, mostly social scientists, also came forth with studies to appraise their scholarly peers about what was going on.[30] Most successful of all the volumes, however, was Graham's *The Jesus Generation*, which sold well over half a million copies.[31] By mid-1972, there were no fewer than forty titles available on, or related to, the movement.[32]

The new flood of publicity marked a significant shift within the direction and nature of the Jesus People movement. While the movement's stronghold had previously been Southern California, the Jesus People center of gravity shifted eastward into the Midwest and through the Great Lakes region. Moreover, as news of the movement spread, it increasingly attracted a new cohort of high school–age "Jesus Teens"—many of them from church youth groups and churched backgrounds—eager to identify with the Jesus People.[33]

As a result of these new developments, the primary organizing mechanism of the Jesus movement shifted away from the communal house that had been the core of the earlier counter-cultural phase. Increasingly centered upon a constituency of more rooted young people living at home with their parents, the new focal point for the movement became the coffeehouse. Serving as a gathering place, a focus of evangelistic activity, and a venue for concerts and sanctified entertainment, the Christian coffeehouse became a cultural fixture of the 1970s and the visible manifestation of the Jesus movement in towns and cities across the country.[34] Bearing colorful names with some sort of biblical allusion—the Upper Room, the Mustard Seed, the Belly of the Whale, the House of the Risen Son—it is probably safe to say that every town of any size or importance had one or more coffeehouse for at least a while during the 1970s. While most of the Jesus People coffeehouses were hole-in-the-wall operations surviving on a shoestring budget or a limited amount of financial backing from a local church or churches, a few major coffeehouses such as the Adam's Apple (Fort Wayne, Indiana), the Avalon (Akron, Ohio), and the Holy Ghost Repair Service (Denver, Colorado) emerged as important regional centers of influence in the larger Jesus movement.[35]

Defining Characteristics of the Jesus People

The Jesus People movement was unquestionably far-flung, unorganized, and often semi-isolated. Nonetheless, a set of six readily identifiable shared markers—some clearly evangelical, some stemming from the counterculture—set the Jesus People apart as an actual movement with a readily recognizable contour.

Three elements of their evangelical heritage stood out as particularly central to the Jesus People. First, the movement was decidedly Pentecostal in its overall orientation. The baptism in the Holy Spirit, glossolalia (speaking in tongues), prophecy, "words of knowledge," "singing in the Spirit," and healing were everywhere in the Jesus movement.[36] Part of this was the direct result of interaction with Pentecostal and charismatic ministers, as well as contact with books like John Sherrill's *They Speak with Other Tongues* and Wilkerson's *The Cross and the Switchblade*.[37] However, much of the impetus arose simply from the Jesus People's literal understanding of the Bible: the early Church had received the baptism of the Spirit and spoken in tongues, so they felt it only natural that they should too. Not all Jesus People groups were Pentecostal, but if there was a default Jesus People setting, it definitely leaned toward the Pentecostal end of the spectrum.[38]

A second defining characteristic of the Jesus People, dovetailing with their Pentecostal inclinations, was the movement's general preoccupation with the supernatural. Signs, miracles, instances of divine provision, and encounters with angels and the forces of spiritual darkness were the stuff of the Jesus Peoples' worldview.[39] One of the most common manifestations of this miraculous mindset was the belief that God was regularly meeting their needs for food, money, and materials in near-instantaneous answers to prayer. For example, Ross, from the upstate New York commune and ministry the Love Inn, recounted instances where they believed God answered a specific prayer for a much-needed commercial freezer that arrived in mid-prayer.[40] Such were expectations of divine intervention that when a member of the Lighthouse Ranch commune near Redding, California, was killed by a drunken driver in 1973, one member was overheard by a reporter from the *Eureka Time–Standard* to earnestly ask, "And the Lord didn't raise him from the dead? I expect he would have."[41]

A third characteristic which most Jesus People groups held in common was an apocalyptic orientation that expected the imminent return of Jesus Christ to Earth. "Maranatha" (Aramaic for "the Lord comes") was ever on the hearts, minds, and bumper stickers of the average Jesus freak. Disillusioned with both the evils of the establishment and the shortcomings of the counter-culture, the Jesus People found it very easy to accept the Bible's warnings of judgment. That expectation became a central feature of their devotional life, motivated their evangelistic efforts, and served as an interpretive filter for events around them. Almost without exception, the movement as a whole confidently expected the Second Coming to take place—

if not momentarily—probably in the immediate future and surely within their lifetimes.[42] The penetration of dispensationalism—the system of biblical interpretation which looks for the Rapture of the Church immediately before the seven-year tribulation prior to the Second Coming—among the Jesus People was given a major boost with the appearance of Hal Lindsey's multi-million-copy best-selling book on Bible prophecy, *The Late Great Planet Earth* (1970).[43] As scholar Robert Ellwood observed among the Jesus People in the early 1970s, that book was "one of the few volumes besides the Bible found in virtually every movement commune, home, and church parlor. Next to the Scriptures, probably no other book is more read."[44]

While the three characteristics mentioned above would be categorized as falling under an evangelical cluster of attributes, three other major characteristics of the Jesus movement could be classified as inherited from the counter-culture. The first obvious and widespread attribute the Jesus People brought with them from their hippie background was a penchant for communal living. While most Jesus People did not live communally (and the overall percentage undoubtedly dropped a great deal as the movement expanded into the nation's heartland), the ubiquity of communal houses and communes within the movement was so radically at odds with normal American lifestyles—particularly those of the middle-class evangelical "Silent Majority"—that it definitely set the Jesus movement apart.[45]

A second major characteristic from the countercultural side of the ledger was a decided preference for informality in dress and behavior.[46] Jesus People were just as likely to wear their workaday blue jeans, t-shirts, tennis shoes, or sandals (or bare feet) to a worship service as they were to a Jesus Rock concert. Women—while urged by most Jesus People groups to dress chastely—frequently sported much the same attire or inexpensive "granny" dresses. All of this was, of course, a far cry from the reigning attitude among churchgoing Americans that had traditionally emphasized wearing one's "Sunday best" to the "Lord's House." In addition to clothing, posture and the arrangement of the congregation in Jesus movement gatherings were also decidedly informal. As the good parishioners of Smith's Calvary Chapel in Costa Mesa, California, had discovered to their perplexity and sometime discomfort, the young enthusiasts were given to plopping down on the floor, cross-legged and sprawled out as space would allow. Used to the informal coziness of communal houses and private homes, circles and face-to-face arrangements were often preferred in almost any Jesus People context.[47] But undoubtedly the most significant defining characteristic the

286 Evangelical Christians and Popular Culture

Jesus People carried over from the counter-culture was the one most at odds with reigning attitudes and practices within the evangelical subculture in the 1960s—their comfort with, and utilization of, popular culture.

The Jesus People and Popular Culture

Unlike older evangelicals, who had been battling to keep "worldly entertainments" at arms' length for years,[48] the Jesus People reflexively used and adapted various elements of popular culture within the movement in their attempts to connect with their youthful peers. The resulting hybrid, while striking many in both the church and the counter-culture as curious, outrageous, and ridiculous, nonetheless positioned the Jesus People much closer to the broader world inhabited by American youth.

To visit a Jesus freak coffeehouse or commune was enough to relieve any casual observer of the suspicion that the Jesus People advocated a grim Protestant cultural separatism. Taking their cues from the counter-culture as well as the realm of popular entertainment and advertising, the Jesus People happily decorated their world. Artwork, from posters to home-made murals to thrift-store paintings of Christ, covered their walls. The Jesus People decorated themselves in colorful buttons announcing "Jesus Is Lord" or "Have a Nice Forever," as well as religious jewelry (generally denounced by most evangelicals up until this time), ranging from simple

JPUSA Bus and witnessing group, ca. 1976. (Used with permission, Jesus People USA Covenant Church.)

wooden crosses on leather straps to—as the movement matured—silver "ICHTHYS" ("fish," the old Greek acronym for "Jesus Christ, Son of God, Savior") and "One-Way" pendants and pins. Meanwhile, their ever-present Bibles became an object of beautification via hand-tooled leather bindings and leather and fabric Bible covers.[49]

Another aspect of the popular culture the Jesus People embraced was reflected in the splashy underground newspapers they adapted from their counter-cultural peers. Reborn as the "Jesus paper," dozens of individual papers were published between 1969 and the late 1970s, including Los Angeles's *Hollywood Free Paper; Truth*, from Spokane, Washington; *Cornerstone*, by the Jesus People USA (JPUSA) in Chicago; and the Berkeley, California–based Christian World Liberation Front's (CWLF) *Right On!* The quality, circulation, and lifespan of these papers varied due to the interplay of local personalities and circumstances, yet their general tone and content was similar. Filled with artwork, cartoons, ads, and the occasional photograph, the Jesus papers were multi-purpose tools within the Jesus People community, serving at once as a news source, an evangelistic tract, a venue for edifying scriptural instruction, and an advertising forum for regional and national resources.[50]

However, probably the most important way in which the Jesus People appropriated the larger popular culture was their adaptation of the pop music found in the larger contemporary youth culture. Everywhere one went in the Jesus People movement there was music, from the strictly amateurish folk-guitar plunking at a local Bible study to full-blown rock 'n' roll concerts and, eventually, festivals. By and large it was music that not only incorporated modern styles and phrasings but also new music that arose from within the movement itself. "Rarely do you hear any of the old-time hymns," wrote one contemporary evangelical observer who was struck by the "preoccupation of the Jesus People with new music."[51] Indeed, wherever the Jesus movement flourished there were probably at the least a few competent guitar-strumming singer-composers or "worship leaders" on site, if not a house band or soloists of near-professional quality.

As a grassroots coffeehouse circuit emerged, Jesus People groups and artists sprang up across the United States. and created a national "Jesus music" scene. Increasingly, however, the Jesus People's musical culture began to mirror the world of the secular entertainment industry. With its 1971 release of *The Everlastin' Living Jesus Music Concert*, Calvary Chapel's Maranatha! Music began to record and distribute music by a number of its in-house groups. At about the same time, Word Records in Waco, Texas, released an album by Cincinnati Jesus People musician Randy Matthews and soon created its own specialized Jesus music label (Myrrh), signing artists like Matthews, Honeytree, Barry McGuire, and Petra. The 1974 release of the debut album by a group called the 2nd Chapter of Acts (*With Footnotes*) sold more than a quarter-million albums and provided the impetus for Word's sale to ABC later that year for over $12 million.[52] Prospects for the Jesus music singers and groups making the rounds had quickly grown to include more than the next rally or prayer meeting—concerts, festivals, record contracts, some radio airplay, and even a kind of stardom became a reality.[53]

Conclusion: Long-Term Impact of the Jesus People Movement

Despite its success, by the mid-1970s the Jesus People had begun to fade away for three major reasons. First, the 1970s economy that combined a stagnant business climate with inflation proved a daunting financial challenge for many struggling Jesus People ministries and their youthful constituencies. Second, the Jesus People—along with the rest of the Baby Boomer generation—were growing up. Increasingly jobs, education, marriage, and new families vied with communes, coffeehouses, and "fellowships" for the Jesus People's time, commitment, and finances.[54] Finally, the changing terrain of American youth culture and the rise of new musical styles (heavy metal, disco, punk, and New Wave) and associated youth subcultures were far removed from the peace-and-love hippie ethos from which the Jesus People had originated.[55] This proved an inhospitable cultural climate for the recruitment of younger teens with different ideas of what was "cool." Some Jesus People groups did manage to navigate these treacherous times either by moving in the direction of traditional evangelical church life (Calvary Chapel and their associated congregations), adapting their strategies in the direction of the evangelical parachurch (Jews for Jesus[56]), or by embracing an evolving "edgy" interaction with youth culture (Chicago's JPUSA[57]). But for the most part the Baby Boomer Jesus People were simply absorbed into the nation's churches and became part of the larger story of a resurgent evangelicalism.[58]

Decades later, one might be tempted to look at the twenty-first-century evangelical subculture and conclude that whatever enduring impact the Jesus People might have had was limited to the persistent flirtations with counterculture as embodied in JPUSA's annual avant-garde Cornerstone Festival, the Emergent Church movement, or the ministry of contemporary evangelical activists and authors such as Shaine Claiborne. Certainly, connections with, and similarities to, the old Jesus freaks live on in these and other examples. The Jesus People's impact upon the larger evangelical subculture in the 1980s and beyond actually proved to be more significant, pervasive—and surprising—than might otherwise be imagined.

One of the most important developments to come directly out of the movement was the rise of what sociologist Donald Miller termed "New Paradigm" churches. Absolutely unhindered by the fading of the Jesus movement, Calvary Chapel and the Vineyard Fellowship (a charismatic offshoot of Calvary Chapel under pastor John Wimber in the mid-1980s) adapted their old formulas for success for middle-class suburbanites—an emphasis on Bible-centered teaching, the gifts of the Spirit, contemporary music, and a relaxed, come-as-you-are atmosphere—and experienced tremendous growth from the mid-1970s onward. In Miller's estimation, these new-style congregations were the forerunners of the megachurch movement, which managed to achieve a balance between the therapeutic antiestablishment values of the counterculture while rejecting its inherent narcissistic tendencies through personal accountability and an emphasis upon community.[59] By 2010, Calvary Chapel, the non-denominational "Little Country Church" in Costa Mesa, California, had—via church plants and voluntary affiliations—expanded to over 1,100 affiliated congregations in the United States.[60] Meanwhile, the Vineyard Fellowship had grown to over 550 congregations by 2010.[61]

Another important influence that came out of the likes of Calvary Chapel and the broader Jesus People movement was its impact on congregational musical life through the—often controversial—spread of "praise and worship" music. Across the country and across denominational lines and styles, guitars and rock band–like "worship teams" pushed aside organs and choirs. The music that had once been the heart of Jesus People Bible studies and coffeehouses became an increasingly ubiquitous presence on Sunday mornings.[62] Acceptance was by no means universal, and many churches and seminaries became embroiled in "Worship Wars" from the 1980s onward.[63] However, through the combination of popular appeal and the marketing efforts of Calvary Chapel's Maranatha! Music and other music publishers, the choruses and anthems of praise music became a normative aspect of American congregational worship.

One of the flashiest and—to many outside observers—most striking developments to emerge from the Jesus People movement was the phenomenon of Contemporary Christian Music (CCM) and the industry that grew around it. Jesus music continued to grow even as its parent movement faded away. Increasingly centered around Nashville, Tennessee, a newly defined CCM with new "stars" like Keith Green and Amy Grant continued to expand its sales, record labels, radio airplay, and—in step with a rapidly segmenting pop music scene—the styles and genres of its stable of Christian rock artists. By 1984, CCM was chalking up sales of about $75 million.[64] A little more than a decade later in 1996, gospel music sales (the largest component of which was CCM) had jumped to over $550 million.[65] By the dawn of the new century, gospel music sales (of which CCM continued to represent the lion's share) accounted for 7 percent of total American music sales—double the revenue of Latin music and more than the sales in the jazz, classical, and New Age genres combined.[66] While the idea of Christian rock continued to have its critics, increasingly they came from within the genre as artists and fans questioned the nature of market-driven music and the viability of a distinctly "Christian" genre of music.[67]

The story of Jesus rock/CCM's acceptance within the evangelical subculture spoke volumes about one of the Jesus People movement's most profound impacts: its effect on evangelical attitudes toward youth culture. Prior to the advent of the Jesus People, evangelicals had been extremely suspicious of youth culture and had approached it mainly by attempting to isolate their children from its styles, fads, and music. The general evangelical embrace of the Jesus People movement in the early-to-middle 1970s, however, forever changed that dynamic. While there was still plenty of evangelical resistance to the content of youth culture, the change of direction evidenced in the tolerance of the Jesus movement had fundamentally altered the evangelical subculture. In the wake of the passing of the hippie youth culture style, the controlling assumption within most evangelical circles was that the trappings of youth culture were essentially neutral. When asked about contemporary youth ministry methods in a 2005 interview, Thomas E. Trask, the general superintendent of the Assemblies of God, specifically looked back to the Jesus People movement as casting the mold for youth evangelization:

> I remember when people from the Jesus Movement... began pouring into our churches. The churches that said, "These people don't fit our mold and style" missed a tremendous opportunity for evangelism and discipleship. Churches that welcomed the Jesus people had the joy of seeing a great harvest... It isn't a matter of style, it's the content. We don't compromise the message—that is sacred. Churches need to make adjustments—as long as they don't water down the gospel—to reach young people.[68]

Evangelicals from the 1970s forward responded to the multiplying genres and styles of rock music and youth culture by simply baptizing the new forms and changing the message. The formula proved remarkably flexible and successful.

The principled embrace of youth culture triggered by the Jesus movement also signaled a related change that swept most of the evangelical subculture from the 1970s forward—a growing comfort with the worldly amusements and entertainments proffered by the larger realm of popular culture. This was a huge boon to the Christian bookstore industry, as well as for an expanding array of individuals and corporations that provided "sanctified" entertainment alternatives for evangelical children, teens, and adults alike. But this parallel world of evangelical entertainment options often masked a larger reality—the fact that evangelicals had also greatly relaxed their general resistance to secular entertainment.[69] By 2004, a study cited in *Time* magazine showed that evangelical Christians were among the most frequent movie attendees in the American population, a fact reflected in major Hollywood marketing campaigns targeting born-again audiences.[70] Obviously, such a major shift in attitudes toward popular culture among American evangelicals was the result of a combination of cultural and social forces. Undoubtedly, however, the Jesus People movement was essential to this shift as they were the first sizeable group of evangelicals to disregard traditional conservative Protestant criticisms against popular culture. The approval the Jesus People received from the bulk of the evangelical establishment to "do their own thing" as they followed Christ may well have unintentionally provided the entire subculture—particularly its Baby Boomer ranks—with the evangelical equivalent to a pop culture emancipation proclamation.

Notes

1. Edward E. Plowman, "'Godstock' in Big D," *Christianity Today*, July 7, 1972, 31–32. For the planning and the event, see Paul Eshleman, *The EXPLO Story: A Plan to Change the World* (Glendale, CA: Regal, 1972).

2. Quoted in "EXPLO '72, Show #3" (San Bernardino, CA: Arrowhead Productions International, 1972).

3. Ibid.

4. Edward B. Fiske, "A 'Religious Woodstock' Draws 75,000," *New York Times*, June 16, 1972, 1, 19; and "Rallying for Jesus," *Life*, June 26, 1972, 40–45.

5. See Maurice Allan, "God's Thing in Hippieville," *Christian Life*, January 1968, 20–23, 35–38; and John MacDonald, *House of Acts* (Carol Stream, IL: Creation House, 1970).

6. Ronald Enroth et al., *The Jesus People: Old-Time Religion in the Age of Aquarius* (Grand Rapids, MI: Eerdmans, 1972), 12–15.

7. Arthur Blessitt, *Life's Greatest Trip* (Waco, TX: Word, 1970), 26; see Enroth et al., *The Jesus People*, 73.

8. Because of the development of unusual sexual attitudes and its subsequent branding as a cult, the Children of God (later, The Family) are perhaps the most researched and written-about element to emerge from the Jesus People movement. See James R. Lewis and J. Gordon Melton, *Sex, Slander, and Salvation: Investigating The Family/Children of God* (Stanford, CA: Center for Academic Publications, 1994); and William Sims Bainbridge, *The Endtime Family: Children of God* (Albany: State University of New York Press, 2002).

9. Michael McFadden, *The Jesus Revolution* (New York: Harper, 1972), 59–71; and Enroth et al., *The Jesus People*, 54–65.

10. Don Williams, *Call to the Streets* (Minneapolis: Augsburg, 1972), 23.

11. Chuck Smith with Hugh Steven, *The Reproducers: New Life for Thousands* (Glendale, CA: Regal, 1972), 37–53.

12. Enroth et al., *The Jesus People*, 85–94, and Smith, *The Reproducers*, 55–77.

13. Pictures of Calvary Chapel's ocean baptisms at Corona Del Mar became one of the ubiquitous images of the Jesus People movement. See Enroth et al., *The Jesus People*, 91–93, and Smith, *The Reproducers*, 91–97.

14. Quoted in Paul Baker, *Contemporary Christian Music: Where it Came From, What It Is, Where It's Going* (Westchester, IL: Crossway, 1985), 40.

15. Ibid., 38–40.

16. For an in-depth study of Shiloh, see James T. Richardson et al., *Organized Miracles: A Study of a Contemporary, Youth, Communal, Fundamentalist Organization* (Brunswick, NJ: Transaction, 1979). See also Timothy Miller, *The 60s Communes: Hippies and Beyond* (Syracuse, NY: Syracuse University Press, 1999), 95–96.

17. See Pat King, *The Jesus People Are Coming!* (Plainfield, NJ: Logos, 1971), and Enroth et al., *The Jesus People*, 117–128.

18. See Scott Ross with John and Elizabeth Sherrill, *Scott Free* (Old Tappan, NJ: Chosen, 1976).

19. For a look at some of the other Jesus People groups around the country in late 1969 and 1970, see Glenn D. Kittler, *The Jesus People and Their Leaders* (New York: Warner, 1972), 182–198.

20. Most early media inklings that something akin to a movement was underway did not show up until 1970 and appeared only in the evangelical press. See Brian Bastien, "Hollywood Boulevard—One Way," *Christianity Today*, January 2, 1970, 328; and Carl F. H. Henry, "Evangelical Pathbreaking," *Christianity Today*, May 8, 1970, 746.

21. Quoted in "1,300,000 Greet New Year at 'Biggest' Rose Parade," *Van Nuys Valley News and Green Sheet*, January 3, 1971, in Collection 360: BGEA-

Scrapbooks, Reel #33 (June 1970–December 1971); Graham Press Conference, February 28, 1971, Greenville, SC, Collection 24: BGEA-Billy Graham Press Conferences, Tape T9, Archives of the Billy Graham Center, Wheaton College, Wheaton, IL. See also Billy Graham, *The Jesus Generation* (Grand Rapids, MI: Zondervan, 1971), 13–14.

22. For Graham's relationship to the Jesus People, see Larry Eskridge, "One Way: Billy Graham, the 'Jesus Generation,' and the Idea of an Evangelical Youth Culture," *Church History* 67, no. 1 (March 1998): 83–106.

23. See, for example, Earl C. Gottschalk Jr., "Hip Culture Discovers a New Trip: Fervent, Foot-Stompin' Religion," *Wall Street Journal*, March 2, 1971, 1; and "The New Rebel Cry: Jesus Is Coming!" *Time*, June 21, 1971, 56–63.

24. *First Tuesday: The Ultimate Trip*, NBC News, February 1971, http://www.xfamily.org/index.php/NBC_First_Tuesday:_The_Ultimate_Trip (accessed February 24, 2010).

25. *The Today Show*, NBC News Archives, July 8, 1971.

26. See for example, the AP wire story by Jay Sharbutt titled "Jesus People's Theories Appear to Be Billy Graham Explained by Timothy Leary," *Anderson* (Indiana) *Daily Bulletin*, February 14, 1971, 12. For an example of a local angle on the Jesus movement during the height of media coverage see Gene Hahn, "A Revolution with Jesus for a Leader," *The Post* (Frederick, MD), September 18, 1971, 23.

27. "The New Rebel Cry: Jesus Is Coming!" *Time*, June 21, 1971, 56–63.

28. For articles in evangelical periodicals about the Jesus movement between 1970 and 1972, see David Di Sabatino, *The Jesus People Movement: An Annotated Bibliography and General Resource*, rev. ed. (Lake Forest, CA: Jester, 2004).

29. See for instance Arthur Blessitt with Walter Wagner, *Turned on to Jesus* (New York: Hawthorn, 1971); Pederson with Owens, *Jesus People;* and Williams, *Call to the Streets*.

30. See, for example, Lowell Streiker, *The Jesus Trip: Advent of the Jesus Freaks* (Nashville, TN: Abingdon, 1971); and Robert S. Ellwood Sr., *One Way: The Jesus Movement and Its Meaning* (Englewood Cliffs, NJ: Prentice-Hall, 1973).

31. See banner on the cover of the book's third edition, November 1971.

32. See Di Sabatino, *The Jesus People Movement*.

33. For the Jesus People movement in the Midwest, see Ed Plowman, "Whatever Happened to the Jesus Movement?" *Christianity Today*, October 24, 1975, 46. For contemporary observations about the increasing visibility of high school churched youth in the Jesus People movement, see Enroth et al., *The Jesus People*, 136–150.

34. See Baker, *Contemporary Christian Music*, 67–70.

35. See *Adam's Apple Juicy News* 2, February 1975; and Baker, *Contemporary Christian Music*, 68.

36. See Larry Eskridge, "God's Forever Family: The Jesus People Movement in America, 1966–1977," PhD dissertation, University of Stirling, 2005, 131–134.

37. John H. Sherrill, *They Speak with Other Tongues* (New York: McGraw-Hill, 1964); and David Wilkerson, *The Cross and the Switchblade* (Old Tappan, NJ: Revell, 1963).

38. See for instance Hiley H. Ward, *The Far-Out Saints of the Jesus Communes: A Firsthand Report and Interpretation of the Jesus People Movement* (New York: Association Press, 1972), 122–126.

39. Eskridge, "God's Forever Family," 134–139.

40. Ross, with Sherrill, *Scott Free*, 115–118, 137–138.

41. "Lighthouse Victim 'Blessed Brother' to Former Comrades," *Eureka Times–Standard* (Eureka, CA), May 17, 1973, 5; see also "Eureka Detectives Figure in Nabbing Hit-Run Suspect in Redding Wednesday," *Eureka Times–Standard*, May 17, 1973, 5.

42. For example, see Ellwood, *One Way*, 89–93.

43. Hal Lindsay with C. C. Carlson, *The Late, Great Planet Earth* (Grand Rapids, MI: Zondervan, 1970).

44. Ellwood, *One Way*, 89.

45. Much of the Jesus People's enthusiasm for communal living came straight from their reading of Acts 2:44–46, which describes how the early Church lived together and had all things in common. For 1971 Jesus communes around the country see Ward, *The Far-out Saints of the Jesus Communes*.

46. See Timothy Miller, *The Hippies and American Values* (Knoxville: University of Tennessee Press, 1991), 59–62.

47. See Eskridge, "God's Forever Family," 147–148.

48. See William Ward Ayer, "Jungle Madness in American Music," *Youth for Christ*, November 1956, 19–21; and Robert A. Cook, "What about Hollywood Movies?" *Youth for Christ Magazine*, April 1957, 15–16.

49. See Colleen McDannell, *Material Christianity: Religion and Popular Culture in America* (New Haven, CT: Yale University Press, 1995), 250–260.

50. See Edward E. Plowman, "The Jesus Presses Are Rolling," *Christianity Today*, March 12, 1971, 664.

51. Excerpt from a letter by John R. Sampey, quoted in Ward, *The Far-out Saints*, 29.

52. See William D. Romanowski, "Rock 'n' Religion: A Socio-Cultural Analysis of the Contemporary Christian Music Industry," PhD dissertation, Bowling Green University, 1990, 136; and Russell A. Sanjek, *American Popular Music and Its Business: The First Four Hundred Years. Volume 3: From 1900 to 1984* (New York: Oxford University Press, 1988), 561.

53. For an overview of CCM, see Jay R. Howard and John M. Streck, *Apostles of Rock: The Splintered World of Contemporary Christian Music* (Lexington: University of Kentucky Press, 1999); and Baker, *Contemporary Christian Music*.

54. See Eskridge, "God's Forever Family," 310–316.

55. Ibid., 320–326.

56. Ruth A. Tucker, *Not Ashamed: The Story of Jews for Jesus* (Sisters, OR: Multnomah, 1999), 84–92.

57. See issues of JPUSA's well-regarded paper and magazine *Cornerstone* (published from 1972 to 2003).

58. See Preston B. Shires, *Hippies of the Religious Right* (Waco, TX: Baylor University Press, 2007).

59. Donald Miller, *Reinventing American Protestantism: Christianity in the New Millennium* (Berkeley: University of California Press, 1997), 20–22.

60. See Calvary Chapel's website, http://calvarychapel.com (accessed May 25, 2012).

61. See http://www.vineyardusa.org/site/about/vineyard-history (accessed December 28, 2010).

62. See Michael Hamilton, "The Triumph of the Praise Songs: How Guitars Beat Out the Organ in the Worship Wars," *Christianity Today*, July 12, 1999, 28–35, and Larry Eskridge, "Slain by the Music," *The Christian Century*, March 7, 2006, 18–20.

63. For an influential critique against praise music, see Marva J. Dawn, *Reaching Out without Dumbing Down* (Grand Rapids, MI: Eerdmans, 1995); for counter-arguments, see John M. Frame, *Contemporary Christian Music: A Biblical Defense* (Phillipsburg, NJ: Presbyterian and Reformed Publishing, 1997).

64. Romanowski, "Rock 'n' Religion," 231.

65. Howard and Streck, *Apostles of Rock*, 44.

66. Lorraine Ali, "The Glorious Rise of Christian Pop," *Newsweek*, July 16, 2001, 41.

67. See for example Charlie Peacock [Charles Ashworth], *At the Crossroads: An Insider's Look at the Past, Present, and Future of Contemporary Christian Music* (Nashville: Broadman and Holman, 1999).

68. "Ask the Superintendent—Ministering to Today's Youth," *Enrichment Journal*, http://enrichmentjournal.ag.org/200101/0101_006_superintendent.cfm (accessed June 4, 2005).

69. See, for example, Eileen Luhr, *Witnessing Suburbia: Conservatives and Christian Youth Culture* (Berkeley: University of California Press, 2009), and Daniel Radosh, *Rapture Ready! Adventures in the Parallel Universe of Christian Pop Culture* (New York: Scribner, 2008).

70. A Barna Group research study, cited in "The Gospel According to Spider-Man," *Time*, August 16, 2004, 72; for Hollywood's attempts to tap into the evangelical market, see James Y. Trammel, "Who Does God Want Me to Invite to See *The Passion of the Christ*? Marketing Movies to Evangelicals," *Journal of Religion and Media* 9, no. 1 (January 2010): 19–29.

Chapter 18

Evangelical Women's Movements and Leaders

Kathleen Osbeck Sindorf

A young woman named Nicki was recently assigned to me in a mentoring program at the evangelical Christian university where I teach. She told me about how her mother became a Christian at the first National Women's Convention sponsored by Precept Ministries International. Through her mother's influence, Nicki also became a Christian, or as evangelicals say, "accepted Christ as her savior," and now teaches weekly Bible study on campus.

I was stunned to hear this story because Nicki had no idea of my role—albeit a minor one—in her spiritual journey. As a senior staff member for Precept Ministries International in 2002, I remember well when CEO Kay Arthur announced, "We're going to have a National Women's Convention! I believe God wants a specific group of us to do a conference together so people can see there's no competition in the Body of Christ."[1] With characteristic bravado, Arthur launched the event, giving us barely enough time to pull it together. Amazingly, each of the speakers responded to Arthur's invitation. It was an impressive line-up and an expression of unity in the midst of the evangelical territorialism at the start of the twenty-first century. The Precept Ministries staff was surprised that these speakers and singers all agreed to come, and they were even more amazed when 8,000 women packed out this inaugural weekend event. Evidently, an army of Christian women like Nicki's mother had been growing—not only in numbers but in their readiness to do something meaningful for God.

After decades of being relegated to traditionally "safe" functions such as choir members, nursery workers, and children's Sunday school teachers, evangelical women are becoming deacons, youth pastors, small group leaders, and sometimes even pastors. The end of the twentieth century brought women more opportunities in business, education, and government, and this new breed of evangelical woman, while running the range from liberal to conservative, wanted to make a difference in their local communities and in the world.

Arthur has spoken in numerous churches where the pastors admit she is the first woman ever allowed in their pulpits. Like her contemporaries, Anne Graham Lotz, Beth Moore, and Joyce Meyer, Arthur is known to be a dynamic Bible teacher with the fervor of an old-time revival preacher, while maintaining her femininity and charm. These women have made a name for themselves in places where men have traditionally reigned, not by pushing their "right" to equality but by faithfully preparing for and then pursuing opportunities open to them.

Evangelical Bible teacher, author, and ministry leader Kay Arthur, CEO and cofounder of Precept Ministries International, shown here in 2007. (Copyright Precept Ministries International. Used by permission.)

The number of evangelical women in the United States continues to grow, and their influence is expanding. This chapter explores the historical beginnings of the evangelical women's movement, its key leaders (past and present), reasons for its growth, and the impact of this movement on mainstream culture.

Laying the Foundation

Baptists allowed women to preach during the First Great Awakening in the 1730s, while the Second Great Awakening in the 1830s empowered women to take up causes outside of their homes and families. They founded Sunday schools, orphanages, charities for the poor, and mothers' clubs to promote education. Evangelical women supported the cause of temperance (a crusade against alcoholism), the abolition of slavery, and women's suffrage in the mid-1800s.[2]

Evangelicalism was becoming one of the most dynamic and important cultural forces in the United States—with women a big part of local church activity and mission work overseas. Pentecostalism, especially, encouraged women to become evangelists. At the end of the nineteenth century, however, many women lost their voice as their churches turned into largely male-run denominations. During the battles between fundamentalists and evangelicals in the early twentieth century, conservative mission boards curtailed the freedom of female missionaries. Denominations took control of service societies that women had run for decades. Women could run bake sales, but men decided how to spend the funds they raised.[3]

In this context of diminished roles for women, one woman became one of the most influential evangelicals of the early 1900s with an impact on key young leaders that still continues today. Henrietta Mears was a high school chemistry teacher who taught children's Sunday school at her local church, First Presbyterian Church in Hollywood, California. She was offered a job as their director of Christian education—unheard-of for a woman in 1928. The church already had over 450 children and young people attending Sunday school, but under Mears's guidance, the classes exploded to over 4,000 students within two years. Challenged to find attractive curriculum that taught God's word well, Mears began to write her own materials, birthing the publishing house that became Gospel Light Publications.[4]

Mears also arranged the purchase of Forest Home, a resort in the San Bernardino Mountains that she turned into a Christian retreat center. There Mears's teaching impacted the lives of promising young men including Bill Bright, who later founded Campus Crusade for Christ International; Richard Halverson, who became the chaplain of the U.S. Senate; and Billy Graham, who preached around the world. Graham says of Mears, "I doubt if any other woman outside my wife and mother has had such a marked influence [on my life]. She is certainly one of the greatest Christians I have ever known!"[5]

Her ministry illustrates both the possibilities and limitations evangelical women encountered in the early twentieth century. Mears intentionally avoided offending traditional gender norms. She officially served under a male superintendent and insisted that her expository lessons were "teaching" rather than "preaching." People connected with First Presbyterian Church in Hollywood in those decades recall her as "the power behind the throne" of the powerful pastors she served.[6] With the exception of herself, Mears tried to preserve traditional patterns of male leadership in the church. Citing the church's difficulty in attracting enough men, she claimed to select women as leaders only as a matter of last resort—not just as a matter of biblical doctrine—on the basis of pragmatic expediency. Both men and women would find male leadership in the Church more attractive. She asserted, "I know that if I can get the best examples of young men to attend, then I can always get the beautiful young women to follow!"[7]

While Mears made her impact working quietly behind the scenes, another early evangelical woman was much more public and flamboyant. Aimee Semple McPherson began preaching at the age of 17 in the early 1900s. After several sicknesses and operations, she experienced what she described as "God's miraculous healing" and began holding tent revival healing services, driving up and down the eastern states in her "Full Gospel Car." When not in a tent, she would find the largest auditorium in town to hold the people coming to her meetings. Once she spoke in a boxing ring in San Diego—before and after the fights—and the National Guard had to be called in to help control her crowd of 30,000 people at some venues.[8]

McPherson grabbed the attention of mainstream culture. She purchased a radio station and became the first woman to preach over the airwaves. Her voice was recognizable across the United States, with down-to-earth humor and a straightforward style. McPherson said, "You don't need to be an orator. What God wants is plain people with the Good News in their hearts who are willing to go and tell it to others."[9]

In 1923, McPherson dedicated the 5,000-seat Angelus Temple in Los Angeles—one of the United States's first megachurches—and opened a Bible school. Her flair for dramatic costumes and faith healing drew much media attention. McPherson provided hot meals for more than 1.5 million people during the Great Depression, and her denomination, the Foursquare Church, today has over 1,800 U.S. churches; worldwide, it has over 60,000 churches and meeting places spread across 140 countries.[10]

Following in the flashy footsteps of McPherson, Kathryn Kuhlman also influenced mainstream culture both positively—by drawing attention to evangelicalism and creating curiosity about it—and negatively, by making the movement look somewhat cultish. Kuhlman started speaking at the beginning of World War II when she was 16. At one of her services, a woman was reportedly healed of a tumor, and Kuhlman's "miracle services" began. She held healing and evangelistic crusades around the world for three decades between the 1940s and 1970s. She also had a daily radio ministry and a weekly television program called *I Believe in Miracles*.[11]

Kuhlman held regular services at the Pasadena Civic Auditorium, seating 2,500, then moved to the Los Angeles Shrine Auditorium, where she regularly filled the 7,000 seats for ten years. Oral Roberts University demonstrated Kuhlman's impact on the evangelical movement by awarding her their first honorary doctorate.[12]

A New Activism

By the 1960s and 1970s, the evangelical movement was becoming more visible in mainstream culture. Many evangelicals were active in the right-to-life movement, while organizations like the Evangelical Women's Caucus (EWC)—formed within Evangelicals for Social Action in 1973—worked for more liberal causes. The mission of the EWC was to "support, educate, and celebrate Christian feminists from many traditions."[13] Their first national conference, held in 1975 in Washington, D.C., addressed "Women in Transition: A Biblical Approach to Feminism." The conference attracted some 360 women favoring passage of the Equal Rights Amendment (ERA), the ordination of women, and gender-inclusive language in all communications, including the Bible. EWC added "ecumenical" to its name in 1990, thus becoming EEWC, and when they resolved to support civil rights protection for homosexuals, their more moderate members pulled out, forming an alternative group called Christians for Biblical Equality.[14]

Some evangelical women, however, argued against "women's liberation," saying that secular feminism enslaved women in its ideology while the Bible's truth freed them. Mary Kassian, author of *The Feminist Mistake*, expresses this view that mainstream culture brainwashed women into worshiping the false idols of careers and independence. She says that a "submitted woman" can quit struggling to do things God never intended her to do and focus on using her feminine gifts for God's glory.[15]

As the National Organization for Women (NOW) was forming in the late 1960s to further the cause of feminist equality, it was opposed by many conservative evangelical leaders. Phyllis Schlafly, a lawyer and political activist, started the Eagle Forum in 1972. She led the pro-family movement in a battle against the ERA, appearing on national television and radio talk shows and lecturing on 500 college campuses. She testified before congressional and state legislative committees, all while raising six children. Illinois named Schlafly Mother of the Year in 1992, saying she inspired a generation of young evangelical women to speak out boldly for the family and traditional values.[16]

Beverly LaHaye became another leading spokesperson on family values during the 1960s and 1970s, first teaching marriage and family seminars with her husband Tim, who later authored the *Left Behind* series. In 1979, she founded Concerned Women for America (CWA), a social and political activism organization touted as the nation's largest women's organization with over 600,000 members at its peak, an estimated ten times the size of NOW. Voted Christian Woman of the Year in 1984 and Churchwoman of the Year in 1988, LaHaye also received the Religious Freedom Award in 1991.[17] Her radio program, *Beverly LaHaye Live*, was named National Religious Broadcasters' 1993 Talk Show of the Year.[18] Even after retiring in 2001, LaHaye says she continues her battle for the family. CWA is the nation's largest public policy pro-family women's organization, holding annual lobbying gatherings in Washington, D.C.[19] Not surprisingly, *Time* magazine chose LaHaye and her husband for their list of the "25 Most Influential Evangelicals in America" in 2005.[20]

This "new activism"—both within the Church and in the cultural discourse—attracted many female followers and created public awareness of the evangelical movement. While outspoken women such as Schlafly and LaHaye spoke out on family, social, and justice issues, others focused on strictly spiritual causes. Vonette Bright cofounded Campus Crusade for Christ International (CCCI) with her husband Bill in 1951, working with students at the University of California at Los Angeles. It grew to be one of the largest international Christian ministries in the world. In addition to co-leading more than 27,000 staff members and 225,000 volunteers working in 190 countries, Vonette played a key role in discipling the large number of women who came to join CCCI. She then founded the National

Prayer Committee, served as chairwoman of the National Day of Prayer Task Force, and introduced the 1988 legislation approved by Congress to make the first Thursday of every May the permanent date for the National Day of Prayer.[21] Since her husband Bill's death in 2003, she has continued to travel around the world and speak at major gatherings like Cape Town 2010, sponsored by the Lausanne Committee for World Evangelization.

John Turner, author of *Bill Bright and Campus Crusade for Christ*, says that para-church organizations like CCCI were able to creatively adapt and "market" their faith to modern culture because they were free of denominational restraints. Because they are normally dependent only on their donors and the leadership of their founders, they can alter policies and strategies quickly to promote their faith in mainstream culture.[22] The vitality of American evangelicalism, especially the adaptability and marketing prowess of para-church organizations, helped evangelicals to retain their hold on a substantial segment of the American population in the twenty-first century. "Through their innovative use of technology, their open stance towards popular culture, and their aggressive fund-raising practices," Turner explains, para-church ministries like the Brights' "have been the consummate marketers of the evangelical gospel in modern America."[23]

Radio and Television Presence

One of the most important factors propelling women into high recognition in the last two decades of modern evangelicalism was the proliferation of evangelical radio and television programs. Three women in particular attracted millions of male as well as female viewers. Meyer, included in *Time's* 2010 list of the "25 Most Influential Evangelicals in America," heads a multi-million-dollar international ministry based in Missouri and delivers her uplifting, no-nonsense message over more than 400 radio and 600 television stations, as well as in seventy books and numerous stadium-filling speaking events each year.[24]

Paula White is the senior pastor of the Without Walls International Church in Lakeland, Florida, which she co-founded with her ex-husband Randy. Her television program, *Paula White Today*, appears on the Daystar, Word, and TBN networks and on Sky Satellite. Unlike many of her female counterparts, White takes the title of pastor and also calls herself a life coach and motivational speaker.[25] Her theology and personal life have been criticized as controversial, but she maintains a large following.

Marilyn Hickey, co-pastor of the Orchard Road Christian Center in the Denver, Colorado, area with her husband Wallace, has appeared on national television teaching a "word of faith" message since 1996. She continues to preach with her daughter Sarah Bowling on her current program, *Marilyn and Sarah*, airing on Christian networks around the world.[26]

While these female Bible teachers exert influence in their own right through the electronic media, others like Gloria Copeland and Betty Robison became known to the United States by co-hosting Christian television programs alongside their influential husbands, Ken and James. Victoria Osteen gained prominence simply by association with her husband Joel, the best-selling author and pastor of the largest church in the United States, Lakewood Church in Houston, Texas. She carries the title of co-pastor there and has also written several books of her own.[27]

One of the new role models for evangelical women in the United States is Sarah Palin, the former governor of Alaska and running mate of Republican presidential candidate John McCain. Through speaking tours, Fox News commentaries, and her television program, *Sarah Palin's Alaska*, she is setting a new standard for female evangelicals as political mavericks who can enjoy deep-sea fishing along with beauty-pageant good looks. "To white evangelical women, Sarah Palin is a modern-day prophet, preaching God, flag, and family—while remaking the religious right in her own image," says *Newsweek*'s religion editor, Lisa Miller.[28] Palin's authenticity, she says, makes her a sister-in-arms—a beautiful, fearless, principled fighter—to millions of women who share her struggles. *Charisma* magazine compared Palin to the Old Testament's Queen Esther, who saved her people from annihilation.[29] According to Miller, "Even if she never again seeks elected office, her pro-woman rallying cry, articulated in the evangelical vernacular, together with the potent pro-life example of her own family, puts Palin in a position to reshape and reinvigorate the religious right, one of the most powerful forces in American politics. The Christian right is now poised to become a women's movement."[30]

Despite their strong followings, neither Palin nor most of the other women listed thus far in the chapter were included in *Time*'s "25 Most Influential Evangelicals in America" in 2005. In fact, *Time* chose very few women. In addition to Meyer and LaHaye, financier Roberta Ahmanson made the list with her husband Howard. This wealthy, conservative Republican couple funds evangelism, faith-based activism, and churches in the developing world.[31] The remaining woman *Time* selected was Diane Knippers, president of the conservative Institute on Religion and

Democracy (IRD). She was among the leaders who helped persuade the Bush administration to press for a cease-fire in the Sudan civil war and an end to the oppression of Christians there.[32] Perhaps more lobbying, think tanks, and financial leverage are in the near future for those who are recognized as female evangelical leaders.

A Biblical Mandate?

The evangelical women leaders mentioned herein claim to have a biblical mandate for their public ministry. They point to the fact that Jesus Christ honored women throughout his ministry, and that Priscilla, as well as her husband Aquila, assisted the apostle Paul in the New Testament (Rom. 16:3) and is credited by Luke in Acts 18:26 as having a teaching ministry, paving the way for today's women to be similarly valued and empowered. Opposition to female leadership still remains, however, especially as various evangelicals differ on their interpretations of Paul's writings.[33]

The first full-time female faculty member at Grand Rapids Theological Seminary, Catherine Mueller-Bell, says research shows there is not just one biblically correct position on the subject of women in ministry. In fact, she says five distinct views can be supported by scripture.[34] "Women have always made up a majority of church adherents, so their role was often more public than has often been recognized," says historian Richard Ostrander, provost of Cornerstone University. "In the past 30 years, evangelical women have become more public in their leadership roles in the church. Much of this was the result of the rise of the Religious Right in politics. Because women have traditionally been seen as the guardians of family morality, when 'family values' became a political issue that propelled women to take more public roles in the political realm."[35] Once accustomed to having a public voice, they were not ready to remain silent at church.

Pastors began to notice the new zeal of many of their female congregants in the 1970s. "When a pastor [saw] ... 500 women arriving to spend a weekday morning studying the scriptures ... e said, 'Oh, my goodness, these women are hungry for God's Word, and they can organize,' " says Sue Edwards, who teaches at Dallas Theological Seminary (DTS).[36] Churches had to respond to this new subculture of Bible study that evangelical women had built on their own.

Large para-church organizations also formed to fill the gap these evangelical women expressed. Women's Aglow Fellowship (WAF) took off in 1967, starting as a devotional association related to the Full Gospel

Business Men's Fellowship. It attracted 200,000 women in over 170 countries.[37] DTS created a degree program in 1975 to prepare women for ministry and church service—but not for the pastorate. However, DTS and other seminaries have since expanded their programs for women and even hired them to teach.[38]

Women's Large Events

One of the key evangelical women's movements over the last two decades is the rise of large, weekend arena events enabling women to be enriched, taught, and strengthened to carry on their responsibilities of raising children, coping with family problems, and overcoming fear and depression. One such event, Women of Faith (WOF), began in 1996 with the help of Thomas Nelson, Inc., just a few years after Promise Keepers, a movement founded by Coach Bill McCartney that holds men's events in huge football stadiums.[39] Since the success of that first WOF conference, the roster of speakers has varied but always includes Thomas Nelson authors.[40] WOF weekends are nondenominational. Over 4 million women have attended more than 275 events held in more than eighty-eight cities across North America, and 350,000 attendees have indicated first-time commitments to Christ.[41] InterMedia Partners in New York, led by Leo Hindery Jr., acquired WOF with Thomas Nelson Publishers in 2006.[42] Promoted as the nation's "largest female-bonding event ... part girl-talk, part God-talk," these events have made a significant impact on the lives of many women, as evidenced in the WOF blog.[43]

The trend for large weekend conferences caught on quickly, and other evangelical organizations copied WOF—sometimes because they wanted to try to improve upon it. Lotz, daughter of evangelist Graham, tried increasing the Bible study element with her Just Give Me Jesus arena events, sponsored by AnGel Ministries. She brought together some of the nation's best women Bible teachers—including Jill Briscoe and Arthur—to speak with her at some of the largest sports arenas in the country. Lotz has since developed these events into "Pursuing MORE of Jesus."[44] Her sister started Ruth Graham and Friends: Get Growing and Transparent Ministries, drawing emotionally broken people in the pews and helping them to better handle personal issues and problems.[45] Leadership skills were the emphasis of author John Maxwell's Injoy events, a series of satellite conferences geared for professional women in the early 1990s. Nancy Lee DeMoss, known for her books and *Revive Our Hearts* radio ministry, started True Women, specializing in ministry to single women.

Other similar events were held for a few years but then discontinued. Nevertheless, such events as Desperate for Jesus, Women's Getaway Weekends, Extraordinary Women, Time Out for Women, Women of Virtue, and Winsome Women have all influenced the way evangelical women are perceived by mainstream culture—as a force to be reckoned with, that is, a large and vocal group of Christians who have money and time to spend on books, inspirational speakers, and like-minded fellowship.

The benefits of these large women's events extend to the corporate bottom line, as more Christian book publishers sponsor similar events for profit and to promote their authors. Moody Publishers created Moody Women's Conferences—smaller in size, but "a great encouragement for women in their spiritual walk," according to one of their speakers, Dr. Linda Mintle, who is a licensed clinical social worker and author. As Mintle explains, "Women need refreshing because the cultural voices we hear are not always supportive or in sync with a biblical world view. When you attend an event that articulates a biblical worldview and the people around you have shared values, it's like getting a booster shot for your faith."[46]

Lifeway, the publishing arm of the Southern Baptist Convention, continues to sponsor Deeper Still satellite conferences at multiple venues simultaneously—spawning interest in their Bible study methods, especially those written by Moore. Lifeway has also been sponsoring separate events designed for African American women—not that minority groups are discouraged from attending the large events. In fact, WOF and other large events are racially integrated, not only among their attendees but also among key speakers and singers.

One organization formed primarily to hold large events is Women of Joy (WOJ), started by Phil Waldrep Ministries in 2006 and geared particularly for women from 35 to 40. WOJ events last longer than those of WOF—usually Friday night through Sunday noon—with no outside sponsorships. They encourage attendees to connect with other women, and they have doubled in size every year. Palin was a key speaker at some of their 2010 events, which drew as many as 16,000 attendees per city, and most of them sold out a year in advance.[47]

Organizer and WOJ president Phil Waldrep says, "This is definitely a growing trend.... We want to make a difference in the lives of people by sharing the gospel and providing women with a quality conference." Waldrep acknowledges that while these events contain an element of evangelism, they are primarily concerned with deepening the faith of the attendees and equipping them to live for Christ and be a witness for Christ to mainstream culture.[48]

Some evangelical women, however, are critical of these large events and express several concerns: (1) the focus is too inward instead of outward—very little is being accomplished in the world by these women coming together for the weekend; (2) they foster a cult following of big-name speakers; (3) millions of dollars are being spent on registration, hotels, meals, books, and other expenses that could go instead to relief efforts in needy countries; (4) separating women and men (or any groups within the Church) can cause division and keep members from being united to accomplish the work of the Church together; and (5) they draw attention away from the bigger issues of our time.

Nevertheless, these large events are well received and well attended by evangelical women in general as inspiring and confirming to their faith. There is no time in the foreseeable future that these events, even if they go through changes, are likely to disappear.

Impact of Evangelical Women

Critical concerns like those above as well as traditional theological assumptions regarding the proper role of women in the church are not holding back the energized tidal wave of evangelical women in the twenty-first century. While there is still a contingent of women within evangelicalism who would identify themselves as "Christian feminists," others prefer a less radical concept. "Christian egalitarianism" is the term preferred by some women who advocate gender equality and the elimination of chauvinistic prejudices and practices without being as liberal about certain social issues as some Christian feminists.[49]

However, neither Christian feminism nor Christian egalitarianism characterize the mainstream evangelical woman today, according to Mintle: "Women are getting empowered to be who God has called them to be—not to be anti-establishment. They are biblical, usually conservative—anything but Christian feminists! These women are not burning bras or bashing men. They want to make a difference in their world and circle of influence—as change agents in their homes, neighborhoods, schools, and culture."[50] Some of these women call themselves "complementarians," signaling their belief that God ordained complementary, and not identical or flexible, roles for men and women.[51]

Melinda Delahoyde, president of Care Net—an organization of over 1,150 pregnancy centers nationwide run by committed evangelicals—says that her 30,000 staff and volunteers would not identify themselves as feminists either, especially because the pro-life movement has been a driving force opposing abortion, a core cause of the feminist movement. "They would see themselves as responding to a calling God has given them," says Delahoyde. "Stepping out into a predominantly male world and earning a new set of skills that are usually associated with the male gender would just be part of the package. These women think of themselves more in the tradition of missionary women who did whatever needed to be done to accomplish the mission."[52]

Overall, the impact of this evangelical women's movement on American culture is still to be determined. "American evangelicals are both cultural outsiders and insiders at the same time. They selectively embrace and resist modern American culture."[53] Certainly, the news media exposure and billboards already draw attention to their big events, and as women return from them to their offices and churches demonstrating change in their lives, their sheer numbers have the potential to exert a tremendous influence on their churches and their culture. At the same time, these evangelical women may cause critics in mainstream culture some discomfort—wondering what they are "plotting" while together. So far, however, mainstream culture has probably exerted a greater influence on evangelicals than the imprint they have made on mainstream culture, according to Ostrander: "Evangelical women (as well as men) have been influenced by the mainstream culture's assumption that you can 'have it all' in terms of work and family." Their impact is often limited, he believes, because, "they are overworked and overcommitted in trying to balance a career with raising children,"[54] issues that can perhaps be overcome as evangelical women continue to gather in groups both small and large for support, encouragement, mutual prayer, and Bible study.

Looking Ahead: The Younger Evangelicals

One example of an influential younger evangelical leader is Priscilla Shirer, the daughter of the well-respected African American pastor, Tony Evans. In a *New York Times Magazine* article, Mary Worthen reports that Shirer avoids using words like *feminist* or *career woman* to describe herself. She is an evangelical Bible teacher who makes her living guiding thousands of women through the study of scripture in her books, videos, and conferences. Shirer stresses that the man is the head and the woman must submit in a biblical home and church.[55] "Satan will do everything in his power to get us to take the lead in our homes," Shirer writes in *A Jewel in His Crown*. "He wants to make us resent our husband's position of authority so that we will begin to usurp it.... Women need to pray for God to renew a spirit of submission in their hearts."[56]

On college and university campuses across the nation, young evangelical women are preparing to be the next leaders in many different fields. Nicki, one student I mentor at Cornerstone University, an evangelical Christian university, assesses her fellow students this way: "Our focus is on ministering right now wherever God has us and seeking him for what he wants us to do in the future through prayer and his word—whether we're single or married—ministering to the people around us, surrendered to him." Gender equality is not a factor in the decisions these young women are making, according to Nicki. "After applying what the Bible says to our lives, we're praying for what God wants us to do within the parameters he has already set up in his word."[57]

Nicki's colleagues at Cornerstone agree, perhaps representing others across the United States: "I look at role models like Becky McDonald, founder of Women at Risk International, who saves women from a devastating life of sex slavery all over the world. In the next ten to twenty years, I know I will have the most spiritual impact if I do not let culture decide my spheres of influence, but God," says Andrea, a young woman who graduated in 2010.[58] A college junior, Stephanie cites her grandmother as her role model because she "trains women to lead groups in Bible Study Fellowship (BSF), and she goes to other countries to visit other BSF places around the world. I think there are a lot more opportunities today for women in Christian ministry than there were in previous generations and years."[59] That appraisal is echoed by another college student, Jessica: "I think that God is opening doors for young women today that have not even been imagined in the past. He is giving us revolutionary opportunities!"[60]

Conclusion

The strong evangelical women leaders described in this chapter and their para-church organizations have done much to change the opinion of many Americans who saw all evangelicals as rural, backward, irrational fundamentalists, relics who would disappear as the country progressed into an urban, industrial future.

The future looks bright for evangelical women, if one listens to historians, evangelical women leaders, and young students. Ostrander concludes, "I think ministry—especially defined as service to others and the Kingdom—has always been on evangelical women's minds. I think in some churches and denominations, traditional understandings of gender roles rooted in their interpretation of biblical texts will continue to limit women's opportunities . . . but in the broader culture women's roles will continue to expand."[61] With a rich historical legacy, active leaders, and a strong contingent of young adherents who are confident and hopeful about the future, female evangelicals show great potential to further impact mainstream culture positively in the years ahead.

Notes

1. Kay Arthur, interview by author, December 17, 2010.

2. "Votes for Women: Beginnings of the Movement," Texas State Library and Archives Commission, http://www.tsl.state.tx.us/exhibits/suffrage/beginnings/page2.html (accessed December 20, 2010).

3. Mary Worthen, "Housewives of God," *New York Times Magazine*, November 12, 2010, http://www.nytimes.com/2010/11/14/magazine/14evangelicals-t.html.

4. John G. Turner, *Bill Bright and Campus Crusade for Christ: The Renewal of Evangelicalism in Postwar America* (Chapel Hill: University of North Carolina Press, 2008), 19.

5. Quoted in Cherie Miller, "Henrietta Mears," History's Women: The Unsung Heroines, http://www.historyswomen.com/womenoffaith/mears.html, para. 3 (accessed December 14, 2010).

6. Turner, *Bill Bright and Campus Crusade for Christ*, 20.

7. Quoted in ibid., 20.

8. Jone Johnson Lewis, "Women's History: Aimee Semple McPherson," About.com, http://womenshistory.about.com/od/protestant/a/aimee_mcpherson.htm, para. 5 (accessed December 3, 2010).

9. Quoted in "History," The Canadian Foursquare Church, http://www.foursquare.ca/index.php/2007072018/About-Us/history.html (accessed June 22, 2012).

10. "About," Foursquare Church, http://www.foursquare.org/about/history (accessed July 27, 2011).

11. "Purpose," Kathryn Kuhlman, http://kathrynkuhlman.com, para. 6 (accessed December 1, 2010).

12. "Articles: Kathryn Kuhlman (1906–1976)," God's Word to Women, http://www.godswordtowomen.org/kuhlman.htm, para. 3 (accessed July 27, 2011).

13. "About EEWC, Our Origin and Our Name," Evangelical and Ecumenical Women's Caucus (EEWC), http://www.eewc.com/About.htm (accessed December 20, 2010).

14. Ibid.

15. Mary Kassian, *The Feminist Mistake: The Radical Impact of Feminism* (Wheaton, IL: Crossway, 2005), 198.

16. "Phyllis Schlafely Biography," *Eagle Forum*, http://www.eagleforum.org/misc/bio.html (accessed December 3, 2010).

17. "Mrs. Beverly LaHaye Founder and Chairman, CWA," Concerned Women for America, http://www.cwfa.org/content.asp?id=2114&department=CWA&categoryid= (accessed July 27, 2011).

18. Tim LaHaye, *Capital Report*, newsletter, May, 1993.

19. "About Us," CWPAC, http://www.cwpac.org/aboutus.aspx (accessed November 29, 2010).

20. "25 Most Influential Evangelicals in America, Tim and Beverly LaHaye," *Time.com*, February 2005, http://www.time.com/time/specials/packages/article/0,28804,1993235_1993243_1993291,00.html (accessed July 27, 2011).

21. "Our Founders," Campus Crusade for Christ International, http://www.ccci.org/about-us/our-leadership/our-founders/index.htm (accessed December 10, 2010).

22. Turner, *Bill Bright and Campus Crusade for Christ*, 2–3.

23. Ibid., 11.

24. "25 Most Influential Evangelicals in America, Joyce Meyer," *Time.com*, February 2005, http://www.time.com/time/specials/packages/article/0,28804,1993235_1993243_1993303,00.html (accessed July 27, 2011).

25. Paula White, "Paula's Life Story," http://www.paulawhite.org/about/paula-white-ministries/paula-whites-story (accessed November 29, 2010).

26. "History," Marilyn and Sarah, http://www.marilynandsarah.org/about/history/ (accessed November 29, 2010).

27. Victoria Osteen, http://victoriaosteen.com/ (accessed November 29, 2010).

28. Lisa Miller, "Saint Sarah," *Newsweek*, last updated November 6, 2010, http://www.newsweek.com/2010/06/11/saint-sarah.html.

29. Julian Lukins, "The Faith of Sarah Palin," *Charisma*, last updated January 1, 2009, http://www.charismamag.com/index.php/features/2009/january/20101-the-faith-of-sarah-palin (accessed July 27, 2011).

30. Miller, "Saint Sarah."

31. "25 Most Influential Evangelicals in America, Howard and Roberta Ahmanson," *Time.com*, February, 2005, http://www.time.com/time/specials/packages/article/,28804,1993235_1993243_1993260,00.html (accessed July 27, 2011).

32. "25 Most Influential Evangelicals in America, Diane Knippers," *Time.com*, February, 2005, http://www.time.com/time/specials/packages/article/0,28804,1993235_1993243_1993290,00.html (accessed July 27, 2011).

33. "May a Woman Be a Pastor?" Faith & Gender (blog), January 14, 2007, http://fiveaspects.com/blog/may-a-woman-be-a-pastor/ (accessed May 25, 2012).

34. Catherine Mueller-Bell, email message to author, December 6, 2010. These five different perspectives about the role of women in ministry come from *Women in Ministry: Four Views*, eds. Bonnidell Clouse and Robert Clous (Downers Grove, IL: InterVarsity, 1989), and from Linda Belleville et al., *Two Views on Women in Ministry* (Grand Rapids, MI: Zondervan, 2005). See also Carolyn Custis James, *Half the Church: Recapturing God's Global Vision for Women* (Grand Rapids, MI: Zondervan, 2011).

35. Richard Ostrander, email message to author, December 10, 2010.

36. Quoted in Worthen, "Housewives of God."

37. "Aglow Spreads Faith, Community of Women Conference Set for Milwaukee 2006," *Milwaukee Sentinel Journal*, July 29, 2006.

38. Worthen, "Housewives of God."

39. "About," Women of Faith, http://www.womenoffaith.com/about/. Then, add the following: see also, "Meet Women of Faith," Christianbook.com, http://www.christianbook.com/html/authors/4840.html (accessed June 26, 2012) (accessed January 4, 2011).

40. "The Line Up," Women of Faith, www.womenoffaith.com/events/dallas/ (accessed June 26, 2012)

41. "About Us," Women of Faith, http://www.womenoffaith.com/about/ (accessed January 4, 2011).

42. "Thomas Nelson Hires Exec for Events Unit," *Nashville Business Journal*, last modified September 8, 2006, http://www.bizjournals.com/nashville/stories/2006/09/04/daily22.html.

43. "Women of Faith Event Inspires at Pepsi Center," blackchristiannews.com http://blackchristiannews.com/news/2009/09/women-of-faith-event-inspires-at-pepsi-center.html (accessed June 26, 2012).

44. "About Us," Anne Graham Lotz, http://www.annegrahamlotz.com/about-us/ (accessed November 15, 2010).

45. Linda Mintle, interview by author, March 13, 2010.

46. Ibid.

47. Women of Joy, http://www.womenofjoy.org (accessed March 15, 2010).

48. Phil Waldrep, interview by author, February 28, 2010.

49. Wendy McElroy, http://ifeminists.com (accessed November 29, 2010).

50. Mintle, interview by author.

51. Worthen, "Housewives of God."

52. Melinda Delahoyde, email message to author, December 27, 2010.

53. Turner, *Bill Bright and Campus Crusade for Christ*, 10.

54. Ostrander, email message to author.

55. Worthen, "Housewives of God."

56. Priscilla Shirer, *A Jewel in Her Crown: Rediscovering Your Value as a Woman of Excellence* (Chicago: Moody, 2004), 74.
57. Nicole, interview by author, December 4, 2010.
58. Andrea Ripley, email message to author, December 8, 2010.
59. Stephanie Mills, email message to author, December 5, 2010.
60. Jessica Werstein, email message to author, December 6, 2010.
61. Ostrander, email message to author.

About the Contributors to Volume 3

Editor **ROBERT H. WOODS JR.** is professor of communication at Spring Arbor University in Michigan, where he teaches in the M.A. program. He holds an M.A. and Ph.D. in communication from Regent University, Virginia, and is licensed to practice law in the Commonwealth of Virginia. He recently served as the president of the Religious Communication Association (2009–2010). His articles have appeared in the *Review of Religious Research*, *Journal of Media and Religion*, *Christian Scholar's Review*, *Christian Higher Education*, and several other journals. He is co-editor of *The Message in the Music: Studying Contemporary Praise and Worship* (2007) and *Understanding Evangelical Media: The Changing Face of Christian Communication* (2008). He is co-author of *Prophetically Incorrect: A Christian Introduction to Media Criticism* (2010) and one of the authors of *Media Ethics: Cases in Moral Reasoning* (2011).

Foreword author **MARK A. NOLL** (Ph.D., Vanderbilt University) is the Francis A. McAnaney professor of history at the University of Notre Dame. Most of his teaching and writing treat American religious history and the recent world history of Christianity. Recent titles include *Jesus Christ and the Life of the Mind* (2011), *Protestantism: A Very Short Introduction* (2011), *God and Race in American Politics: A Short History* (2008), *The Civil War as a Theological Crisis* (2006), and, with Carolyn Nystrom, *Clouds of Witnesses: Christian Voices from Africa and Asia* (2011). In 2005, Dr. Noll was named by *Time* magazine as one of "the 25 most influential evangelicals in America."

PHYLLIS E. ALSDURF is an associate professor of English and director of the Johnson Center for Journalism and Communication at Bethel University, St. Paul, Minnesota. She holds a Ph.D. in journalism (University of

Minnesota), an M.A. in humanities (Western Kentucky University), and an M.A. in journalism (Kansas State University). Her research interest is in the area of media and religion, and her dissertation examined the impact of the magazine *Christianity Today* on the development of modern evangelicalism. Among her professional publications is a chapter in *Religion, Media, and the Marketplace* (2007) and "The Founding of *Christianity Today* Magazine and the Construction of an American Evangelical Identity," in the *Journal of Religious and Theological Information* (2010). Alsdurf is the co-author of *Battered into Submission* (1989) and has written numerous articles for a variety of Christian publications. She was editor of *Family Life Today* magazine in southern California for six years and director of publications at Bethel University for five years prior to joining the Bethel faculty.

WILLIAM J. BROWN is professor and research fellow in the School of Communication and the Arts at Regent University in Virginia Beach, Virginia. He received a B.S. in environmental science from Purdue University, an M.A. in communication management from the Annenberg School of Communication at the University of Southern California in Los Angeles, and both an M.A. and a Ph.D. in communication from the University of Southern California. His academic research interests include media effects, entertainment-education for social change, media personalities, and social influence. He has taught communication at the University of Southern California; the University of Hawaii; University of the Nations in Kona, Hawaii; and Regent University. His academic work includes published research in *Journal of Communication*, *Human Communication Research*, *Journalism Quarterly*, *Communication Quarterly*, *Communication Law & Policy*, *Political Communication*, *Mass Communication & Society*, *Journal of Communication and Religion*, *Journal of Media & Religion*, *Health Communication*, and *Journal of Health Communication*. He is also a partner of Brown, Fraser & Associates, a communication research and consulting firm in Chesapeake, Virginia. He and his colleague Benson P. Fraser have conducted more than 100 national media studies in more than thirty countries. Brown is a Fulbright specialist and has collaborated with the Center for Media and Health and the Netherlands Entertainment-Education Foundation on entertainment-education projects.

JUDITH M. BUDDENBAUM holds an A.B. in chemistry, an M.A. in journalism, and a Ph.D. in mass communication from Indiana University.

She is professor emerita in the Department of Journalism and Technical Communication at Colorado State University, where she taught courses on religion and media, communication law, media research, and reporting. She is founder and past president of the Association for Education in Journalism's Religion and the Media Interest Group and co-founder and co-editor of the *Journal of Media and Religion*. A former religion reporter, she has served on the American Academy of Religion's Public Understanding of Religion committee and on the advisory committee for *The Lutheran* magazine and conducted media research for Lutheran World Federation in Geneva, Switzerland. Her scholarly research on religion and media has been published in *Journalism Quarterly*, *Newspaper Research Journal*, and *Journalism History* and as book chapters. Her books include *Reporting News about Religion: An Introduction for Journalists* (1998), *Readings on Religion as News* (2000) with Debra L. Mason, and *Religious Scandals* (2009).

LARRY ESKRIDGE is the associate director of the Institute for the Study of American Evangelicals (ISAE) at Wheaton College. He did doctoral coursework at the University of Notre Dame and earned his Ph.D. from the University of Stirling in Scotland. He has been with the ISAE since 1989 assisting in the creation, management, and content of a number of its projects and was the executive producer of the video series *People of Faith: Christianity in America*. In addition, he has served as a frequent resource for news stories about contemporary evangelicalism, quoted by such outlets as *Newsweek*, *Time*, the *Chicago Tribune*, *Los Angeles Times*, *USA Today*, *Christian Century*, and the Associated Press, as well as giving interviews for broadcast media such as CBS Radio and NPR. His primary research interest lies in the intersections among evangelicalism, popular culture, and the mass media, and he has written a number of articles, essays, reviews, and reference entries on various dimensions of these relationships. With Mark A. Noll, he co-edited *More Money, More Ministry: Evangelicals and Money in Recent North American History* (2000). He is currently working on a history of the Jesus People of the 1960s and 1970s to be published by Oxford University Press in 2012.

DENISE P. FERGUSON is associate professor of mediated communication and director of graduate programs in communication at Pepperdine University in Malibu, California. She earned a Ph.D. in public affairs and issues management at Purdue University, an M.A. in communication at

Bowling Green State University, and a B.S. in communication from Indiana State University. Her research has been published in *Oxford Handbook of Religion and the News*, *Public Relations Review*, *The Handbook of Public Relations*, *Public Relations Journal*, and *Sociological Quarterly* and has been presented at annual conferences of the International Communication Association, National Communication Association, Central States Communication Association, and Public Relations Society of America, where she was awarded the 2008 Top Faculty Paper. Ferguson has several years of experience in professional public relations in higher education, corporate, and non-profit organizations. She holds the Accreditation in Public Relations (APR) from the Public Relations Society of America and is an executive member of the international Commission on Public Relations Education.

BENSON P. FRASER is associate professor in the School of Communication and the Arts at Regent University in Virginia. He has served as chair of the Department of Communication Studies and director of the Center for the Study of Faith and Culture at Regent University. Fraser earned his M.Div. from Fuller Theological Seminary, his M.A. in psychology from Pepperdine University, his M.A. in communications from California State University, Fullerton, and his Ph.D. in intercultural communication from the University of Washington. His academic and research interests are in the area of media effects, celebrity influence, indirect communication, and entertainment-education. He has taught communication classes at the University of Washington, the University of the Pacific, and Regent University. His primarily teaching responsibilities are in the areas of qualitative research, communication and theology, and communication theory. Fraser is also a partner and consultant of Brown, Fraser & Associates, a communication research firm in Chesapeake, Virginia. He and his colleague William J. Brown have conducted more than 100 national media studies in more than thirty countries.

KEVIN HEALEY serves as assistant professor of media studies at the University of New Hampshire in Durham. He has a Ph.D. in communications and media from the Institute of Communications Research at University of Illinois at Urbana-Champaign. He has published research on media concentration and minority ownership, media coverage of religion and politics, and the Christian men's movement Promise Keepers. His articles have appeared in *Journal of Mass Media Ethics*, *Cultural Studies ⇔ Critical Methodologies*, and *Symbolic Interaction*. He received fellowships from the Illinois Program for Research in the Humanities at the University of Illinois at Urbana-Champaign; the School of Criticism and Theory at Cornell University; and the Colloquia 2000 Series in Applied Media Ethics at Colorado State University. Healey is a regular contributor for *Trans/missions*, edited by Diane Winston at the Annenberg School for Communication at the University of Southern California.

MICHAEL A. LONGINOW, originally from Chicago, chairs the Department of Journalism and Integrated Media at Biola University near Los Angeles. He began teaching journalism in 1989 at Asbury University in Kentucky, where he developed specialties in cross-cultural media, interactivity of religion and media, and the connections between journalism's past and its future. He earned a B.A. at Wheaton College in political science and an M.S. in journalism from the University of Illinois at Urbana-Champaign, followed by stints in full-time general assignment and political reporting for dailies outside Chicago and Atlanta. Since entering academia, Longinow has been a freelance writer for national and regional magazines, academic publications, and books. His Ph.D. is from the University of Kentucky, where his dissertation research focused on the interplay of Christian media, higher education, and socioreligious change in the United States between 1888 and 1942. He is active in the Association for Education in Journalism and Mass Communication, College Media Advisers, Inc., and the California College Media Association. He serves as executive director of the Association of Christian Collegiate Media. He has served as a faculty journalist-in-residence with the Council of Christian Colleges and Universities's Washington Journalism center on Capitol Hill and was named the 2009 McCandlish Phillips Chair of the World Journalism Institute.

MARTIN J. MEDHURST is distinguished professor of rhetoric and communication and professor of political science at Baylor University in Waco, Texas. He holds a Ph.D. from Pennsylvania State University and has taught at the University of California–Davis and Texas A&M University. He is the author or editor of thirteen books, including *Words of a Century: The Top 100 American Speeches, 1900–1999* (2009, with Stephen E. Lucas); *Before the Rhetorical Presidency* (2008), *The Rhetorical Presidency of George H. W. Bush* (2006); *Presidential Speechwriting: From the New Deal to the*

Reagan Revolution and Beyond (2003, with Kurt Ritter); and *Critical Reflections on the Cold War: Linking Rhetoric and History* (2000, with H. W. Brands). His articles have appeared in leading disciplinary and interdisciplinary journals, including the *Quarterly Journal of Speech*, *Communication Monographs*, *Critical Studies in Mass Communication*, *Rhetoric & Public Affairs*, *Presidential Studies Quarterly*, *Armed Forces & Society*, and *Journal of Church and State*. He is the founder and editor of the award-winning interdisciplinary quarterly *Rhetoric & Public Affairs* and serves as a series editor at Michigan State University Press and Baylor University Press. In 2005, he was named a distinguished scholar of the National Communication Association.

STEPHEN J. NICHOLS earned an M.A. both in theology and in philosophy and holds a Ph.D. from Westminster Theological Seminary. He is research professor of Christianity and culture at Lancaster Bible College in Pennsylvania. He also serves as adjunct professor for Reformed Theological Seminary and as a visiting lecturer at London Theological Seminary. He is the author of over a dozen books. His earlier books were on church history and historical theology. More recently, he has been exploring the intersection of Christianity and culture in such books as *Jesus Made in America: A Cultural History from the Puritans to "The Passion of the Christ"* (2008) and *Getting the Blues: What Blues Music Teaches Us about Suffering and Salvation* (2008). He also wrote a children's book, *Church History ABCs: Augustine and Twenty-Five Other Friends* (2010). Among his current projects is a look at Dietrich Bonhoeffer, *Bonhoeffer on the Christian Life: In Christ, in Community, in Love* (2012), and a look at the current landscape of evangelicalism, *Mapping Evangelicalism: Who We Are and Where You Can Find Us* (forthcoming).

PAUL D. PATTON has graduate degrees in counseling and religious education and a Ph.D. in communication with an emphasis in theater arts from Regent University. He is professor of communication and chair of the Department of Communication and Media at Spring Arbor University, where he teaches courses in media, popular culture, and theater. He was a pastor until 1993, ministering in the Detroit area at Trinity Church in Livonia. It was at Trinity, while a youth pastor, that he founded Trinity House Theater in 1981. He is the author of over thirty produced stage plays, radio plays, and performance essays; his latest play, *The Celebrity*, is published by

Heuer Press (2009). He is involved in several academic writing projects and has lectured on topics ranging from "The Idolatry of the Cult of Celebrity" to "God Talk: Lessons in the Manipulative Use of Religious Language." He is co-author of *Prophetically Incorrect: A Christian Introduction to Media Criticism* (2010) and authored a chapter on evangelical theater in *Understanding Evangelical Media: The Changing Face of Christian Communication* (2008). He regularly attends the National Communication Association conventions, is involved in Christians in Theater Arts (CITA), and has hosted CITA's Great Lakes Theater Conference for several years. He has published articles in *Christianity and Theater* and *The Banner*.

QUENTIN J. SCHULTZE is the Arthur H. DeKruyter chair in faith and communication as well as a professor of communication arts and sciences at Calvin College. His books include *American Evangelicals and the Mass Media: Perspectives on the Relationship between American Evangelicals and the Mass Media* (1990), *Televangelism and American Culture: The Business of Popular Religion* (1991, 2003), *Habits of the High Tech Heart: Living Virtuously in the Information Age* (2001), and *Christianity and the Mass Media in America: Toward a Democratic Accommodation* (2003); he edited, with Robert H. Woods Jr., *Understanding Evangelical Media: The Changing Face of Christian Communication* (2008). He has written over 100 scholarly and general-interest articles and delivered hundreds of speeches to academic groups, business associations, and non-profit organizations. He has been quoted in most of the major North American media, including the *Wall Street Journal, Newsweek, U.S. News & World Report, Fortune*, the *New York Times*, and the *Chicago Tribune*. He has been interviewed by such broadcast media as CNN, CBS Radio, NBC TV, NPR, the CBC, and Radio New Zealand.

KATHLEEN OSBECK SINDORF, associate professor of communication and media studies at Cornerstone University in Grand Rapids, Michigan, has served on the Board of Directors for National Religious Broadcasters, Concerned Women for America, and the Evangelical Council for Financial Accountability. She has been a pioneer among women in evangelical broadcasting, including *World Religious News* on 1,300 radio stations, the Walter Bennett Advertising Agency with Billy Graham crusade broadcasts and James Robison's television ministry, and the Christian Broadcasting Network (CBN). She was CBN's first acting news director, first regular female cohost of *The 700 Club* with Pat Robertson and Ben Kinchlow, and first senior international correspondent. Sindorf was editor, voice talent, and co-host for the Luis Palau Evangelistic Association and executive producer for all "Lausanne II in Manila" plenary videos. Nominated for two Emmy awards while at WCFC-TV38 in Chicago, she then served as vice president of communication for Precept Ministries International with Kay Arthur in Chattanooga, Tennessee, where she coordinated the successful National Women's Conventions. A contributor to *Understanding Evangelical Media: The Changing Face of Christian Communication* (2008), Sindorf and her husband Joe led the church media track at the COICOM conferences in 2009 in Argentina and in 2010 in the Dominican Republic, teaching pastors and media directors from across Latin America.

MICHAEL RAY SMITH earned a Ph.D. from Regent University and has taught at state and private universities at graduate and undergraduate schools. He is professor of communication studies at Campbell University. An award-winning writer and photographer, he has been quoted in the *New York Times*, the *Boston Globe*, the *Chicago Tribune*, the *Arizona Republic*, *Editor & Publisher*, *Christianity Today*, and many other periodicals and appeared on French24 TV and other broadcasts. He has written five books, twelve journal articles, and hundreds of articles for the popular press. In 2011, he published *A Free Press in Freehand: The Spirit of American Blogging in the Handwritten Newspapers of John McLean Harrington 1858–1869*. His others books include *FeatureWriting.Net* (2002) and *The Jesus Newspaper: The Christian Experiment of 1900 and Its Lessons for Today* (2002). His earlier books explore history in south-central Pennsylvania where he worked as a journalist. Smith spent a decade working in the newsroom and more than two decades working in the classroom. He has presented workshops on writing in the United States and overseas. He works with the Association for Education in Journalism and Mass Communication on issues of equity and disability and teaches for the World Journalism Institute among others. Smith and his wife Barbara have two daughters, both involved in media and entertainment. His personal theme is "We're saved to be spent."

TERRENCE R. WANDTKE earned his Ph.D. at Saint Louis University, specializing in twentieth-century literature, film, and critical theory. He joined the division of communication arts at Judson University in Elgin,

Illinois, where he teaches classes in literature, film, and popular culture. His scholarship has consistently focused on the connections between literature and film. In recent years, he has been writing about heroic narratives in literature, in film, and especially in popular media such as comic books. His work includes a collection of essays, *The Amazing Transforming Superhero* (2007), on the history and cultural impact of superheroes, and his current project, *The Meaning of Superhero Comic Books*, examines the significance of the ideas and structure of comic books in an Internet culture. In recent years, seminars presented at the Cornerstone Festival include C. S. Lewis's argument for open endings and the post-modern heroism of *Watchmen*. He directs the Imago Film Festival, an event designed to explore the intersections between faith, film, and culture. In addition, he has served on the selection committee for the St. Louis International Film Festival's Interfaith Award and on the jury for the Elgin Film Festival.

ANNALEE R. WARD is interim director of distance education at the University of Dubuque Theological Seminary, where she oversees the M.Div, the M.A. in missional christianity, and the commissioned lay pastors online programs. A former chair of the Communication Arts Department at Trinity Christian College in Palos Heights, Illinois, she earned her Ph.D. from Regent University and her M.A. from Colorado State University. Her scholarly work includes *Mouse Morality: The Rhetoric of Disney Animated Films* (2002), which led to the Carl Couch Center's 2004 Clifford G. Christians Award. She has also contributed to *Understanding Evangelical Media: The Changing Face of Christian Communication* (2008), written articles and reviews, and guest edited *Journal of Communication and Religion* (March 2004). A community speaker and contributor to popular and scholarly publications, Ward's interests lie at the confluence of media, rhetoric, and ethics in the context of a Christian worldview. That has led to work as diverse as consulting with pastors on preaching, visits to theme parks, popular media reviews, and research on popular culture.

KENNETH E. WATERS earned his Ph.D. from the University of Southern California. For the past two decades he has been a professor of journalism at Pepperdine University, and in 2010 he began serving as chair of the Communication Division. He has also advised the student newspaper, magazine, and online publications at the university. His scholarly articles have appeared in *Journalism and Mass Communication Quarterly*, *Journal of Mass Media Ethics*, *Journalism History*, *Catholic Historical Review*, and *American Journalism and Newspaper Research Journal*. He has also contributed book chapters to *Popular Religious Periodicals in the U.S.* (1995), *Good News, or Dupes and Reactionaries?: The Promise Keepers* (1999), *Understanding Evangelical Media: The Changing Face of Christian Communication* (2008), and *The Oxford Handbook of Religion and the News Media* (2012). He is an active member of the Association for Education in Journalism and Mass Communication and the National Communication Association. He is currently working on a book about the future of Christian periodicals.

Index

Abernathy, Ralph, 156
Abortion, 18, 19, 21, 23, 25, 27, 28, 42, 44–48, 51, 54, 62, 163
Abortion providers, murder of, 111–12
Activism, 233
Advertising, 103
Africa
    AIDS epidemic in, 202–4
    spiritual mapping in, 67–68
African American Episcopal Church, 197
African American evangelicals, xxiv–xxv, 50, 156–57
Ahmanson, Roberta, 303
AIDS epidemic, 11, 36, 39, 202–4
Air Force Academy, 119–20
Alamo, Susan, 280
Alamo, Tony, 280
Alliance Defense Fund, 22
Allitt, Patrick, 18
American Bible Society, 197
American culture
    changes in, 18, 19, 86
    consumerism and, 97
    evangelical magazines and, 196–98
    evangelicals and, 20
    media and, 144–45
    See also Culture; Popular culture
American Family Association, 22, 41
American Idol (TV show), 219
Anabaptists, 17
Analytical criticism, xx–xxii
Angelus Temple, 299–300
Answers in Genesis (AIG), 253
Anti-war movement, 19
Anti-white racism, 70
Apocalyptic orientation, 284–85
Applied Theater, 266
Arguello, Christine, 120
Aristotle, xx

Arminian (magazine), 196–97
Arthur, Kay, 296, 297
Artistic quality, lack of, xxiii–xxiv
Art museums, 254
Arts, 264, 265
Art Within, 273
Asians, xxv
Assembly of God, 117
Associated Baptist Press, 173
The Audacity of Hope (Obama), 35
Augustine, Saint, 144, 269
Authenticity, 69, 70, 72, 86, 88, 247
Ave Maria Grotto, 248

Babin, Pierre, 137
Bakker, Jim, 110, 113, 114, 117, 133, 137, 139, 158, 161, 174–75, 251–52
Bakker, Tammy Faye, 113, 114, 139, 174–75, 251–52
Balmer, Randall, 231
Baptist Press, 173
Barrett, John, 111
Bauer, Gary, 25, 37
Baylor University, 119
Bebbington, David, 85, 233
Beckmann, David, 203
Beecher, Henry Ward, 116
Beecher, Lyman, 152
Beers, Gilbert, 221
Bell, L. Nelson, 214–15
Bell, Rob, 86
Belz, Mindy, 169
Bennett, James Gordon, Sr., 151–52
Berg, David, 280
Bible
    authority of, 33, 54
    translations of, 200–202
    women and, 304
Biblicalism, 233–34

Biblical justice, 51
Billy Graham Library, 253
Black church, 72
Black evangelicals, xxiv–xxv, 50, 156–57
Blake, Charles, 50
Blessitt, Arthur, 280
Blogs, 7, 182
Bok, Sissela, 112–13
Bonhoeffer, Dietrich, 89, 103
Bono, 6
Boorstin, Daniel J., 94, 96
Born-again Christians, 19, 33, 157. *See also* Evangelicals
Born Alive Infant Protection Act, 44, 46
Branch Davidians, 161
Brandi, xxiii
Branson, Missouri, 249–50
Brethren, 51
Bright, Bill, 279, 299
Bright, Vonette, 301–2
Brokaw, Joanne, 219
Brownback, Sam, 36
Brushaber, George, 221
Bryan, William Jennings, 154–55
Burke, Kenneth, 98
Bush, George H. W., 21
Bush, George W., xxiii, 16, 24–27, 33, 34, 36, 37, 39, 42–43, 51, 90, 163, 204
Butler, John W., 154
Butler Act, 154

Caldwell, Kirbyjon, 50
Call to Renewal, 35, 37, 39, 47
Calvary Chapel, 280–81, 288, 289
Campbell, Alexander, 197
Campbell, Minnie Lee, 116–17
Campbell, Thomas, 197
Campolo, Tony, 38–39, 47, 50, 52–53
Campus Crusade for Christ, 225, 278, 299, 301–2
Caner, Ergun, 113
Capitalism, 35, 54, 96–97, 100
Capper, Arthur, 184
Care Net, 308
Carter, Jimmy, xxiii, 16, 19, 20, 23, 25, 44, 157–58
Cash, Johnny, xxiii, 79–93, 278
 conversions of, 82–85
 dark side of, 84
 evangelicalism and, 86–92

 Graham and, 79–81
 later career of, 84–86
Cash, June Carter, 82, 86
Catholics, 23, 42, 152, 156
Celebrity culture, 94–109, 130, 219
 characteristics of, 95–99
 consumerism and, 102–3, 104
 defined, 94–95
 influence of, on evangelicals, 99–105
Celebrity endorsements, 96–97
Celebrity worship, 98–99
Centrist evangelicals, 40–41, 44, 50, 53
Chancellor, John, 157
Charisma, 143–44
Charisma & Christian Life (magazine), 201
Charismatics, 128–29, 135–38
Charity, 49
Chautauqua, 251
Chevaldayoff, Les, 244
Chicago Declaration, 19
Chipps, D. E., 111
"Christ and Culture" paradox, xx, xxv, 17
Christian Baptist (newspaper), 197
Christian bookstores, 291
Christian Broadcasting Network (CBN), 19–20, 141–42, 174
Christian Century (magazine), 200
Christian Church, xx
Christian Coalition, 16, 22–26, 41
Christian film festivals, 229–43
Christian Films Distributors Association (CFDA), 234
Christian Herald (newspaper), 200
Christian History (magazine), 196
Christian Identity survivalists, 161
Christianity, 53, 72, 88
Christianity Today (magazine), 6, 18, 41, 52, 62, 135–36, 174, 182, 200–206, 212–28
 Graham and, 212–13, 214–15
 influence of, 217–21
 launch of, 214–17
 new model of, 221–22
 purpose of, 213, 220–21, 223–24
 role of, in evangelical resurgence, 224–26
 sister publications, 222–23
 success of, 216–17
Christianity Today International (CTI), 216–17, 222–23
Christian Life (magazine), 200
Christian newspapers, 172–73, 184–91

Christian Post (newspaper), 173
Christian realism, 88–90
Christian Recorder (magazine), 197
Christian Right, 18–29, 34, 37, 41–43, 62–64, 159–60
Christian rock, 83, 290–91
Christians
   born-again, 19, 33, 157
   early, xx
Christians in Theater Arts (CITA), 266–67
Christian Voice, 19–20, 159
Christ the Transformer of Culture, 263–64, 265
Chrzan, David, 6
Churches
   architecture of, 131
   New Paradigm, 289
   use of media by, 7–9, 104
   See also Megachurches
Church of God of Prophecy, 248
City of the Angels Film Festival, 237–38, 241
Civil discourse, 71
Civil rights movement, 19, 38, 156–57
Clairborne, Shaine, 288
Clapp, Rodney, 91
Clinton, Bill, 23, 54, 117, 122, 161
Clinton, Hillary, 4, 27, 39
Coffeehouses, 283
Coley, Bryan, 273
Colleges, 175
Colson, Charles, 23, 144
Committee of Bible Translators (CBT), 201
Commodification, 102–3, 106
Communal living, 285
Community impact committees, 22
Compass Direct, 177
Compassionate conservatism, 40
Concerned Women for America (CWA), 18, 22, 42, 301
Congressional elections
   of 1994, 23
   of 2010, 28
Conservative evangelicals, 50, 52, 53, 62, 63
Consumerism, xviii, 95–97, 102–3, 104, 105
Contemporary Christian Music (CCM), xxiv, 83, 87, 289–91
Contract with the American Family (Christian Coalition), 16
Conversion, 82, 233, 240
Coomes, Tommy, 281
Copeland, Gloria, 303

Copeland, Kenneth, 115, 136
Cordeiro, Wayne, 4
Cortes, Luis, 36–37
Coughlin, Joseph, 132
Council of Christian Colleges and Universities (CCCU), 175
Council of Trent, 143
Counterculture, 278–91
Covenant Players, 266
Creation care, 40
Creation Museum, 253–54
Creation Science, 161
Crosswalk.com, 182
Cruci-centrism, 234
C Street House, 121–22
Cult of saints, 143
Cult of the martyrs, 251
Cultural criticism, xx–xxii
Cultural engagement, 17, 87–91, 217–19, 225, 254–56
Culture
   celebrity, 94–109, 130, 219
   consumer, 103, 104, 105
   transformation of, 218–19, 263–65
   withdrawal from, 87, 263–64
   youth, 280, 288, 290–91
   See also American culture; Popular culture
Culture wars, 11, 18
Cyber-communities, 104

Daddy Grace, 114, 116–17
Damah Film Festival, 240
Darrow, Clarence, 154
Daughtry, Leah, 35
Davis, George T. B., 184
Dawn, Marva J., 255
Dean, Howard, 35
Decision (magazine), 200
Declaration of Independence, 130
DeCurtis, Anthony, 86
Delahoyde, Melinda, 308
DeLay, Tom, 120–21, 122
Democratic National Committee (DNC), 35
Democratic Party
   abortion issue and, 54
   evangelicals and, 27–28, 33–35, 37, 39, 43–48, 54
DeMoss, Nancy Lee, 305
Depeche Mode, 90
Dispensationalism, 285

Distraction, 106
Divorce, 18
Dobson, James, 22, 25, 37, 41, 46, 64, 90, 201
Dole, Bob, 21
Dollar, Creflo, 115
Doomsday cults, 161
Dooyeweerd, Herman, 264
Dortch, Richard, 113
Drama, 250–51. *See also* Theater
Drucker, Peter, 9
Dual-loyalty organizations, 267–68
DuBois, Joshua, 35
Dutch Reformed Protestants, 264
Dylan, Bob, 280

Eagle Forum, 18, 301
Economic justice, 40–41, 50
Education, 42
  evolution and, 154
  higher, 175
  vouchers, 25
Edwards, John, 27
Edwards, Jonathan, 196
Eighteenth Amendment, 153
Ein Geistliches Magazien (magazine), 196
Elections. *See* Congressional elections; Presidential election
Ellul, Jacques, 105
Ellwood, Robert, 285
Elshtain, Jean Bethke, 53
Elvgren, Gillette, 267
Emergent Church movement, 47
Enron, 119
Ensign, John, 122
Entertainment, 96, 106, 232–33, 250–51, 255, 291. *See also* Theater
Environmental movement, 19
Environmental policy, 40, 62
Equal Rights Amendment (ERA), 18–19, 157, 300, 301
Esperanza USA, 36
Eternity (magazine), 200
Ethics and Religious Liberty Commission, 42
Ethnic diversity, lack of, xxiv–xxv
Ethnic pluralism, 62
Eureka Springs, 248–49
Euthanasia, 27
Evangelical celebrities, 130–31
Evangelical churches. *See* Churches; Megachurches

Evangelical clergy
  media and, 1–9, 130–31
  on radio, 131–32
  Rick Warren, 1–15
Evangelical colleges and universities, 175
Evangelical film festivals, 229–43
Evangelicalism
  in eighteenth century, 150–51
  film and, 230–32
  Johnny Cash and, 86–92
  loss of influence of, in twentieth century, 153–57
  in nineteenth century, 151–53
  political demographics, 37–44
  return to prominence of, 157–63, 200, 224–26
  struggles within, 62–63
Evangelical magazines, 190–91, 195–211
  American culture and, 196–98
  Christianity Today, 200–206, 212–28
  online, 205–8
  Sojourners, 200–26
  World, 169–71, 182, 190–91, 195, 200–206
  See also specific magazines
Evangelical media
  lack of ethnic diversity in, xxiv–xxv
  as "preaching to the choir," xxii–xxiii
  See also specific media types
Evangelical news, 169–81, 182–94
Evangelical Press Association, 190
Evangelicals
  African American, xxiv–xxv, 50, 156–57
  centrist, 40–41, 44, 50, 53
  conservative, 41–43, 50, 52, 53, 62, 63
  Hispanic, 34, 36–37, 54
  influence of celebrity culture on, 99–105
  with mass appeal, xxiii
  media coverage of, 149–68
  political engagement by, 16–32, 33
  post-modern, 86
  progressive, 19, 27, 37–39, 43, 47–50, 52–53
  scandals involving, 110–27
  young, 27, 33–34, 37, 51, 54, 62, 200, 208, 308–9
Evangelicals for Social Action (ESA), 19
Evangelical television, 128–48
Evangelical theater, 261–77
Evangelical women, 296–313
Evangelical Women's Caucus (EWC), 300
Evolution, 154, 198

EXPLO '72, 278–79
Ezines, 205–8

Facing the Giants (film), 234
Faith, 35
Faith healing, 135, 136, 140, 200, 284, 299
Faith in Action, 35
Faith Working Group, 35
Falwell, Jerry, 20, 22, 25, 27, 41, 90, 133, 136, 158–60
The Family, 121–22
Family, threats to, 18
Family issues, 42
FamilyNet, 182
Family Research Council, 22, 25, 42
Fandom, 99, 100
Father Divine, 114
Federal Council of Churches (FCC), 155–56
The Fellowship, 121–22
Feminists, 201, 300–301, 307
Fennig, Brice, 234
Fields, Echo Ellen, 159–60
Film festivals, 229–43
Films, xxiv, 230–32, 265, 291
Financial scandals, 119
Finney, Charles, 8, 231
Firebone Theatre, 272
First Amendment, 129
Fiscal policy, 50
Flickerings Film Festival, 238, 241
Focus on the Family, 22, 25–26, 41, 46, 225, 234
Focus on the Family Action, 22
Folger, Janet, 45
Ford, Gerald, 44, 157
Foreign policy, 19, 28, 41
Forest Home, 298–99
"For the Health of the Nation" report, 40–41
Fosdick, Harry Emerson, 153, 154
Fox News, 66, 69
Franklin, Benjamin, 150, 183
Franklin, James, 189
Free Congress Foundation, 20
Free will, 197
Frisbee, Lonnie, 280–81
Fuller, Charles E., 131–32
Fuller Theological Seminary, 18, 213–14, 237
Fundamentalism/fundamentalists, 87, 90, 153–55, 158, 162, 198, 200, 220, 298

Galli, Mark, 110, 217–18
Gates, Bill, 6
Gay marriage. *See* Same-sex marriage
Gay rights, 42
Gerson, Michael, 45, 50
GetReligion.org, 182
Gibson, Charles, 66–67
Gideon Media Arts conference, 236–37
Giffords, Gabrielle, 112
Gingrich, Newt, 16, 67, 120, 122
Glossolalia, 129, 136, 153, 284
Godfrey, Arthur, 131
God gap, in politics, 35
Godstock, 278
Gore, Al, 120
Gorman, Marvin, 117
Gospel Advocate (magazine), 197
Gospel Herald, 177
The Gospel Road (1972), 83
Graham, Billy, 2, 5, 11, 72, 85–87, 92, 156, 174, 200, 279, 299
  Christianity Today and, 212–15
  Jesus People and, 282, 283
  Johnny Cash and, 79–81
Graham, Franklin, 92
Gramm, Phil, 16
Grant, Amy, 87, 290
Grant, Marshall, 82, 83
Grassley, Charles, 115
Great Awakening, 150–51, 196, 197, 298
Greek theater, 268
Greeley, Horace, 152
Green, Keith, 290
Griggs, Russell, 282
Guiliani, Rudy, 37
Guns, 112
Gushee, David, 39, 41, 66

Hagee, John, 37
Haggard, Ted, 110, 117–18, 175
Hahn, Jessica, 113, 117
Haitian earthquake, 115, 169
Hale, Tony, xxiii
Halverson, Richard, 299
Hannity, Sean, 69
Harbinson, Colin, 266
Harris, Benjamin, 183
Hatch, Nathan O., 8
Healing, 135, 136, 140, 200, 284, 299
Hearst, William Randolph, 156

Heaton, Patricia, xxiii
Henry, Carl F. H., 17–18, 174, 214, 215, 218–21
Herald of Gospel Liberty (newspaper), 172
Heritage USA, 251–52
Heroes, 95–96, 130
Hertenstein, Mike, 238
Hickey, Marilyn, 303
Higgins, John, 280
Hill, Paul Jennings, 111
Hinn, Benny, 115
Hippies, 279–81, 285. *See also* Jesus People
Hispanic evangelicals, xxv, 34, 36–37, 54
HIV/AIDS epidemic, 11, 36, 39, 202–4
Hollywood, 130, 232–33, 291
Holmes, Amy, 68
Holy Land Experience (HLE), 244–47, 256
Holy Land USA, 247
Homosexuality, 11, 18, 19, 23, 39, 51, 163, 203
Hoover, Stewart M., 10
Huckabee, Mike, 63–64
Hucksters, 114–15
Hudson, J. K., 189–90
Humbard, Rex, 133, 158
Hume, Brit, 66
Hunter, James Davidson, 224
Hurricane Katrina, 6
"Hurt" (Cash), 87
Hybels, Bill, 3, 52
Hype, 96
Hypocrisy, 160

Identification, 98
Images, 103–4, 106
Imago Film Festival, 229–30, 239, 241
Immigration reform, 34, 36–37
Inauguration, invocation at, 5
Inception (2010), 195
Individualism, 129–30
Industrialization, 151
In-group, xxii–xxiii
In His Steps (Sheldon), 184, 185, 191
International Bible Society (IBS), 201
International Christian Video Media (ICVM), 234, 241
Internet, use of, by churches, 7–9
Investigative reporting, 174–76
Iraq War, 25, 34, 37, 39, 40, 51, 66
IVoteValues.org, 26

Jackson, Jesse, 117, 161
Jakes, T. D., xxv, 3, 50
Jesus Christ, poor and, 38
The Jesus Generation (Graham), 283
Jesus Movement, 83, 265
Jesus People, 278–95
Jesus People Army (JPA), 281–82
Jews, 158, 160
Jinwright, Anthony, 113–14
John Paul II (pope), 137
Jones, Bob, III, 37
Jones, Mike, 118
Jones, Terry, 112
Journalism, 171–72, 174–76, 182–83. *See also* News media
Judeo-Christian values, 18
Jump, Herbert A., 231–32
Justice, 51
Just-war theory, 39, 51

Kalnins, Ed, 65
Kantzer, Kenneth, 221
Kassian, Mary, 300–301
Kemp, Jack, 21
Kennedy, D. James, 136
Kennedy, John F., 156
Kent, Frank R., 154
Kerry, John, 33
Kid Rock, 90
King, Bernice, 118
King, Coretta Scott, 118
King, Larry, 6
King, Martin Luther, Jr., 38, 118, 156
Kinkade, Thomas, xxiii
Knippers, Diane, 303–4
Know Nothing movement, 152
Kranda, Jay, 8
Kristofferson, Kris, 83, 89, 92
K Street Project, 121
Kuhlman, Kathryn, 300
Kuo, David, 72
Kurtz, Howard, 65
Kuyper, Abraham, 264

LaHaye, Beverly, 18, 42, 301
LaHaye, Tim, 301
Lamb's Theater Company, 270–71
Land, Richard, 42
The Late Great Planet Earth (Lindsey), 285

Lay, Kenneth, 110, 119
Leadership (magazine), 222
Left Behind series, 301
Levi, Zachary, xxiii
Lewinsky, Monica, 117, 122
Lewis, C. S., 21
Liberalism, 88
Libertarianism, 50
Lies, 112–15
Lifeway, 306
Lighthouse Club, 280
Lillenas Press, 267
Limbaugh, Rush, 70, 71
Lindsell, Harold, 221
Lindsey, Hal, 285
Lindvall, Terry, 231
Little Country Church, 289
Lobbyists, 121
Local politics, 23
Loder, Kurt, 91
Logos Books, 190
Long, Eddie, 115, 118
Lott, Trent, 16
Lotz, Anne Graham, 297, 305
Love, David, 111
Love Song, 278, 281
Lucado, Max, 3
Luntz, Frank, 70

MacDonald, John, 279
Maddow, Rachel, 66
Magazines, 190–91, 195–211.
    See also specific magazines
Mainstream media, 149, 169–72, 182–85
The Man in White (Cash), 84
Marsh, Molly, 203
Marty, Martin, 119
Mather, Increase, 196
Matthews, Randy, 278, 288
Mattingly, Terry, 182
McArthur, John, 10
McCain, John, 4, 25, 27, 34, 37, 40, 43, 52, 54, 62, 64–65, 204–5
McGee, J. Vernon, 143
McLaren, Brian, 38, 47, 48, 52
McPherson, Aimee Semple, 113, 131, 155, 299–300
Meacham, H. C., 111
Mears, Henrietta, 298–99

Media
    American culture and, 144–45
    celebrity culture and, 104, 106
    evangelical approaches to, 169–81
    evangelical clergy and, 1–9, 130–31
    mainstream, 149, 169–72, 182–85
    new, xx
    news, 1–2, 4, 6, 12
    online, 7–9, 144–45, 205–8
    Sarah Palin and the, 62–73
    social, xviii, xx
    use of, by churches, 7–9, 104
    See also News media
Megachurches, 289, 299–300
    international ministries of, 12
    pastors of, 128, 139–40
    use of media by, 7–9
Meissner, Linda, 281–82
Mencken, H. L., 154
Mennonites, 17, 51
Messer, Allan, 89
Methodists, 151
Meyer, Joyce, 115, 297, 302
Millennial Harbinger (magazine), 197
Millennium Challenge Account, 39
Miller, Donald, 47–48, 53, 103, 289
Miller, Vincent, 102
Mintle, Linda, 306
Mitchell, Mary, 69–70
Modernism, 231
Modernists, 153–55, 158
Modesett, Jack, Jr., 222–23
Moehler, Albert, 201–2
Money, 97, 130
Moody, Dwight L., 8, 130–31, 153
Moody Monthly (magazine), 200
Moore, Beth, 297
Moore, Roy, 119
Moore, Russell, 86
Moralistic criticism, xx–xxii
Morality plays, 250–51, 269
Moral Majority, 16, 20, 22, 41, 90, 136, 158–59
Moral values, 26
Morgan, Tim, 6, 223
Morton, MeLinda, 118
Mother Angelica, 132
Mouw, Richard, 71, 237
Movement politics, 17
MTV, 87–88
Muck, Terry, 221

Mueller-Bell, Catherine, 304
Muggeridge, Malcolm, 133
Murders, 110–12
Murphree, Debra, 117
Murray, Matthew, 111
Museum of Biblical Art (MOBiA), 254
Museums, 252–54
Music, 87, 278–79, 281, 287–91
Muthee, Thomas, 67–69
Myra, Harold, 221, 222–23, 225
Mystery plays, 250–51, 269

National Association of Evangelicals (NAE), 17, 18, 34, 36, 40–41, 118, 213–14
National Courier (newspaper), 190
National Organization for Women (NOW), 301
Neff, David, 41, 202, 220, 221, 223
Neo-evangelical movement, 18–19, 200, 213–14
New Birth Baptist Church, 118
New Christian Right, 19–20, 159–60
New International Version (NIV), of Bible, 201–2
New Life Church, 117–18
New media, xx
New Paradigm churches, 289
News media, 1–2, 4, 6, 12
   audience interest and, 176–77
   coverage of evangelicals by, 149–68
   in eighteenth century, 150–51
   evangelical, 169–81, 182–94
   magazines, 190–91, 195–211
   mainstream, 170–72, 182, 183–85
   in nineteenth century, 151–53
   online, 182, 205–8
   in twentieth century, 153–57
Newspapers, 151–53, 172–73, 183–91, 196, 287
Niebuhr, H. Reinhold, 17, 19, 88–90, 218
Norman, Edward, 184
Norman, Larry, 278
Norris, J. Frank, 111
Notoriety, 130
Nuclear family, 18

Obama, Barack, 4, 5, 27–28
   abortion issue and, 44–48
   courting of evangelicals by, 35–40
   evangelical magazines and, 204–5
   Iraq War and, 51–53
   Jeremiah Wright and, 69, 70, 72
   presidential campaign of, 34–54
   racism and, 71
Ockenga, Harold John, 214
Office of Faith-based Initiatives, 25, 39
Olasky, Marvin, 149, 171–72, 175, 201, 202
Olbermann, Keith, 66, 68
Olsen, Ted, 224
168 Hour Film Project, 235–36, 241
Online churches, 158
Online media/news, 7–9, 144–45, 182, 205–8
Operation Rescue, 112
O'Reilly, Bill, 66, 67, 70
Originality, lack of, xxiii–xxiv
Osteen, Joel, 4, 101–2
Osteen, Victoria, 303

Pacifism, 51
Pagano, Ken, 112
Palestine Park, 251
Palin, Sarah, xxiii, 54, 112
   ambition of, 72
   media coverage of, 62–78, 161
   racial issues and, 69–71
   religious faith of, 62, 65–67, 69
   as role model, 303
   Tea Party and, 71
Para-church movements, 132, 225, 302, 304–5
Parasocial interaction, 97
Parks, Carl, 282
Parsley, Rod, 37
Partial-birth abortions, 45–46
Passion plays, 250–51
Patriotism, 70
Paul (apostle), xx, 84
Peale, Norman Vincent, 156
Pelosi, Nancy, 35
Penny papers, 197
Pentecostalism, 67, 68, 135, 153, 201, 284, 298
Perkins, Luther, 82
Perkins, Tony, 41–42, 64
Personal authority, 129–30
Personality cults, 128, 129, 132, 138–40, 143–44
Petersen, Jonathan, 201
Petty, Tom, 90
Pew, J. Howard, 215
Phillips, Doug, 236
Phillips, Sam, 82
Pickering, Chip, 122
Pilgrimage, 251

Pious frauds, 114–15
Piper, John, 3
Plato, 269
Plugged-in (magazine), 195
Pluralism, 62–63, 71, 129
Political demographics, 37–44
Political engagement
    in 1970s, 18–20
    in 1980s, 20–22
    in 1990s, 22–24
    of 2000s, 24–28
    by evangelicals, 16–33
    philosophies of, 17–18
Political issues
    abortion, 44–48
    poverty, 48–51
    war, 51–53
Political scandals, 119–22
Politics
    2008 presidential campaign, 33–61
    debates over, 90
    evangelical clergy and, 4
    evangelical involvement in, 157–63
    local, 23
    movement, 17
    quiescent, 17
    regularized, 17
    Rick Warren and, 11–12
    See also Presidential election
Popenos, Frederick O., 184
Popular culture, 254–55, 265
    evangelicals and, xx–xxii
    historical precedent and, xx
    Jesus People and, 286–88, 291
    See also American culture; Culture
Pornography, 18
Postman, Neil, 144
Post-modern evangelicals, 86
Poverty, 27, 28, 38, 40–41, 48–51, 62
Praise the Lord (PTL), 113
Prayer, 67–68, 284
Precious Moments Chapel, 252, 256
Pre-emptive war, 51–52
Presbyterian Church, 153–54
Presidential campaign, of 2008, 33–61, 62–73
Presidential election
    of 1976, 19, 33, 157
    of 1980, 20, 159–60, 161
    of 1988, 21
    of 1992, 23, 161

    of 2000, 24–25, 33
    of 2004, 25–26, 33, 34, 35, 40, 42, 162–63
    of 2008, 4, 27–28, 54, 161, 204–5
Prison Fellowship, 225
Pro-choice movement, 163
Progressive evangelicals, 19, 26–27, 37–39, 43–50, 52–53
Pro-life movement, 300
Promise Keepers, 305
Prosperity gospel, 115
Publick Occurrences Both Forreign and Domestick (newspaper), 183
Puritans, 269–70
Purpose Driven Connection (magazine), 9
The Purpose Driven Life (Warren), 1, 9–11

Quakers, 51
Quiescent politics, 17
Quinn, Sally, 5

Racial pluralism, 62
Racial prejudice, 69–71
Radio personalities, 131–32, 143, 231, 302–4
Ragamuffin Film Festival, 238–39
Rapture, 284–85
Rasmussen, Scott, 69
Reagan, Ronald, 20–21, 90, 160
Rededication, 82–83
Red Letter Christians (RLC), 39
Reed, Ralph, Jr., 16, 22–24, 26, 120
Reed, Ron, 265
Reeves, Vaughn, 114
Regularized politics, 17
Relevant (magazine), 176–77, 206–8
Relief organizations, 49
Religion, science and, 154
Religious celebrities, 100–104
Religious community, 104, 105
Religious conservatives, 16, 18–29, 34, 37, 41–43, 62, 63, 159–60
Religious freedom, 40
Religious leaders, personas of, 128–29
Religious pluralism, 129
Religious Right. *See* Christian Right
Religious Roundtable, 20, 159
Religious theme parks, 244–50
Religious tourism, 244–57
Republican Party
    abortion issue and, 44–48, 54
    Christian Right and, 20–29, 63–64

evangelicals and, 34, 35, 37, 40–43, 44, 47–48, 53–54
Rice, John, 200
Rivers, Eugene, 50
Robbins, Paul, 222
Roberts, Oral, 133
Robertson, Pat, 19–23, 25, 37, 41, 115, 133, 141, 158, 161, 174
Robertson, Tim, 141–42
Robinson, Eugene, 5
Robison, Betty, 303
Rock music, 83, 290–91
Rocky Hock Playhouse, 272
Roe v. Wade, 18, 42, 157, 163
Roloff, Lester, 143
Roman Catholic Church, 161, 268–69
Romanowski, William D., 232
Roman theater, 268–98
Romney, Mitt, 37
Ross, A. Larry, 6, 7
Rove, Karl, 26
Rubin, Rick, 83, 90

Saddleback Church, 1–2, 4, 7–9, 27, 36
Safire, William, 205
Saints, 143
SaltWorks Theater, 267
Salvi, John C., 111–12
Same-sex marriage, 25, 27, 37, 40, 42, 62, 118, 163
San Antonio Independent Christian Film Festival, 236, 241
Sanford, Mark, 110, 122
Sawyer, Diane, 66
Scandals, xxiii, 110–27, 138, 161
Schaeffer, Francis, 18, 21
Schlafly, Phyllis, 18, 20, 159, 301
School prayer, 42
School Prayer Amendment, 21
Schudson, Michael, 226
Schuller, Robert, 133, 136, 137, 158
Science, 154, 198
Scopes trial, 154–55, 198
Second Coming, 284–85
Second Great Awakening, 197, 298
Secularism, 254–55
Self-criticism, xxiii
Self-improvement movement, 251
Senkbeil, Peter Lucas, 262–64, 267–68
Sex scandals, 115–18, 122, 161

Shaw, Jack, 85
Sheen, Fulton J., 132, 133
Sheldon, Charles M., 153, 173, 182–94
Sheldon, Lou, 41
Sherrill, John, 284
Shiloh Youth Revival Center, 281
Shirer, Priscilla, 308–9
Shulman, George, 71
Sider, Ron, 205
Sight and Sound Theatre, 249, 272–73
Silsby, Laura, 115
Silver Dollar City, 250, 255
Slavery, 197
Smith, Alfred E., 155
Smith, Bailey, 158, 160
Smith, Chuck, 3–4, 280
Smith, Elias, 172
Smith, Harold, 217, 220, 223
Smith, Liz, 130
Smith, Michael W., 87
Snow, Jimmy, 83
Social agency, 105
Social gospel movement, 153
Social issues, 20–21, 25, 27, 36, 42, 62–63
Social justice, xxiv, 19, 29, 35, 38, 49–50, 71–72
Social media, xx
Sojourners, 16, 19, 26–27, 35, 49–50
Sojourners (magazine), 200–206
Souder, Mark, 122
Sound bites, 9
South-Carolina Gazette (newspaper), 183
Southern Baptist Convention (SBC), 26, 158, 173, 306
Southern Methodist University, 119
Speaking in tongues, 129, 136, 153, 284
Spiritual mapping, 67–68
Springer, Dan, 66
Stafford, Wess, 223
Stanford, Karin, 117
Stanley, Charles, 3, 137
Stem cell research, 25
St. Louis Fair, 251
StopERA, 18
Strang, Cameron, 206, 208
Strategic prayer, 67–68
Strider, Burns, 50
Success, 130
Summer of Love, 279
Sundance Film Festival, 232, 233
Sunday, Billy, 8, 153

Supernatural, 284
Swaggart, Jimmy, 117, 136, 137–38, 140, 158, 161
Sweeney, Douglas, 220
Sword of the Lord (magazine), 199–200

Taproot Theater, 271
Tax policy, 28, 50
Taylor, W. David O., 238–39
Tea Party movement, 28, 63, 71
Televangelism, 132–45
Televangelists, 128–31, 231
    charisma of, 143–44
    charismatics, 135–38
    cult following of, 138–40
    intimacy created with, 133–35, 138
    media coverage of, 158, 161–62
    personas of, 134
    scandals involving, 21, 113, 117, 138, 161
    success of, 133
    successors of, 140–43
Television, xviii, xxiv
    charismatic movement and, 135–38
    evangelical, 128–48
    intimacy created by, 133–35
    women on, 302–4
Ten Commandments, 119
Tertullian, 268
Theater, 250–51, 261–77
Theater 315 (playhouse), 270
Themed destinations, 244–52, 254–56
Thompson, Fred, 37
Threads New Works Series, 273
Tierra Santa, 247
Tilton, Elizabeth, 116
Tilton, Robert, 115
Timberlake, Justin, 88
Topeka Daily Capital (newspaper), 185–90
Touched by an Angel (TV show), xxiv
Tourist attractions, 244–57
Traditional values, 18
Traditional Values Coalition, 22, 41
Trask, Thomas E., 290
Trinity Broadcasting Network (TBN), 245–46
Trinity Evangelical Divinity School, 37–38
Trinity House Theater, 261–62, 273–74
Turner, John, 302
Turner, Steve, 83

U2, xxiii
Uganda, 11–12
Underwood, Doug, 171
The Uneasy Conscience of Modern Fundamentalism (Henry), 214, 218–19
Universities, 175
U.S. Air Force Academy, 119–20
U.S. Constitution, 129
Utopianism, 88

Values vote, 26, 163
Van Susteren, Greta, 70
VeggieTales (videos), xxiv
Vienna Fair, 251
Vietnam War, 38
Vineyard Fellowship, 289
Violence, against abortion providers/clinics, 111–12
Voter registration drives, 26

Waldrep, Phil, 306–7
Wallis, Jim, 19, 26–27, 35–39, 49–51, 54, 205
War, 39, 51–53
Ware, John, 235–36
Warren, Kay, 7
Warren, Rick, 1–15, 27, 36, 43
    influence of, 12–13
    media credibility of, 3–7
    media messages of, 7–9
    politics and, 11–12
    The Purpose Driven Life, 1, 9–11
Washington for Jesus rally, 158–59
Wasilla Assembly of God, 65–66, 67
Wealth, 97
Web media, use of, by churches, 7–9
Websites, xxiv, 182
Wedge issues, 64
Weekend conferences, 305–7
Weigel, George, 53
Wesley, Charles, 8, 196–97
Wesley, John, 8, 196–97
Weyrich, Paul, 20, 37
What would Jesus do? (WWJD), 184, 185–86, 191
White, Paula, 115, 302
White, Randy, 115
Whitefield, George, 150–51, 196
Whitmarsh, Thomas, 183
"Why I Wear Black" (Cash), 89
Wildmon, Donald, 41, 158

Williams, Don, 280
Williamson, Martha, xxiv
Willow Creek Church, 267
Winfrey, Oprah, 6, 102
Wise, Ted, 279–80
Witch hunts, 68
Women
    changing role of, 18–19
    evangelical, 296–313
Women of Faith (WOF), 305
Women of Joy (WOJ), 306–7
Women's Aglow Fellowship (WAF), 304–5
Women's events, 305–7
Women's movements, 19, 296–313
Woodhull, Victoria, 116
Woods Bible Park, 248
World (magazine), 169–71, 182, 190–91, 195, 200–206

World fairs, 251
World Vision (magazine), 200
Woroniecki, Michael Peter, 112
Worship, celebrity, 98–99
Worship music, 289
Wright, Jeremiah, 69, 70, 72
Wright, Wendy, 45
Wurzelbacher, Joe, 70–71

Yates, Andrea, 112
Young, Scott, 237–38
Young evangelicals, 27, 33–34, 37, 51, 54, 62, 200, 208, 308–9
Youth culture, 280, 288, 290–91
Youth for Christ, 200
Youth vote, 27

Zondervan, 201, 202, 234